I0454135

THE ART OF THE OCCULT

Quarto

First published in 2020 by White Lion Publishing
This published in 2024 by Frances Lincoln
an imprint of The Quarto Group.
1 Triptych Place, 2nd Floor,
London, SE1 9SH,
United Kingdom
T (0)20 7700 9000
www.Quarto.com

EEA Representation, WTS Tax d.o.o.,
Žanova ulica 3, 4000 Kranj, Slovenia

Text © 2020 Sarah Walter

Sarah Walter has asserted her moral right to be
identified as the Author of this Work in accordance with
the Copyright Designs and Patents Act 1988.
All rights reserved. No part of this book may be
reproduced or utilised in any form or by any means,
electronic or mechanical, including photocopying,
recording or by any information storage and retrieval
system, without permission in writing from Frances
Lincoln.

Every effort has been made to trace the copyright
holders of material quoted in this book. If application is
made in writing to the publisher, any omissions will be
included in future editions.

A catalogue record for this book is available from the
British Library.

ISBN 978-0-7112-4883-0

12

Design by Paileen Currie

Printed in China

*This book is dedicated to
the seekers, dreamers and
magic makers. May you
find inspiration, delight and
a breathless rekindling of
curiosity each and every time
you open the book anew.*

Front cover
Group X, No. 1, Altarpiece
Hilma af Klint, 1915, oil and
metal leaf on canvas.
The Picture Art Collection/Alamy

Back cover
The Crystal Ball
John William Waterhouse,
1902, oil on canvas.
Heritage Images/Getty

THE ART
OF THE OCCULT

A Visual Sourcebook
for the Modern Mystic

S. Elizabeth

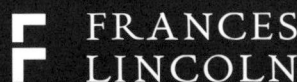

FRANCES
LINCOLN

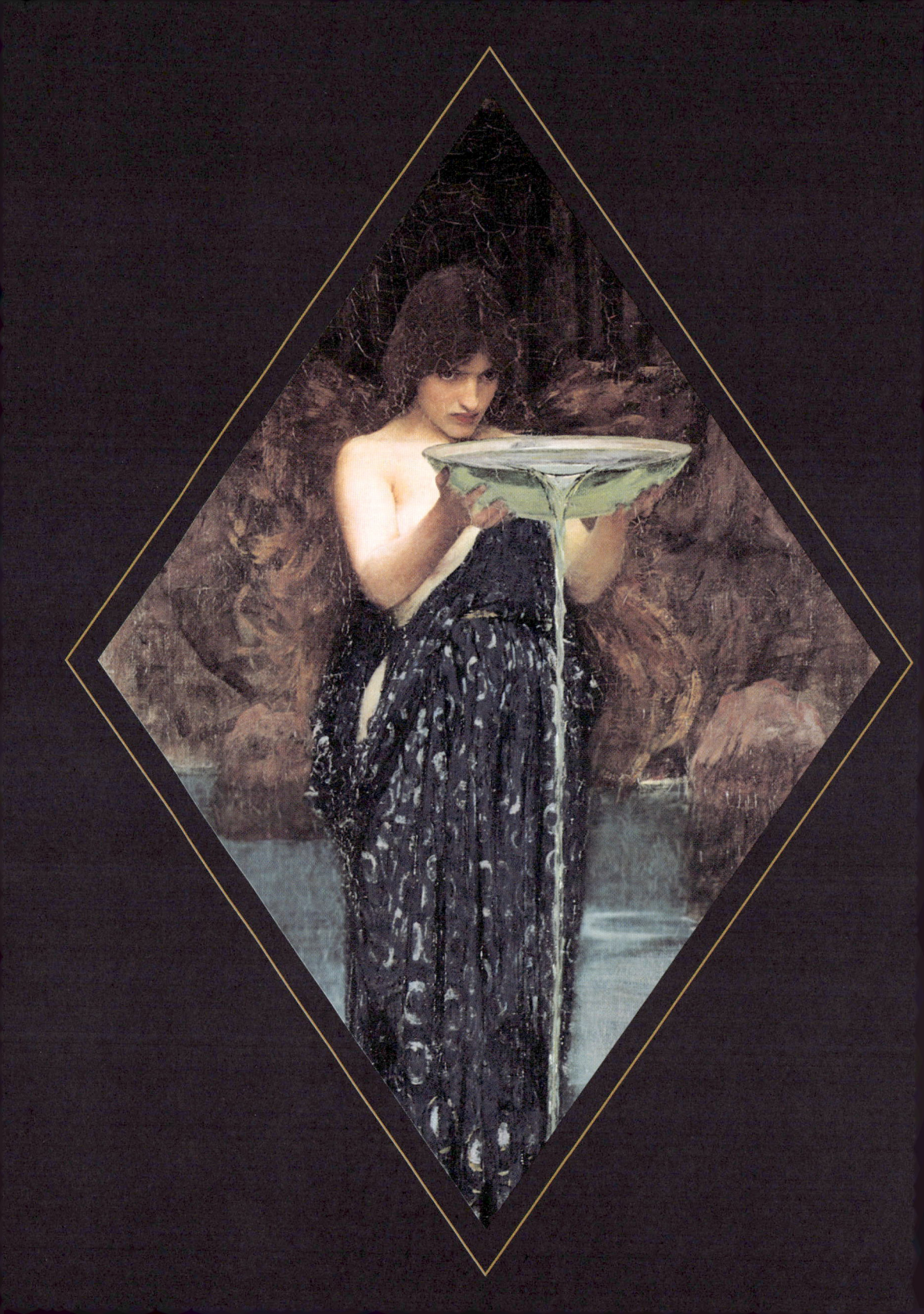

CONTENTS

INTRODUCTION

O UR BELIEF IN MAGIC AND mysticism is a thread that runs glimmering throughout human history, and woven uncannily throughout that history are practitioners of the arcane arts as well as hands-on visual artists, who have been drawn to these unknown spheres and have created curious artworks that transcend time and place. Both artist and magician – sometimes in the same role – use the medium of creativity and art to illuminate mystical beliefs and philosophies, revealing to us all of those mysteries that cannot be easily seen.

If we consider magic as the practice of manipulating these invisible forces to shape our visible world, it could be said that the link between art and magic is one that reveals the hidden rules of nature and our world – and beyond – and also explores the shadowy inner realms of dreams and desires. 'Magic in its earliest form is often referred to as "the art" ', declares writer, occultist and ceremonial magician Alan Moore. 'Art is, like magic, the science of manipulating symbols, words or images, to achieve changes in consciousness.'

Art-making, then, is magic-making.

There is transformative magic present in both the creative artistic process and the participatory act of observing an artistic creation. Both sides of the coin stem from the need to better understand the world around us, and in doing so to connect what is familiar and what we know to be true with glimpses from the world of the unknown. Knowledge is power, as everyone is so fond of saying, but it's an artful cliché that is no less true for its ubiquity; there is a great deal to be learned from both the process and practice of actively conjuring a work of art from the blank slate of the ether, and passively witnessing its form, function and details – and from your interpretation of its meaning, learning as much about yourself as you do about the actual work. Losing yourself in the creation and contemplation of a work of art and gaining insights into yourself in the process, is a fine bit of magic on its own, if you ask me.

It seems silly at this point to bring up the fact that, throughout history, for a good segment of the population the term 'occult art' has tended to conjure up pictures of devils, demons and shocking Satanic imagery. I don't know that this is necessarily still the case today, but this is a good moment to point out that the term 'occult' simply means 'hidden', and is derived from the Latin *occullere*, meaning to cover over, to hide, or conceal. In essence, occult art is derived from our search for hidden knowledge of ourselves and our place in the universe.

The resulting imagery created by artists exploring these ideas stems from a soul-deep desire for truth and awareness – a longing that connects us all regardless of creed or culture – and echoes through the many different religions and philosophies of our world; in fact, since the very beginning of human creativity itself. Small carved figurines, ancient cave paintings, and the primitive masks used for rituals and celebrations all hint at the very roots of art and magic and intersect in a realm that is deeply emotional and very human. For ancient tribal people emerging from their base origins and attempting to make sense of the strange and unpredictable world they found themselves in, these artifacts created by shamans, prophets and artists are some of the earliest examples of the use of visual art as a means of entering other realms for the answers they sought and the records made of what they encountered there. For our ancestors, this magical art was powerful, wondrous, transformative – both a catalyst that caused changes in life (births, deaths, seasonal changes, the movement of the stars . . .) and a consequence, resulting in profound changes within the artists themselves.

'Architecture in its earliest forms was also concerned with realities beyond the everyday', suggests author and musician Gary Lachman. Studying the very shape and contours of such visionary structures and spaces may offer us a cosmic glimpse into the hidden pattern embedded in everything: from the enormous stone slabs of Stonehenge reaching mysteriously towards the heavens, to the precise planes of the pyramids of Ancient Egypt, which are thought to contain much in the way of esoteric, occult knowledge, to the Gothic cathedrals of Chartres and Notre Dame, whose very stones are said to whisper alchemical secrets about man, God and the cosmos.

From Antiquity to the Enlightenment, the mysteries and practices of astrology, magic and alchemy were believed instrumental in unravelling the secrets of nature and human destiny; in the wake of the West's exposure during the Middle Ages to the astrological beliefs of Arab philosophers and the mystical writings of late Antiquity, these occult traditions became vibrant sources of inspiration for artists. During the Renaissance, we find evidence of occult influence, due greatly in part to the rediscovery of the works of the most famous magician of all time, Hermes Trismegistus, 'thrice greatest Hermes'. The result was a steeping of Hermetic and occult ideas, a transformational brew of magic and alchemy, which infused and invigorated the work of a wide range of artists, including Bosch, Bruegel, Dürer and Caravaggio.

The Enlightenment eventually gave way to the wildness of Romanticism, which rejected eighteenth-century rationalism and reason, and emphasised the irrational and the imaginative, the visionary and the transcendental. The occult found revived expression in the visions of nineteenth-century artists, such as Henry Fuseli, who explored the darkness of the human psychology in his macabre paintings, and the imagery of poet and mystic William Blake, whose uncanny, dream-like works convey a significant inner mythology of his very own. During Paris's belle époque, artistic styles influenced by the esoteric flourished. Symbolism and those who thought art and the developments of technology didn't come at the expense of spirituality (both Symbolism and Theosophy claimed an affinity with science) and Art Nouveau, at the root of which was a preoccupation with 'sensitivity to the psyche' and which combined aspects of fantasy, dreamworlds and nature, offered respite from the anxieties of the industrial age. Brilliant visual renderings of these themes can be seen in the woozy, luminous visions of Symbolist painter Odilon Redon and the lavish, mystical Art Nouveau elegance of Alphonse Mucha.

Twentieth-century Surrealists conceived of practices and generated works that defied reason and denounced a rationalist mindset. Tapping into the unconscious mind and the power of imagination were the likes of the renowned and prolific artist Salvador Dalí and artist, Surrealist painter and novelist Leonora Carrington who wrote, 'The task of the right eye is to peer into the telescope, while the left eye peers into the microscope.' This quote, from a creator of bold, transcendental visions, reveals an artist who is not content with peeking only at part of reality and, at least to me, speaks to what can be glimpsed in so many iconic and powerful pieces of occult art: a space in which the agonising and the marvellous

are equally combined. Spirit and matter, life and death, the past and the future – and in between, as mediator between the macrocosm and the microcosm, the artist / magician translating and transmuting for us the Big and the Small, without which we'd have no Whole. Carrington continues, 'To possess a telescope without its other essential half – the microscope – seems to me a symbol of the darkest incomprehension.' It is the practitioner of the art – however you choose to interpret 'art' – that utilises these tools in tandem and draws forth what is found there.

A belief in magic and the hope that there is more dreamt of than in our familiar philosophies is a vital aspect of the human condition, and it is through those practices that delve into divining and decoding the unknown that we begin to throw light on the hidden knowledge that our very souls seek (and maybe some surprises we weren't seeking!). This longing for illumination has been evident in cross-cultural artistic ideas and powerful archetypal images and symbols since time immemorial. This eternal human yearning for answers is an especially powerful desire in times of turmoil and upheaval. Over history, time and again, people turn to spirituality and the study of the occult for self-empowerment during times of uncertainty and chaos. When we practice magic (or art) we turn within to reconnect with ourselves, reclaim our power, wrest control from instutions and establishments and to begin manifesting seeds of change.

While *The Art of the Occult* does not necessarily take a chronological approach to these arcane and artistic explorations, and nor is it meant to provide a comprehensive historical study of the various artists and schools of thought referenced herein, my intention is to introduce important occult themes and showcase the artists who have been influenced and led by them. And though much of the art featured in this book is informed by various belief systems and occult traditions (Hermetic, Alchemical, Kabbalistic, Masonic, Theosophist, Spiritualist, or all or none of the above), one does not need to adopt or even practise these beliefs to appreciate the results. It is, however, also my intention to wind all of these strands together to weave a space for both practitioners of the hidden arts and visual art enthusiasts alike to explore their occult interests.

The following chapters (divided thematically into The Cosmos, Higher Beings and Practitioners) act as a lively and enlightening introduction to the art of mysticism while providing a visual feast of eclectic artwork informed and inspired by spiritual beliefs, magical techniques, mythology and otherworldly experiences. My hope is that the imagery and information presented in this book covers a wide range of artists and creations, from iconic to obscure, and provides a wealth of inspiration to incite your curiosity, excite your senses, and perhaps inform your own practice – whether you incorporate them into your personal search for the truth, make them part of your magical philosophies, or experiment with them as part of your artistic techniques and processes.

Perhaps Leonora Carrington's surrealist interpretations of myth, alchemy and Kabbalah might inspire a focus for your ritual practice; learning more about the automatic drawings of Hilma af Klint and Madge Gill may move you to channel the artistic spirit as you sketch out your dreams; you may spend some time redecorating your magical space with the symbolic and mythical images of the Pre-Raphaelites; or even relax with some mindless spiral doodling as art therapy, later scrying the scraps for sacred shapes (or, you know, just frame it and put it on your altar).

However you choose to explore the artists and their creations, in revealing the elements and philosophies hidden in these works of occult art, as well as sharing insights and information on the artists who have created these pieces, I hope that you will consider *The Art of the Occult* a valuable tool in your arcane arsenal, an oft reached-for sourcebook of mythic, magical imagery for the modern mystic. Whatever you choose to take away from these words and symbols, these paintings and illustrations, whatever worlds you discover within them, I wish you truth and transformation and a canvas awash with limitless possibility.

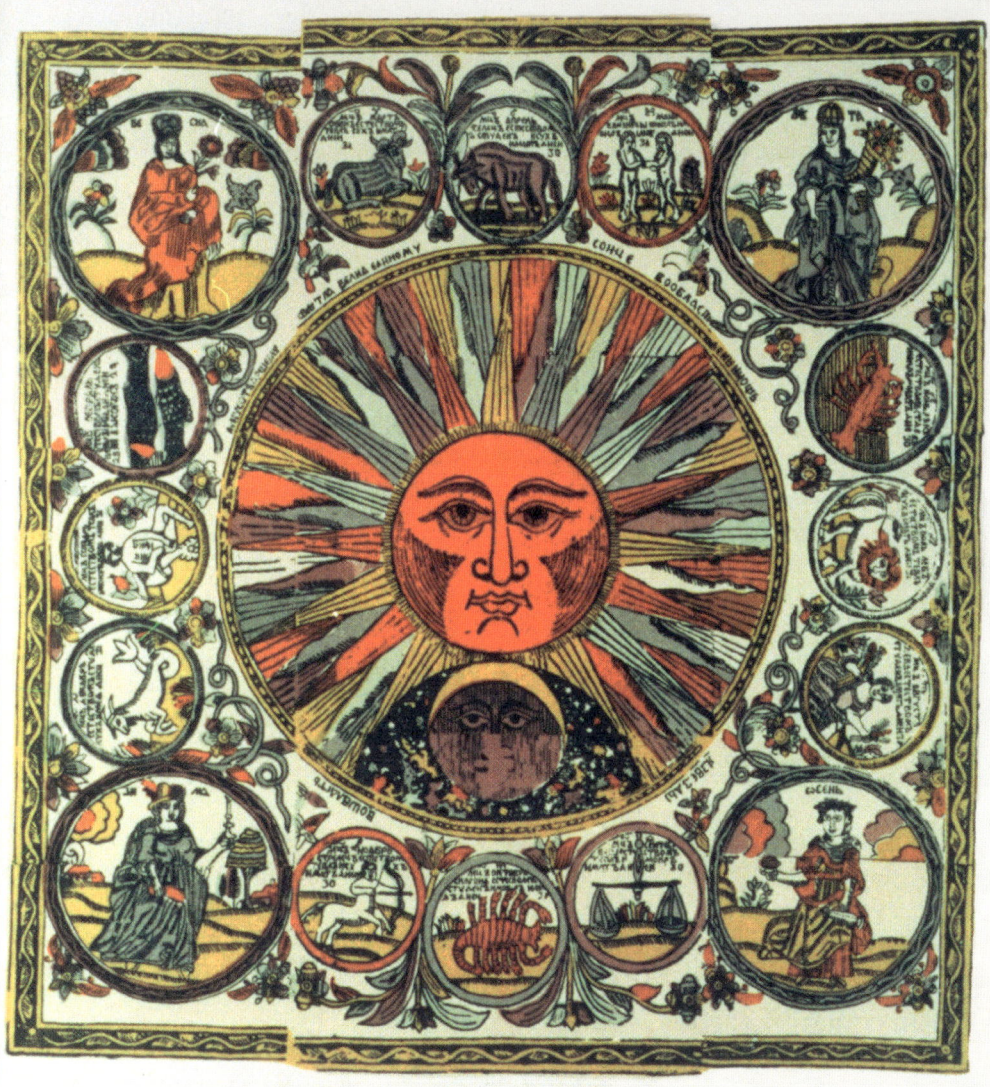

1. СОЛНЦЕ С ЗОДИАКАМИ

▲ **The Sun and the Zodiac**
Russian School, late 18th
century, woodcut print.

PART ONE

THE
COSMOS

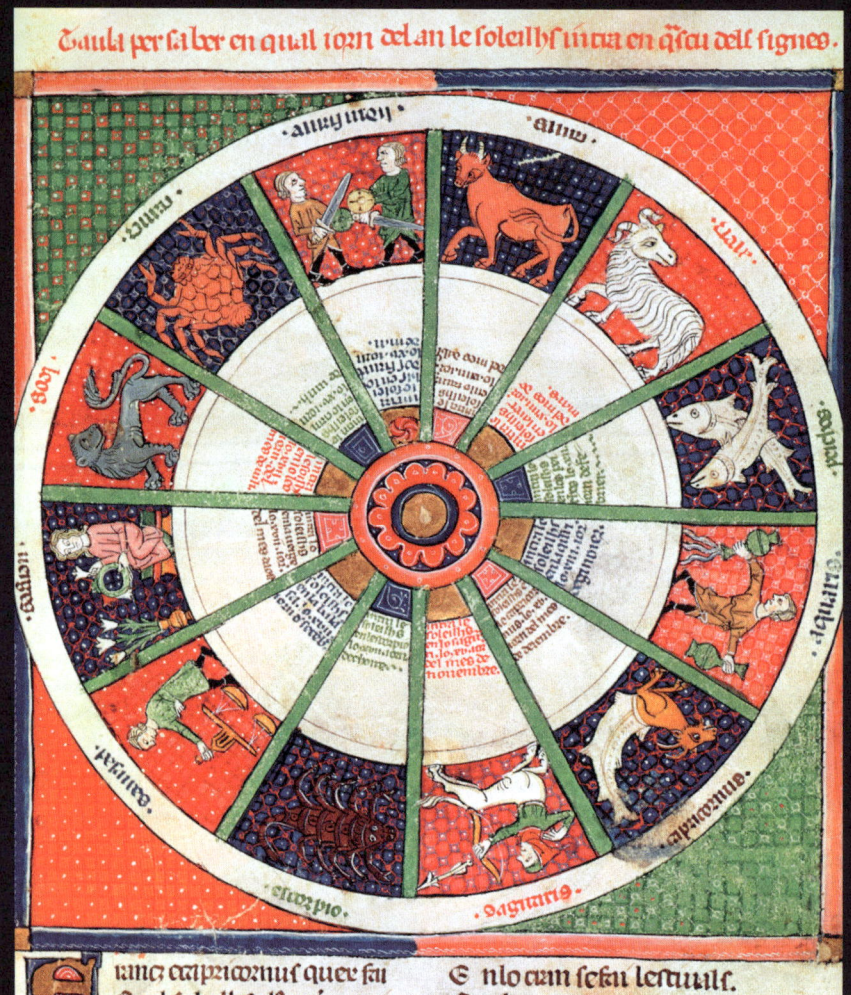

▲ **Fol.38r The Twelve Signs
of the Zodiac and the Sun**
Matfre Ermengaut, 13th
century, vellum.

'Creativity is that marvellous capacity to grasp mutually distinct realities and draw a spark from their juxtaposition.'

— MAX ERNST

❛ OUR FEEBLEST CONTEMPLATIONS OF THE Cosmos stir us,' declared scientist Carl Sagan, 'there is a tingling in the spine, a catch in the voice, a faint sensation, as if a distant memory, of falling from a height. We know we are approaching the greatest of mysteries.'

Lift your eyes up into the vast sky: the sun's dazzling rays pierce the billowing clouds at noon; the moon's mistily glowing halo illuminates the shadowy midnight darkness; the incomprehensibly vast distance of starlight reaches us from the deep void of space. The universe is a panoramic painter's palette of indescribable celestial beauty, but even with these remarkable visual cues it is difficult to conceive of its expansive frontiers, and many of its aspects are still too abstract for us to fully grasp or understand.

As the astrologers and alchemists once probed the universe through observation, experiment and theory, so too did the artists questioning the world we live in. From early fascinations with constellations, the zodiac and humankind's place within that larger universe of lifecycles, fate and destiny, to the hidden patterns and spiritual truths present in the smallest atom to the largest spiralling galaxy; from attempting to understand the connections between the elements – earth, air, fire and water – in order to explain the nature and complexity of matter and spirit, to expanding upon these fundamental elemental building blocks in the exploration of alchemical ideas of transformation and arcane spiritual acts in the quest for immortality and eternal life. The cosmos and all it encompasses has long intrigued visual artists, and its myriad mysteries remain a recurring subject in our society and culture.

Through these artists' eyes and various painterly interpretations of their brushstrokes, we can see how humankind has attempted to capture the immeasurable poetic grandeur of the cosmos, as well as the manifold changes in how we understand the universe and our place within it. The following chapters present introductions to these ancient and transformative ideas of alchemy, sacred geometry, the elements and the zodiac and, as Carl Sagan was also wont to say, the 'contemplations' by those learned scholars upon how these 'greatest of mysteries' were approached, analysed and assimilated. Reflective of an enduring captivation with these mystical cosmic themes and the philosophers who made it their life's work to understand them, the paintings included here feature a vivid and diverse range of the mesmerising artistic representations inspired by these sacred occult concepts.

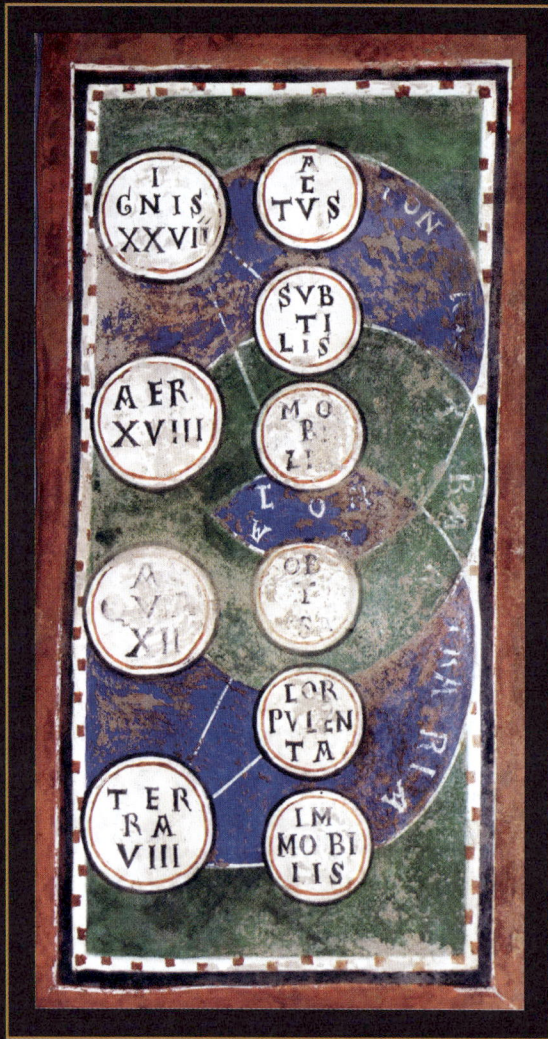

◄ **Theory of the elements: the four elements**
13th century, fresco.

▶ **Zoroaster standing atop a fire-breathing salamader or similar mythological creature**
From the alchemical manuscript *Clavis Artis* (1738).

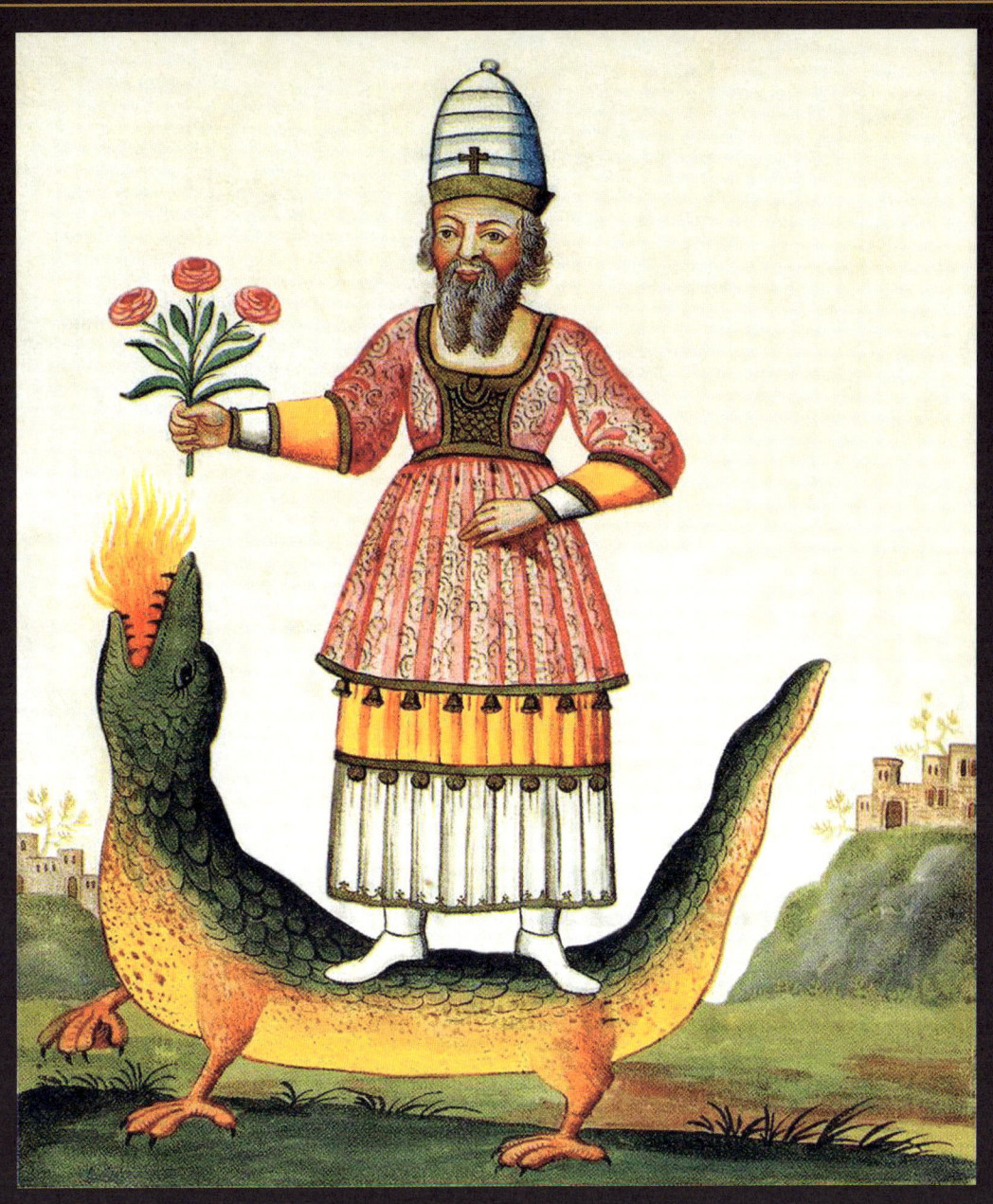

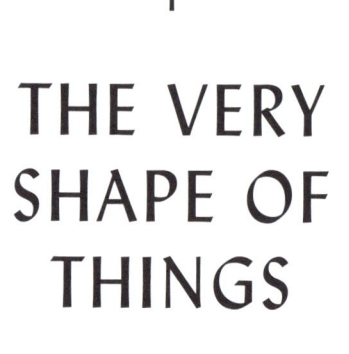

I

THE VERY
SHAPE OF
THINGS

Sacred
Geometry
in Art

SILVERY, FROST-TIPPED SNOWFLAKES AND the prismatic, hexagonal wax cells of golden honeycomb; the iridescent overlap of fish scales and the dizzying spiral of a nautilus shell; the vast neural networks of our brains, and a fresh new tattoo depicting the delicate interlocking circles of the Flower of Life . . . What could these things possibly have in common? If you noted that they are each composed of intricate patterns, hinting at an underlying significance and synchronicity between seemingly disparate elements, from the smallest atom to the infinite universe itself, you have a keen eye and remarkable skills of deduction.

These wondrous displays of universal pattern recognition reveal to us certain proportions, cycles and patterns woven into the fabric of all natural creations – patterns which, at their core, contain certain mathematical constants that appear again and again, in myriad forms, across the span of centuries and everywhere in the world. It is believed that by studying the nature of these patterns and the relationships between them, insight and perspective may be gained into the mysteries of the universe itself. This ancient idea that mathematical principles and spiritual truths are profoundly interlinked is referred to as 'sacred geometry', a term used to encompass the religious, philosophical and spiritual beliefs that have emerged around geometry in various cultures throughout the whole of human history.

In a closer examination of what form these mathematical constants take, we look first to numbers. The Greek mathematician Pythagoras believed that reality is primarily mathematical and declared that the numbers themselves were sacred, ascribing divine meaning to numbers one through ten. But one of the most sacred numbers, which has puzzled mathematicians, sculptors and artists for millennia, is the Golden Ratio, otherwise known as phi (Φ). Phi (1.6180339887) can be used to divide a line or rectangle into two unequal parts so that the proportion of the two new parts is the same as the proportion of the larger part to the original line or rectangle. This is also known as the Golden Mean, and it is a principle that is revered by nearly every culture on the planet. It is possible that the Egyptians used phi in the construction of the great pyramids, and the Greeks may have applied it to the design and sculptures of the Parthenon. On a smaller scale, the pentagram which you may wear around your neck, a holy symbol for many religions, is a shape in which the Golden Ratio appears in abundance.

Elsewhere, in approximately 1202, Leonardo of Pisa conceived of the enigmatic Fibonacci series, a sequence of numbers in which the next number in the series is found by adding the two numbers before it. You may recognise its mention from Dan Brown's cryptographical thriller *The Da Vinci Code*, but its origins are rooted in the less thrilling calculations of burgeoning local rabbit

Leonardo da Vinci's (1452–1519)
drawing of a male figure perfectly
inscribed in a circle and square,
known as the *Vitruvian Man*,
illustrates what he believed to
be a divine connection between
the human form and the universe.
Beloved for its beauty and symbolic
power, it is one of the most
famous images in the world.

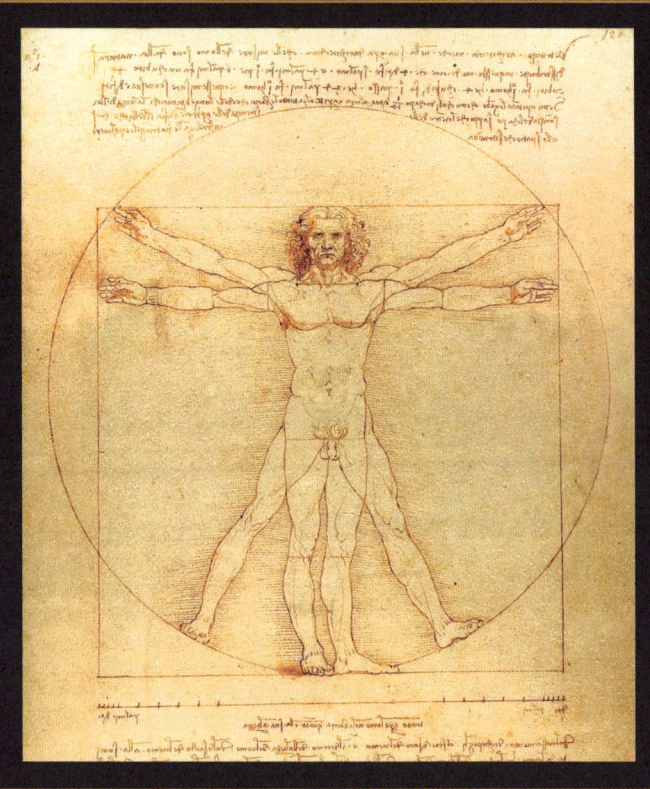

populations. It is fascinating to note that in this series of numbers, when you divide each number by the one immediately before it, each successive division gets closer and closer to converging on 1.6180339887 – thus linking it to the value of phi, or the Golden Ratio, the number that lies at the heart of sacred geometry. Fibonacci series can appear in a variety of uncanny phenomena in mathematics and science, art and nature: the number of petals on a plant, the shell of a snail, a spider's web – from something as small as the cochlea of our inner ear to a thing as immense as the spiral arms of the Milky Way galaxy.

From sacred numbers we move on to sacred shapes, as we look to the Platonic and Archimedean solids: 3D, multi-sided figures whose faces are made up of either one type of polygon or two or more types of polygon, respectively, both of which are important historical pieces of practical and mystical geometry. The Greeks believed that a handful of these solids were the core patterns of physical creation and thought to be the pattern behind the life force itself. Other shapes and symbols associated with sacred geometry include the Vesica Piscis, Metatron's Cube and the Flower of Life; the nineteen interlocking circles of the latter represent perfect form, proportion and harmony, and are said to represent the connection of life that runs through all beings.

Over the centuries, architects have relied on these constants, ratios and shapes to build sacred structures such as temples, mosques, megaliths, monuments and churches; astronomers have utilised geometry to determine holy seasons; and philosophers have beheld the harmony of the universe in the numerical properties of music. Sacred geometry is a vital aspect in the creation of religious art and iconography, and the use of divine proportions, symbolic numbers and geometric perspective can be observed in such classical imagery as Leonardo da Vinci's *The Last Supper* or *Vitruvian Man*. Piet Mondrian, a Dutch painter of the early twentieth century and a dedicated Theosophist who shared Da Vinci's views that mathematics and art are closely linked, often exhibited the concepts of sacred geometry in his abstract works, employing the image of the golden rectangle, a frequently used compositional tool that falls under the golden ratio rule.

In exploring the principles and ideologies of sacred geometry, and how these mathematical ratios, harmonics and proportions manifest time and again in nature and science, how they are found in music, light and cosmology, and how they have inspired the greatest works of art, we begin to see the smallest glimpse of how this illuminating study reveals the universal codes that connect us to the infinite and the sublime.

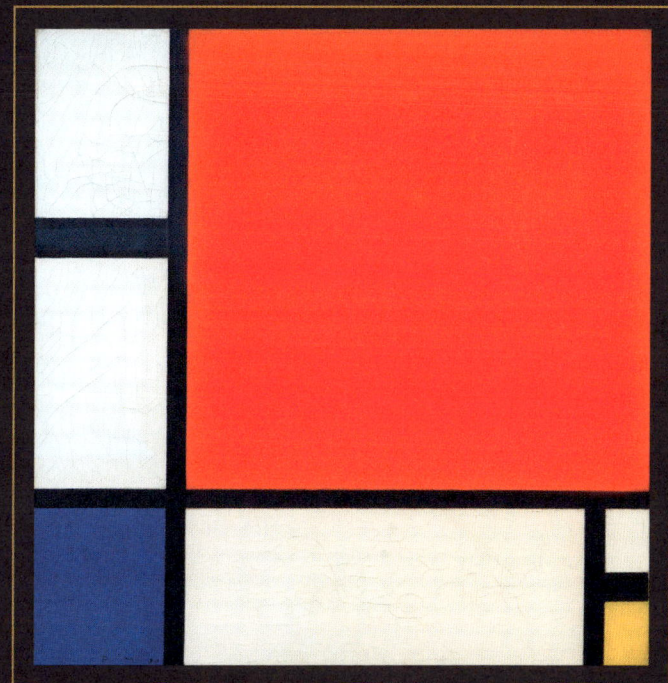

▶ **Composition with Red Blue and Yellow**
Piet Mondrian, 1930.

Piet Mondrian (1872–1944) was one of the greatest painters and the leading abstract artist of the 20th century. His abstract art consisted of white ground, upon which he painted a grid of vertical and horizontal black lines and the three primary colours. There is some argument as to whether he deliberately incorporated concepts of the golden mean into his paintings – he was said to be an intuitive artist who arrived at his results through the harmonies and balance of trial and error. It is up to us, as individuals, to decide how to interpret the spirit of the work.

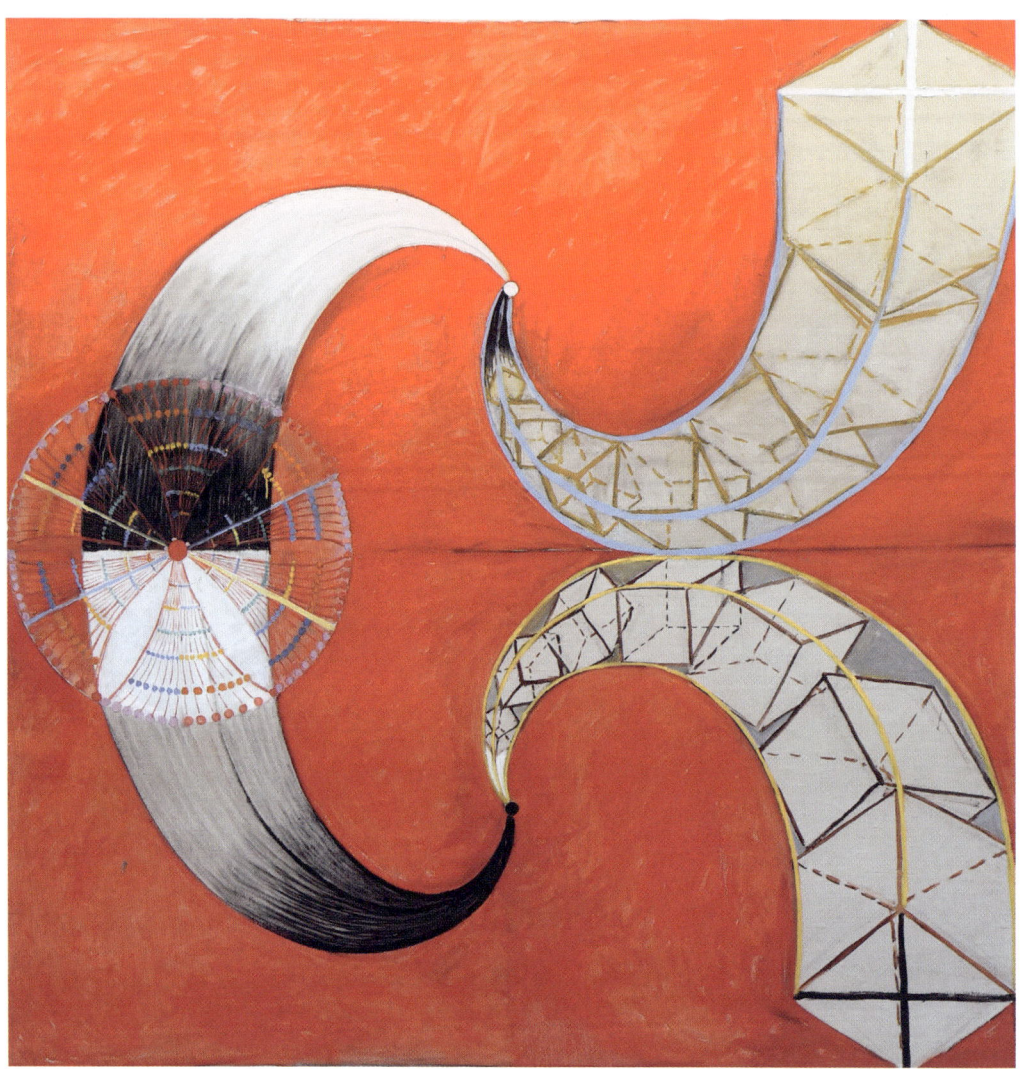

▲ **Group IX/SUW, The Swan, No. 9**
Hilma af Klint, 1915, oil on canvas.

Hilma af Klint (1862–1944) was a Swedish artist, medium and mystic. Her powerful, abstract paintings drew upon mathematics, scientific research and religion and represented complex spiritual concepts. Organically inspired images and mystical symbols, diagrams, words, and geometric series, all form part of af Klint's body of work.

▼ Eternal Cosmos
Daniel Martin Diaz,
undated, graphite
on paper.

Daniel Martin Diaz (b.1967) is a Tuscon-based artist whose work is steeped in both cryptic, recurring symbols and scientific and philosophical concepts – such as anatomy, computer science, maths, cosmology, biology, quantum physics and consciousness. He believes that there is an underlying dichotomy in the power of technology and our quantum connection to it and our universe.

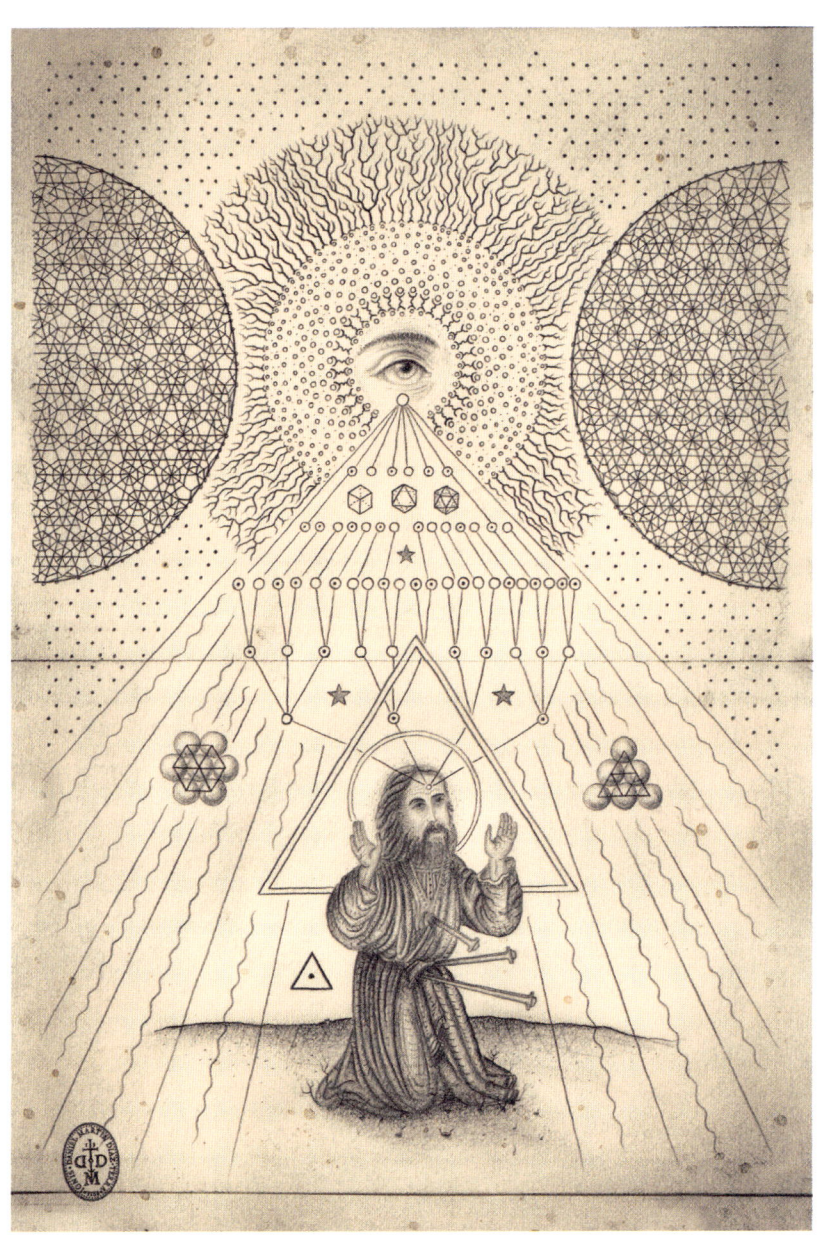

▼ Vesica Piscis
Joe Goodwin, 2015, acrylic
on canvas on board.

Presented at a conference on art and psyche in Siracusa, Italy – *Vesica Piscis*, by contemporary artist Joe Goodwin, is an exercise in synchronicity. The work, not then complete, was noted by the artist as having a 'glaring compositional problem', in the form of empty space. The addition of an off-centre circle, overlapping the one already on the canvas, resulted in an important symbol in sacred geometry, representing the intersection of the world of the divine with the world of matter and also the beginning of creation. Given that this conference held an audience mostly comprised of Jungian analysts, this process and experience was well understood.

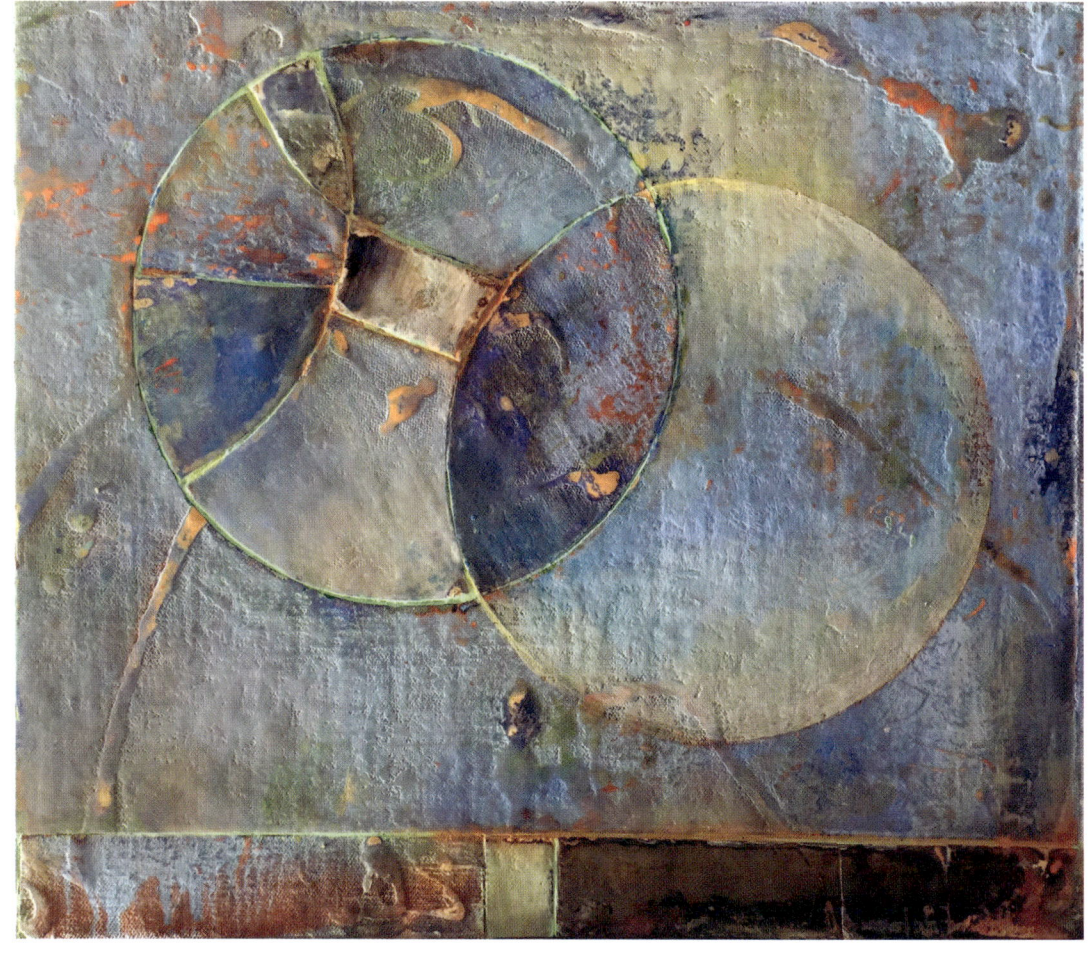

THE COSMOS

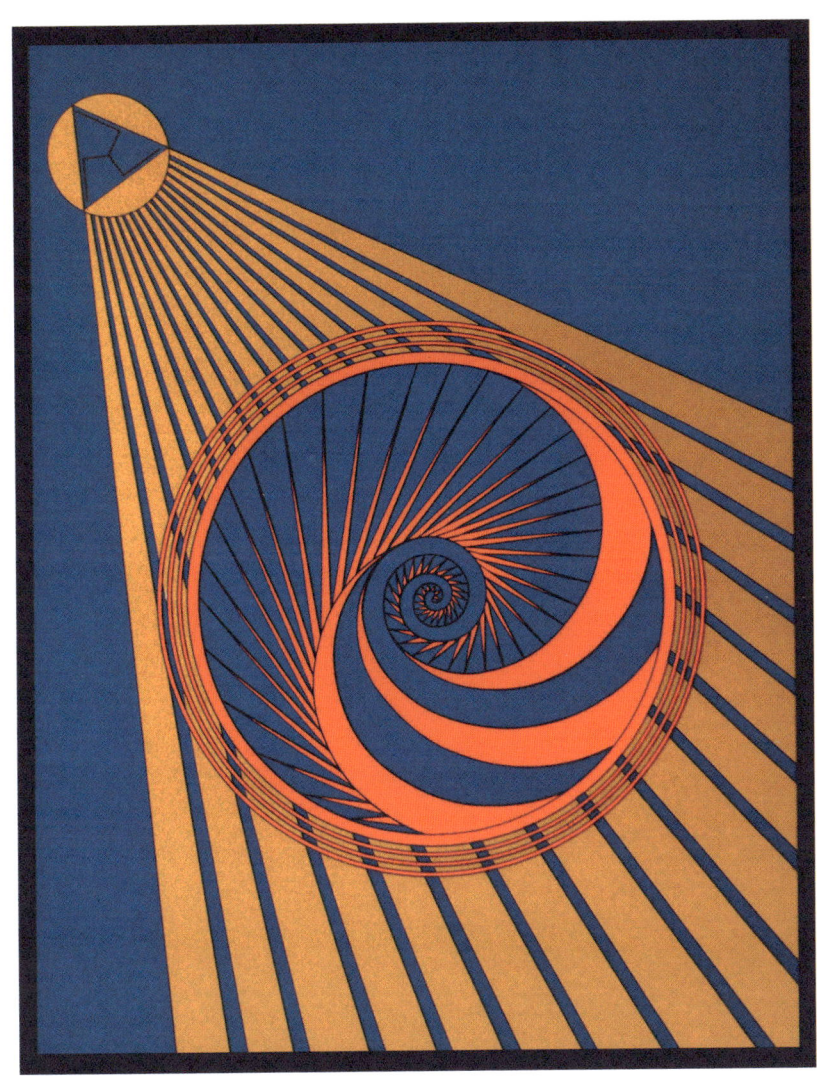

▲ The Divine Breath
Olga Fröbe-Kapteyn,
c.1930, screenprint.

With roots in the Art Deco movement of the 1920s,
Dutch artist and Theosophist Olga Fröbe-Kapteyn's
(1881–1962) precise and geometrical work is
reminiscent of impossible and yet wonderfully organic,
structures and motifs. They reference the principals of
sacred geometry and the secret form of the divine.

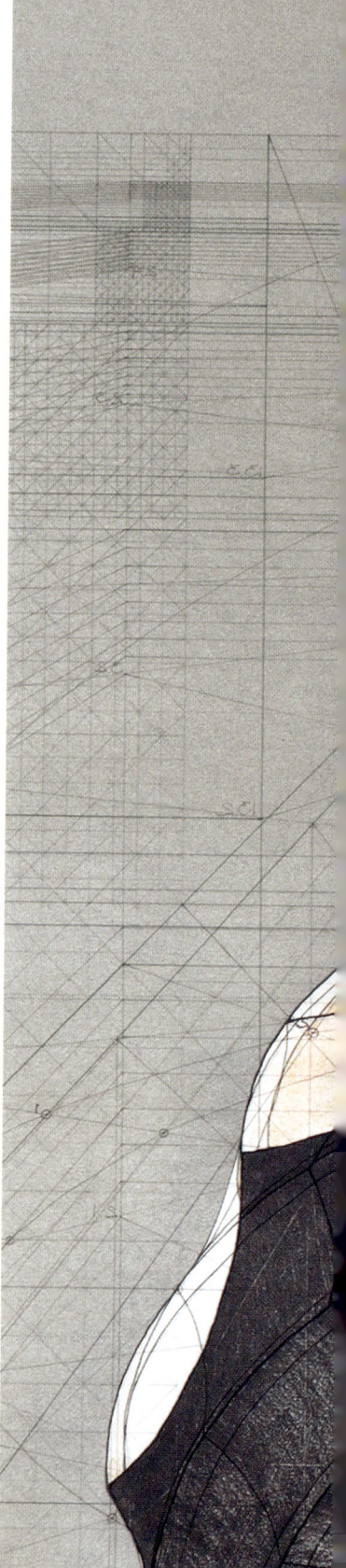

▶ **The Fibonacci Sequence**
Rafael Araujo, c.2015, acrylic
and ink on canvas.

Autodidact artist Rafael Araujo's
(b.1957) work is the outcome of
years of persistent trial and error
upon the theme of tridimensional
geometry and the 'platonic' search
of the illusion of the 'Truth'. In doing
so, he has developed structures
that could perfectly be described
as illustrated equations of natural
subjects. To that end, he works with
the concept of the Golden Ratio
to produce the perfect results.

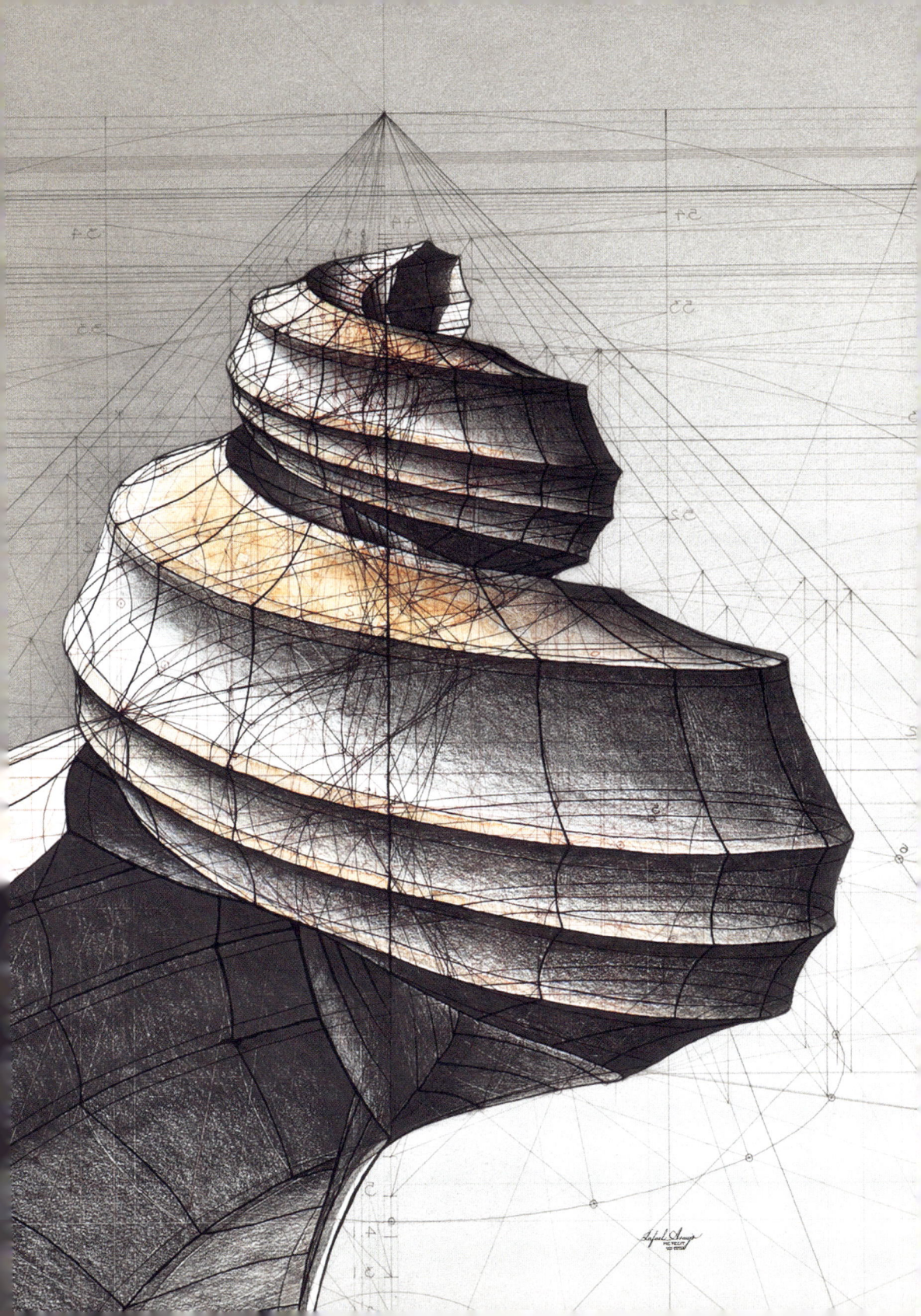

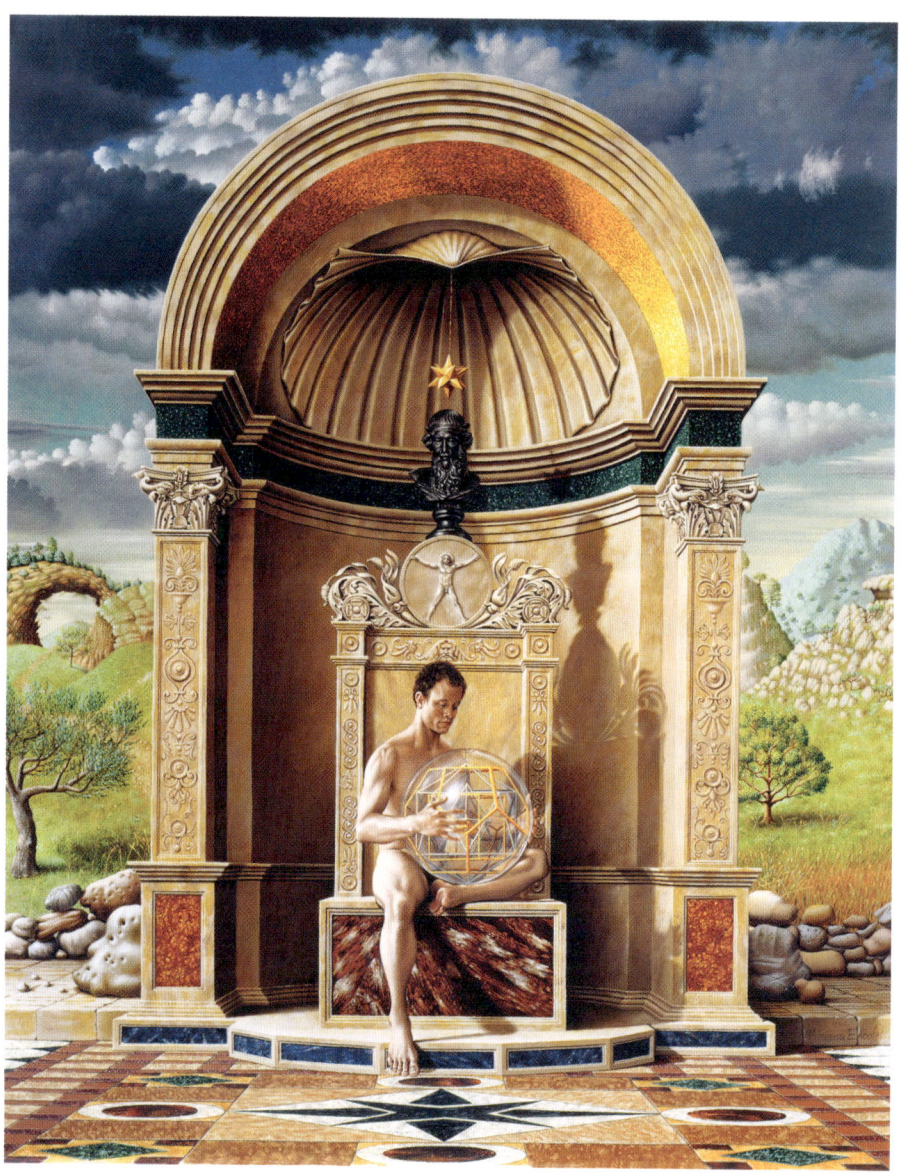

▲ The Five Platonic Solids
Miriam Escofet, 2005, oil on canvas.

Barcelona-born artist Miriam Escofet's (b.1967) has explored many themes, mediums and ideas in her vast body of work – and the unifying passion linking everything she creates is the search for a kind of 'hyper real expression'. In *The Five Platonic Solids* we observe a young man seated in surroundings brimming with wonders both sumptuous and natural, gazing upon an orb containing the artistic motifs of the five platonic solids.

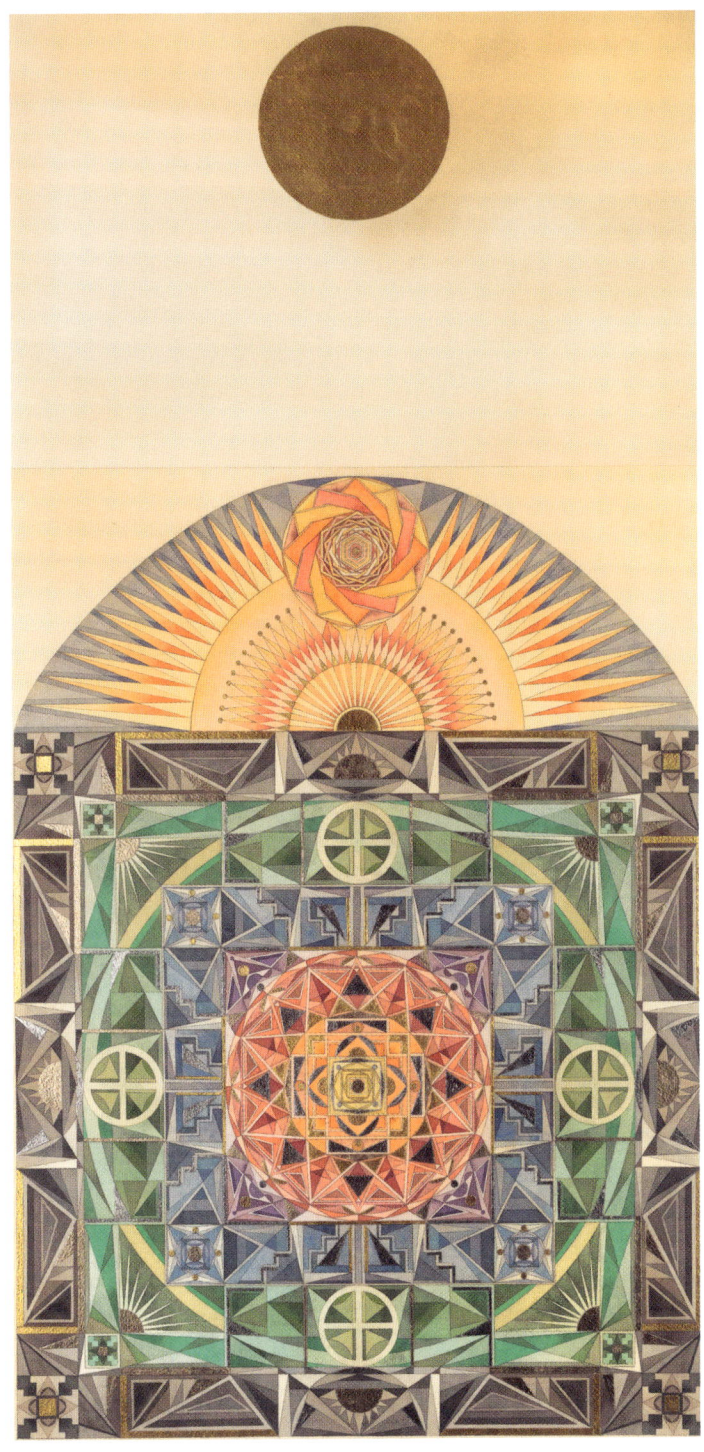

◄ **Mandala With Sun-disk**
Fredrik Söderberg, 2012, watercolour and gold leaf on paper.

Fredrik Söderberg's (b.1972) vibrant, symmetrical compositions are, according to the artist, often based on existing images within the esoteric and mystical traditions and can be seen as a map of their symbols and archetypes. To the viewer, the balanced geometries and the recurring visual implication of cosmic forces evoke feelings of a holy experience in a sacred space.

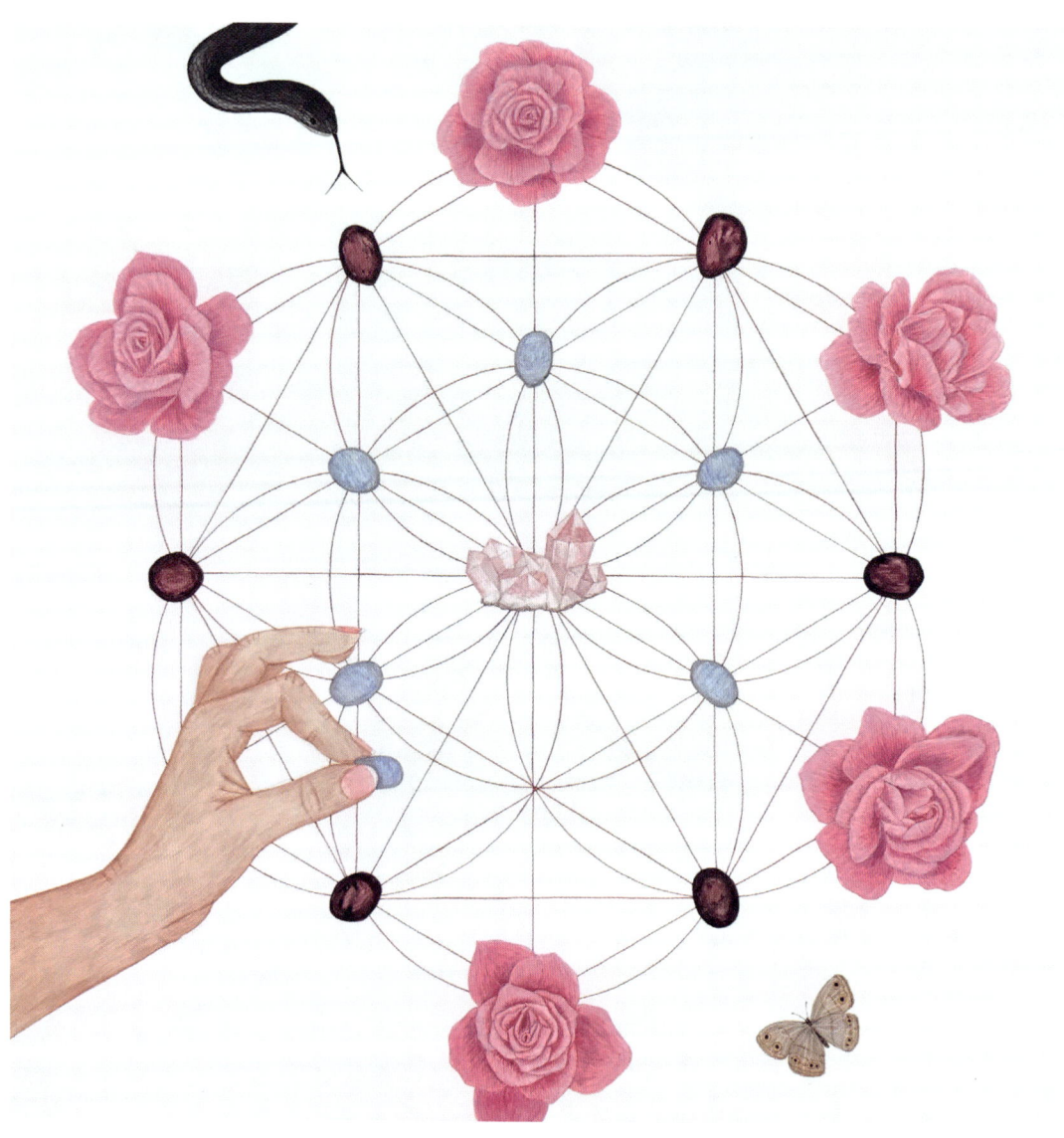

▲ Under The Rose
Susan Jamison, 2017,
egg tempera on panel.

Susan Jamison's feminine iconography spans several media – including painting, drawing, textile based sculpture and installation – all steeped in ritualistic and mythological associations. Her *Rocks and Threads* series pairs classical shapes and symbols associated with sacred geometry, alongside natural elements, intertwining both the ephemeral and the eternal.

**▼ The Choir
of Angels**
**Hildegard of Bingen,
miniature from** *Liber
Scivias* **(1151–1152).**

Hildegard of Bingen (1098–1179) was a German Benedictine abbess, writer, composer, philosopher, Christian mystic and polymath. She is one of the best-known composers of sacred monophony and has been considered by many in Europe to be the founder of scientific natural history in Germany. Her visions – from the design and construction of the monastery that she directed, to her cosmic mandalas full of myth, memory and symbolism that she 'art directed' – all broadly engage with the timeless principals of sacred geometry.

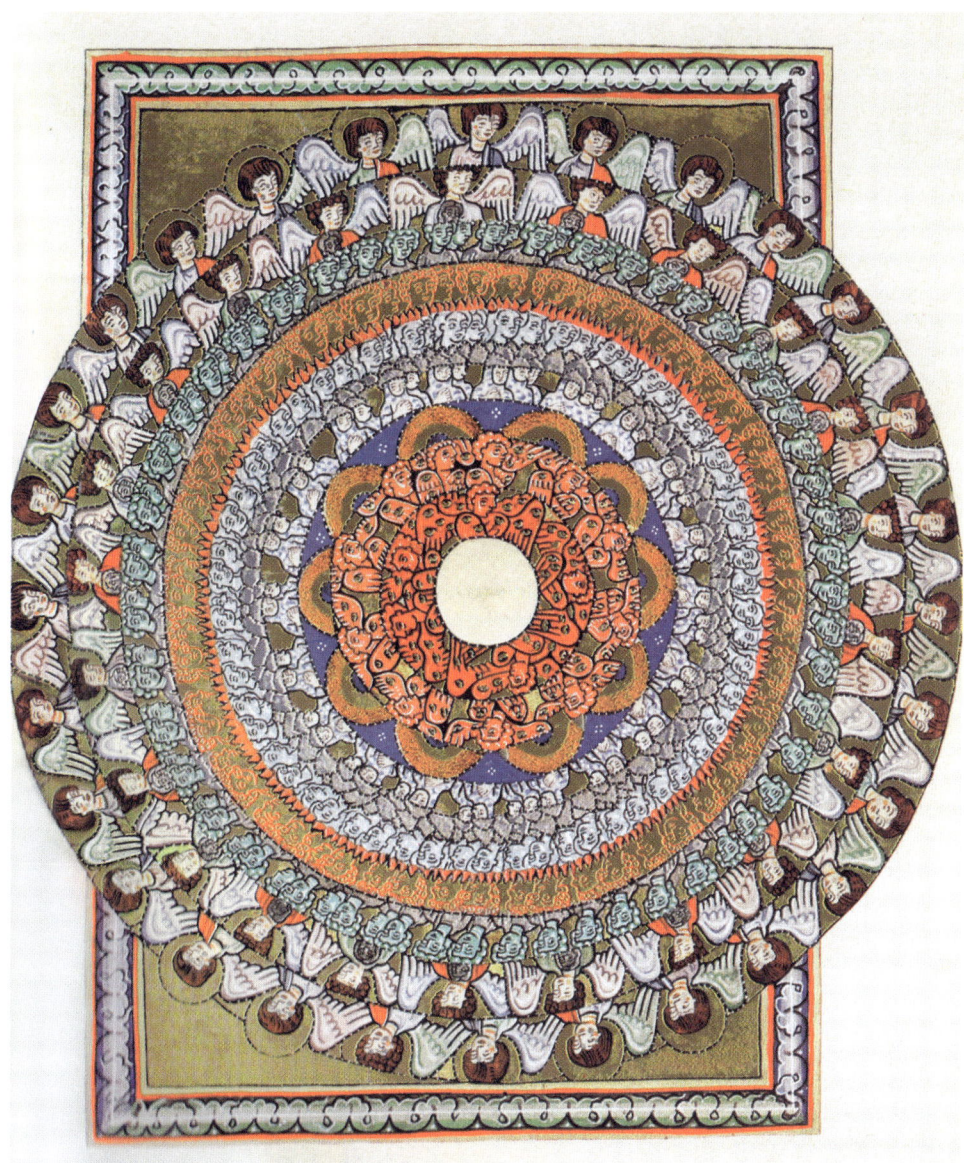

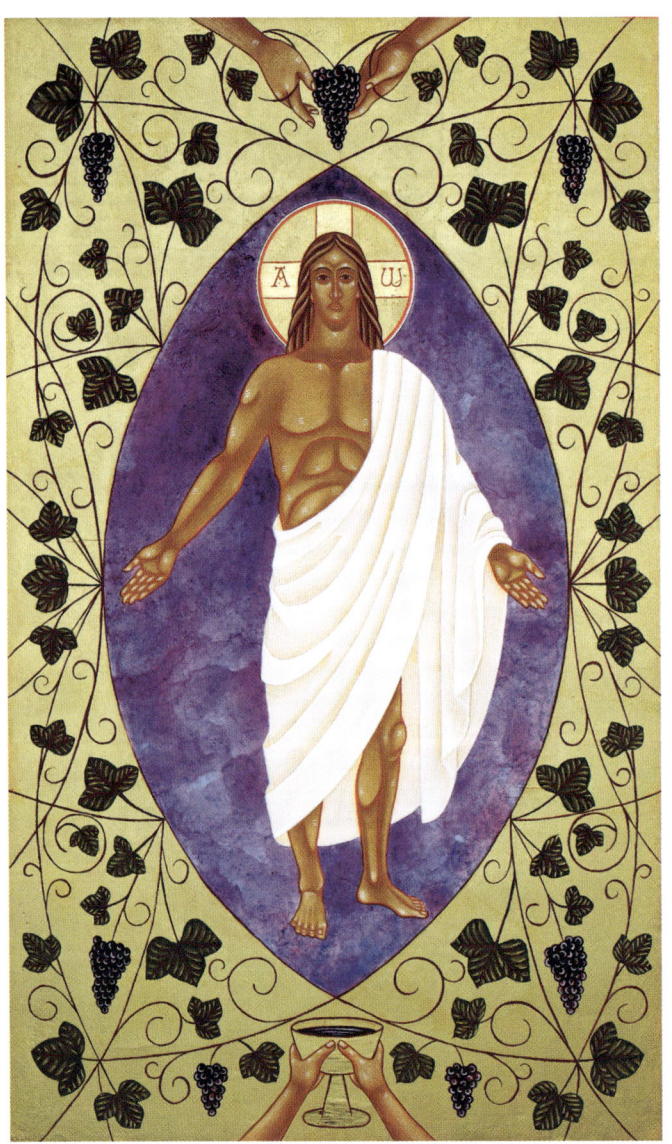

Ernst Heinrich Philipp August Haeckel (1834–1919) was a German zoologist, naturalist, philosopher, physician, professor, marine biologist and accomplished artist whose published works includes hundreds of detailed illustrations of animals and sea creatures. It is said that Haeckel's idol was Goethe, who maintained that art as well as science could unearth the underlying truths of nature.

◄ **Christ the True Vine**
Jodi Simmons, 2012, egg tempera and 24k gold on wood.

Artist of contemporary icons and sacred subjects, Jodi Simmons has depicted the Christ figure in a gently welcoming gesture. For Simmons, Christ is 'the blueprint of all creation, the fixed point in the circle of eternity from which lines radiate out in all directions, creating new shapes and forms, wherever they are intersected.' In this painting, the central figure is enclosed in the aureole of the *vesica pescis* (the conjunction of two equal circles passing through each other's centres) – a frame that frequently surrounds the totality of an iconographic figure.

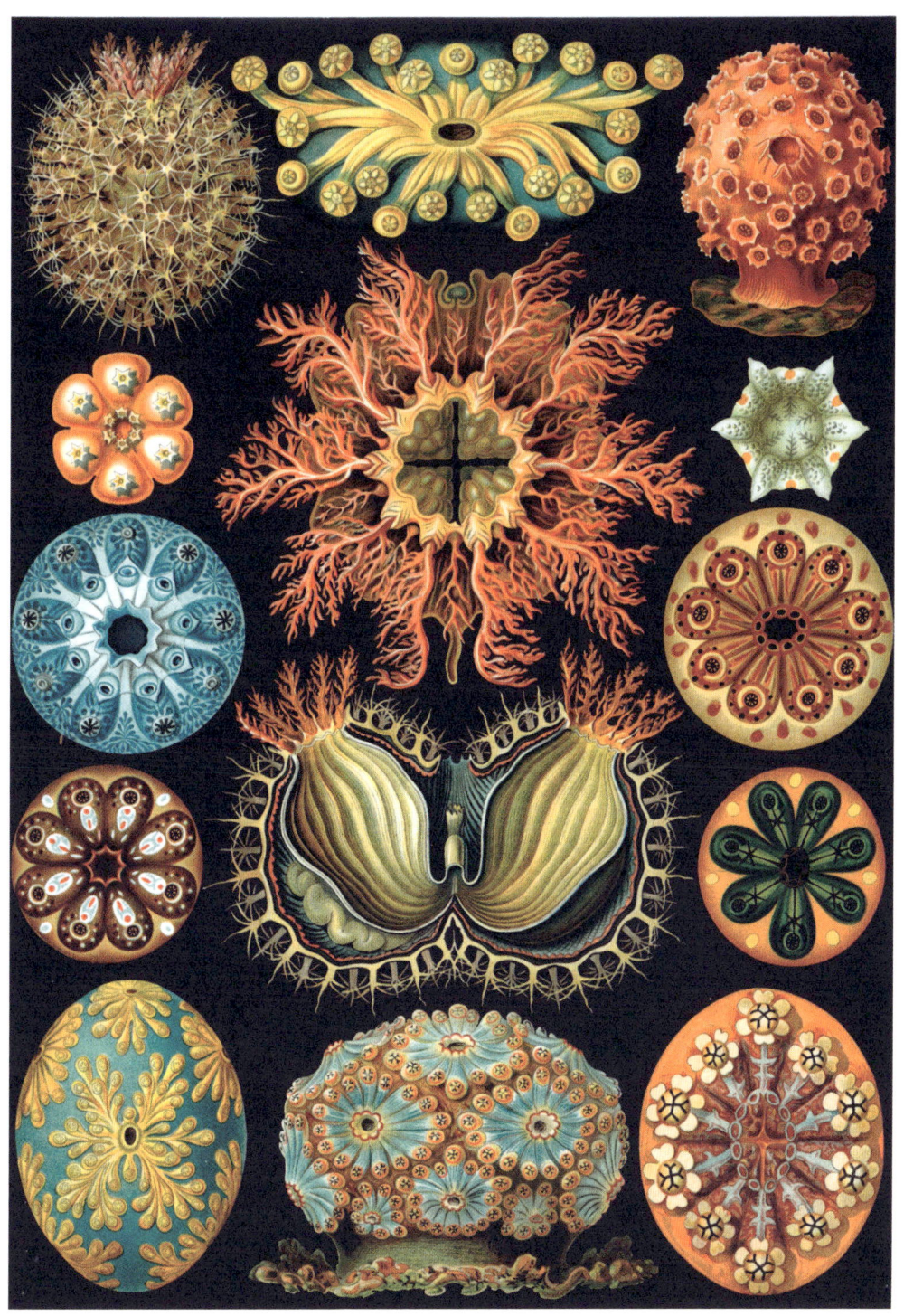

II

GAZING AT THE STARS

Astrology and the
Zodiac in Art

ART THEORIST, INTELLECTUAL HISTORIAN and cultural scientist Aby M. Warburg mused: *'Was bedeutet es, sich im raum zu orientieren?'*, a physical and spiritual mouthful which roughly translates as, 'What does it mean to orient oneself in space?'

In pondering this question, one may look to Warburg's wildly ambitious and, sadly, unfinished last project, the Mnemosyne Atlas, a metaphoric mood board comprised of a constellation of symbolic images, created to stimulate the viewer's memory, imagination and understanding of what Warburg called 'the afterlife of antiquity'. Through these cosmographic and art-historical images (or his 'thought space'), Warburg attempts to illuminate how fundamental visual motifs pass from one culture to another over time.

On the subject of space in a more literal sense, Warburg was keenly interested in astrological motifs as pictoral forms that guide and influence humanity in its quest to orientate itself in the cosmos. It was during his speech at the Tenth International Congress of Art History held in Rome in 1912 that he shared a critical interpretation of the mysterious frescoes that had been uncovered in the early nineteenth century in the Palazzo Schifanoia in Ferrara. He saw astrology as representing 'an important development on the road to human enlightenment', and theorised that certain cryptic figures in the frescoes were derived from 'decans', or astrological figures, the gods ruling ten-day periods (the term originates from the division of the signs of the zodiac into three parts of ten degrees each). Referring to them as 'the missing links' between image and symbol, Warburg traced the route of this astrological imagery back through Persian, Indian, Egyptian and Greek mythology. Scholars declare that this revelation had a 'formative influence on our idea of astrology-based iconographic symbolism'.

One can hardly blame Warburg for his fascination. Our fierce need to understand the universe and our place in it through the study of the zodiac and practice of astrology permeates our cultural consciousness. And much as they are today, fate and astrology were popular notions with the ancient world as well. For many thousands of years, humans have looked upon the stars as living things, capable of influencing our destinies and bringing a sense of order out of chaos – from predicting weather patterns and natural disasters to guiding the policies of nations and ruling even the smallest daily actions of individuals. Today we mourn the fates of 'star-crossed lovers', we thank our 'lucky stars', we read our horoscopes in the newspapers and say soothing things to our friends after a bad breakup, like, 'Well, it makes sense that he was crazy, he was a Scorpio, you know?'

The concept of astrology and the signs of the zodiac did not originate fully formed in the back column of a women's interest magazine, hard as that might be to believe. The apparent birthplace

▶ **The Zodiac Man**
Unknown Persian artist, 19th
century, watercolour.

Sometimes depicted in writings and
drawings from ancient classical,
medieval and modern times, the
Zodiac Man (Homo Signorum,
or 'Man of Signs') represents a
roughly consistent correlation
of zodiacal names with body
parts. The Zodiac Man appeared
most frequently in calendars,
devotional Books of Hours and
treatises on philosophy, astrology
and medicine in the Medieval era.

of astrology was Mesopotamia. For thousands of years before Christ, Assyrians and Babylonians scrutinised the heavens for omens of their fate. Babylonian star lore was introduced to the Greeks early in the fourth century BC and, through the studies and writings of Plato, Aristotle and others, astrology came to be regarded as an essential science. It was soon adopted by the Romans (the Roman names for the zodiacal signs are still used today) and the Arabs, and eventually spread throughout the entire world.

Of course, as pointed out by Aby Warburg, the symbolism of the stars and the zodiac has long been reflected in various cultures' illustrations of astrological motifs, in their artful attempts to visually capture the cosmos. Art historians, for example, have spoken on possible astrological interpretations for Leonardo da Vinci's famous fresco *The Last Supper*, with each of the twelve apostles representing the twelve signs /

constellations of the zodiac and Jesus, the sun; in other interpretations, the astrological energies are rearranged, and Jesus becomes a Pisces. Visionary Surrealist artist Salvador Dalí, with his enthusiastic interest in archetypal imagery and fascination with mysticism and freeing the unconscious from the constraints of everyday reality, depicted the twelve signs of the zodiac in 1967 in a series of watercolours. In a wonderfully absurd example of artistic licence (or perhaps paying homage to an earlier, well-known work), he portrayed Cancer the crab as a melancholy polka-dotted lobster.

In examining this centuries-old relationship between astrology and art, we can see some of the fascinating and provocative ways in which astrology, mythology and symbolism intersect, and gain deeper insight into the question of how art reflects astral and heavenly influences.

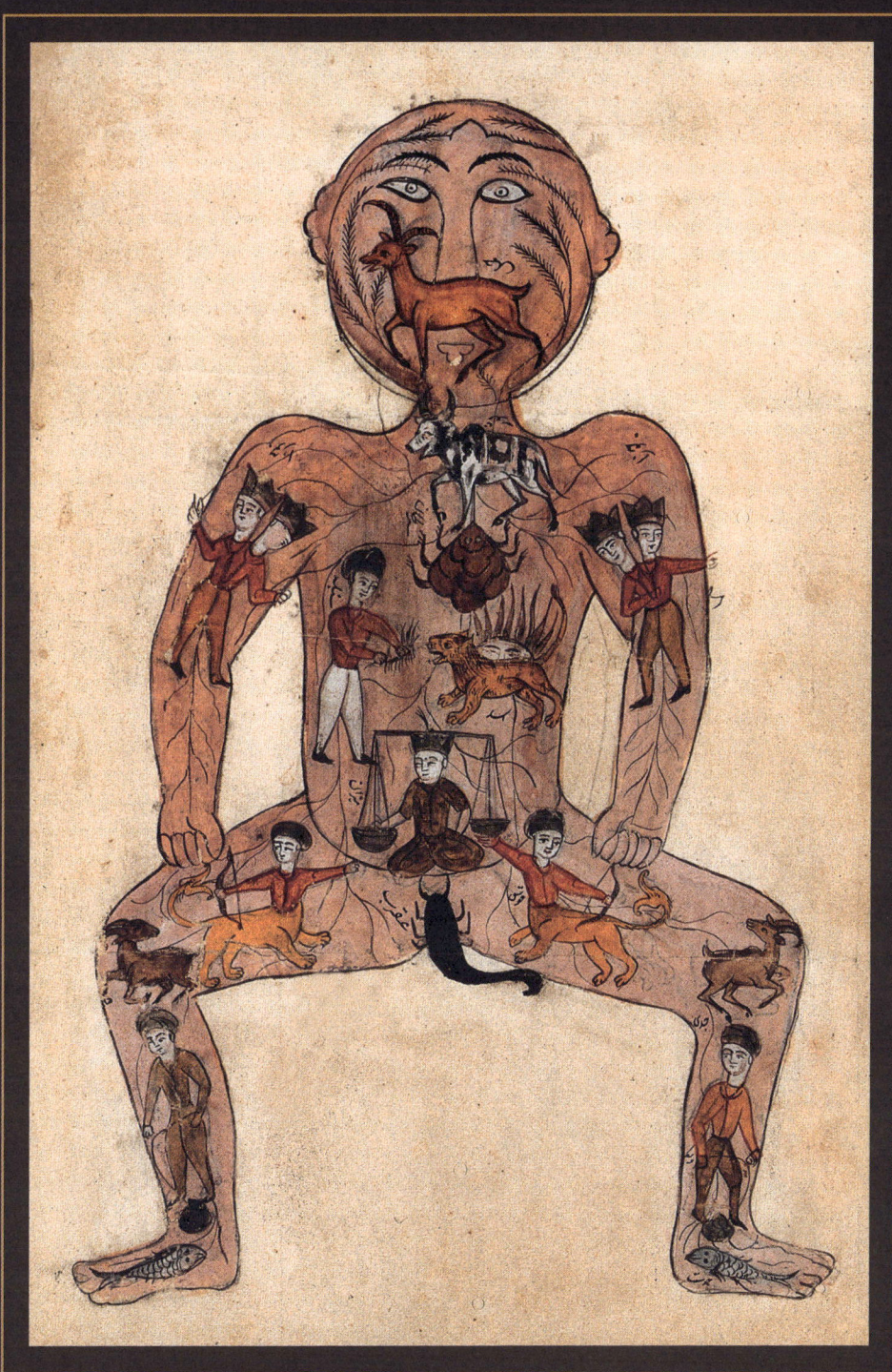

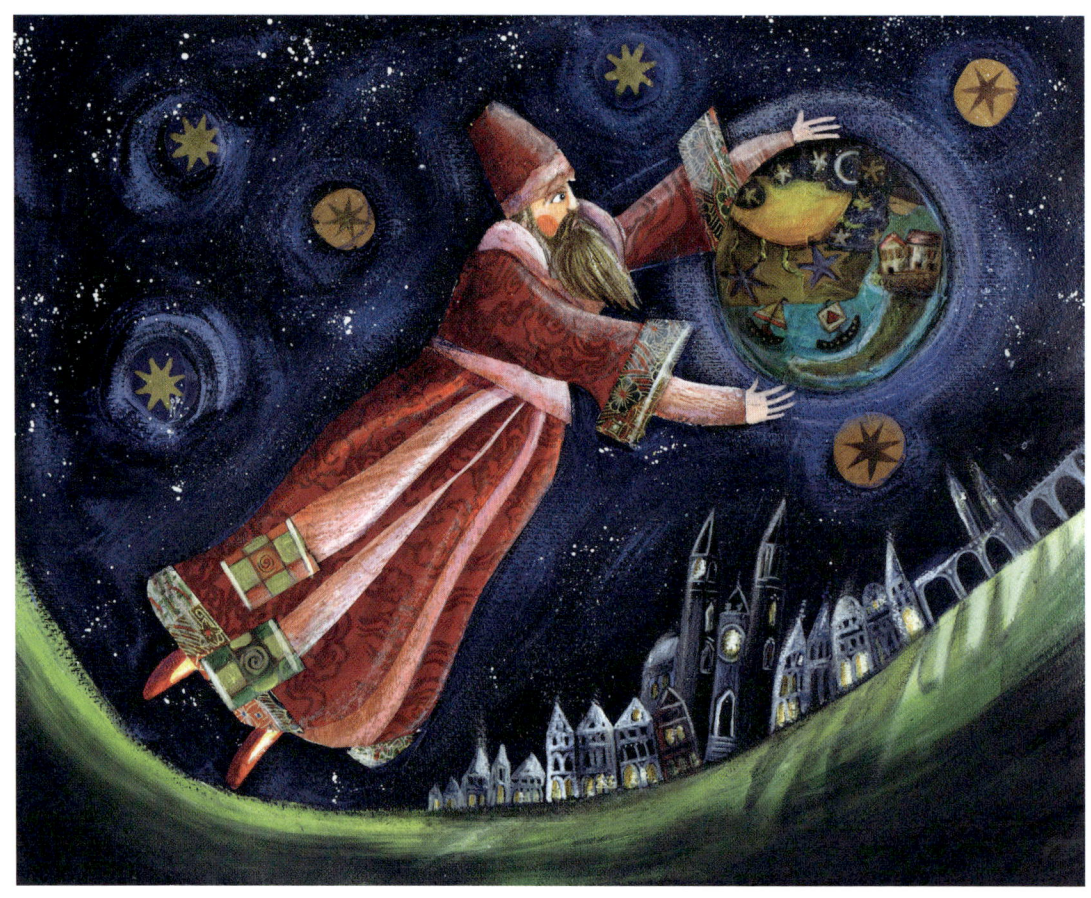

▲ **Michel de Nostradamus, Astrologer.**
Patrizia La Porta, undated.

Contemporary illustrator Patrizia La Porta's colourful
rendering of Nostradamus (also called Michel de
Nostredame) depicts the French astrologer, physician and
most widely renowned seer of the Renaissance, flitting
whimsically throughout the night sky, ostensibly consulting
the stars and engaging in prophetic mediations.

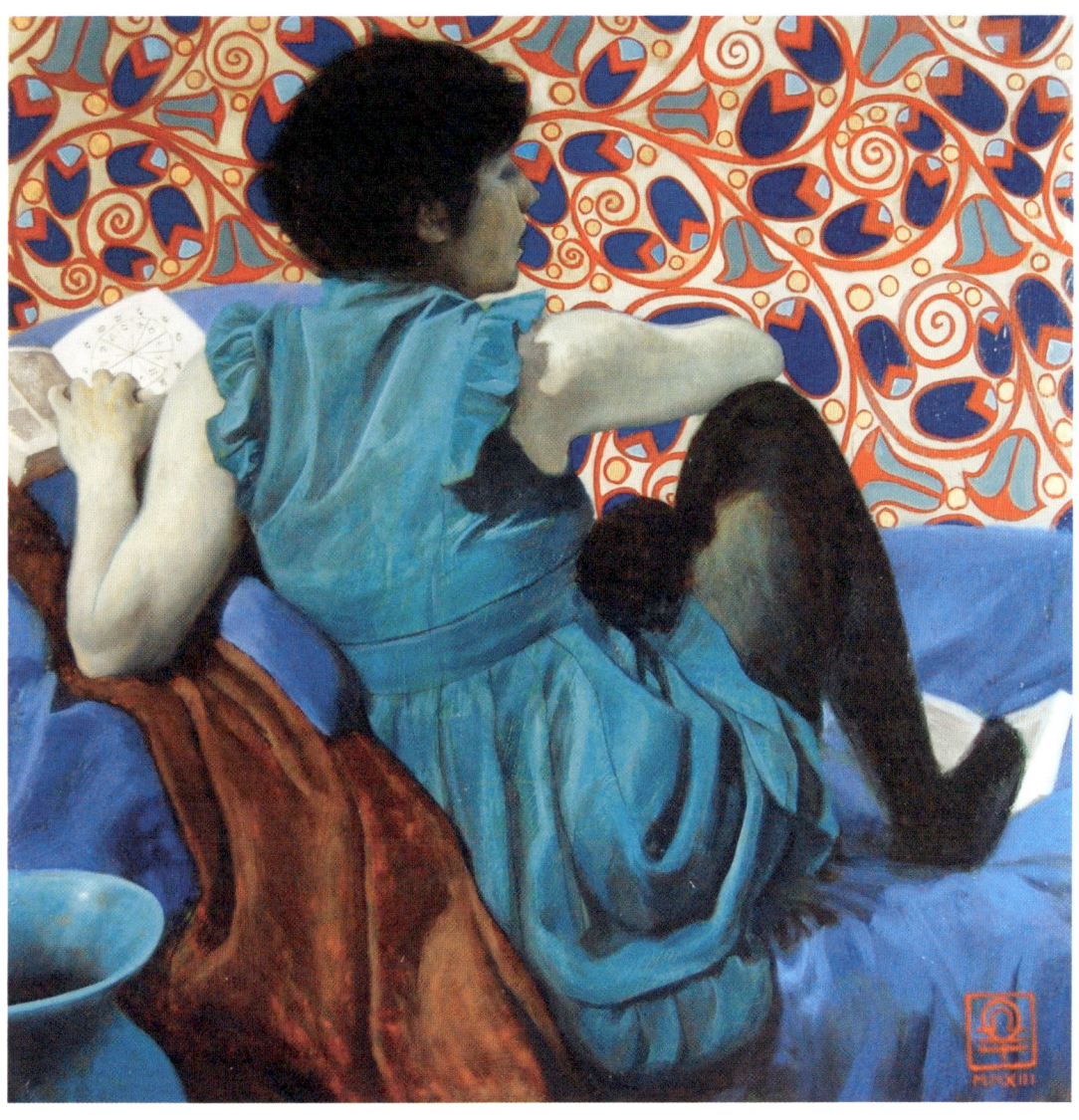

▲ The Astrologer
Damian Chavez,
undated, oil on
linen.

Damian Chavez (b.1976) is an artist and instructor from Los Angeles who studied in Florence, Prague and Paris before he attended the School of the Art Institute of Chicago and the ArtCenter College of Design, CA. His signature style consists of allegorical portraits incorporating a strong emphasis on ornament and richly intricate background textures.

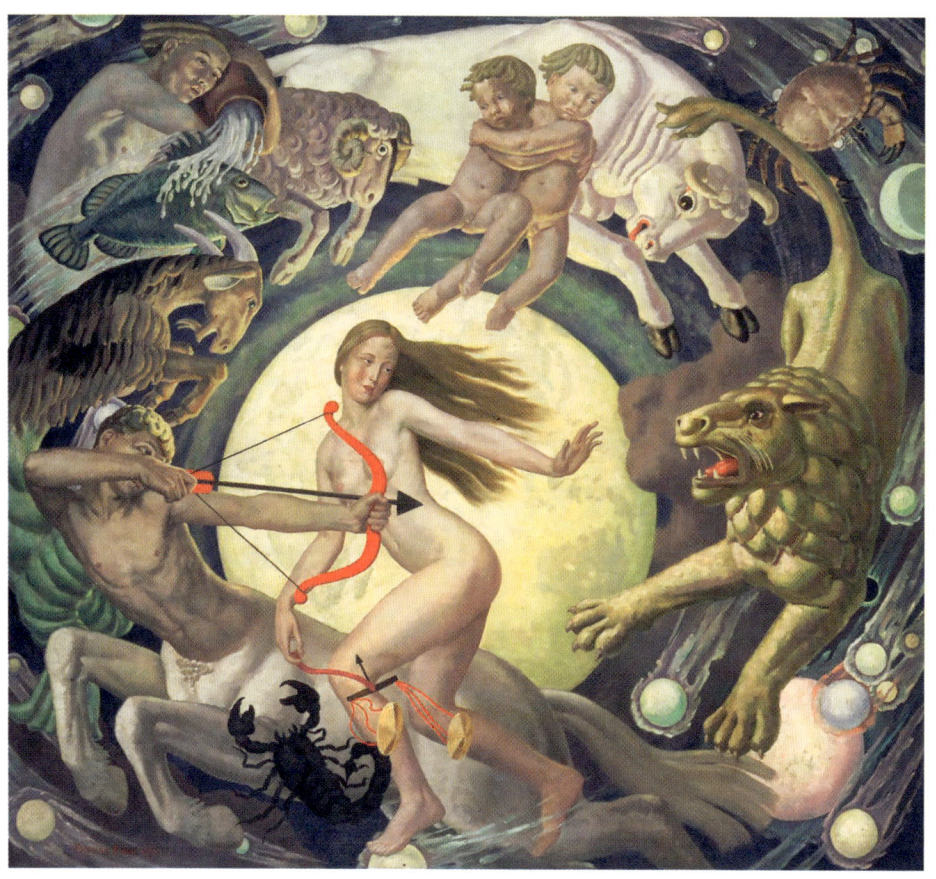

▲ The Zodiac
Ernest Procter, 1925,
oil on canvas.

Ernest Procter (1885–1935) was an English designer,
illustrator and painter. His 1925 painting *The Zodiac*
cleverly combines representations of the twelve animal and
human symbols of the zodiac into a spirited composition
of elements, amidst the chaos of the swirling cosmos.

▼ Astrology. The Myth of Creation
Timur D'Vatz, 2016, oil on canvas.

Merging ancient legends and symbols with modernist form and vivid colours, Timur D'Vatz (b.1968) is a Russian artist whose figurative and emblematic works draw inspiration from ancient histories, early Byzantine art, medieval tapestries and mythology. D'Vatz believes that artists 'will always find rejuvenation in the eternal youth of the ancients; in core ideas that do not lose meaning as time passes, but rather gain new significance with each historical transition.'

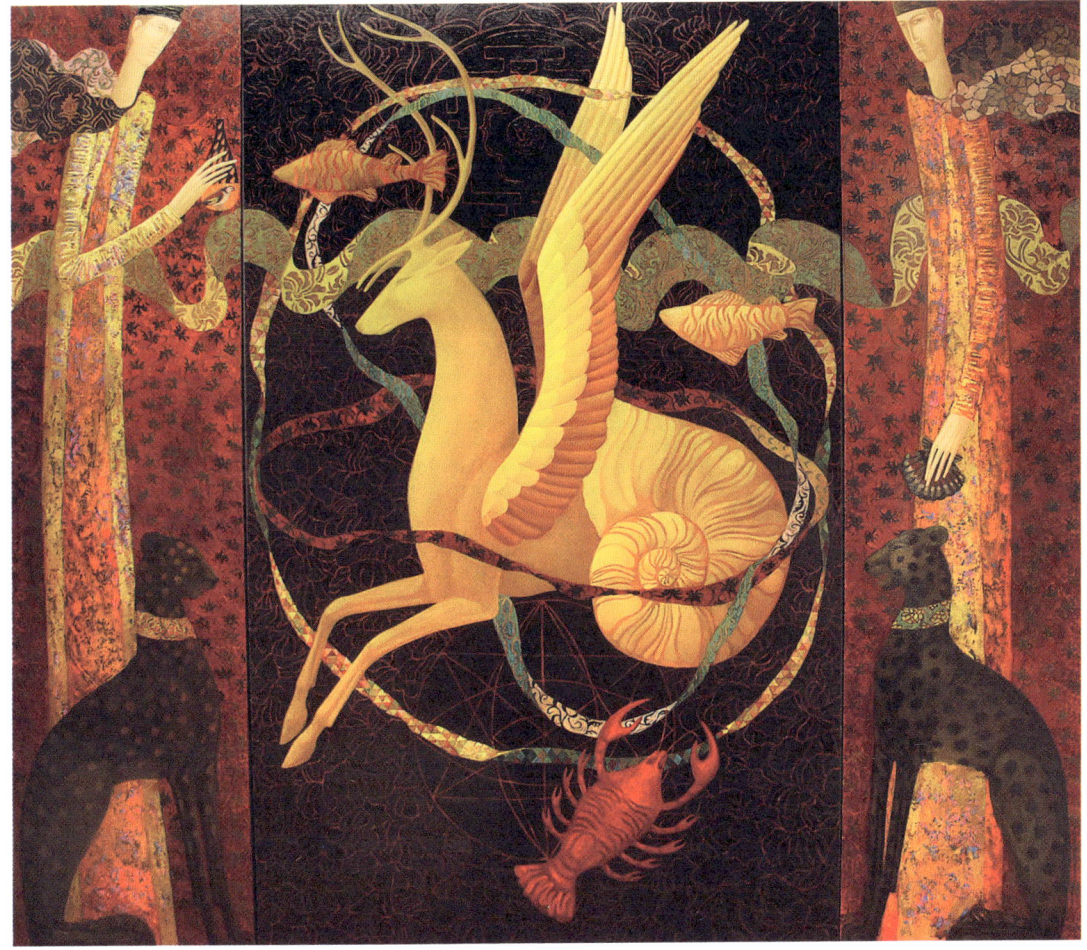

► Several Circles
Wassily Kandinsky, 1926, oil on canvas.

An avid student and sometimes practitioner of occult and mystical teachings, abstract artist Wassily Kandinsky (1866–1944) was deeply interested in spiritual pursuits. While composed as a purely abstract arrangement of various-sized circles, this canvas is full of suggestions of the cosmos and, with imagination, some interesting interpretations of the constellations and the zodiac.

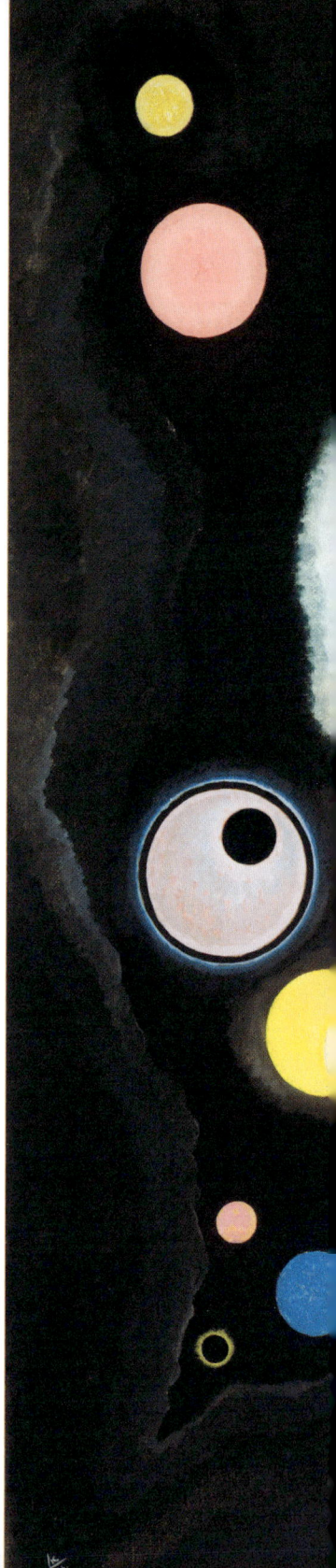

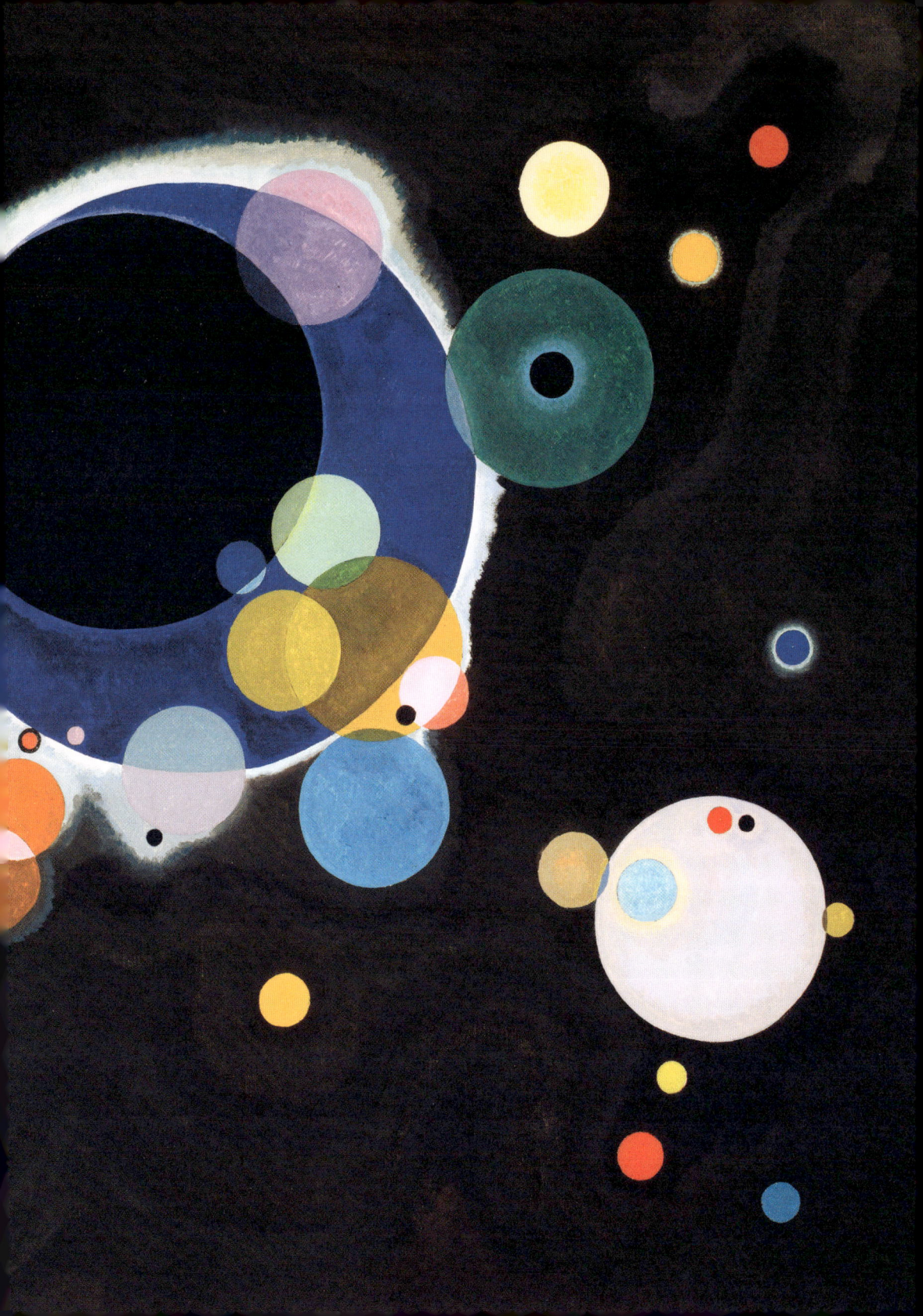

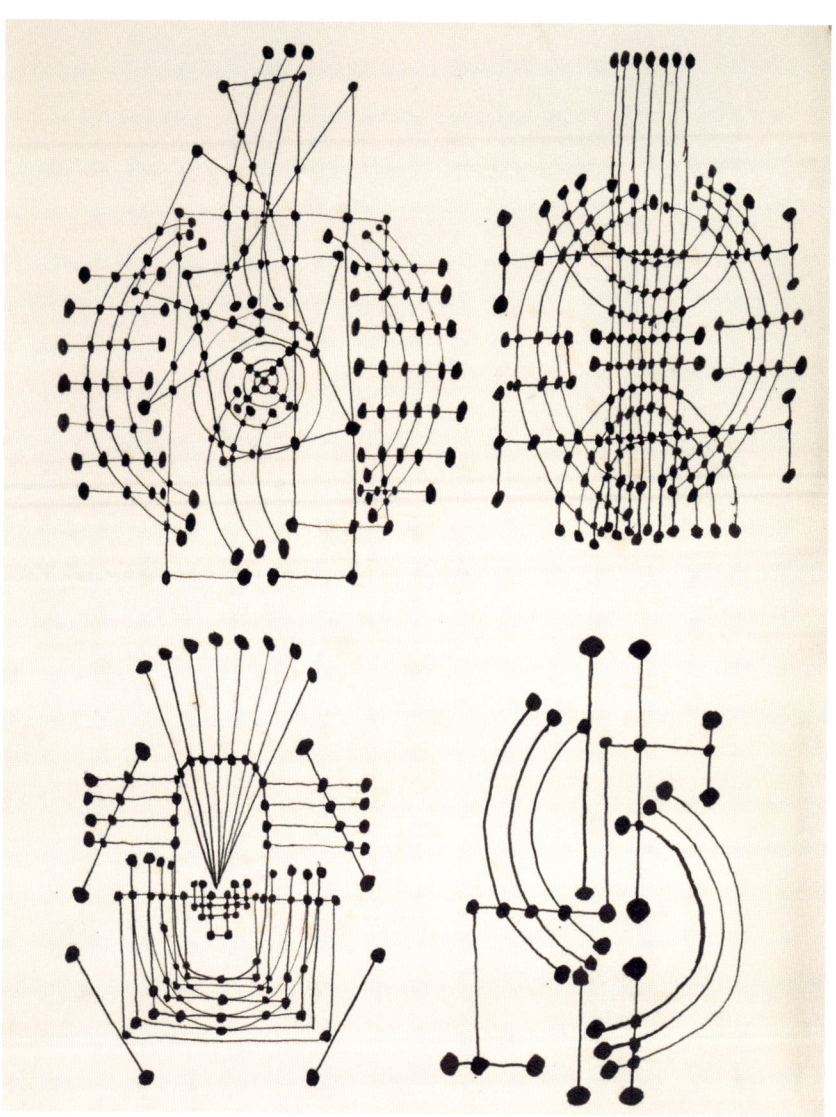

▲ **Four Studies
of a Guitar**
**Pablo Picasso, 1924,
from the *Constellations
drawings*, pen
and black ink.**

The *Constellations drawings* are a series of evocative line
and dot ink sketches drawn on sixteen pages of a notebook.
For these small drawings, Pablo Picasso (1881–1973)
took inspiration from sky charts and aimed at an artistic
exploration of the limit between abstraction and figuration.

I initially spied these Persian astrological diagrams with reference
to their inclusion in the 1966 book of striking occult imagery,
History of Occult Sciences, written by engineer and historian of
alchemy and Freemasonry, René Alleau (1917–2013). Further
research revealed that they originated in *The Book of Fixed Stars*,
an astronomical text written by Abd al-Rahman al-Sufi, c.964. The
diagrams illustrate different cultures' converging ideas of astrology.

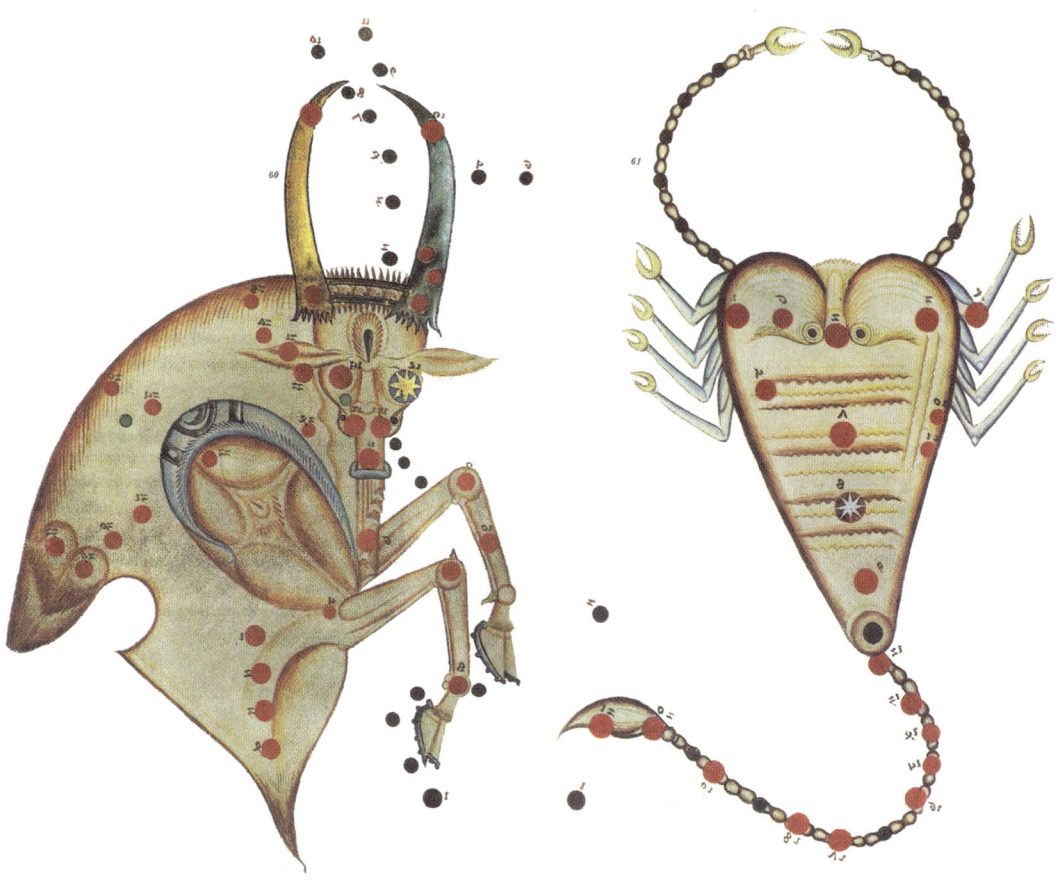

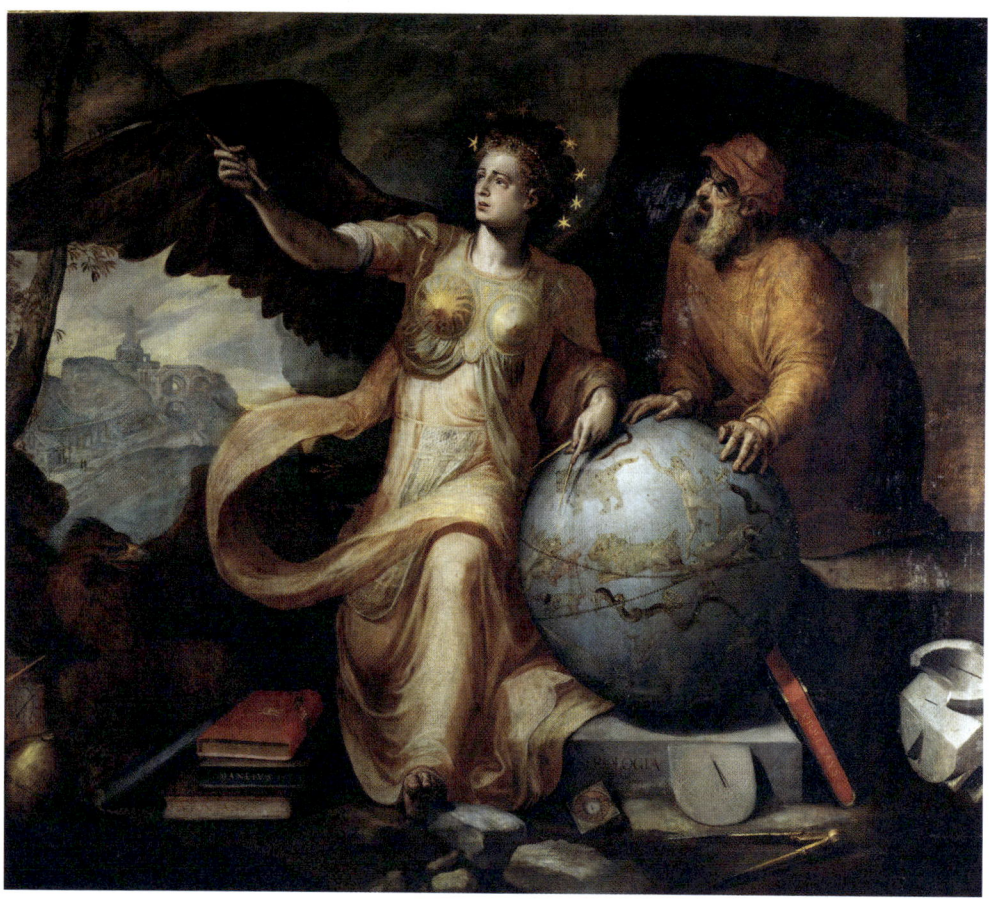

▲ Astrology
Frans Floris, 16th century.

Frans Floris (c.1519–1570) was Flemish painter, draftsman and etcher who greatly influenced the Northern Renaissance and was well known for portrayals of a broad range of allegorical subject matter. In this painting – exploring the operation of celestial influences on human bodies and terrestrial events – Astrology, a winged female personification, leans besides a globe with zodiacal star symbols. On the ground are various scientific instruments and sundials. This is one among a series of paintings by Floris for the villa of merchant and art-collector Nicolaas Jongelinck.

▶ The Sun is Passing the Sign of Virgo
M. K. Čiurlionis, 1906/7, from *The Zodiac*, tempera on paper.

Mikalojus Konstantinas Čiurlionis (1875–1911) was a Lithuanian painter, composer and writer and has been considered one of the pioneers of abstract art in Europe. Čiurlionis was interested in the structure of the universe and man's place in it. The most famous of Čiurlionis' series is his 12 paintings named *The Zodiac*. This theme was inspired by the ancient myths of the constellations and it was supported by the artist's interest in astronomy.

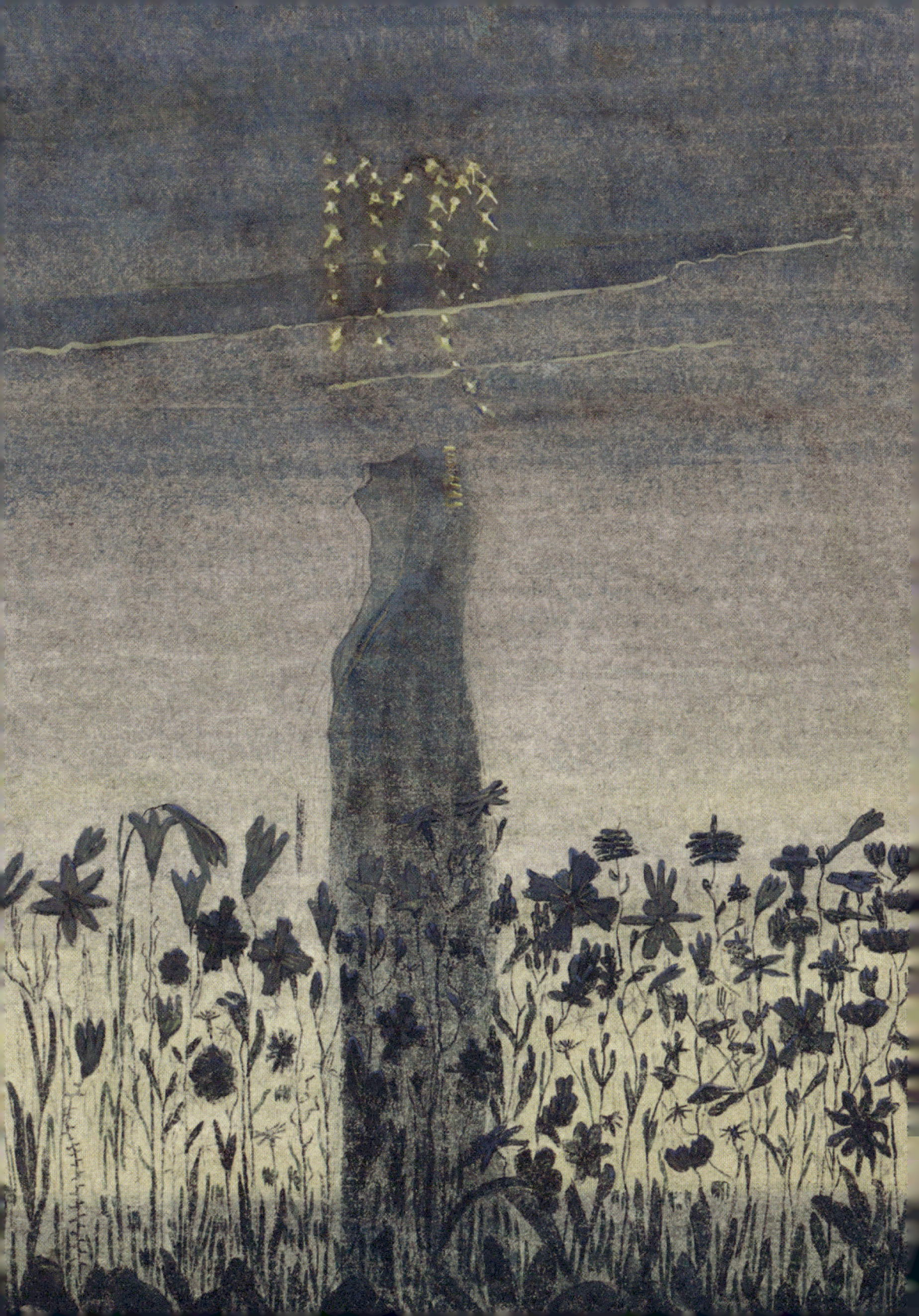

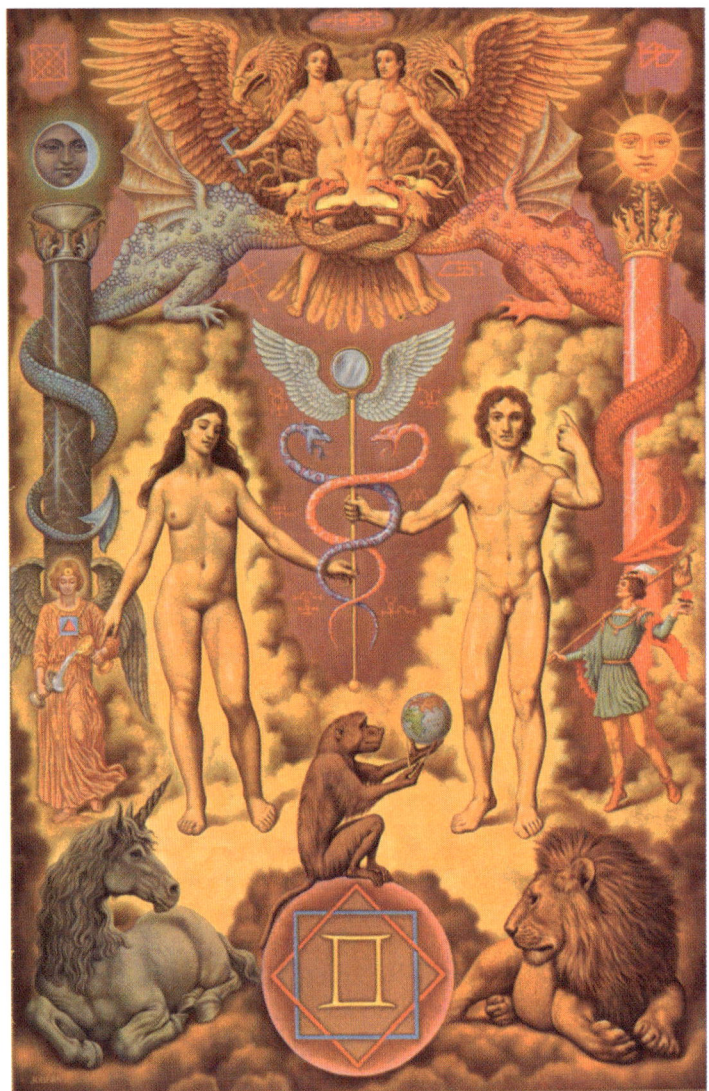

Jake Baddeley (b.1964) draws his inspirations from many sources: the Ancient Greeks, the Italian Renaissance Masters, the Dutch Masters, iconography, mythology, psychology and philosophy. But most of all the artist relies on his own subconscious and intuition, which has proven many times to have a logic and curious independence of its own. The depiction of Libra with a pair of scales, notes the artist, is very old. The balance corresponds to an Egyptian deity, Ma'at, the goddess of measure and balance. The key traits for a Libra personality type is said to be the qualities of balance harmony and diplomacy. The constellation itself is also in the shape of a pair of scales.

▲ **Gemini**
Johfra Bosschart,
1974/5, from
The Zodiac Series.

Johfra Bosschart (1919–1998) was a Dutch painter who described his own works as 'Surrealism based on studies of psychology, religion, the Bible, astrology, antiquity, magic, witchcraft, mythology and occultism'. His series of zodiac paintings, brimming with symbolism, was produced between 1974 and 1975.

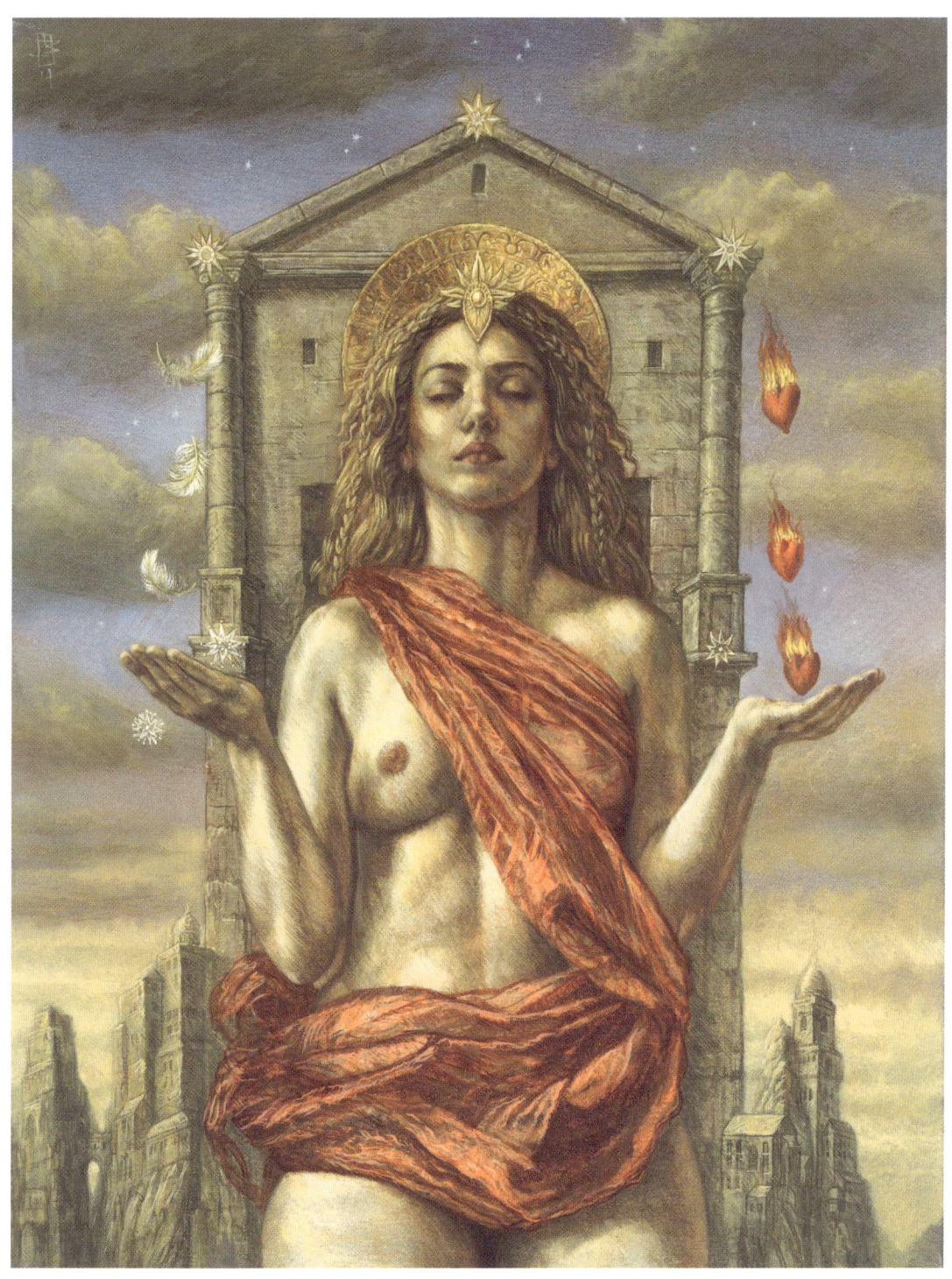

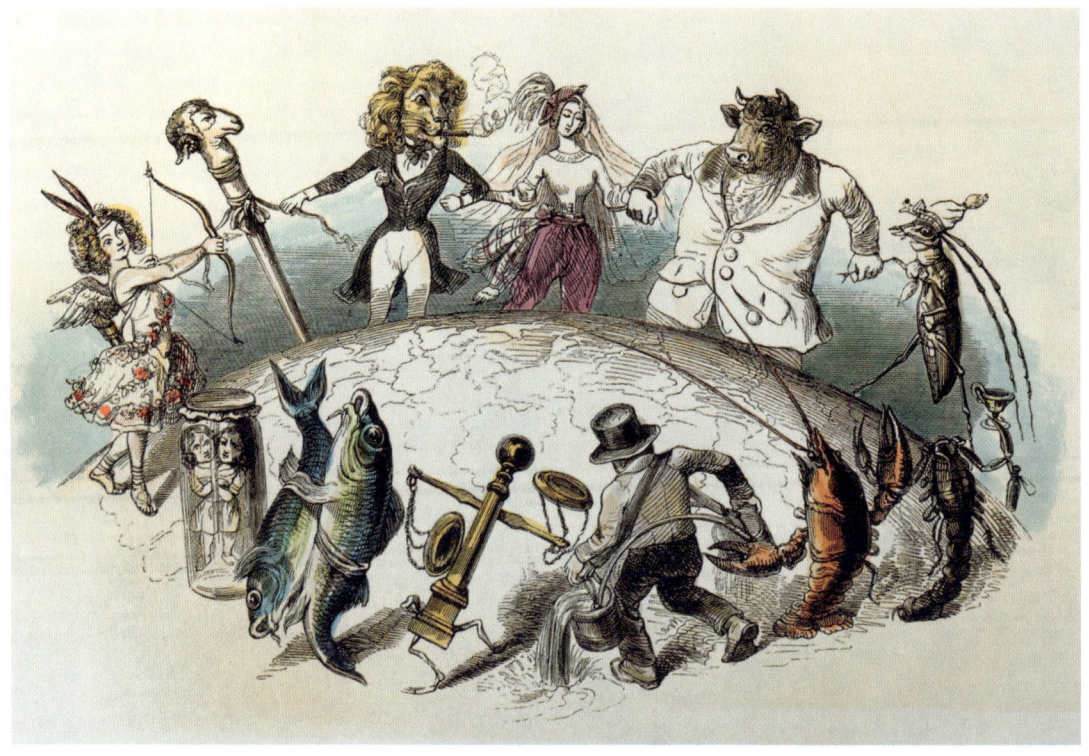

▲ The zodiac in a round dance around the world
J. J. Grandville, 1847, from *Les etoilles animées*, coloured engraving.

► Zodiac
Alphonse Mucha, 1896, colour lithograph.

Influential and prolific French illustrator and caricaturist J. J. Grandville (1803–1847) created delightful, discordant and anthropomorphised imagery which 'captured the foibles and follies of humanity with the metaphor of the menagerie.' Grandville's work is now recognised as a major precursor and inspiration to the Surrealist movement. In this dancing circle of astrological archetypes, we can make out the attributes of each of the signs of the zodiac. As for artist himself, born on September 13, 1803 – Grandville was a Virgo.

Alfonse Maria Mucha (1860–1939) known internationally as Alphonse Mucha, was a Czech painter, illustrator and graphic artist. Living in Paris during the Art Nouveau period, he is best known for his distinctly stylised and decorative theatrical posters. *Zodiac* was Mucha's first work under his contract with the printer Champenois, and was originally designed as an in-house calendar for the company. In this piece, Mucha integrated twelve zodiac signs in the halo-like disk behind the woman's head, one of Mucha's customary motifs. It became one of his most popular designs.

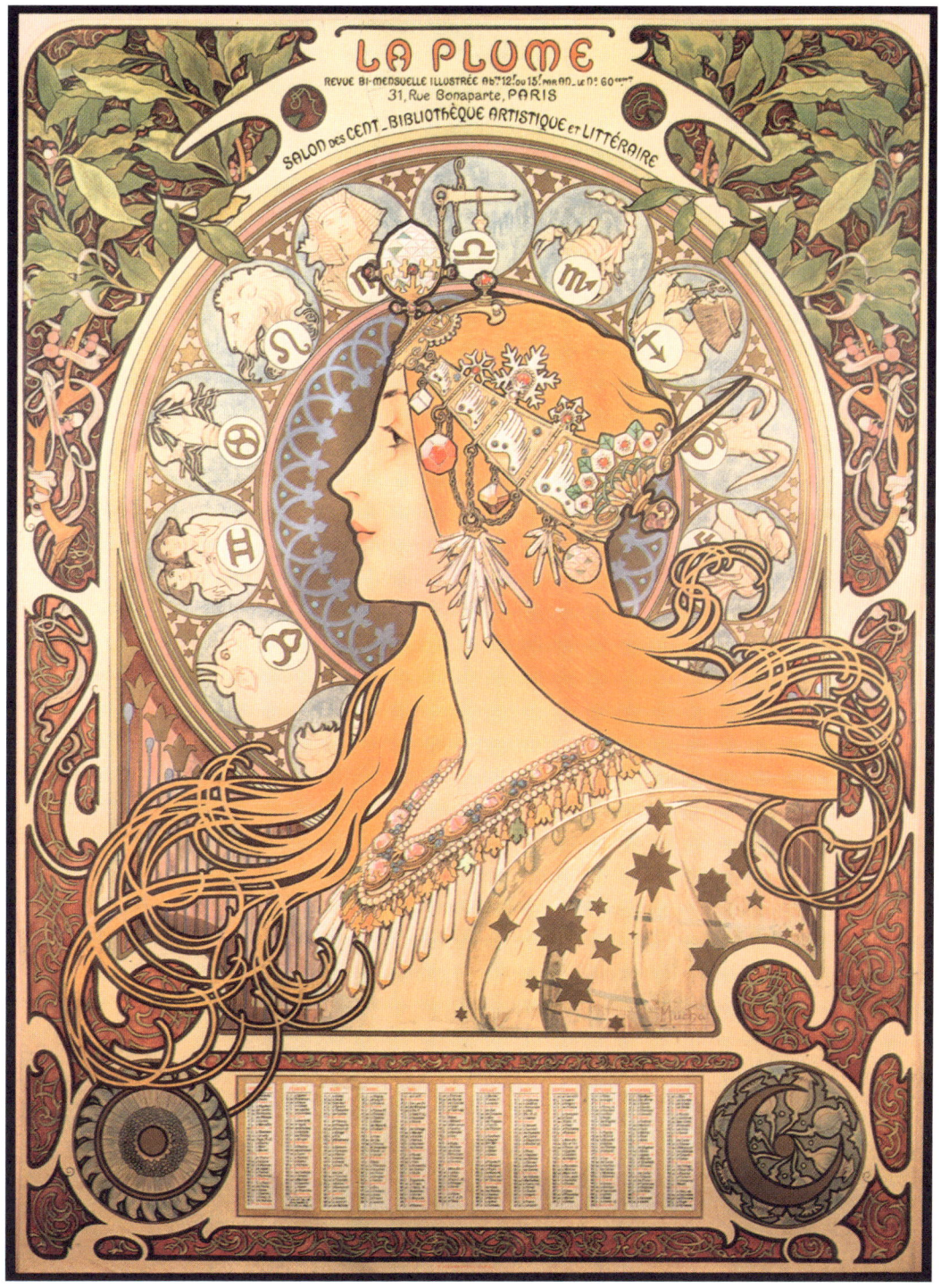

III

THE IMAGERY
AND
INSPIRATION
OF THE
ELEMENTS

Times, Mexican novelist and screenwriter Laura Esquivel revealed the following intimate tidbit concerning her daily rituals and the altars at which they are performed: 'I acknowledge the four elements . . . Water in the north; incense to recognise the air in the east; flowers for the earth in the south; a candle for light from the west. It helps me keep perspective.' This artful and evocative description of the surrealist storyteller's magical, perspective-keeping practices provides lovely imagery for the reader and draws upon an idea that is foundational to nearly all Western occult philosophies: the classical elements.

The Greeks proposed the existence of five essential elements, four of which were the physical elements – fire, air, water and earth – of which the entire world is composed. These four physical elements are considered the cornerstones of all life, not only on earth but throughout the universe, linking humans to nature and the divine. The fifth element goes by a variety of names; some refer to it as 'spirit', others call it 'aether' or 'quintessence' (literally 'the fifth element' in Latin), or 'akasha' in India.

Different cultures had varying explanations concerning the attributes of the elements and how they related to widely observable phenomena, as well as the origin and evolution of the universe. Sometimes these ideas overlapped with mythology and they were personified as deities or 'elemental beings'. Swiss alchemist Paracelsus

with each element. Gnomes are chthonic earth elementals, often depicted guarding mines and underground treasures; undines are water elementals, usually found in forest pools and waterfalls; salamanders are fantastical creatures that correspond to the element of fire; and sylphs are invisible air elementals. Plato divided all beings into four groups based on the elements: air/birds, water/fish, earth/pedestrians and fire/stars. The alchemists and magicians of the Middle Ages derived their philosophy of humoral constitutions around Aristotle's four-element theory, whereby these qualities determined the behaviours and temperaments of the human body: earth corresponds to melancholic/black bile; water to phlegmatic/ phlegm; air to sanguine/blood; fire to choleric/ yellow bile. Admittedly, it's more than a little repulsive if you spend too much time thinking about it!

These elemental relationships and correspondences extended to various gems, minerals and metals, planets and constellations, the Four Horsemen of the Apocalypse, multiple species of the animal and plant kingdoms, human personality traits, as well as geometrical shapes.

Ancient cultures in Persia, Greece, Babylonia, Japan and India had similar lists of elements, although some referred to air as 'wind' and the fifth element as 'void'. The Chinese Wu Xing system lists Wood, Fire, Earth, Metal, and Water

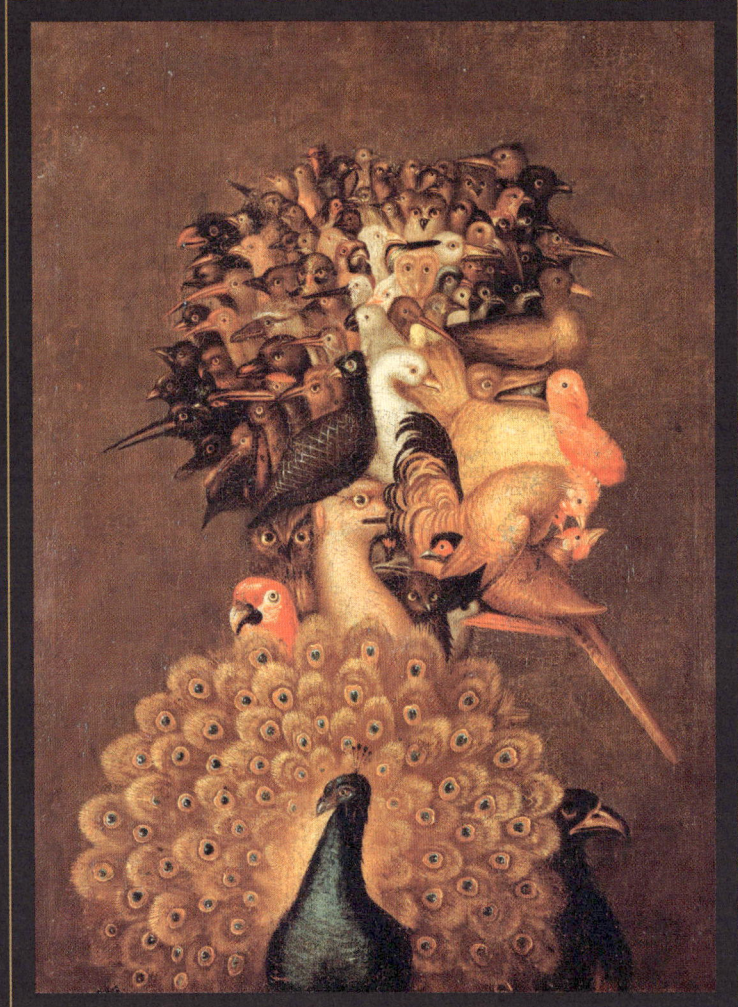

► **Elementals**
Balthasar Schwan,
from *Philosophia
Reformata* (Johann
Daniel Mylius, 1622).

Johann Daniel Mylius
(c.1583–1642) was a
composer and a writer
on alchemy, as well as
scholar of theology and
medicine. A plate from his
Philosophia Reformata,
created by German engraver
and printmaker Balthasar
Schwan (d.1624), depicts
four woman, or goddesses,
balancing upon spheres
which bear the symbols
of the four elements –
from left to right, Earth,
Water, Air and Fire.

▲ **Air**
Giuseppe Arcimboldo, c.1566, from *The Four Elements*.

In his allegorical series of *The Four Elements* Giuseppe Arcimboldo
(1527–1593) assigned a face formed by the animals or objects
most characteristic of each element. Traditionally known for his
religious works, it is thought that with these faces, Arcimboldo
catered to the era's penchant for puzzles and the bizarre.

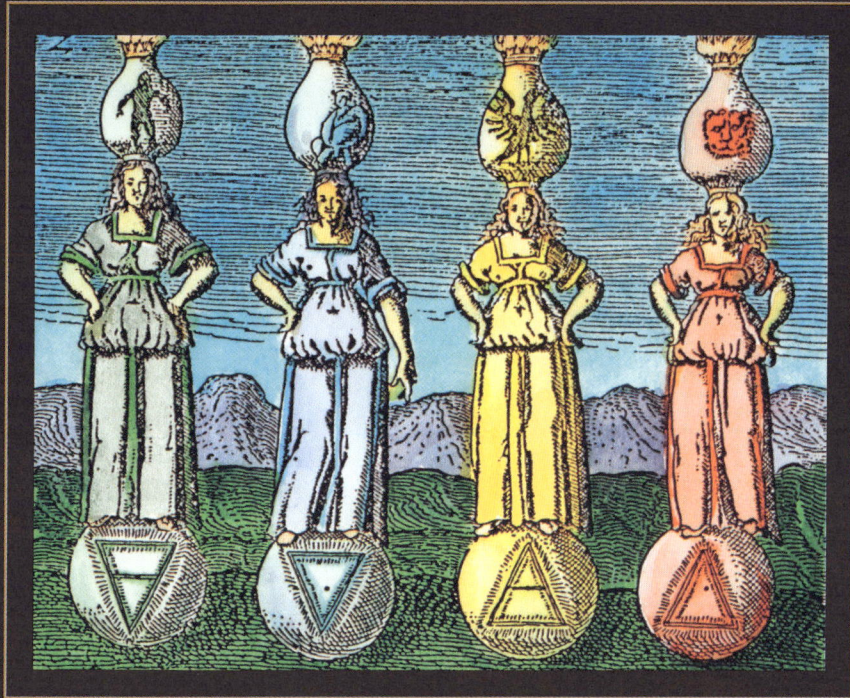

though these are described more as energies than types of material.

Being considered sacred, vital forces of nature, the elements often serve as inspiration for artists and those who are tapped into the divine. In the latter sixteenth and the seventeenth centuries, it became common to symbolise the elements using references to the natural world. In a series of paintings by Joachim Beuckelaer, *Earth* was depicted as an abundance of vegetables, tumbling from baskets; *Fire* as still-life haunches of meat and poultry being prepared for cooking on the fire; in *Air*, several varieties of fowl are offered for sale; and in *Water*, street vendors offer a dozen different kinds of fish. In a less aggressively terrestrial fashion, Surrealist artist Leonora Carrington's *The Garden of Paracelsus* portrays what could be viewed as a delicate alchemical dance amongst ethereal elemental creatures in the dim pallor of a twilit garden.

Sadly, we are not all imaginative writers of magical realism, like author Laura Esquivel; nor are most of us visual artists who splash watercolours masterfully on canvas or sculpt majesty from stone. I believe, though, that we can (even if we are only creatives at heart) be moved by the poetry and philosophy of the elements. We can find evidence of this instinct in the phantom perfume of incense lingering in the air, the fallen petals of a rose recently plucked from the earth, the warm wax of a candle flame just snuffed, and the soft glimmer of water droplets disappearing into the woollen cables of our sweaters on a misty morning's walk around our neighbourhood.

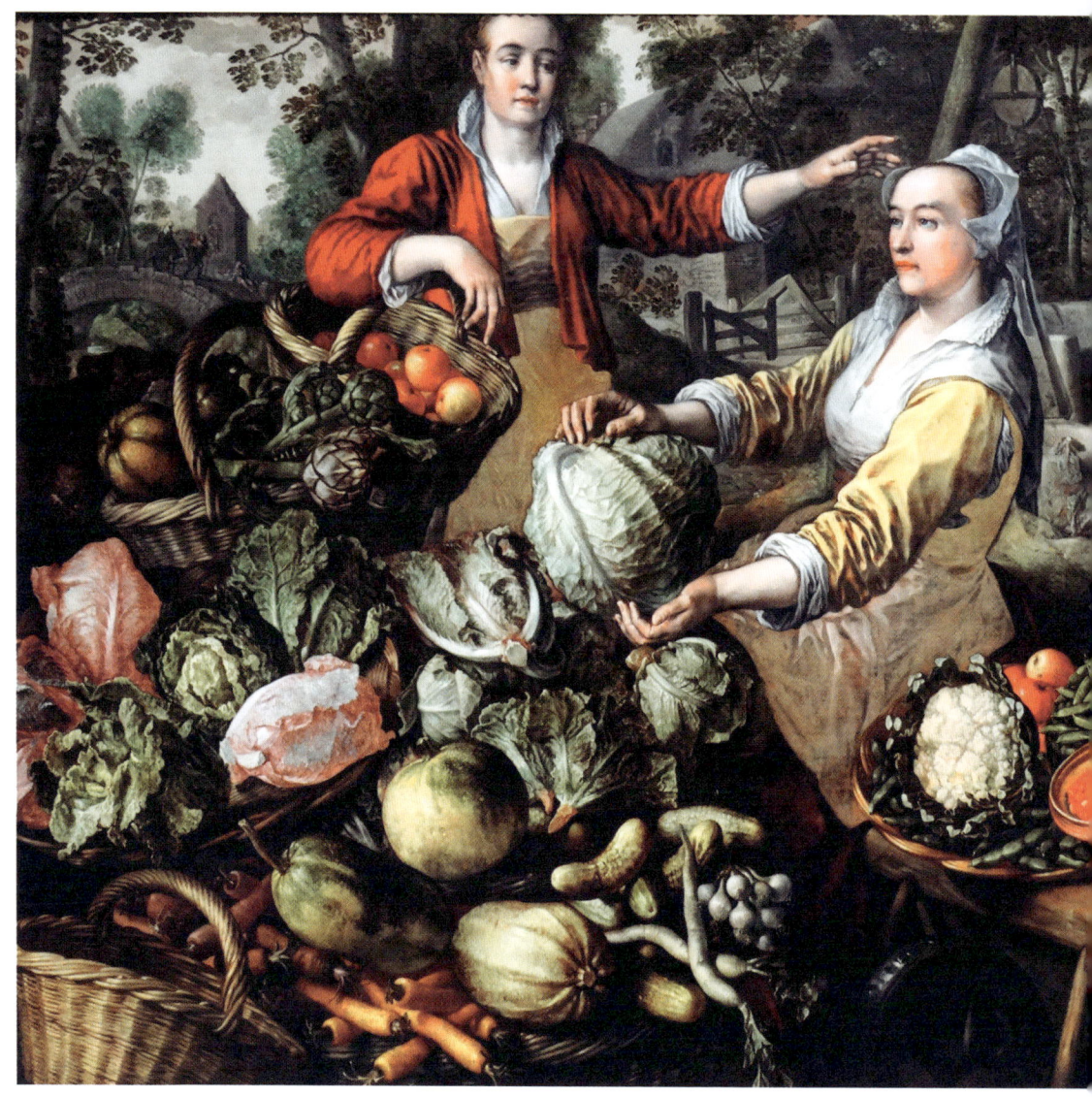

▲ The Four Elements: Earth
Joachim Beuckelaer, 1569, oil on canvas.

Although superficially market and kitchen scenes packed with fish, fruit, vegetables, birds and animals – in this series of works by Flemish painter Joachim Beuckelaer (1533–1574) the different types of food represent the four elements: vegetables for earth, fish for water, poultry for air and game for fire.

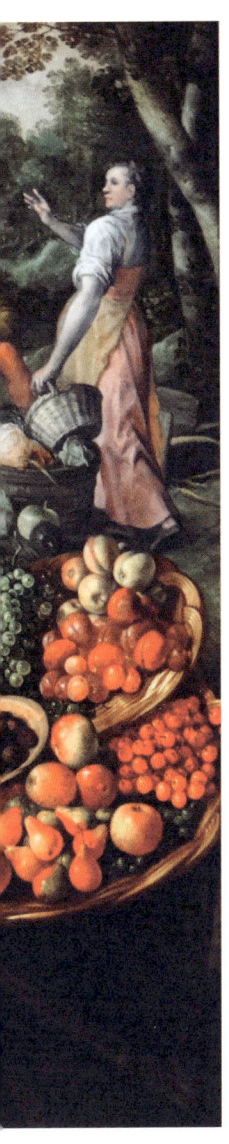

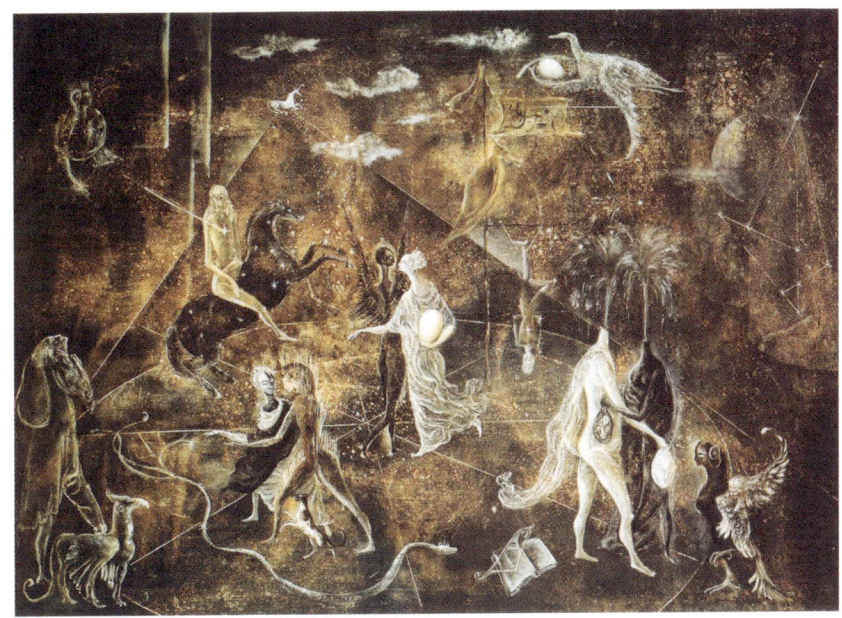

▲ **The Garden of Paracelsus**
Leonora Carrington, 1957, oil on canvas.

In the muted yet decadent dreamscape of her work *The Garden of Paracelsus*, Surrealist artist Leonora Carrington (1917–2011) depicts a magical bestiary of arcane symbolism where all manner of elemental beings slither and prance. Paracelsus described the four elemental beings, each corresponding to one of the four elements: salamanders, which correspond to fire; gnomes, corresponding to earth; undines, corresponding to water; and sylphs, corresponding to air.

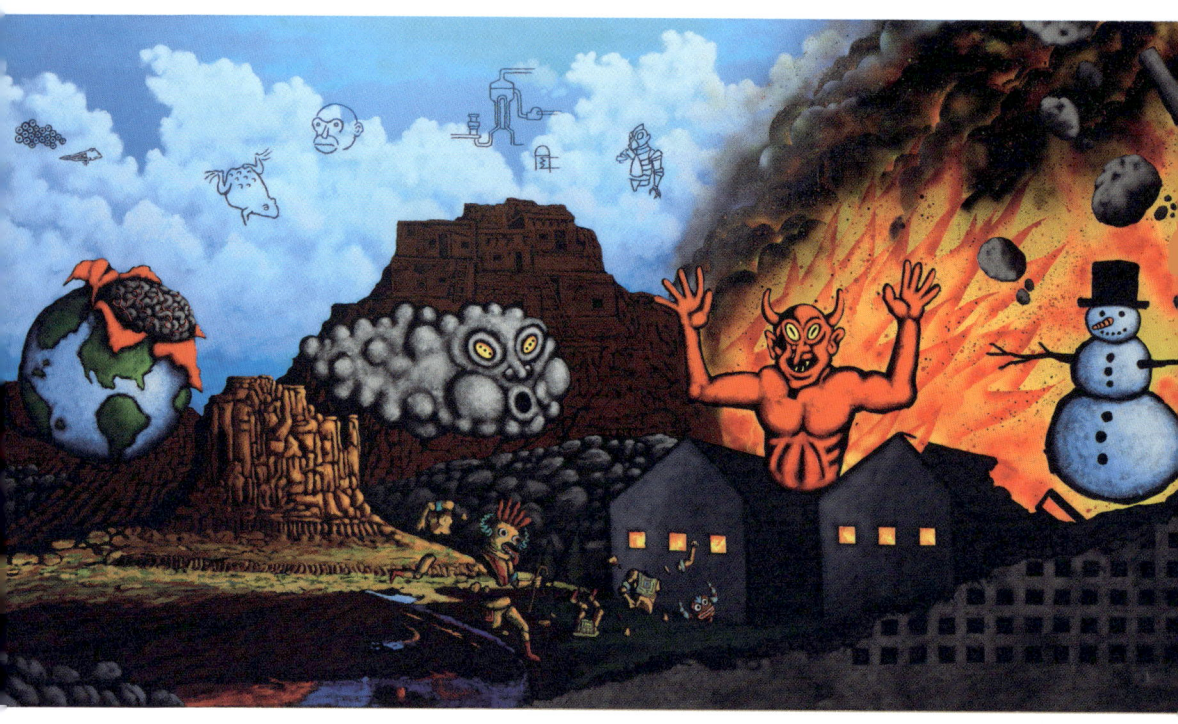

▲ Earth, Wind, Fire and Water
David Wojnarowicz, 1986, acrylic,
spraypaint and collage on canvas.

David Wojnarowicz's (1954–1992)
diverse body of work spans performance,
photography, painting, sculpture and
time-based media. It is unified by an
'underlying political urgency and a
highly personal visual symbology'.

▶ Four Elements: Water
Patricia Ariel, 2018, graphite ink
and acrylic on paper.

Patricia Ariel (b.1970) creates images full of symbolism, spirituality
and mysticism. She believes in promoting consciousness and a
perception of the spiritual and sacred in the mind of the viewer
through her images, in which beauty and communion with nature
are always present. In her *Four Elements* series, she works with
each one of the classical elements used in the ancient traditions
to describe the compositional foundation of the natural world.

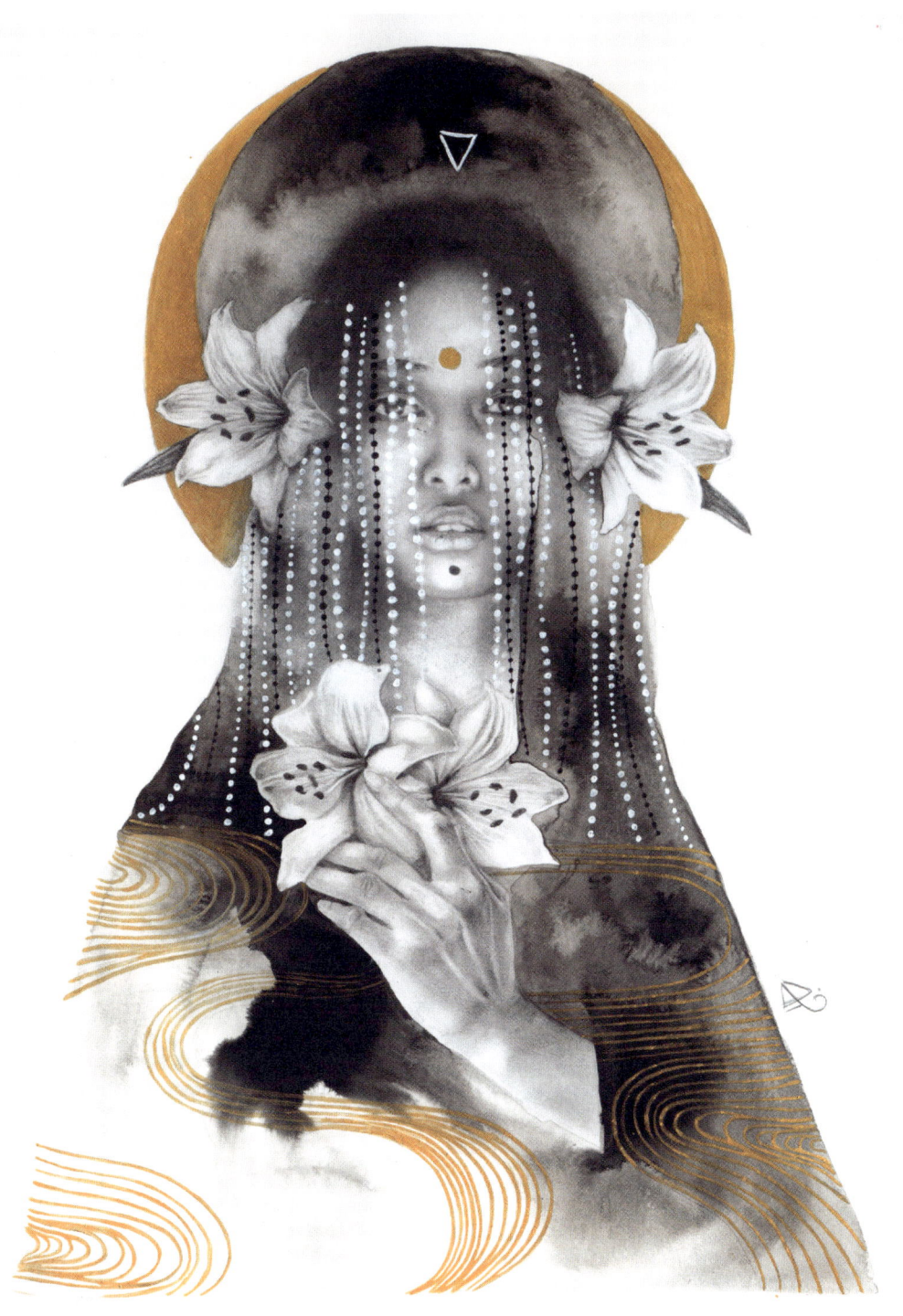

► Water
Matteo Mauro, 2018,
digital painting.

In his elemental series, Italian artist, architect and designer
Matteo Mauro takes a conceptual journey through the
myriad ways in which the components of nature have
been interpreted – from the realistic to the abstract.

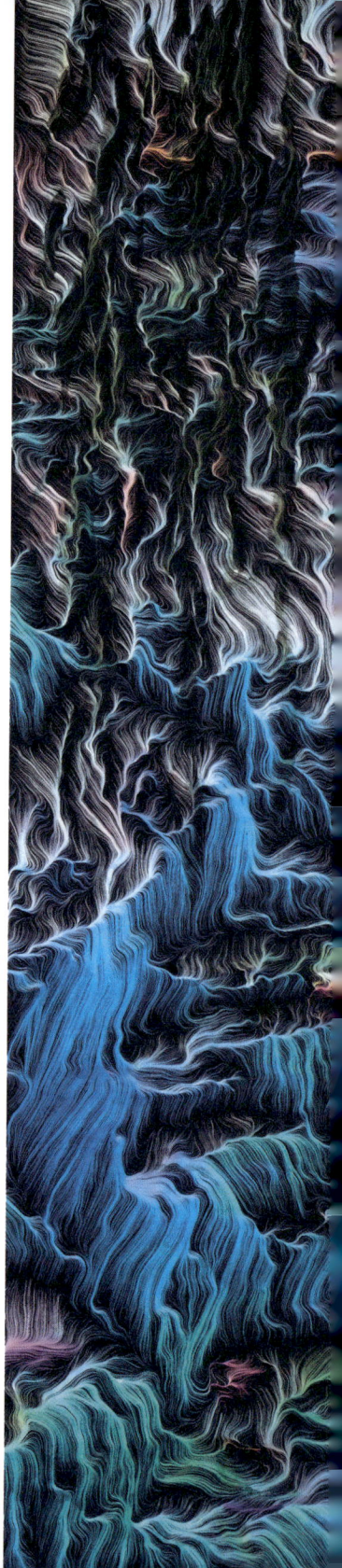

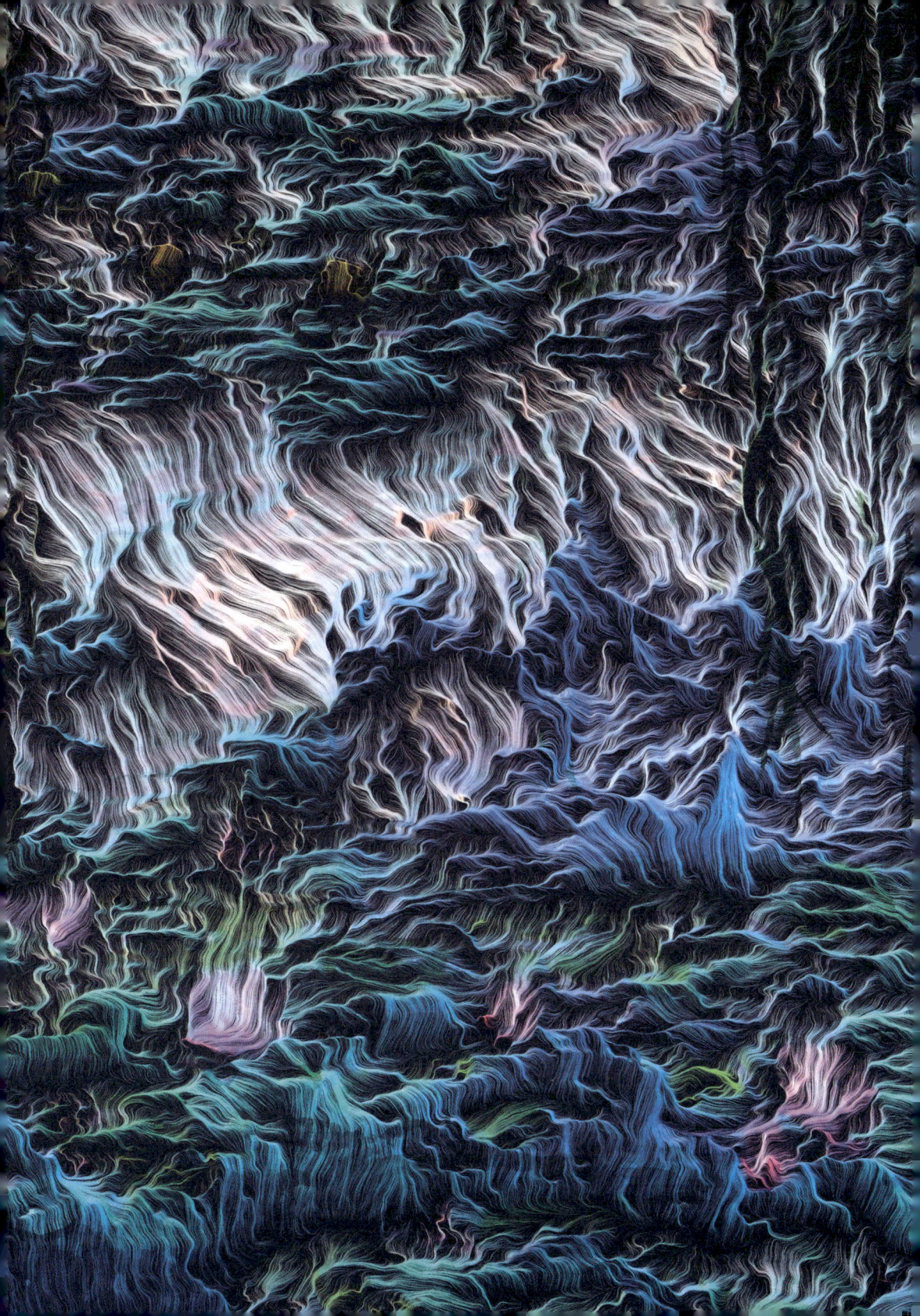

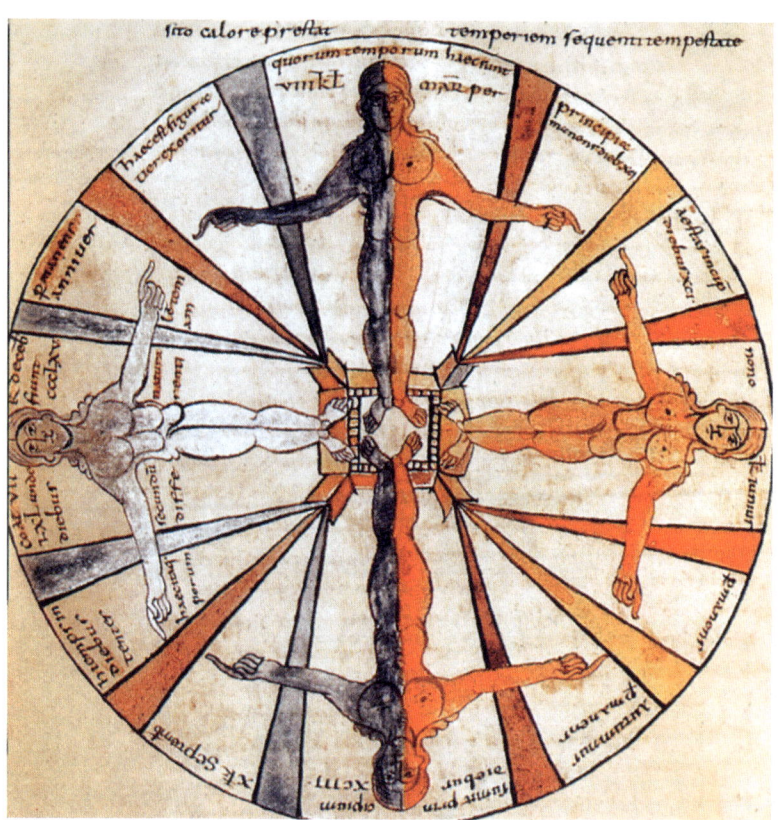

▲ **The wheel of
seasons and months**
From *De natura
rerum* (Isidore of
Seville, c.612–615).

Isidore of Seville (560–636), was a scholar, prolific writer,
and, for over three decades, Archbishop of Seville. He
is regarded as 'the last scholar of the ancient world',
in the oft-quoted words of the 19th-century historian
Montalembert. As it happens, Isidore of Seville is also
widely considered 'the patron saint of the internet'.
This is perhaps because he wrote a 20 book opus *The
Etymologies*, also known as the *Origins*, in which he tried
to record everything that was known. In book 11, Seville
writes on the body as it corresponds to the four elements:
earth (flesh), air (breath), water (blood) and fire (vital heat).

THE COSMOS

▼ Allegory of the Four Elements
Mark Ryden, 2006, oil on Canvas.

Mark Ryden (b.1963) – a contemporary artist dubbed as 'the godfather of Pop Surrealism' – is known for his compelling combinations of kitsch and preciousness juxtaposed with esoteric symbolism, mysticism and occultism. About this, the artist readily acknowledges, 'my paintings do arouse many questions'. In his enchanting painting, *Allegory of the Four Elements*, four nymphs gather around a tree stump. Each has the alchemical symbol for their respective element (earth, water, fire, air) on their dress.

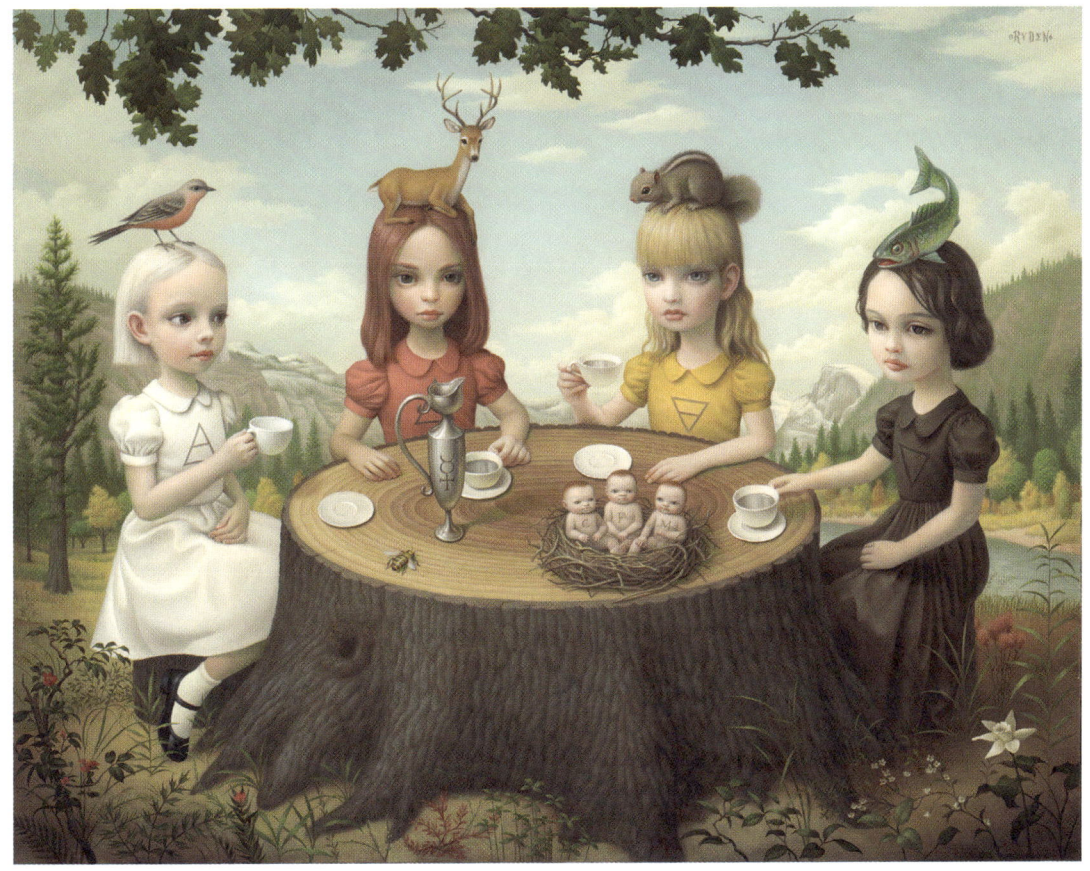

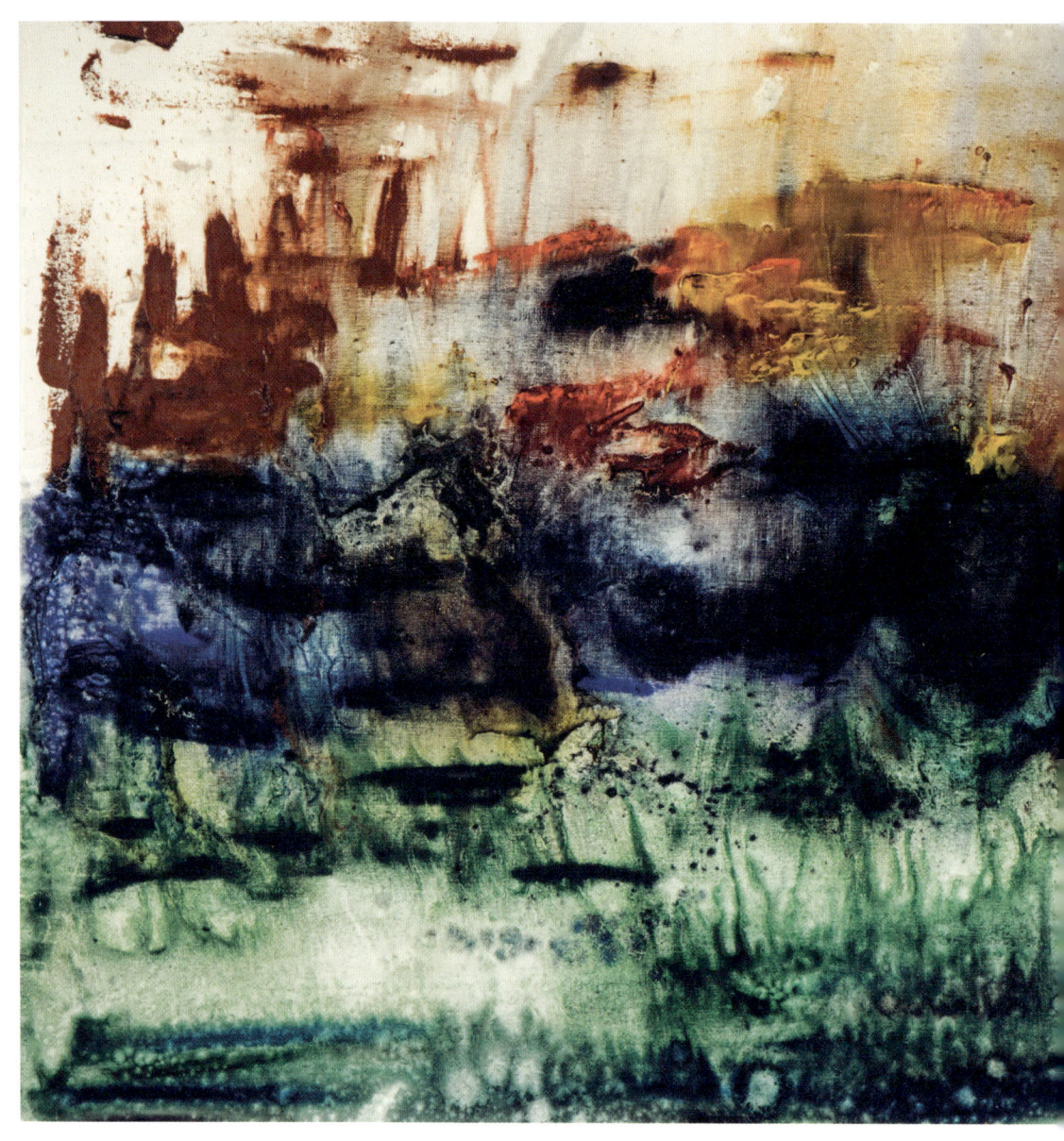

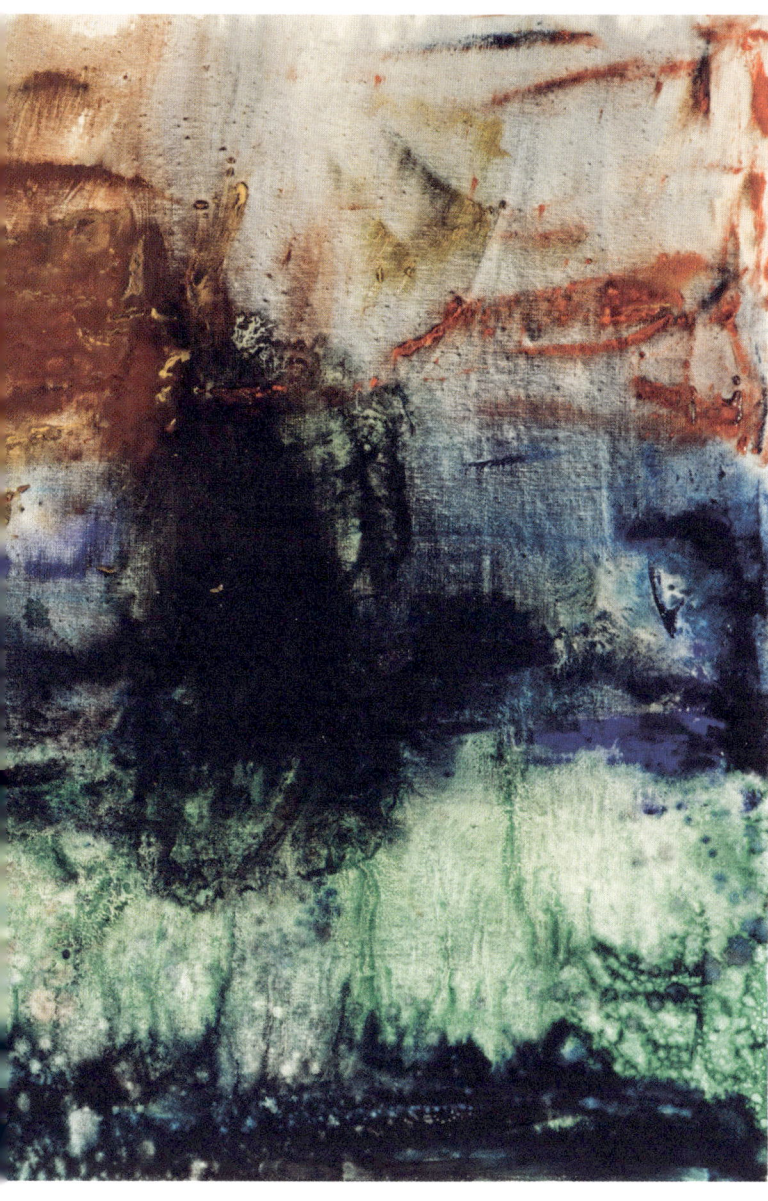

◄ **Celebration of Earth, Air, Fire and Water**
William Johnstone,
1974, oil on canvas.

Scottish artist and writer William Johnstone's (1897–1981) work *Celebration of Earth, Air, Fire and Water* was painted in the spring of 1974 during a burst of creativity inspired by the spirit of growth and renewal. The artist stated that he worked 'with tremendous speed, almost unconsciously' and the resulting imagery exudes energy and life due to this dynamic method of painting as well as the combination of rich, vibrant colours used to represent the elements. Johnstone's work was heavily influenced by the Abstract Expressionists in the US, in addition to the notion of the unconscious, as inspired by Surrealism.

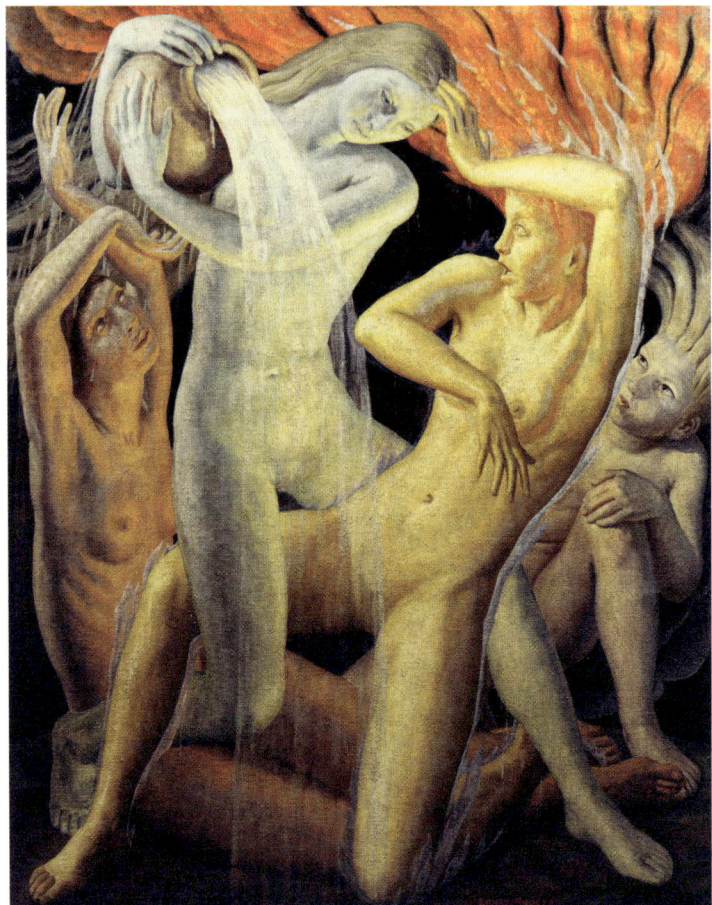

▶ **The Four Elements**
machumaYu, 2019,
oil on Canvas.

Using art to probes the
depths of the human mind,
the enigmatic machumaYu
explores the imagery of
the four elements in her
signature pop-surrealist
style. The artist's works are
interpretations of 'bright
darkness' that depict the
loneliness, desperation, hope,
joy, sadness and conflict at
the root of peoples' hearts.

▲ **The Four Elements**
Ernest Procter, 1928, oil on canvas.

In *The Four Elements* by English designer, illustrator and painter
Ernest Procter (1885–1935) we can observe the artists portrayal
of the classical four elements of earth, air, fire and water depicted
as four women dynamically displaying some of the characteristics
of the different elements. Varying beliefs regarding the sacred
elements are common to most ancient philosophies, to include
that the elemental composition of a substance determines
its particular nature and attributes, properties and actions.

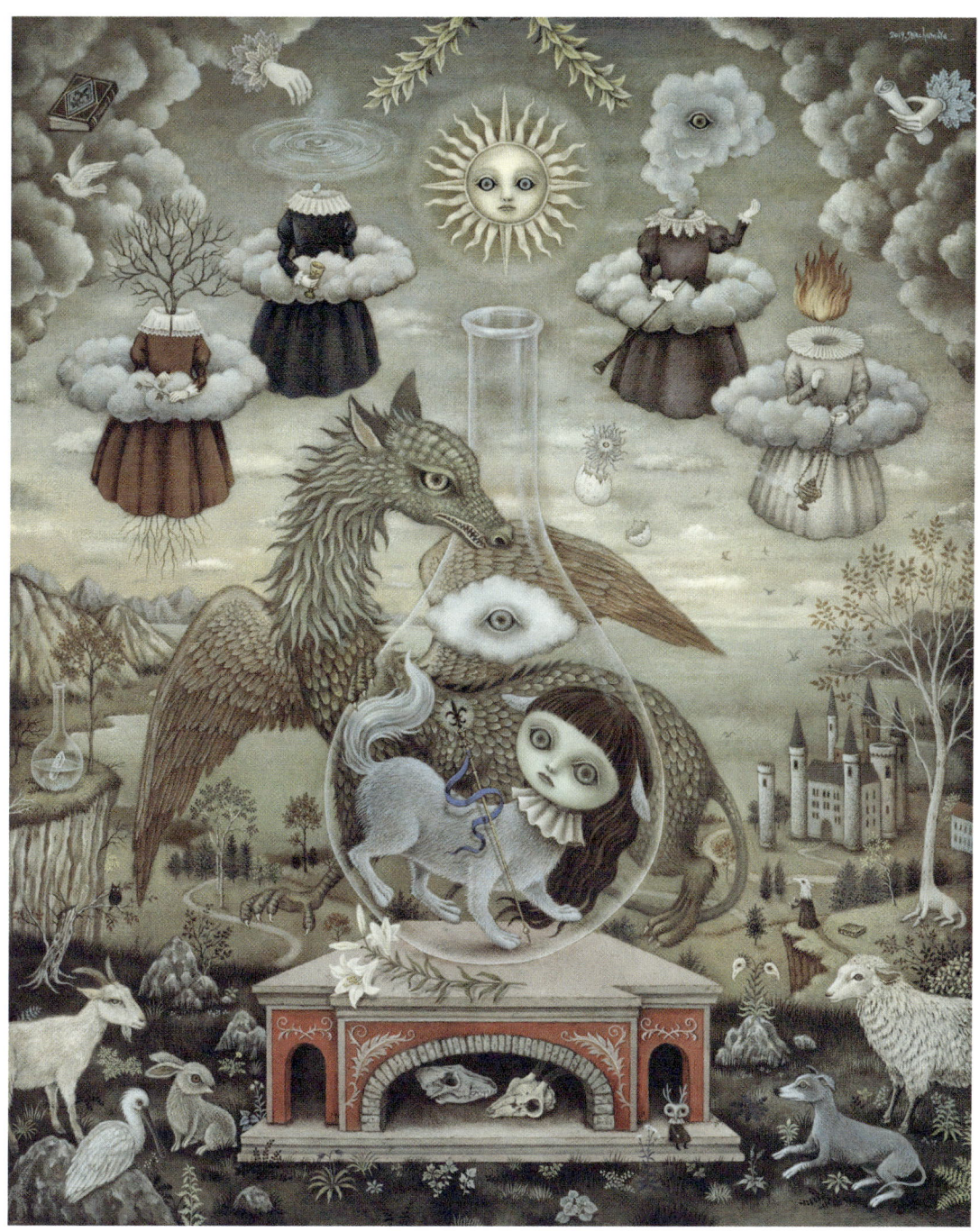

IV

ALCHEMY
AND THE
ARTISTIC
SPIRIT

A SHADOWY SCENARIO UNFOLDS AS a lone wax candle burns deep into the night. Various lenses and prisms refract the faint glow of the flickering flame to vaguely illuminate a crude, darkened laboratory, an oaken table, dusty flasks, precariously balanced, bubbling with a disquieting phosphorescence, and engines of distillation chugging and clanking murkily nearby. Brittle scrolls and yellowed manuscripts, embellished with colourful emblems and arcane symbols scribbled hastily in the margins, are scattered haphazardly on a dirt floor to further illustrate this scene of curious chemical phenomena and scholarly chaos. A wan, stocking-footed man with a funny cap alternately pores pensively over massive tomes, or perhaps pumps a small bellows to encourage a sullen, smoking fire, lost in analytical reverie.

One might be inclined to believe that the vivid picture evoked above is the description of a mystifying scene I had personally chanced upon – which is not entirely inaccurate – but, in truth, these were not cryptic goings-on witnessed first-hand. Instead, this montage is a peculiar jumble, a puzzle-piece pastiche of imagery plucked from my head, selected and composed quite at random, from observations of dozens of sixteenth- and seventeenth-century oil paintings such as Thomas Wijck's *The Alchemist*, steeped in alchemical knowledge and symbolism. It is fascinating to note that although this mental imagery initially references a specific timeframe, the artistic

works inspired by alchemy – a mysterious and often misunderstood ancient tradition mingling science, philosophy, faith and artistic spirit – can be traced through many civilisations, spanning several millennia. To glean an understanding of artists' timeless fascination with the ancient art of alchemy, we must begin to explore the practice and its philosophies.

Alchemy was concerned with the attempt to purify and perfect certain materials, so in a very broad sense we could describe this proto-scientific practice as 'taking a lesser thing and making it a better thing'. Or, for a more academic viewpoint, we will consult Michela Pereira's definition of alchemy from the Routledge Encyclopedia of Philosophy: 'the quest for an agent of material perfection, produced through a creative activity . . . in which humans and nature collaborate'. Alchemical ventures, both in the speculative sense and hands-on practice, took several forms: metallic metamorphosis (transmuting lead into gold); the creation of an elixir to prolong/ create life; the production of a universal cure-all; or the development of a universal solvent. Philosophically speaking, these chemical and material processes were metaphors for spiritual states and transformations. Perhaps you have heard of the legendary Philosopher's Stone? This Western alchemical concept represented a mystic key variously connected to all of these notions, and an obsession that greatly preoccupied the fourteenth- and fifteenth-century European

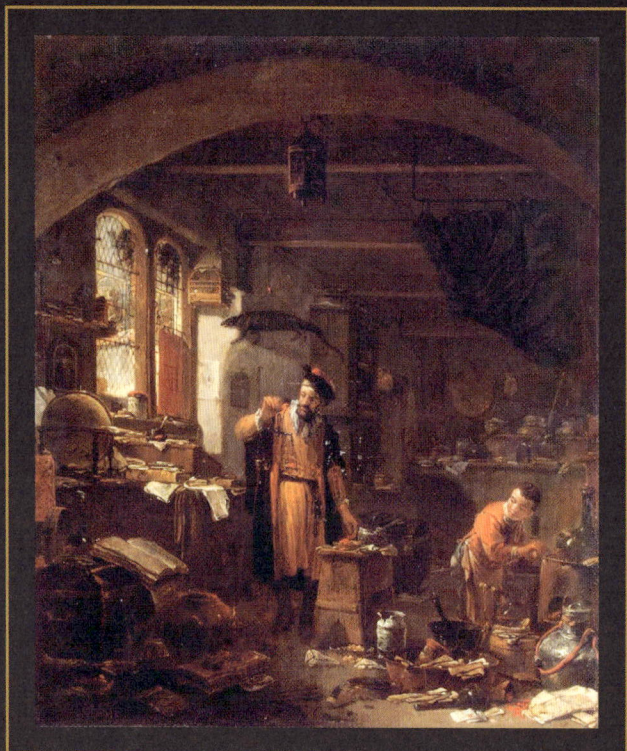

◀ **An Alchemist**
Thomas Wijck, late 17th
century, oil on panel.

In the latter years of his life, Dutch
painter of ports and landscapes
Thomas Wijck (1616–1677)
produced a great number of
paintings portraying the curious
figure of the alchemist – a theme
extremely fashionable in genre
painting in the 17th century.
He delighted in depicting the
bearded and venerable alchemist,
in amidst a murky confusion of
laboratory equipment, intent
in his clandestine quest.

alchemists who feverishly sought it out for their research and experiments.

The Ancient Egyptians, of course, were some of the first practitioners of alchemy, until Alexander the Great conquered Egypt, shifting the major hub for alchemical pursuit to Alexandria, where Egyptian, Greek and Jewish knowledge and culture accumulated. After the destruction of the Library of Alexandria in 48BC, most alchemical texts were lost, and the focus of alchemical development moved to Islamic civilisation, then travelled to Europe with the Crusades, where it regained popularity in the Renaissance period. The decline of European alchemy was precipitated by the popularity of a more modern type of science, with its focus on empirical, quantitative experimentation, detached from archaic beliefs and principles of magic, mythology and religion. In the twentieth century, a revival of alchemical thought was brought about through psychoanalyst Carl Jung, who, in re-evaluating the alchemical symbols, postulated that there is a direct relationship between them and the psychoanalytical process, as can be seen in the works of such contemporary artists as Karena Karras.

Though their notoriety for attempting to turn lead into gold is an impression to which we still default today – and setting aside mythic quests for the elixir of life and the elusive Philosopher's Stone – the goals of the alchemists were often more ambitious than simply the increase and accumulation of worldly goods. And, it might be said, more humanitarian, regarding their concerns with revealing the relationship of humans to the cosmos and using that understanding to improve the human spirit. And despite its mystical overtones, alchemy played a considerable part in laying much of the groundwork for the advancement of modern chemistry and medicine, led by the efforts of serious-minded, dedicated practitioners such as Paracelsus, Albertus Magnus, Raymond Lully and Nicolas Flamel. Alchemy spoke to a wide range of scientific uses and applications, including metallurgy, distillation and chemical medicine; inventions developed from alchemical laboratories include metal alloys, oil paints, glassmaking effects and chemical baths for photography.

Today, contemporary artists continue to be inspired by the extraordinary efforts, practices and beliefs of early alchemists; artists such as Laurie Lipton or Sveta Dorosheva incorporate alchemical principles and symbols into their work, engaging with the system of thought on a more metaphorical level, even by way of experimentation and innovation with their materials and processes. After all, when it boils down to its very purest notion, the scientists and scholars were toiling away to unlock the very secrets of how the world is made, and is there any more enduring influence on artistic practice and expression over the centuries than this?

▶ **The Alchemist Discovering Phosphorous**
Joseph Wright of Derby, 1771, oil on canvas.

Joseph Wright of Derby (1734–1797) was an English landscape and portrait painter, notable for his use of chiaroscuro effect and his paintings of candlelit subjects. Originally completed in 1771 then reworked in 1795, It has been suggested that *The Alchymist* refers to the discovery of phosphorus by the Hamburg alchemist Hennig Brand in 1669. The alchemist, illuminated, kneels in front of a shining vessel appears remarkably unsoiled for working with processes which involves the 'reduction by boiling of urine'.

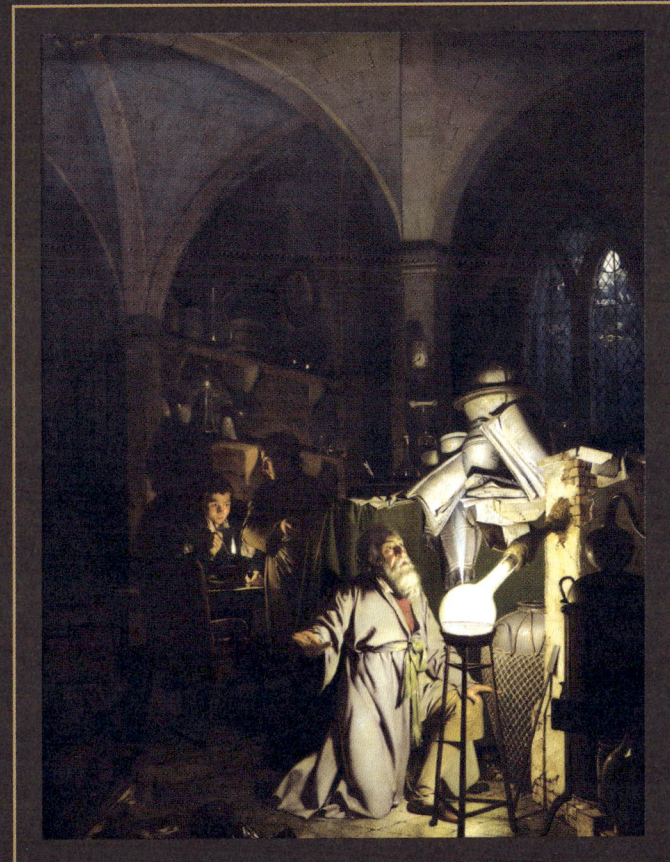

▼ Alchemist's Laboratory
Giovanni Domenico Valentino, 17th century, oil on canvas.

Giovanni Domenico Valentino (1630–1708) was an Italian painter of the late-Baroque period who specialised in a mix of genre and still-life painting. In this particular alchemical scene, we are so focused on the jumble of shining copper laboratory instruments and implements, that it would be easy to miss the alchemists busy at work in the background. At the forefront, a cat perches atop an indistinct object, both alert and idle, as only cats can be. 'Fuck this thing in particular', it seems to say, regarding the toppled container at its feet.

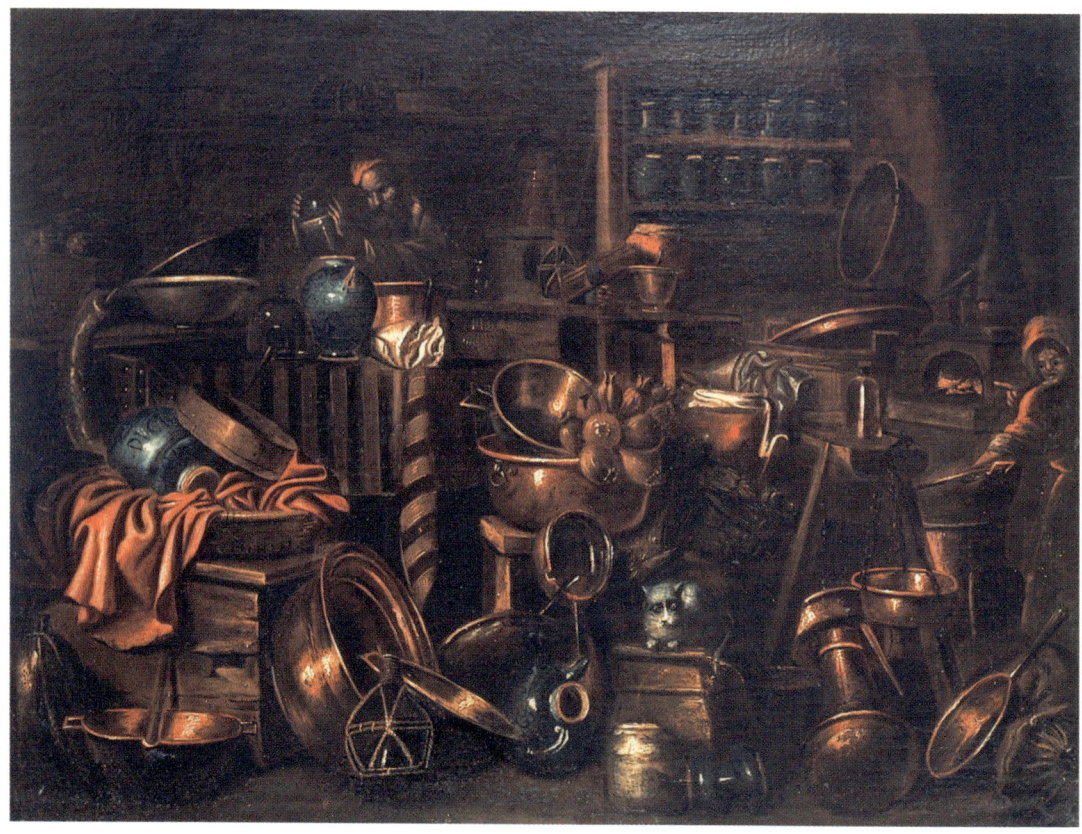

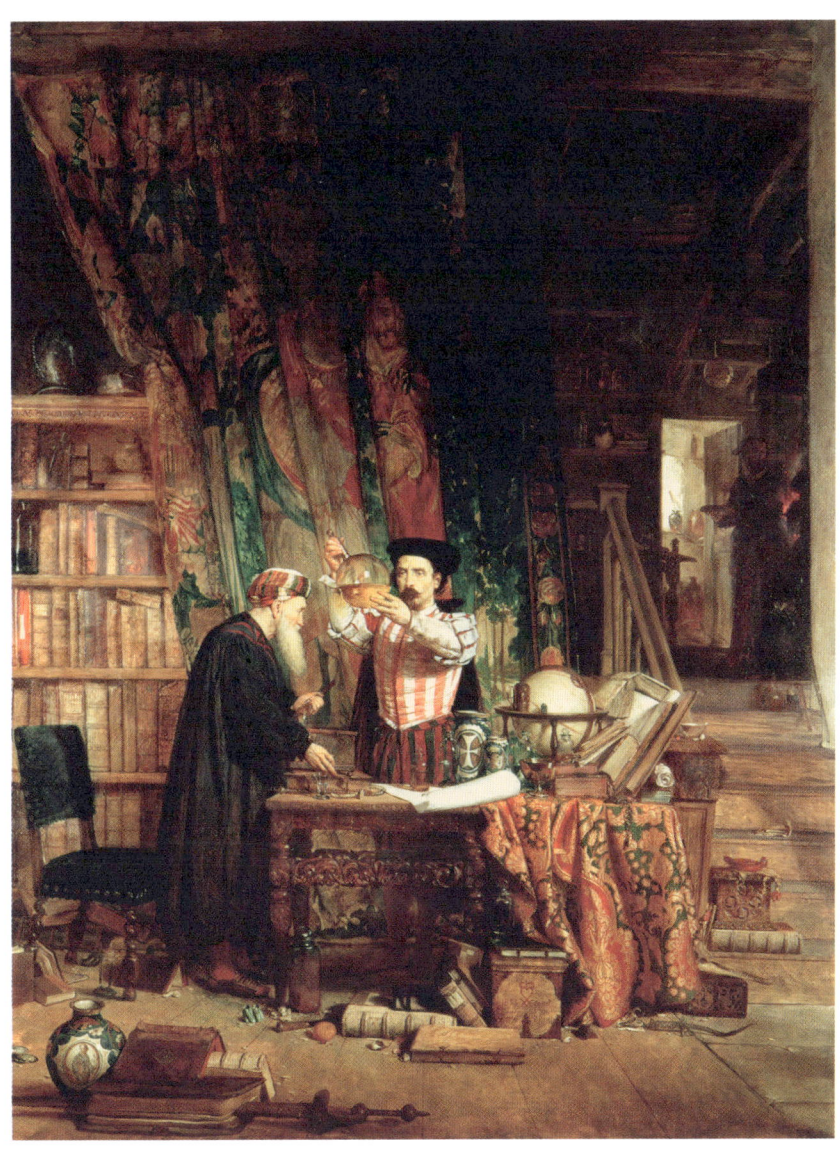

▲ The Alchemist
William Fettes
Douglas, 1853,
oil on canvas.

Scottish painter Sir William Fettes Douglas (1822–1891) was a keen art connoisseur and collector and has been described as a man 'greatly in love with the past'. The artist was fascinated by alchemy and mysticism, as clearly visible in his painting. Richly glowing colours to subtle effect, and remarkably perfect details, reflect much of the Pre-Raphaelite spirit and render this an extraordinary scene to gaze upon.

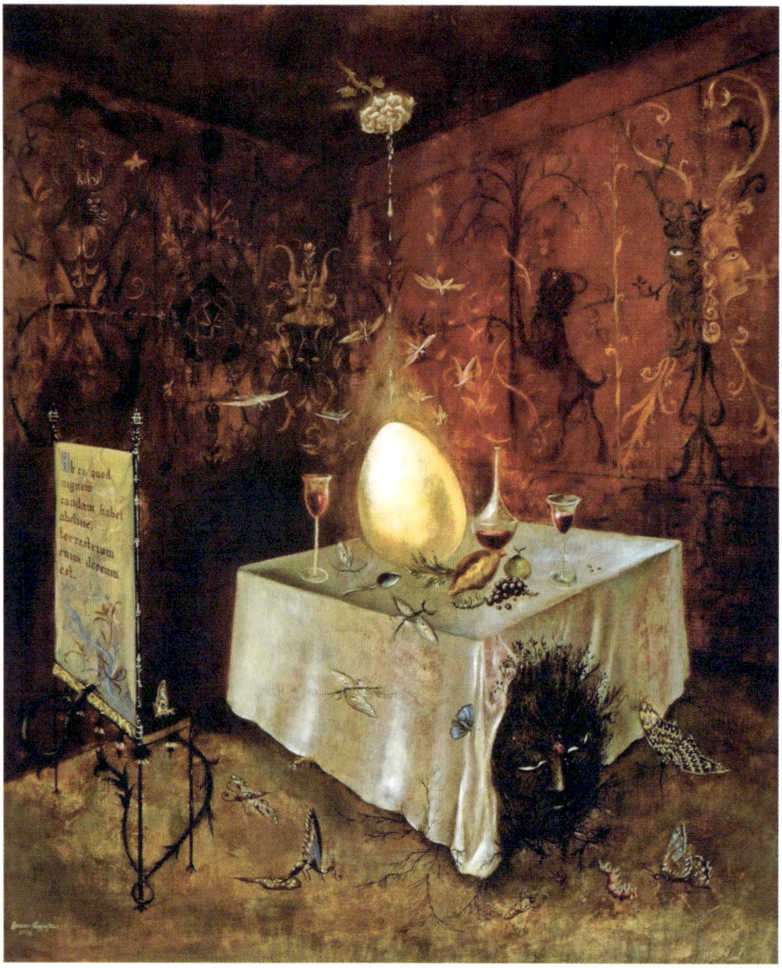

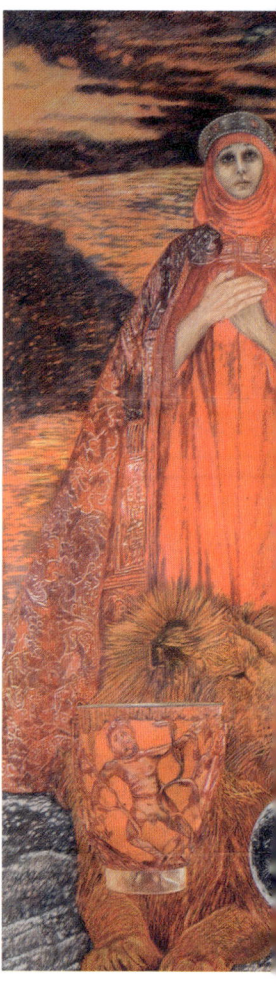

▲ AB EO QUOD
Leonora Carrington,
1956, oil on canvas.

Leonora Carrington (1917–2011) was a British-born Mexican Surrealist painter and student of the esoteric and magical arts. Her ideas of art as alchemical transformation were for a time tied to the feminine domestic sphere, in which the kitchen becomes a sacred place of magic and power. *AB EO QUOD* (1956), with its potent symbolism and arcane diagrams, hints at a precisely-timed alchemical drama developing to unfold just in time for invisible guests to arrive.

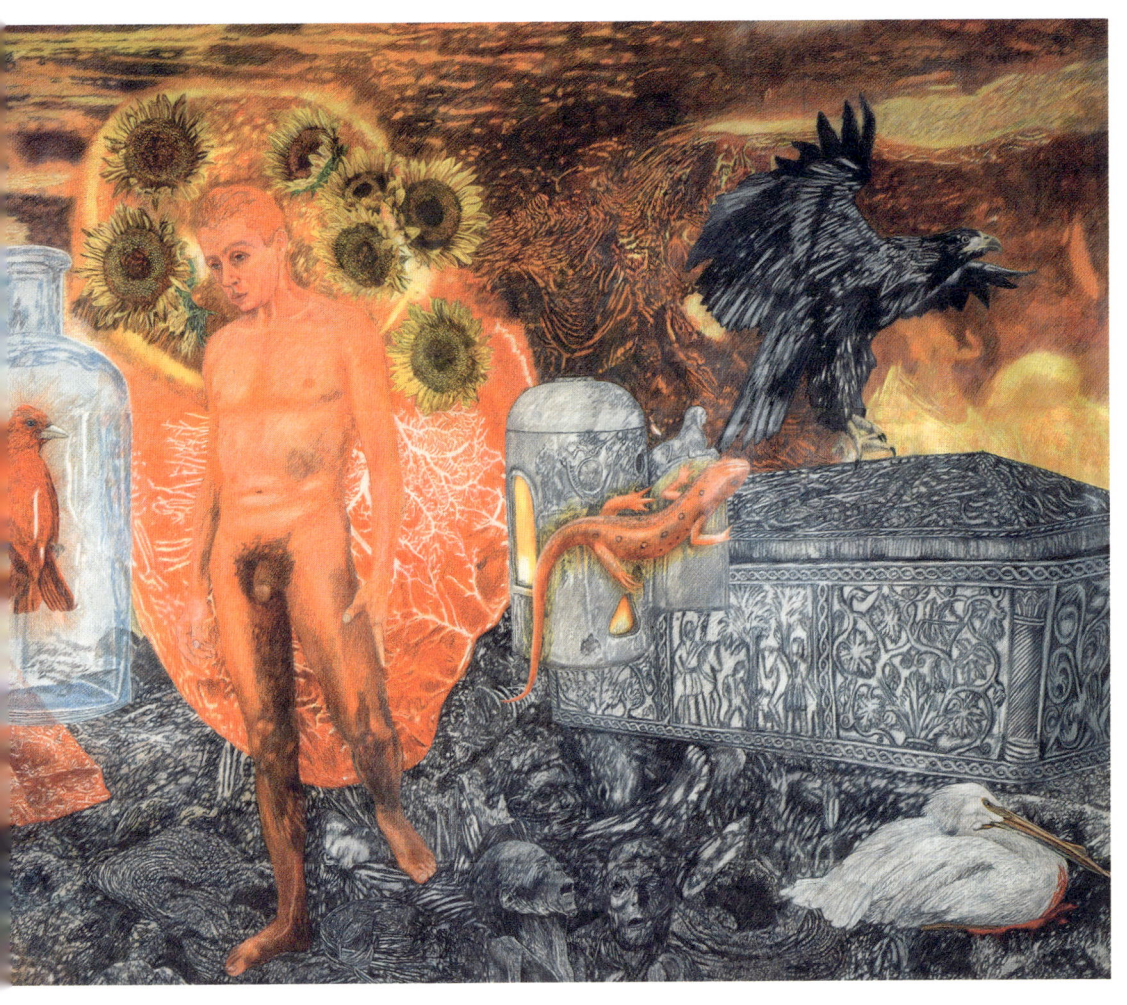

▲ Splendor Solis
Ann McCoy, 1995,
coloured pencil on
paper on canvas.

Ann McCoy (b.1946) is an artist deeply studied in
alchemy and whose lush, dreamlike imagery is much
influenced by Jungian ideas on alchemy. *Splendor Solis*
(1995), a work of delicate details rendered lushly in
coloured pencils was, according to the artist, inspired
by a dream which closely resembled plate eight of the
Splendor Solis, an illuminated alchemical manuscript.

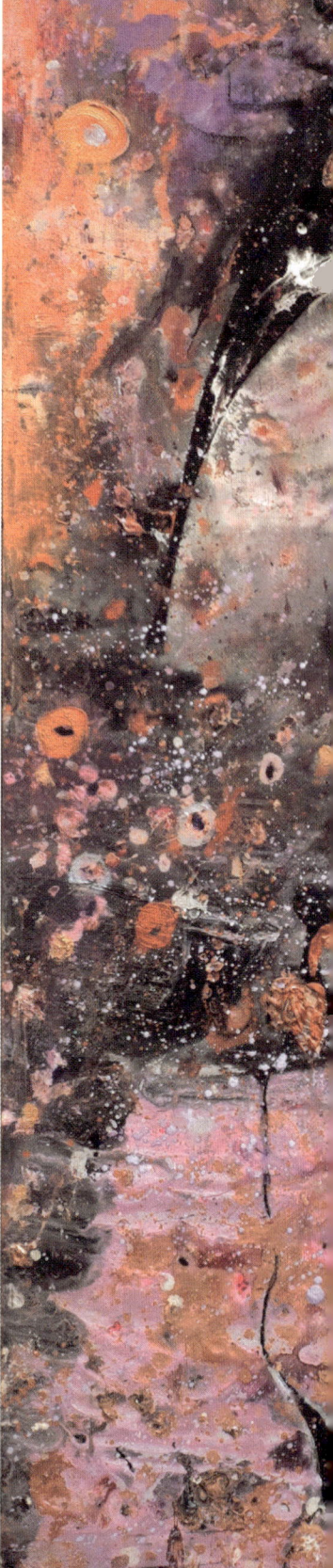

▶ **Alchemy**
Carolyn Mary Kleefeld, 1991,
acrylic and gouache on board.

Contemporary artist, poet and writer
Carolyn Mary Kleefeld's (b.1945)
passion for creative experimentation –
and a lifelong fascination with spiritual
transformation – can be experienced
in her extensive and diverse body of
paintings and drawings. In her language
of symbolic imagery, ranging in style
from romantic figurative to abstract,
Kleefeld's works explore spiritual,
psychological and ecological themes
in ways that reveal infinite vistas of
possibility, and encourage viewers
and readers to create, define and
live their own personal mythology.

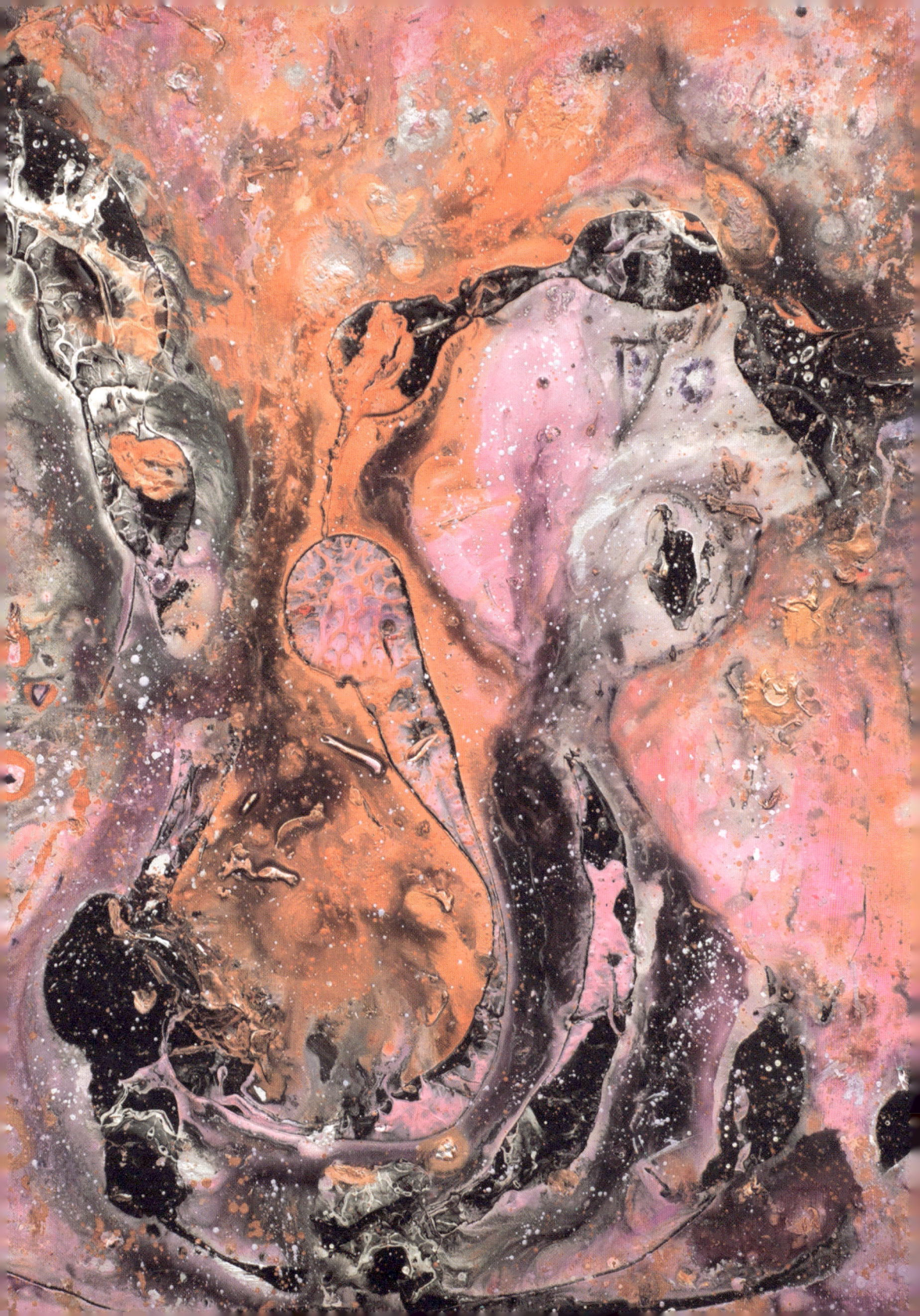

▶ The Alchemyst
Sveta Dorosheva, 2013, ball
pen and ink pen on paper.

Originally from Ukraine and currently based
in Israel, artist Sveta Dorosheva notes a keen
interest in alchemy, Hermetic engravings
and mysterious emblems. Much resembling
the intricacy of medieval illuminated
manuscripts, this richly detailed work in
its entirety portrays an alchemical adept
toiling inside an ancient turtle, upon which
grows a tree with emblemata depicting
various stages of alchemical work.

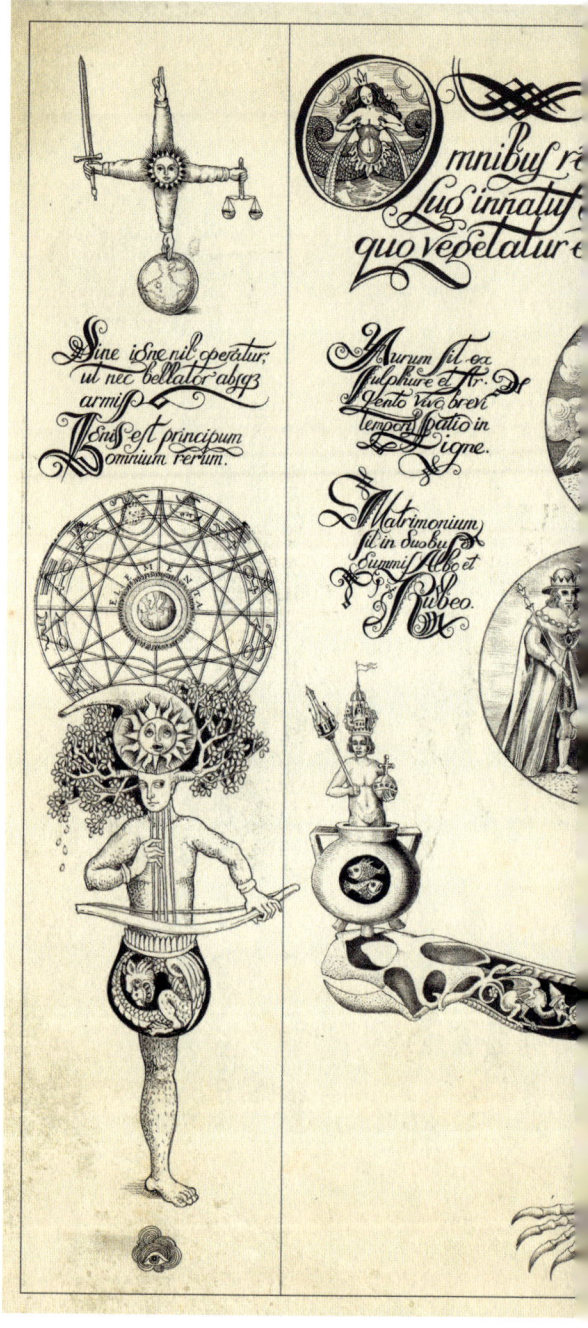

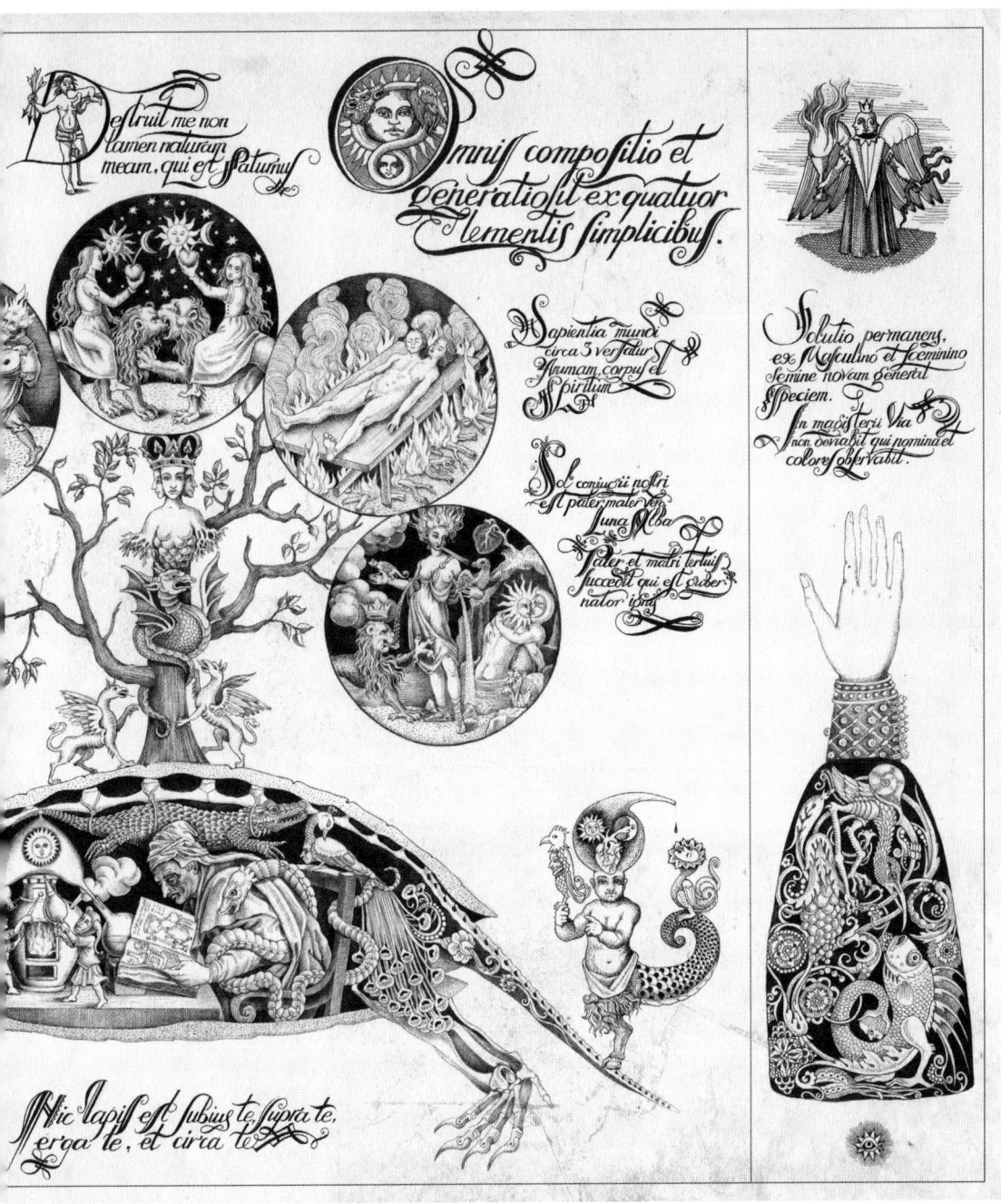

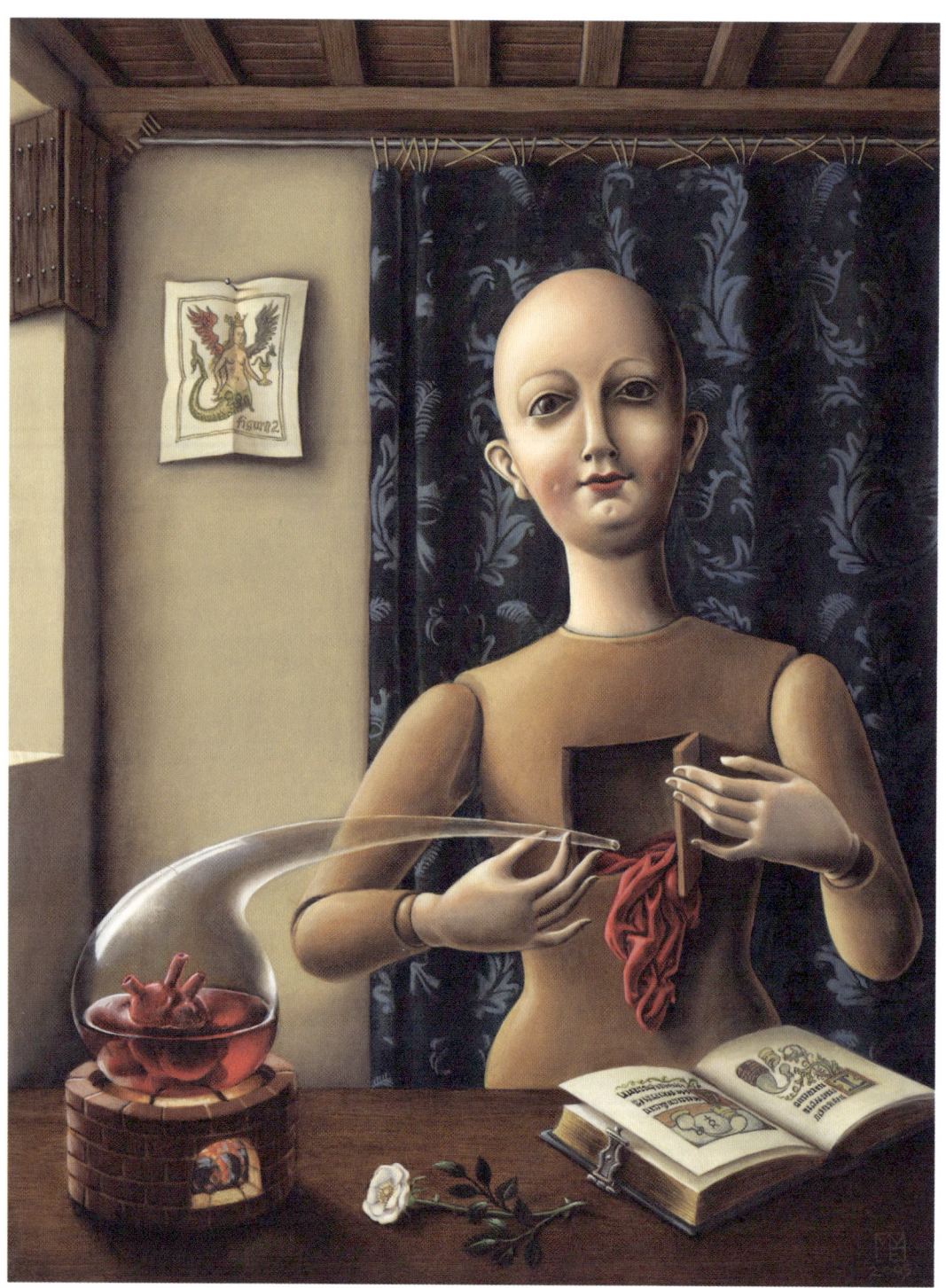

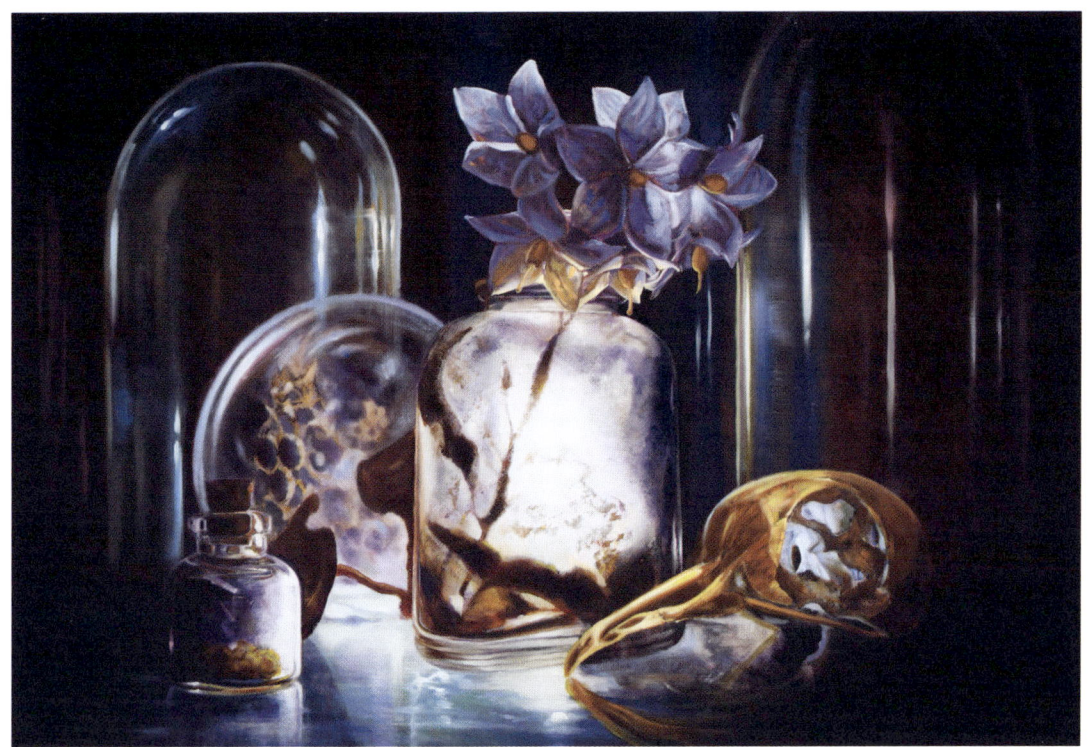

◄ Essentia Exalta
Madeline von Foerster, 2006, oil
and egg tempera on panel.

About *Essentia Exalta*, artist Madeline von
Foerster (b.1973) states, 'This painting
comes out of my love for alchemical texts and
illustrations. The alchemists of old inspire
me greatly with their metaphoric language
and their endless quest for knowledge!
While the alchemists were obsessed with
the distillation and transmutation of inorganic
elements, I imagined that a non-biological
being might be just as interested with our
animal parts and their elusive workings.'

▲ Alchemy Alchemia
Gatya Kelly, 2016,
oil on linen.

'Even in the deepest darkness there is light',
declares contemporary artist Gatya Kelly. 'It's
a reminder that the unpredictability and lurking
chaos of the outside world is only transient.'
With a perspective that reflects the domestic
and the feminine and using a glowing nocturnal
tableau of familiar objects, in *Alchemy Alchemia*
the artist pays tribute to this ancient branch
of natural philosophy and invites us to step
back and reconnect with who we are.

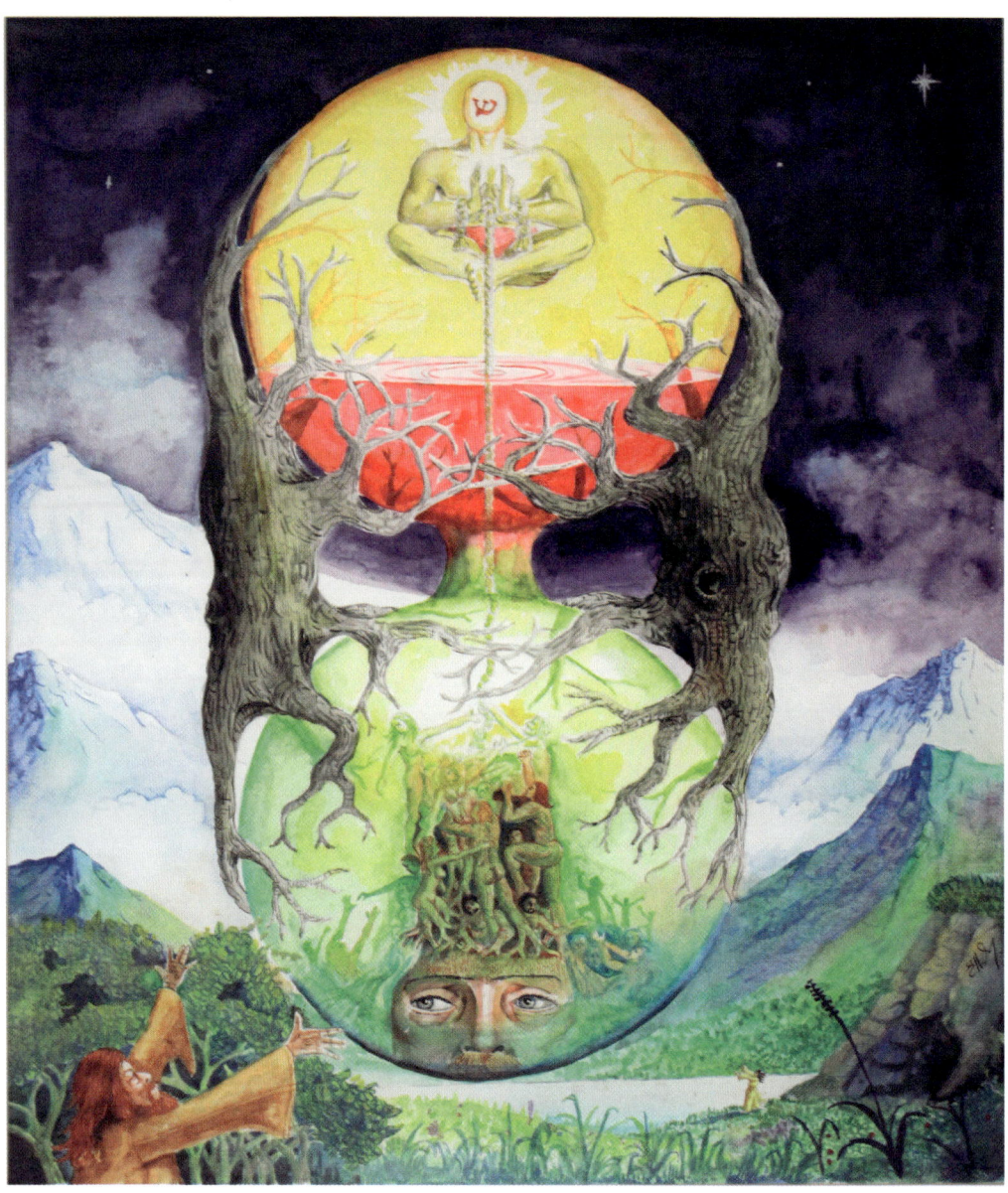

▲ The Chemical Wedding
Robert Ellaby, undated.

British Surrealist artist, Robert Ellaby (b.1964), is much influenced by kabbalah, alchemy and other esoteric systems of ideas. He has been a student of the Western Mystery Tradition for over thirty years. His passion for kabbalistic and alchemical concepts are at the heart of his studies, informing and inspiring such paintings as *The Chemical Wedding*.

▼ The Hermaphrodite with the World Egg Laurie Lipton, 1989, coloured pencil on paper.

Artist Laurie Lipton's (b.1953) luminous, dramatic work is the effect of a self-developed technique involving thousands of fine cross-hatching lines to build up tone, 'like an egg-tempura painting'. The artist was commissioned by the Bibliotheca Philosophica Hermetica to do a series of drawings recreating legendary alchemical works, to include *The Hermaphrodite with the World Egg*.

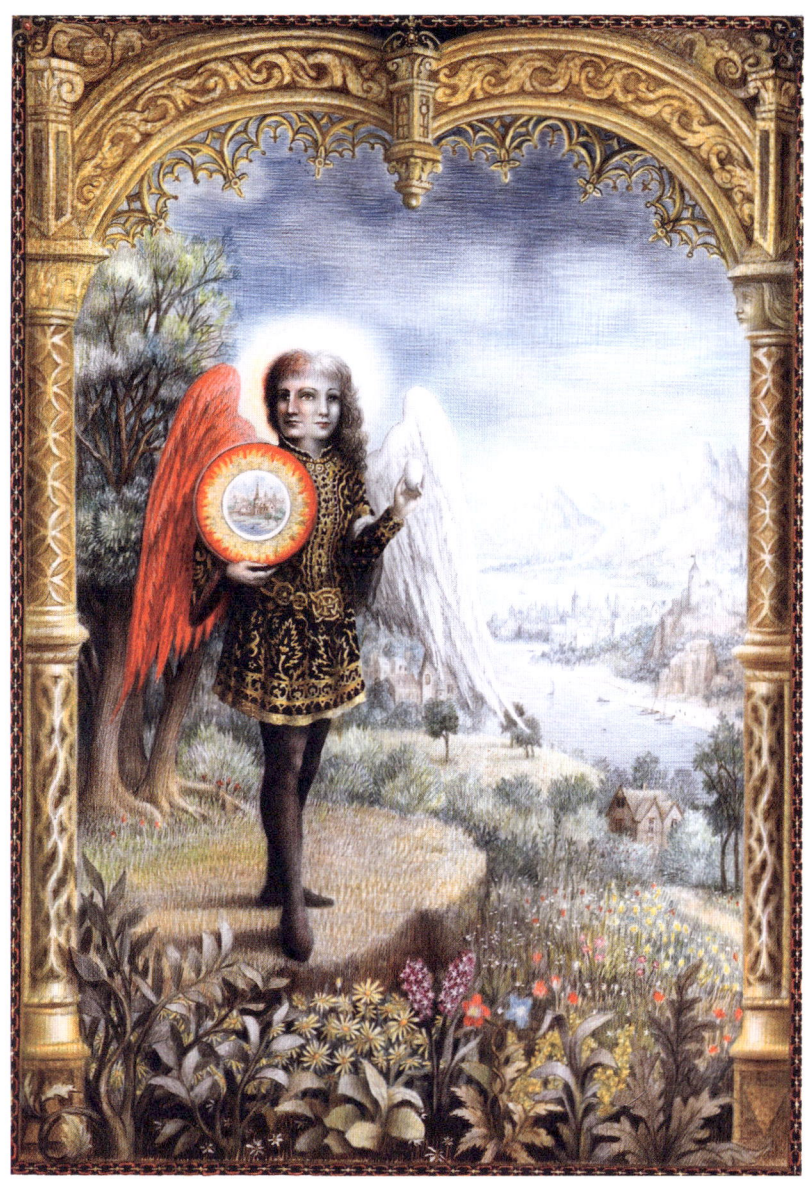

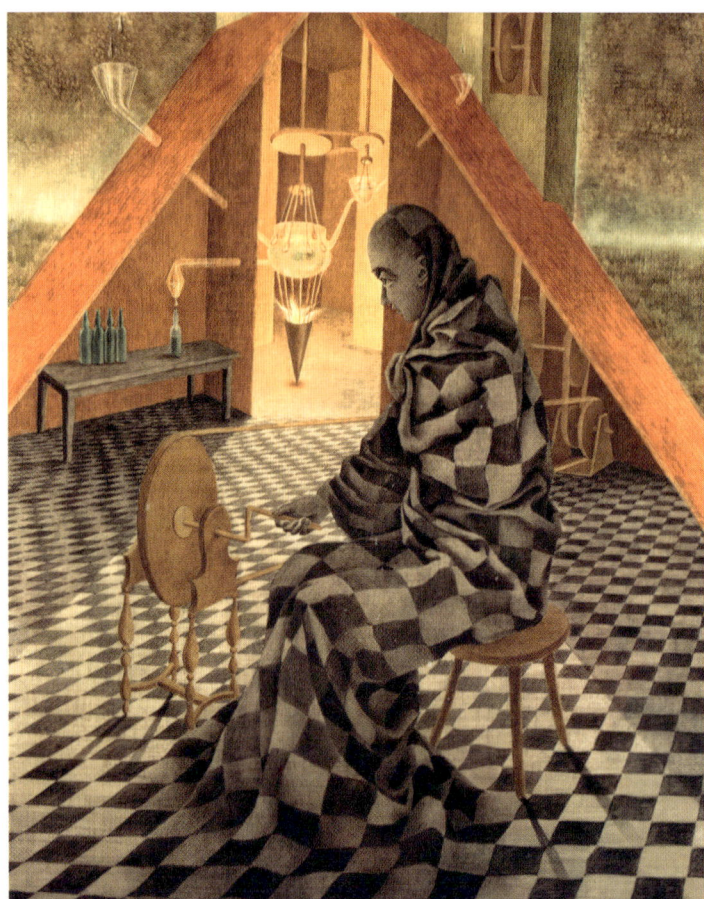

Orryelle Defenestrate-Bascule is an esoteric artist who creates in many mediums, including painting, writing, sculpture, sound, film and performance art. *Alchemist with Golden Dragon* is from *Coagula*, the second of four volumes, with each book carrying the alchemical work into the field of art by colour association with the magical steps to the Philosopher's Stone.

▲ **Alchemy or the Useless Science**
Remedios Varo, 1958, oil on masonite.

Born in the town of Angles in the province of Girona in Spain and forced into exile from Paris during the Nazi occupation of France, Surrealist artist Remedios Varo Uranga (1908–1963) moved to Mexico City at the end of 1941. Although she initially considered Mexico a temporary haven, she remained in Latin America for the rest of her life. Leonora Carrington, another painter and Surrealist in Mexico, was her close friend. A knowledgeable seeker and naturalist, Varo's deeply intuitive, and multi-sensory imagery explored the intersection of science, magic and the spiritual. *Alchemy or the Useless Science*, depicts a lone subject swathed in a cloak of black and white chequered flooring, turning the handle of a fanciful machine full of gears and funnels that is producing droplets of strange green liquid.

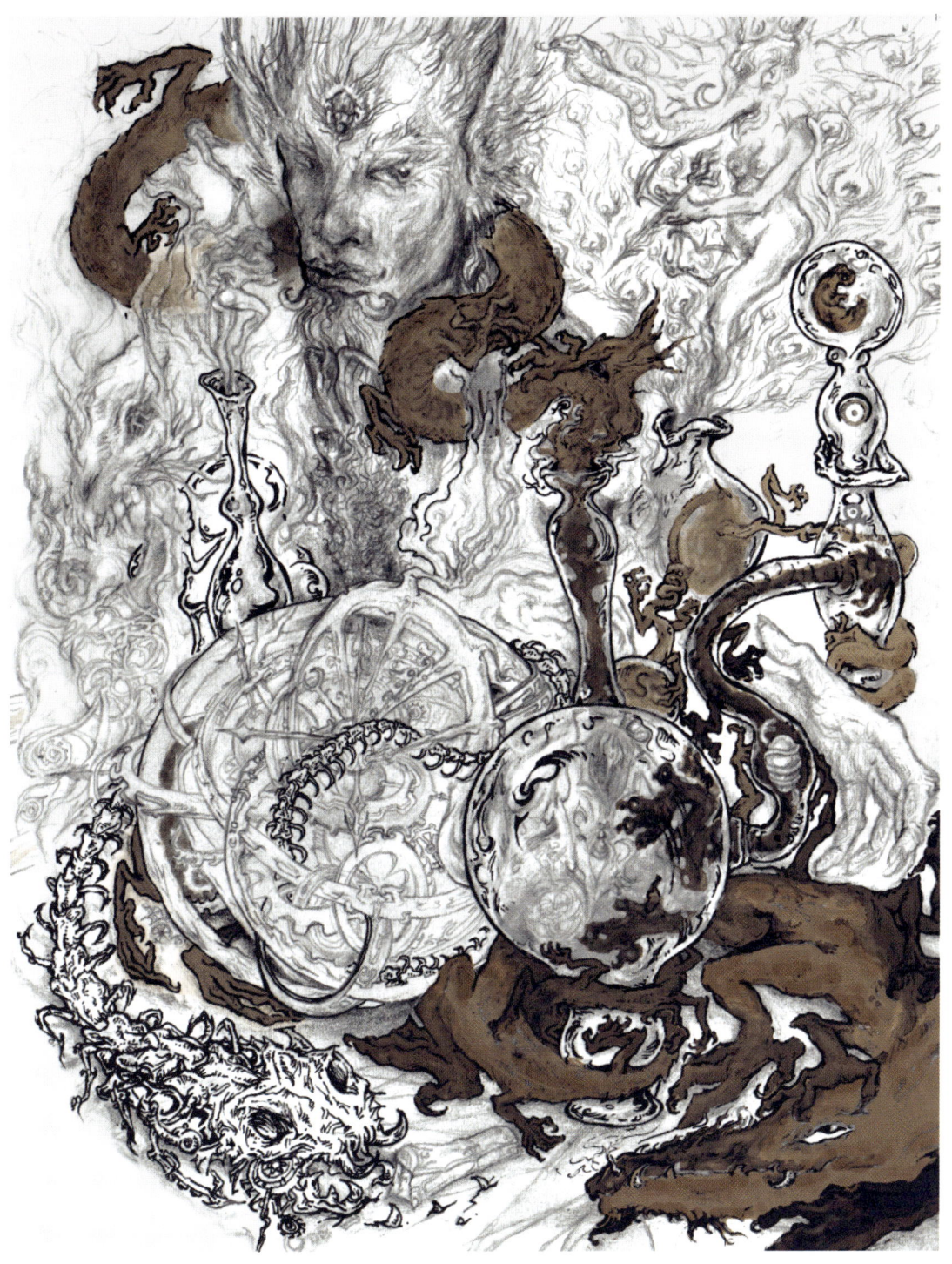

PART TWO

HIGHER
BEINGS

'The pictures were painted directly
through me, without preliminary drawings
and with great power. I had no idea
what the pictures would depict and still
I worked quickly and surely without
changing a single brushstroke.'

— HILMA AF KLINT

M ANY THOUSANDS OF YEARS OF religious iconography and
museums spanning the globe full of human art and artifacts
glorifying the gods, would imply that we are eternally awestruck,
terrified and, well, maybe just a bit concerned with our relationship
to a higher power.

Looking to the past, we can see countless depictions of how
ancient cultures imagined their gods and goddesses in different
ways, reflecting their own needs and environments, hopes and
threats, beliefs and traditions at various points in the timeline
of human history. As these works evolved and became more
sophisticated in their execution, we can follow the growth and
change in artists' perceptions and understandings of the holy
in their sublime portrayals of gods and goddesses – from their
superhuman engagement in the heroic world of epic, to their
complex religious function in culture and society, as well as their
transformation from divine corporeality into metaphors in aesthetic
and philosophical thought painted on canvas, illustrated in
manuscripts or carved in stone.

As we study these classic works in an effort to examine the
relationship of the gods to human perception and imagination,
we can also take a moment to observe how these religious and
philosophical questions gave rise to several occult organisations
and movements.

What is the essence of God and how can the greatest intimacy
with the divine be achieved? Is there a spark of the divine hidden
within us and by what means can we access that precious kinship?
In our quest for inner self-knowledge and understanding, can
we reveal these higher cosmic truths? The esoteric doctrine of the
Kabbalah, the school of ideas and systems in the Hermetic tradition,

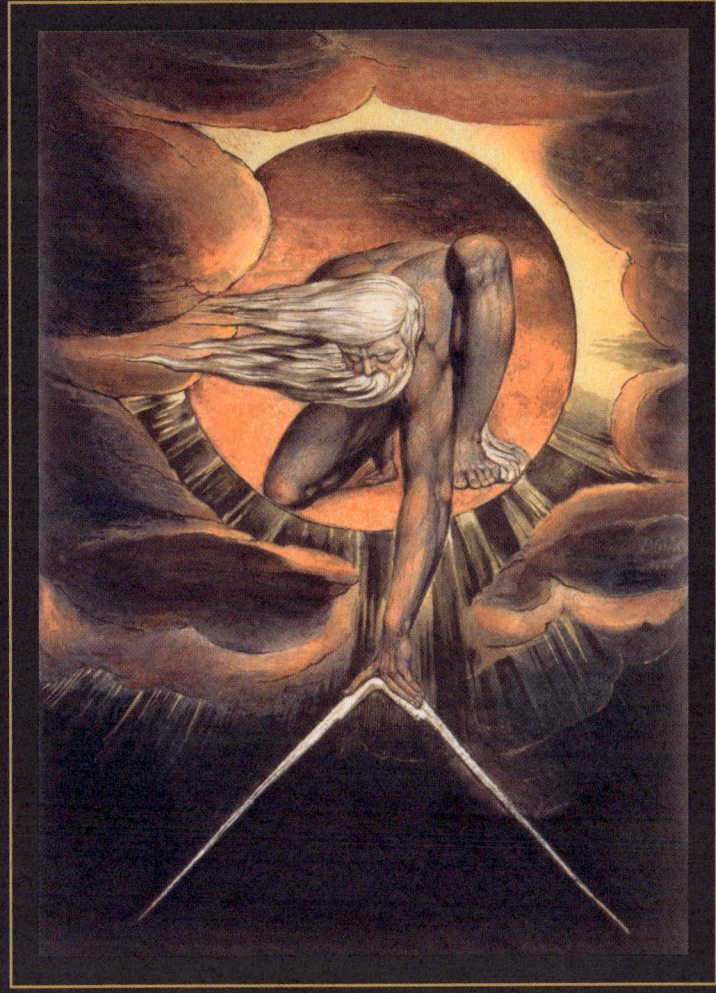

► The Ancient of Days
William Blake, 18th century, etching with pen and ink, watercolour and bodycolour on paper.

and the wisdom and tenets of Theosophy all seek to address these questions. And along with them, of course, were the artists inspired by these esoteric spheres of thought, who generated visionary responses to what they saw in these mystical traditions.

As you'll see in the following pages, artists, in collaboration with whatever deities or higher powers they may choose to call upon – even if it is just the sacred flame within their own passionate, beating heart – remain as deeply compelled by such powerful questions today as did their counterparts worlds away and in times long past.

INTRODUCTION

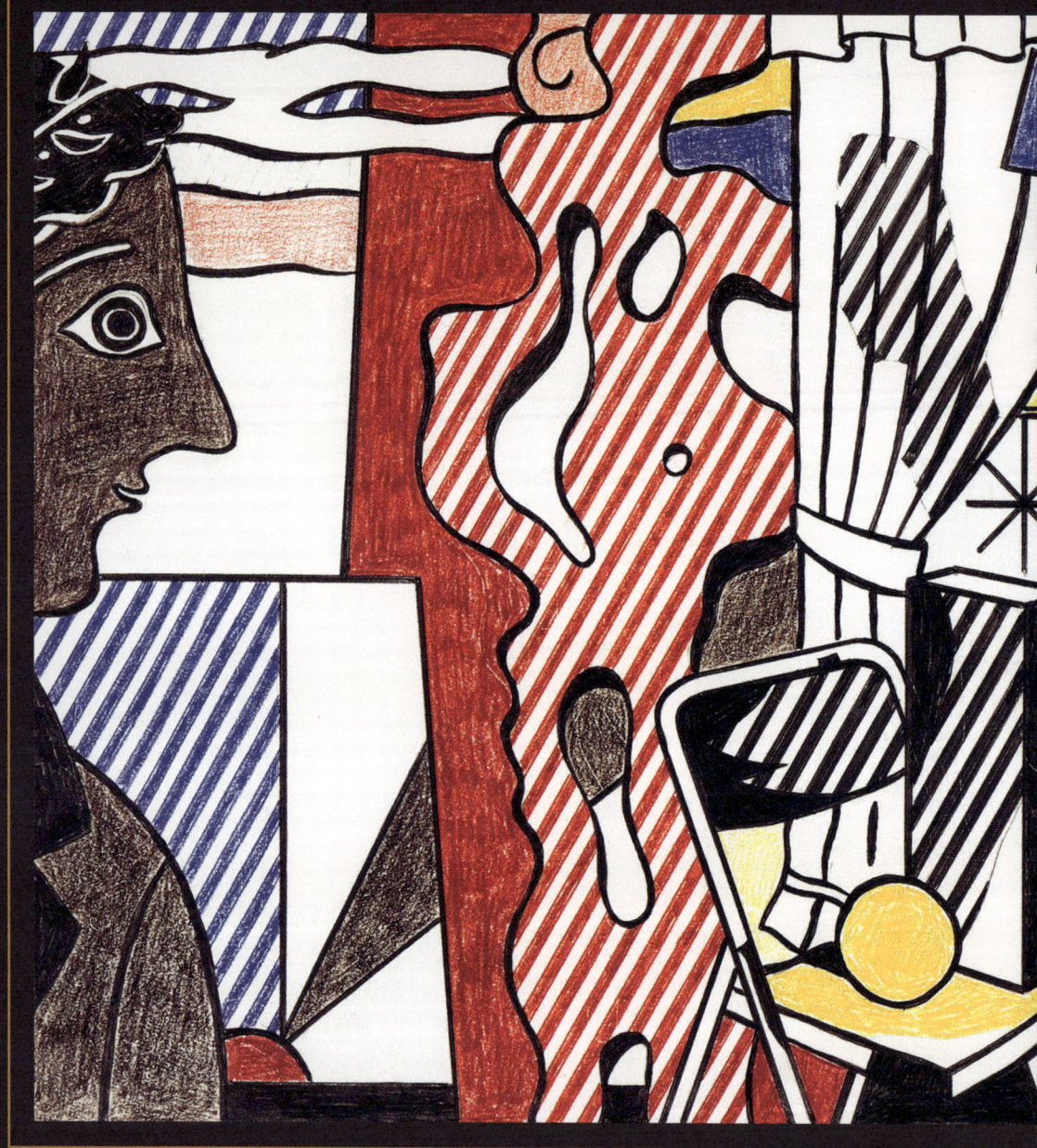

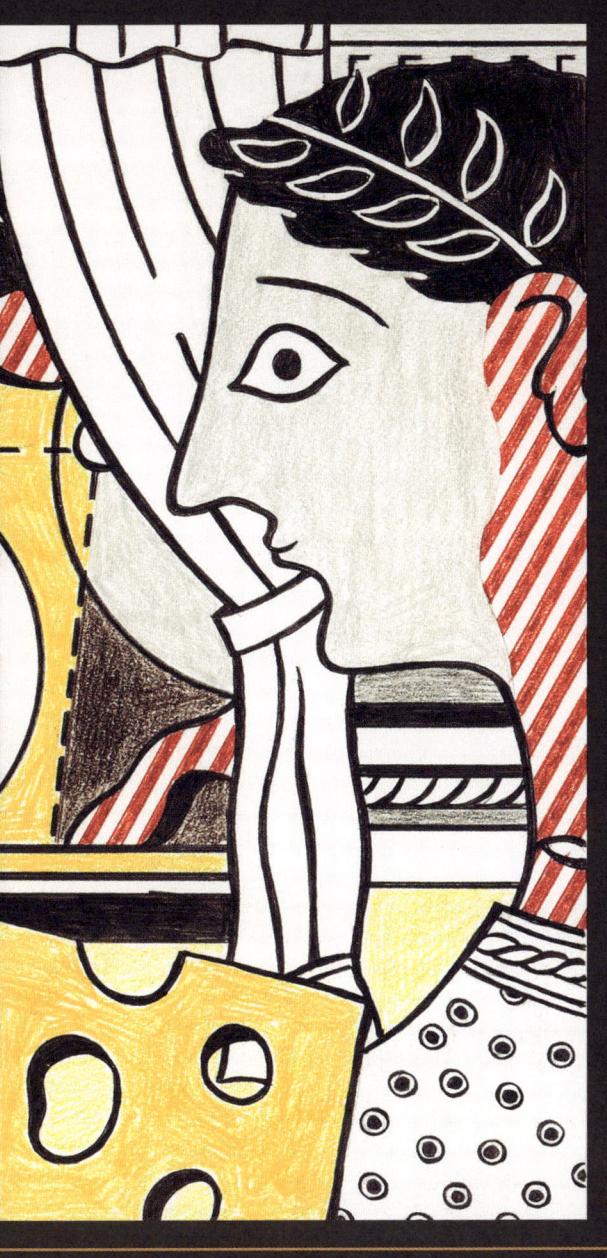

V

GODS AND IMMORTALS

Divine Expression Through the Arts

I N THE ANCIENT WORLD, ALL aspects of
life were steeped in the supernatural; it was,
initially, the only way that humans could explain
the curious, inexplicable and unseen forces of
the universe. Through attributing unexpected or
exceptional occurrences to the agency and actions
of all-powerful, all-knowing, wild and wily
deities, those who lived in long-gone eras might
begin to make sense out of the chaos of the world
in which they lived.

In the beginning, these primordial gods were
tied to fundamental natural forces: light and
dark, birth and death, masculine and feminine.
These primary notions of divinity and providence
were critical to early man's understanding of the
world around him. As societies advanced, these
divine beings came to represent a much more
comprehensive array of ideas and concepts, and
became allegorical personifications of both natural
forces and human emotions. Old gods evolved
and assumed new aspects. New gods arrived to
personify new ideas. And as societies developed,
so the pantheon of gods and goddesses grew.
These complex, mythological beings guided
and judged a wide range of circumstances, both
mortal and immortal, and societal belief in their
existence provided answers and gave context to
the passion, ambition, greed and suffering that
comprised the human condition.

Different cultures visualised their gods and
goddesses in different ways, reflecting their own
needs and environments, beliefs and traditions.

This imagery might attempt to make the spiritual
world present, to define the very nature of a deity,
or to depict rituals or practices dedicated to the
divine. In many instances, visual images and
objects assisted humans in communicating with
the world of the gods. And what an immense and
beautiful palette of divinity there was to choose
from, with stylistic, iconographical, narrative and
ritual aspects varying tremendously from culture
to culture.

Many deities were conceived as animals
or as beings with zoomorphic attributes – the
Ancient Egyptians often depicted their gods as
half-animal, half-human – and it is easy to see
how certain animals with physical abilities that
far exceeded those of humans were thought to
be closely related to the gods of the sky, earth
and sea. However, this did not mean they saw
their gods as cats or hawks or jackals, but instead
that the animal served to illustrate particular
characteristics of the god. Other deities were
depicted as super-human, the fantastical addition
of multiple arms, for example, emphasising their
immense power, such as the Hindu goddess of
feminine energies, Kali. Or perhaps we can look
to Greek Goddess Hecate, with three heads / faces,
indicating various aspects of her nature, or, some
say, the new moon, half-moon and full moon.

And certainly, many gods and goddesses in
both traditional and contemporary visual arts
are portrayed as disarmingly, devastatingly . . .
human. No animal parts, no extra limbs, just the

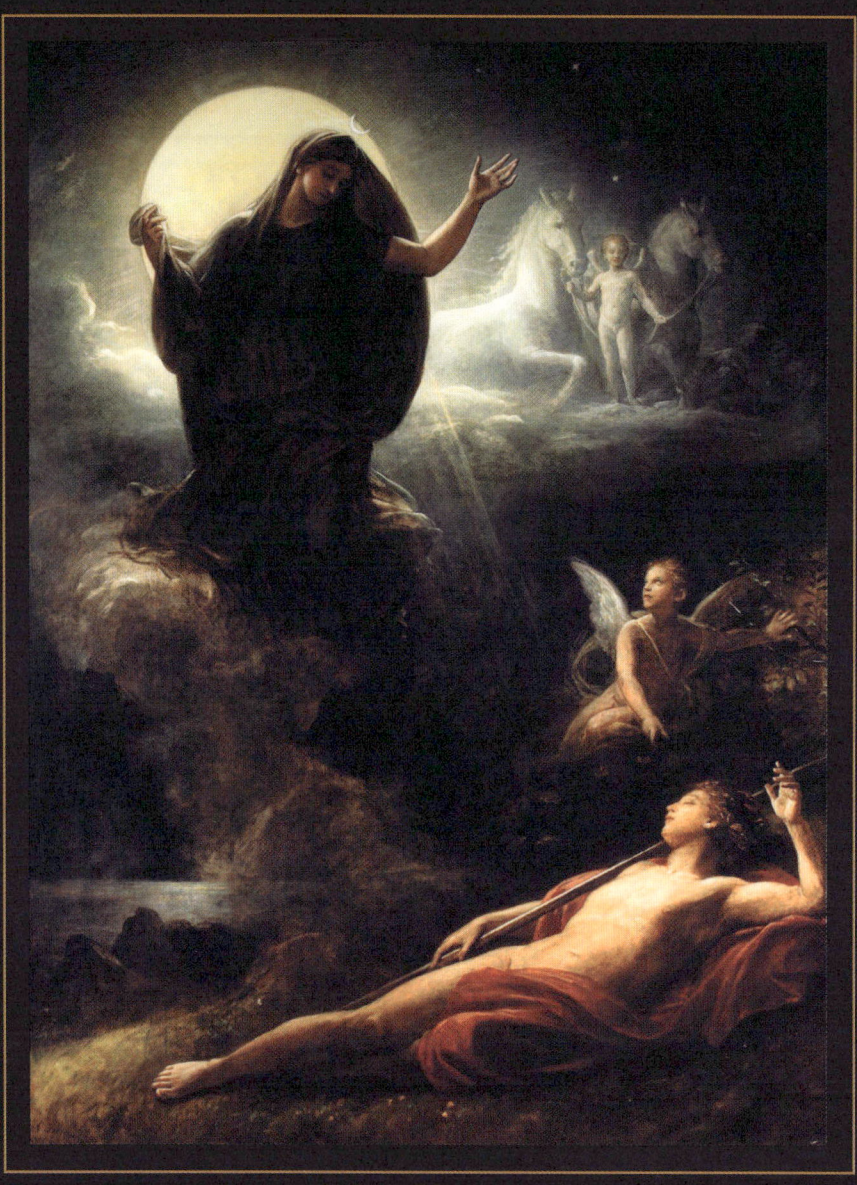

▲ **Diana awakening Apollo**
Carl Bertling, 1910, oil on canvas.

Diana awakening Apollo, as depicted by Carl Bertling (1835–1918), reveals the goddess looming in the moon's shadow as its light falls gently on her brother, below. Born on the island of Delos with her twin brother, Apollo the god of light, Diana was revered as the goddess of the hunt, the woods, children and childbirth, fertility, chastity, the moon and wild animals.

Diana, Goddess of the Hunt
Willem van Mieris, 1686, oil on panel.

Painter, sculptor and etcher Willem van Mieris' (1662–1747) works were highly sought-after affairs. This was painted in 1686 when he was about 24 years old. The woman is certainly meant to represent Diana, the goddess of the hunt. Although lacking her primary attribute, the crescent moon, Diana is depicted holding an arrow taken from the quiver lying on the rocky ledge before her.

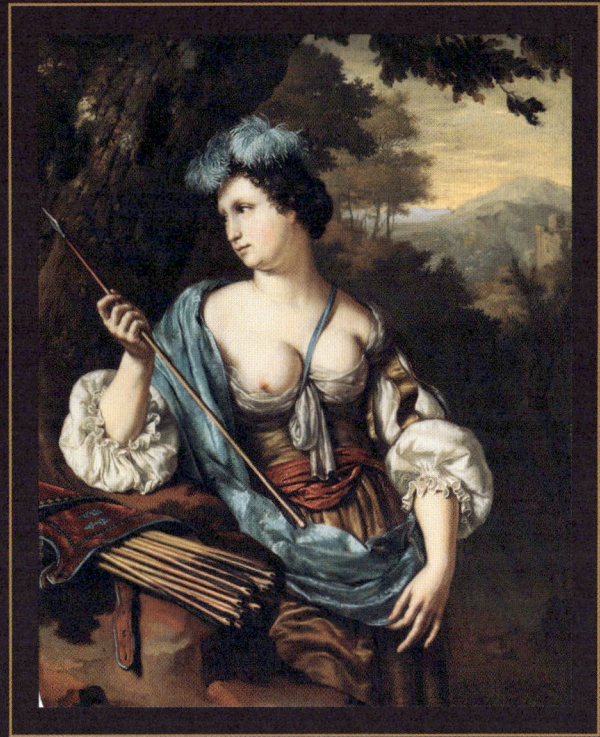

essence of the divine contained in a fragile mortal vessel, in inks or oils, or sculpted from stone, illustrating our conquests, victories and failures in a manner that we cannot fail to relate to. After all, the gods in the art we admire and cherish look exactly like us, and the themes and motifs explored in these pieces depict the vast drama of all human nature.

French Symbolist Odilon Redon, fascinated by the motif of the mythological horses of the sun often driven by Apollo, god of light and poetry, made over thirty depictions of the motif. In *Osiris for Patsy O'Hara*, Ann McCoy examines themes of rebirth and renewal via Egyptian mythology and the resurrection of the god Osiris. The Hindu goddess Kali is rendered by Prokash Karmakar in her iconic stance: sword aloft, a great and terrible protector vibrating with a bright, cleansing rage.

Lust, longing, fury, grief, compassion – these are undying, enduring themes that continue to inspire and influence the canvases of modern artists, just as they did the artists of our ancestors.

In viewing a painting or sculpture in a museum today, or a totem or altar cloth from centuries ago, we contemplate the creators of these objects (creation, of course, being a spark of the divine in and of itself) along with our part in the creation of all of these belief systems. After all, did the gods create us, or did we in fact create them? And the fact remains that these images of gods, divinities and spirits, expressing the ancient belief that the world is controlled by powerful non-human forces, are as compelling today as when they were first interpreted millennia ago.

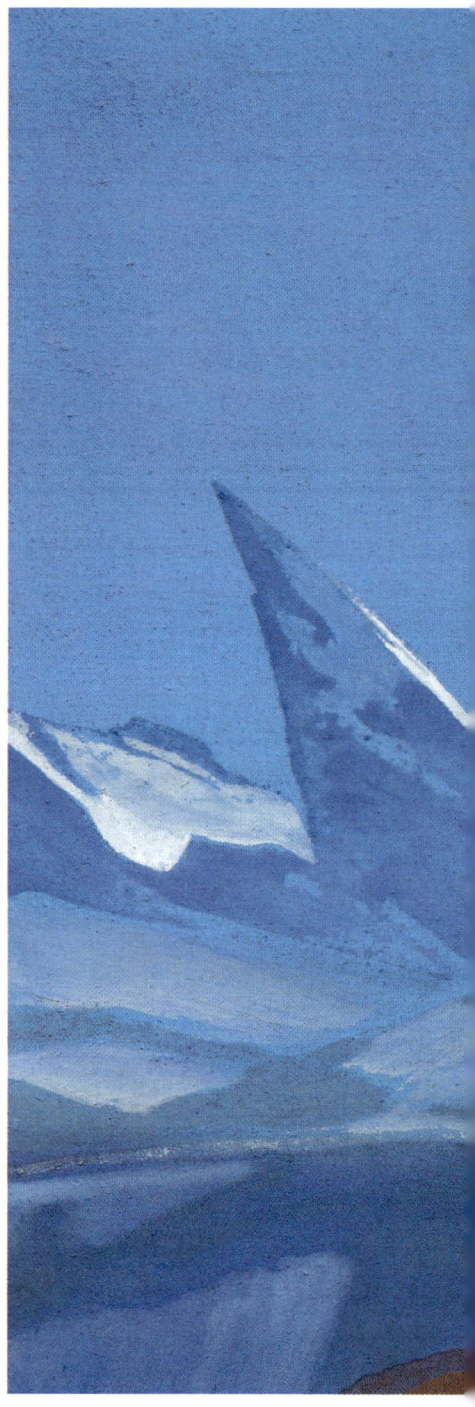

► Kuan-yin,
Nicholas Roerich,
1933, tempera
on canvas.

Celebrated Russian painter
Nicholas Roerich (1874–1947)
was also a writer, archaeologist,
Theosophist, philosopher and
public figure – thrice nominated
for the Nobel Peace prize. His
creative legacy is enormous, with
thousands of paintings scattered
around the world. Though his
earlier works reflected the
splendor of a primeval pagan
Russia, a quest for Eastern
spirituality led to the themes of
India and the East appearing
increasingly more frequently in
Roerich's later artistic output.

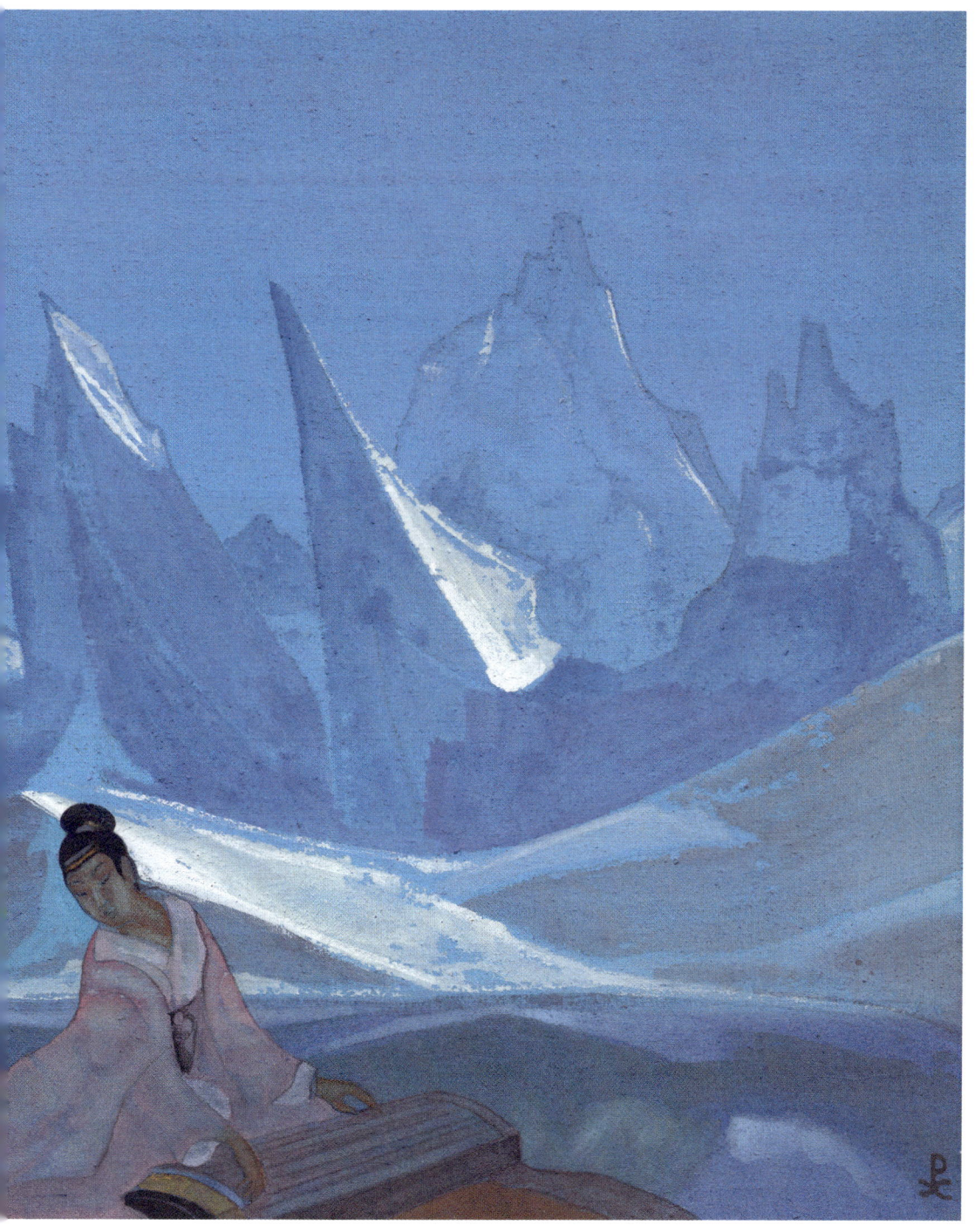

▼ Hathor-Horus
Orryelle Defenestrate-
Bascule, 2013.

A prolific visual and sonic artist, Orryelle Defenestrate-Bascule creates in many mediums, including poetry, art, music, theatre, Magick, Alchemy and self-transformation. Of this painting, the artist points to the ancient Egyptian text 'The Contendings of Horus and Seth' (*Chester Beatty Papyri*), which tells a strange tale of the healing of Horus's eyes by Isis after his epic battle with Seth. Where lay Horus's sundered eyes, Lotuses grew from mounds in the earth, and on these fed a Gazelle.

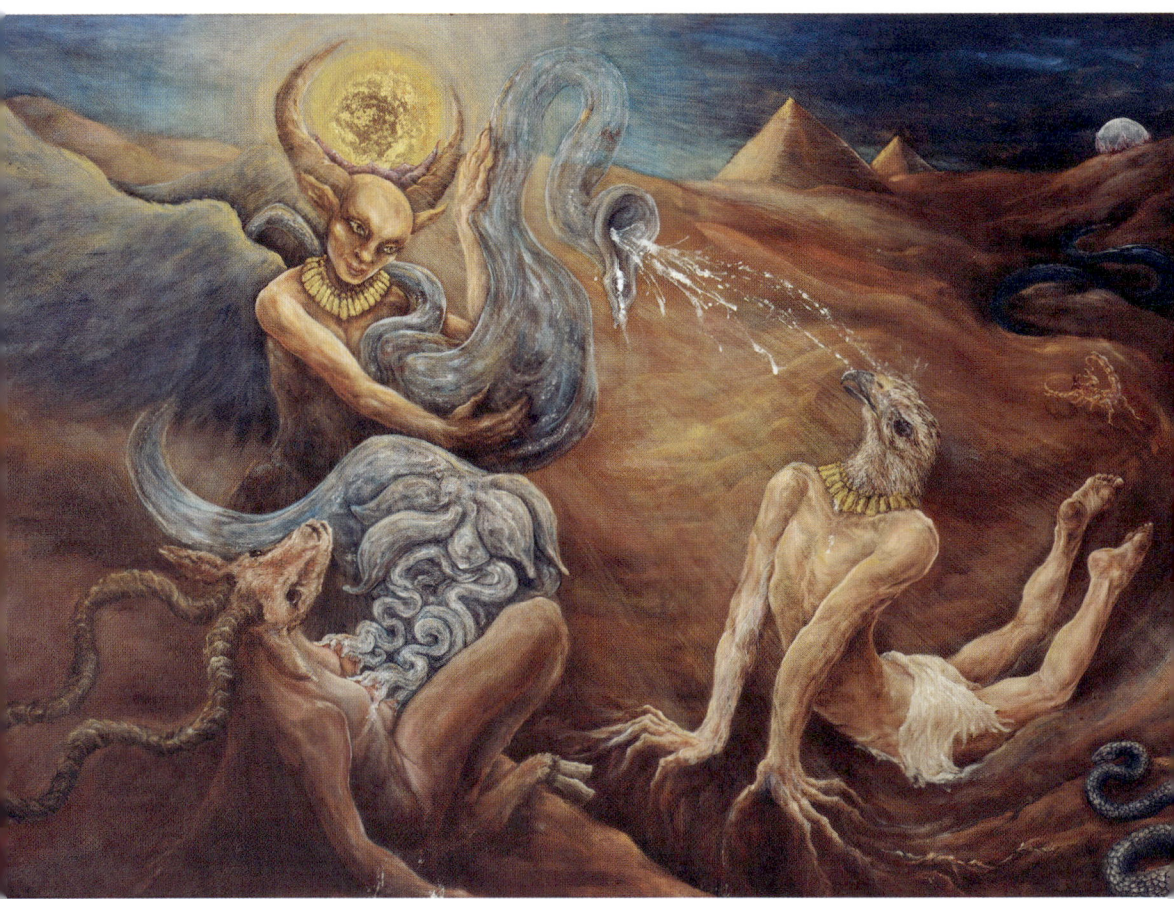

▼ Hekate
Maximillian Pirner,
1901, pastel on paper.

Described as both a 'mastery of the sinuous line' and an 'over-sophisticated mystic' (is that supposed to be a bad thing?) Czech artist Maximillian Pirner's (1853–1924) usual themes were classical mythology and the macabre. These can be seen to great effect in his gloomy, moonlit depiction of triple-faced Greek goddess, Hekate.

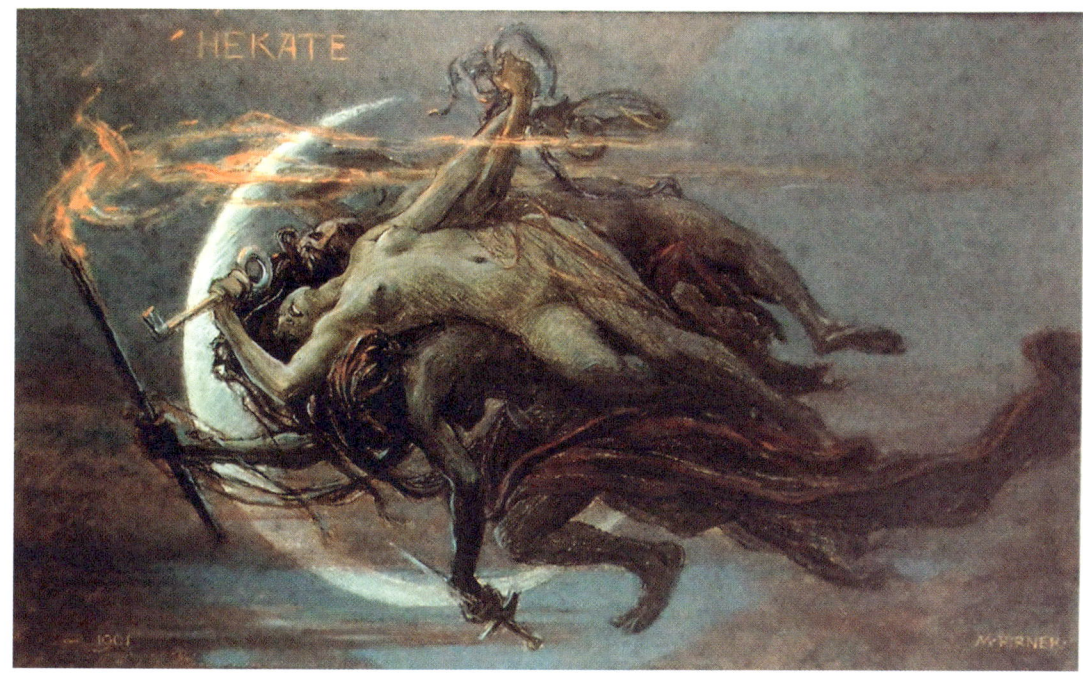

**▶ Osiris for
Patsy O'Hara**
Ann McCoy, 1981, pencil
on paper on canvas.

Notes artist Ann McCoy
(b.1946), 'Resurrection has
been a reoccurring theme
in my work … . In the life of
the individual we are always
resurrecting the spiritual forces
within ourselves, after periods
of annihilation and defeat. The
tomb is the first step; Christ is
resurrected from the tomb as
is Osiris. The Egyptian religion
was an important prototype
for the resurrection of a god,
renewal, and the role of the
feminine in the process.'

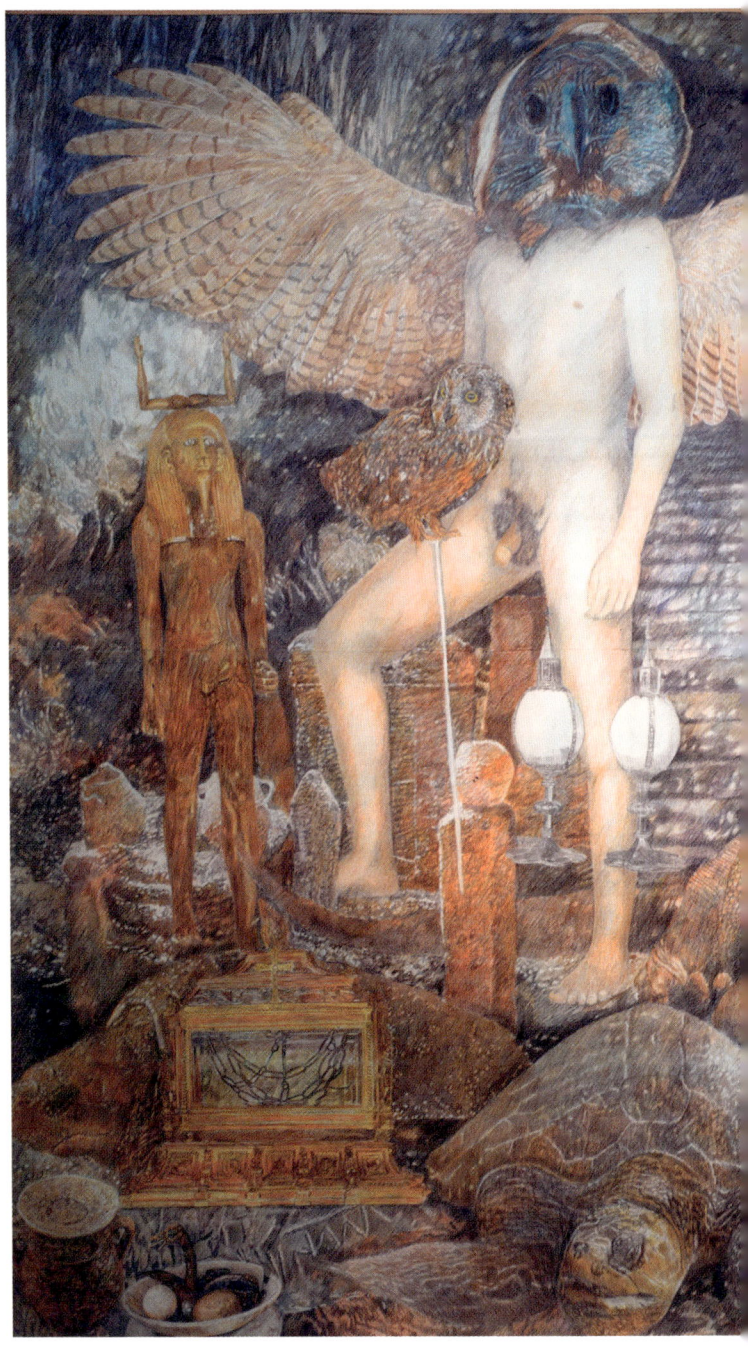

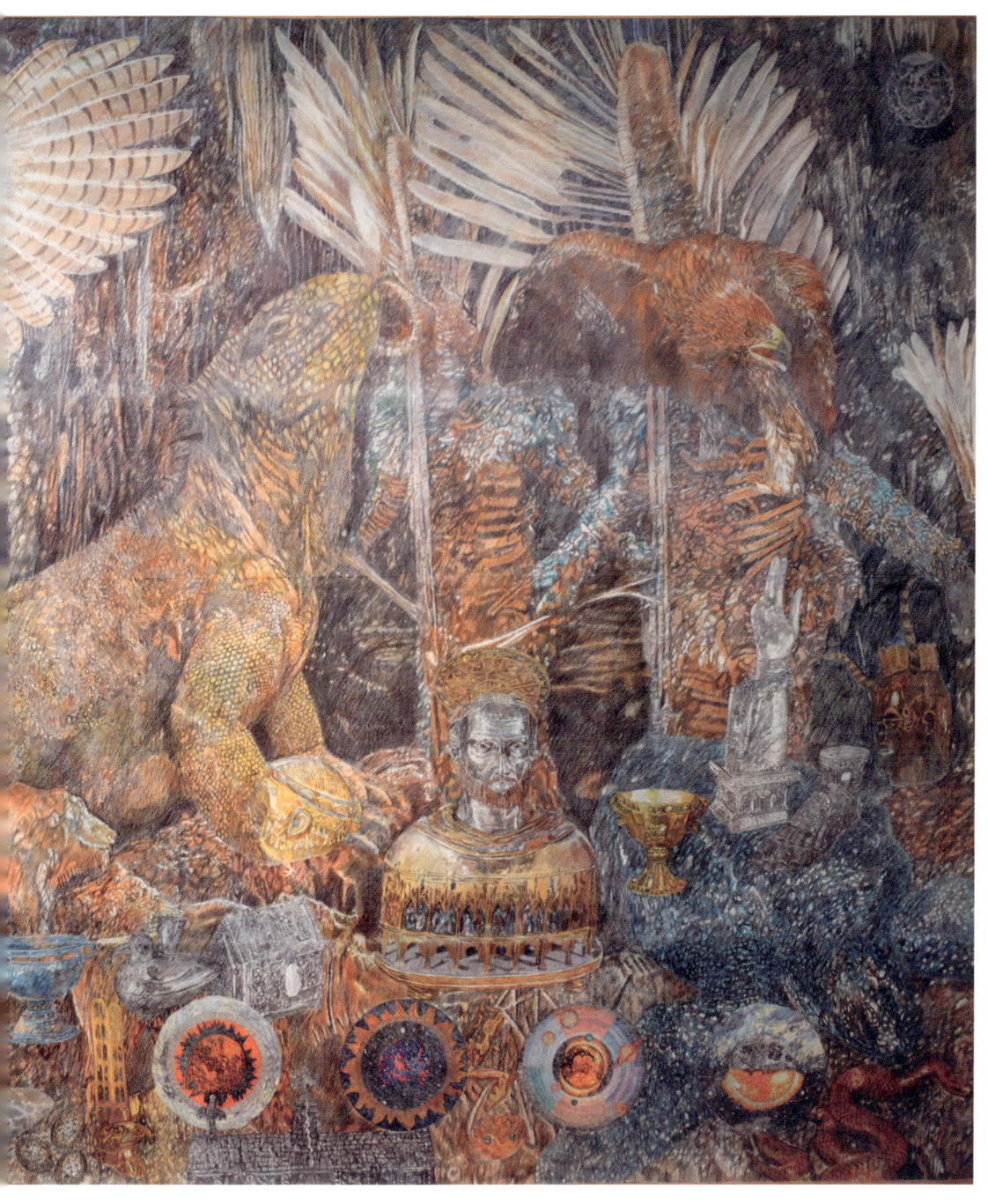

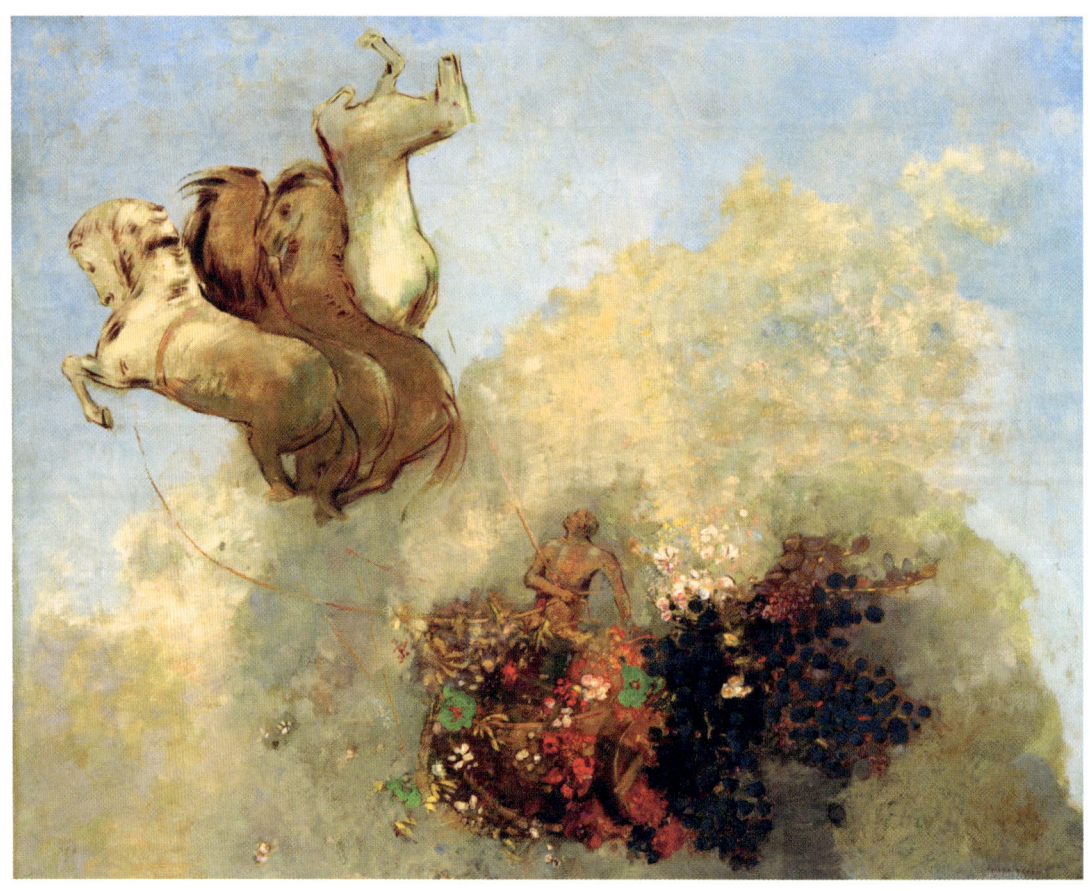

▲ Quadrige
Odilon Redon, 1910, oil on canvas.

▶ The Household Gods
John William Waterhouse, 1880, oil on canvas.

Odilon Redon (1840–1916) was a French Symbolist painter whose evocative works are the stuff of mysteries and nightmares. In 1878, while visiting the Exposition Universelle in Paris, Redon was dazzled by the *Phaeton* by Gustave Moreau (1826–1898), in the form of a large preparatory watercolour for the decoration of a ceiling. Towards the end of his life, Redon explored the mythological subject of the sun chariot of Apollo by creating different versions that strongly echoed Moreau's work.

John William Waterhouse (1849–1917) was an English painter of classical, historical and literary subjects, and themes associated with the Pre-Raphaelites – particularly tragic or powerful femme fatales. *The Household Gods* holds no such drama, but instead depicts a quietly luminous moment of ritual and reverence in which two women refresh their offerings to the Lares, Roman guardian spirits of a family and home.

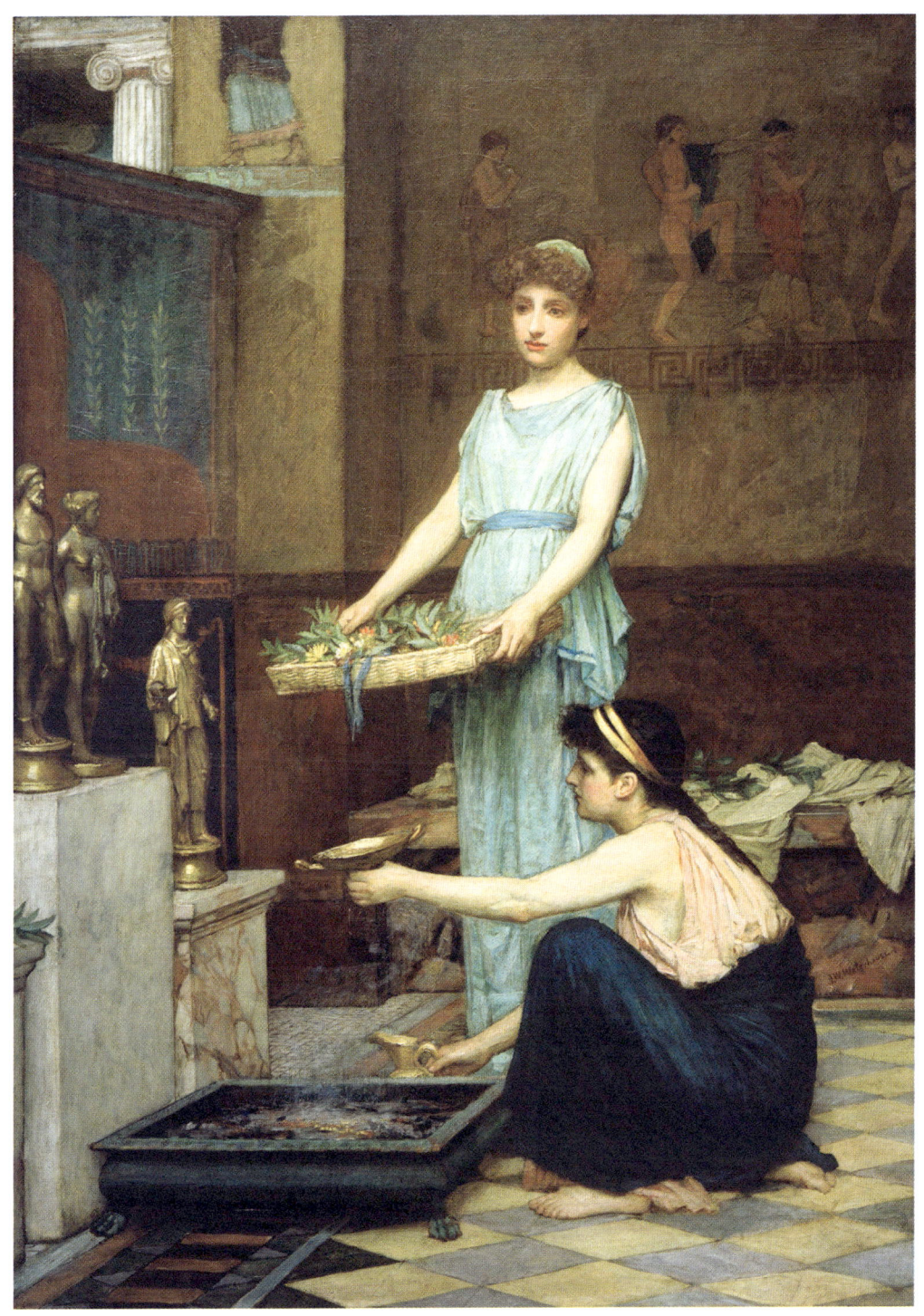

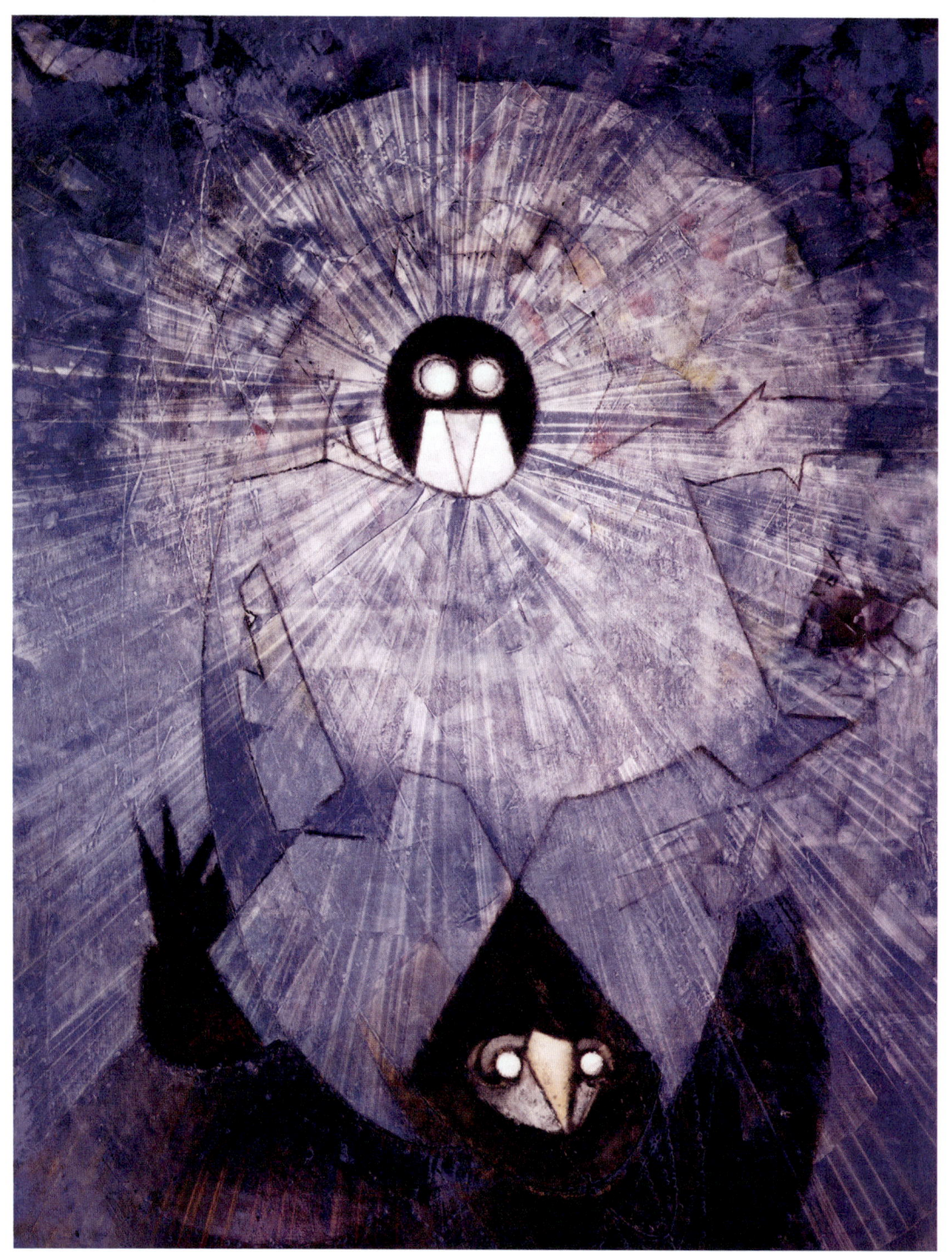

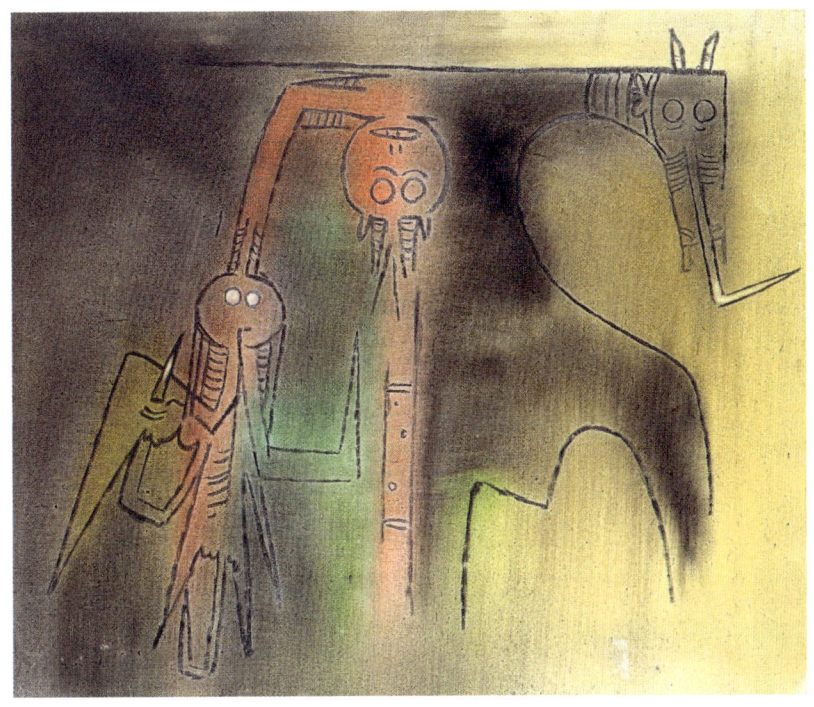

◄ Die Dunklen Götter (The Dark Gods)
Max Ernst, 1957, oil on canvas.

Surrealist Max Ernst (1891–1976) was not a formally trained artist, but his experimental attitude resulted in his invention of frottage – a technique that uses pencil rubbings of objects as a source of images. Ernst no doubt was inspired by alchemical and occult ideas, as can be glimpsed in this eerie and luminous work, a projection of simple lines and forms emerging from the shadows.

▲ Totem
Wifredo Lam, 1973, oil on canvas.

Wifredo Óscar de la Concepción Lam y Castilla, better known as Wifredo Lam (1902–1982) was a Cuban-born artist, best known for his large-scale, distinctive paintings which reference modernist aesthetics and Afro-Cuban imagery to explore themes of social injustice, spirituality and rebirth. Through his work, Lam challenged assumptions about non-European art and examined the effects of colonialism. The lush and strange nature of his native land had a strong impact on Lam from early childhood. At the age of five, he was startled by the eerie night-time shadows cast on the wall of his bedroom of a bat in flight. He would later describe the incident as his first magnificent awakening to another dimension to existence.

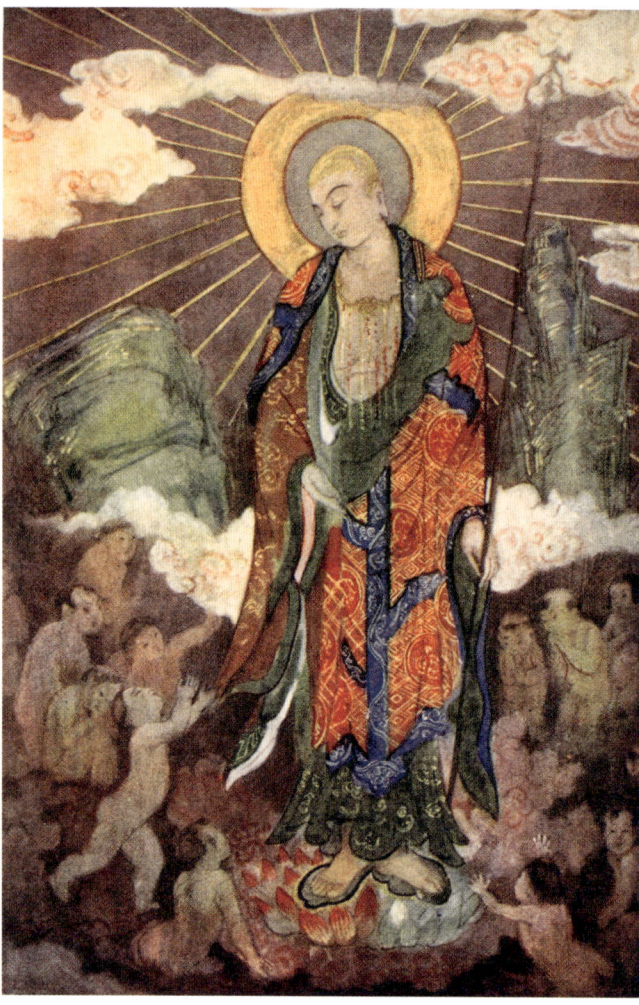

Carrie Ann Baade (b.1974)
is a contemporary painter
whose work quotes from,
interacts with and deeply
relates to art history.
Working allegorically with
layers of meaning, personal
biographical intensity and
strong ties to the divine
feminine she paints 'in
dialogue with relevant
masterpieces from the
Modern period to antiquity,
in order to reclaim them in a
surreal narrative.' In *Artemis*
we can observe repeating
motifs of the crescent moon
and arrowhead-shaped forms,
two symbols commonly
associated with this goddess.

▲ **Jizō, the children's god**
Evelyn Paul, 1925, from *The Book of Myths*
(Amy Cruse, 1925), colour lithograph.

Evelyn Maude Blanche Paul (1883–1963) was known for her
book illustrations, including those replicating the style of medieval
illuminations. A variety of influences can be seen in her work, including
Gothic, Art Nouveau, Arts and Crafts and the Pre-Raphaelite
artist Dante Gabriel Rossetti – who has been named one of Paul's
most consequential influences. This illustration is from *The Book
of Myths*. In Japanese culture, Jizō or Ojizō-sama. is the guardian
of children and patron deity of unborn and deceased children.

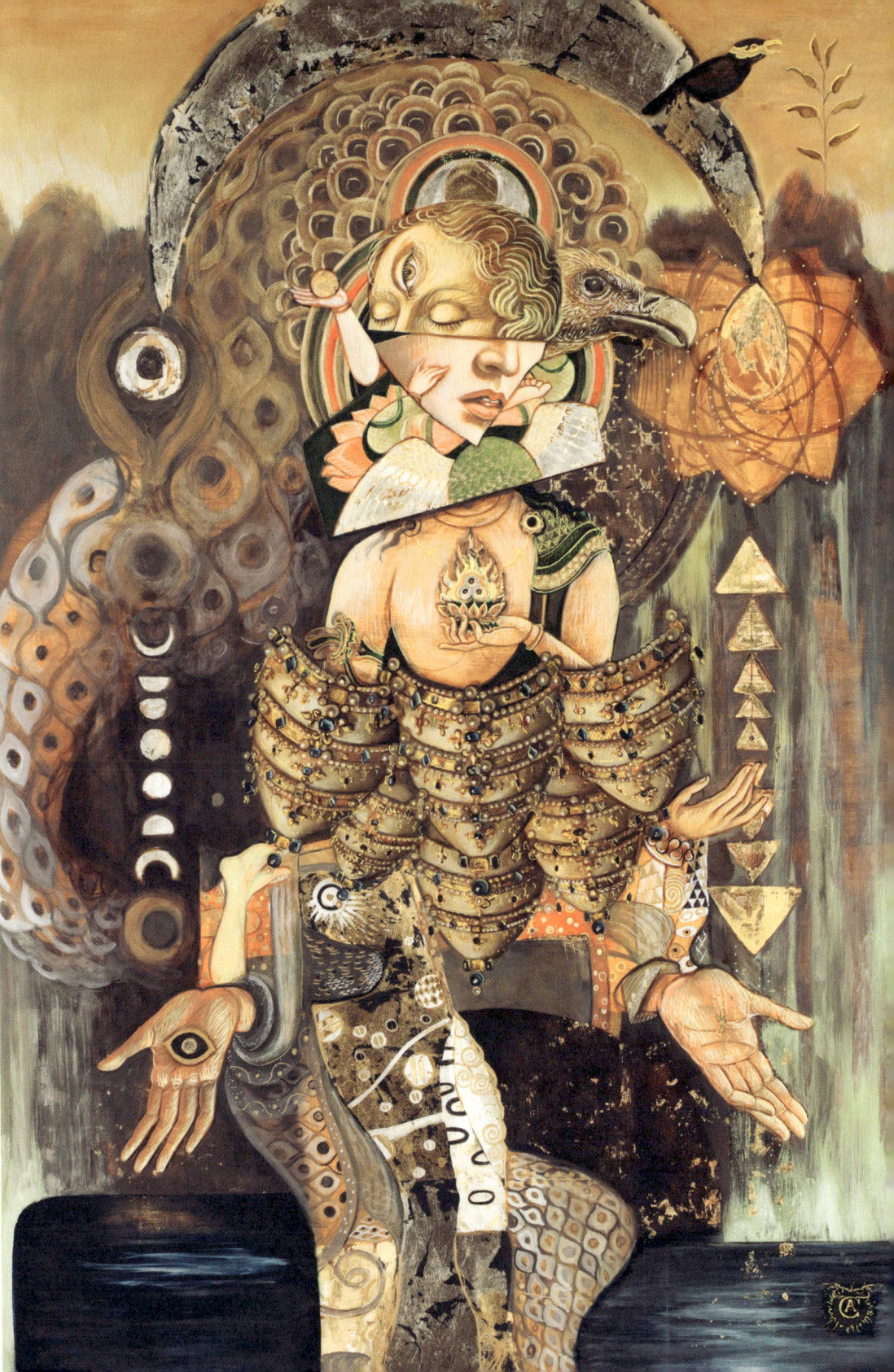

VI

THE
KABBALAH
AS A SOURCE
OF ARTISTIC
INSPIRATION

T HE KABBALAH (ALSO SPELLED KABALAH, Cabala, Qabala) is an esoteric Jewish doctrine and mystical tradition that concerns the essence of God and attempts to explain the relationship between the infinite and divine, as well as the finite and temporal. Kabbalists believe that God moves in mysterious ways, whether it involves a sacred text, an experience, or the manner by which things work. However, Kabbalists also believe that true knowledge and understanding of that mysterious process is obtainable, and through that knowledge, the greatest intimacy with God can be attained. This desire is especially intense because of the powerful sense of kinship that Kabbalists believe exists between God and humanity. Within the soul of every individual is a hidden part of God that is waiting to be revealed.

In Alexander Gorlin's *Kabbalah in Art and Architecture*, Gorlin notes that the Kabbalah is a source of evocative ideas that have either inspired or are illustrated by significant works of art and architecture, and asserts that the idea of an esoteric Jewish mysticism is deserving of a place at the table of contemporary art. Even a cursory glance at a gallery of Kabbalistic art – by an eye untrained in either the fundamentals of art or the deep mysteries of Kabbalah – will reveal a rich abundance of symbolic image and emblem. And, of course, an intense desire to learn more of the origins and insights of the Kabbalah itself.

Stretching back at least 3,500 years, the word 'Kabbalah' originates from the Hebrew root 'QBL',

meaning 'to receive', and refers to the passing down of secret knowledge through an oral transmission – though later it was communicated in ciphers, thereby making it more of an occult science. The secrets of the Kabbalah were handed down 'since the time of Abraham' and culminated in the Zohar, a collection of written, mystical commentaries on the Torah (the teachings of the Five Books of Moses which form the basis of all Jewish law and practice), which is considered to be the underpinning of Kabbalah. Written in medieval Aramaic and medieval Hebrew, the Zohar is intended to guide Kabbalists in their spiritual journey, helping them attain the greater levels of connectedness with God that they desire. In the Kabbalah, the Torah and its Hebrew words and letters are synonymous with God himself; it is the seeker's sacred objective to study, reveal, and understand the hidden meanings enfolded into the literal words of the Torah.

The most important graphic symbol of the Kabbalah is the Tree of Life, an ultimate symbol of creation with all of nature included in its schema. Composed of ten spheres representing the numbers one through ten, and twenty-two paths, corresponding to the twenty-two letters of the Hebrew alphabet, together they form the thirty-two paths of wisdom described in the *Sepher Yetzirah*, an early Kabbalistic text. The ten numbers are significant as a numerical description of our known universe prior to creation, with one being a manifestation of 'the point', and ten

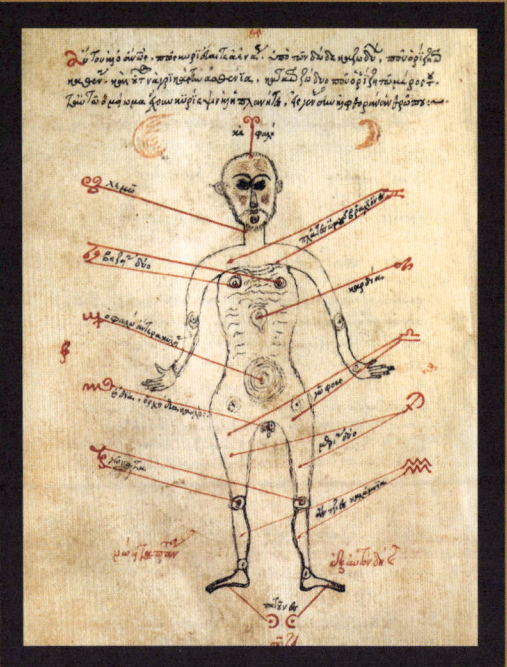

◄ **Influence of various kabalistic signs on the organs of the human body**
16th century, miniature from a Kabbalistic treatise, Greek manuscript.

arriving at a fully developed self-consciousness in the physical world. The twenty-two letters of the Hebrew alphabet are considered to be the vehicle by which God progressively called forth the physical universe through sound.

There is yet another symbolic grouping of numbers within the tradition of the Kabbalah, and that is of the four worlds, or planes of reality: '*Atziluth*', the archetypal world of pure idea; '*Briah*', the creative world which contains all patterns of general ideation; '*Yetzirah*', the formative world of specifics of individual design; and '*Assiah*', or the material world of tangible manifestations.

The evolution of Kabbalah into a more widespread phenomenon in European esotericism took place from the Renaissance onwards, when these texts were studied and translated by Christian specialists in Hebrew studies, and Hermetic occultists who adapted related traditions independently of Jewish Kabbalah,

reading the Jewish texts as 'universal ancient wisdom'. These eventually merged with other theologies, religious traditions and magical associations such as Rosicrucianism (whose manifestos do not elaborate but contain references to the Kabbalah) in the sixteenth and seventeenth centuries, becoming popularised in the books of nineteenth-century occultist Éliphas Lévi, and becoming the primary symbolic language of the Hermetic Order of the Golden Dawn.

The Kabbalah is awash with metaphor and meaning as it relates to art and architecture, and much of that imagery is both abstract and abundantly literal in its description of the heavenly realm; the Zohar is 'a poem of light and dark and a rainbow of colours and materials'. The Kabbalistic idea of creation, as expressed through light, space and geometry, has sparked inspirations and revelations in many an artist and has without doubt left a profound impact, and an unmistakable mark on our civilisation.

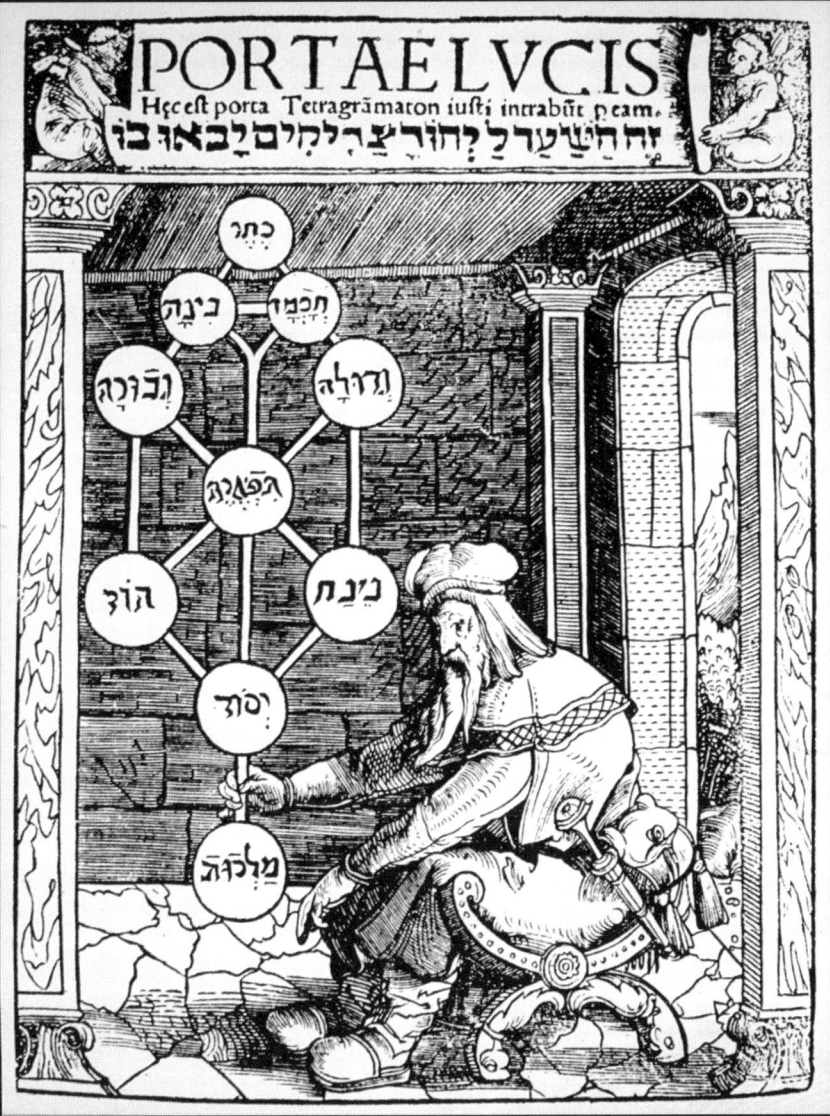

▲ **Jewish cabbalist holding a sephiroth**
copy of an illustration from *Portae Lucis*
(Paul Ricius, 1516) used in a *History of
Magic* (late 19th century), engraving.

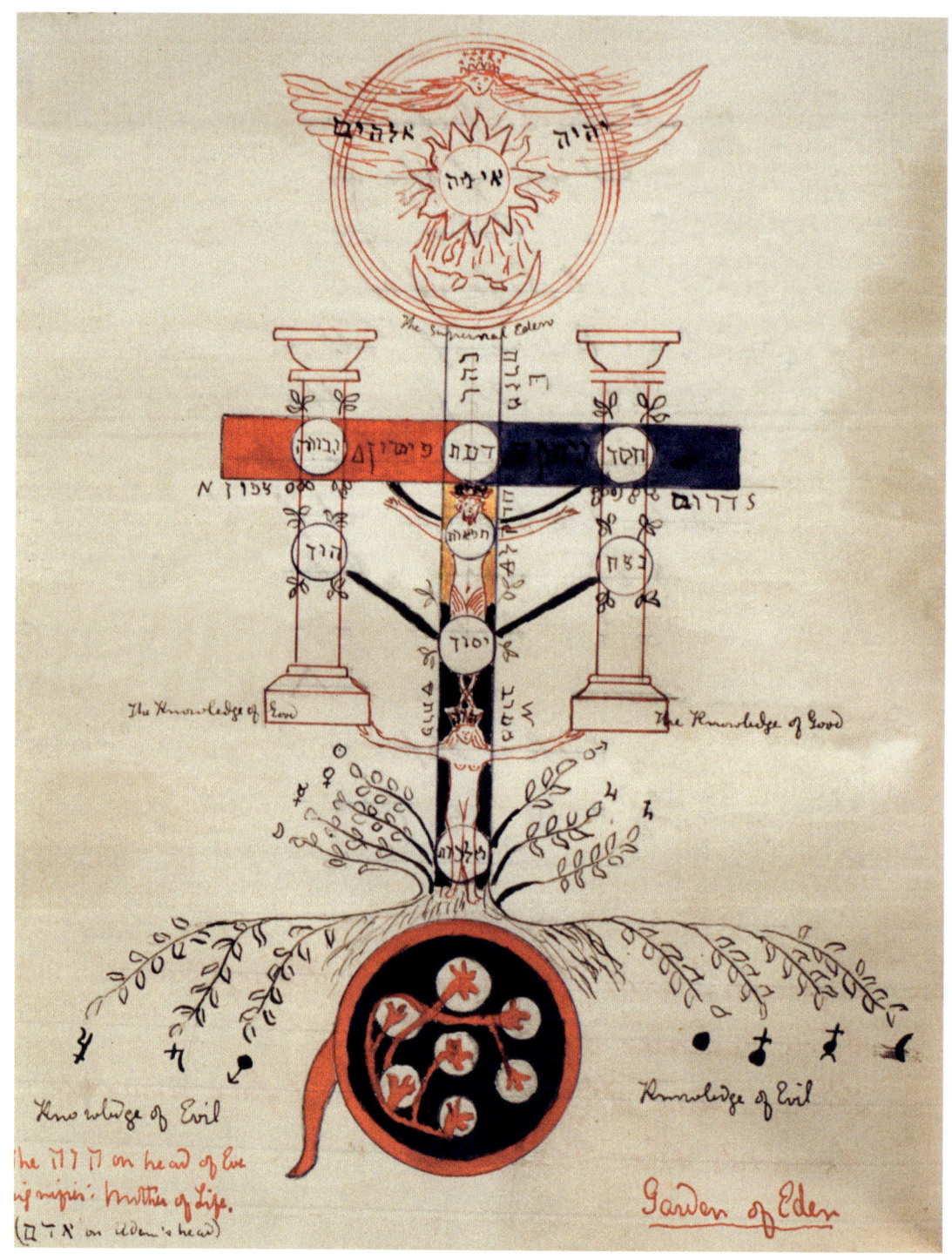

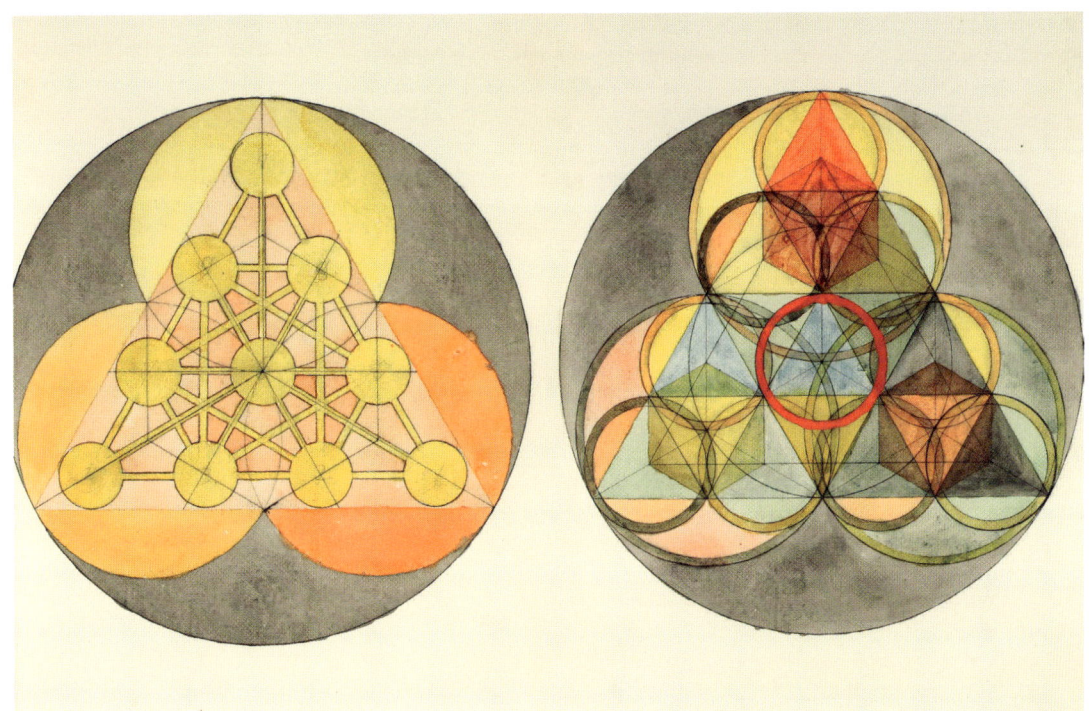

**◄ Symbolic diagram
of the Garden of Eden
before the Fall of Man**
Elizabeth Burnett, c.1892,
coloured ink on paper.

Created by Elizabeth Burnett (fl.1890s)
– the wife of ceremonial magician
and co-founder of the Golden Dawn,
William Wynn Westcott (1848–1925)
– this image depicts the earliest phase
of the first degree of initiation in the
Golden Dawn tradition, called 'The
Garden of Eden before the Fall'. The
diagram, which is presented to the
initiate, represents a stage of primordial
innocence and the bliss of ignorance.

▲ Geometric cabbalistic illustrations
From *Cabala* (c.1700).

Manly Palmer Hall (1901–1990) was a Canadian-born author,
lecturer and researcher in the realms of mysticism and the occult.
He is perhaps best known for his comprehensive 1928 work
The Secret Teachings of All Ages. These geometric cabbalistic
illustrations are part of a collection of 243 manuscripts detailing
the arts of Alchemy, Hermeticism, Rosicrucianism and Masonry.

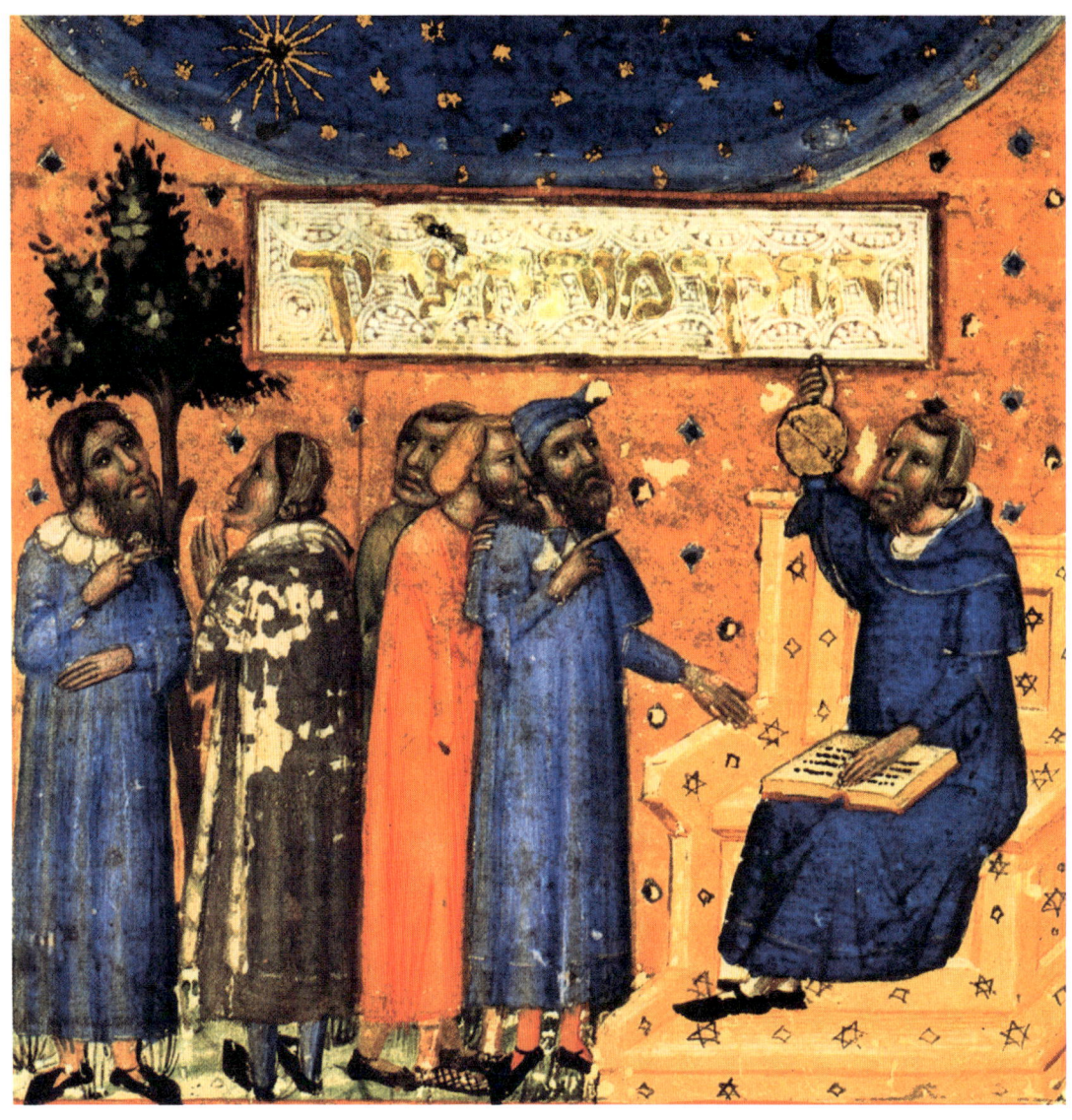

▲ Cabala, Master and Students
From a spiritual treaty of Maimonides, (14th century).

Moses Maimonides, original name Moses Ben Maimon (1135–1204) – Sephardic philosopher, jurist and physician – was regarded as a foremost intellectual figure of medieval Judaism and one of the most influential Torah scholars of the Middle Ages. His prolific work comprises a cornerstone of Jewish scholarship.

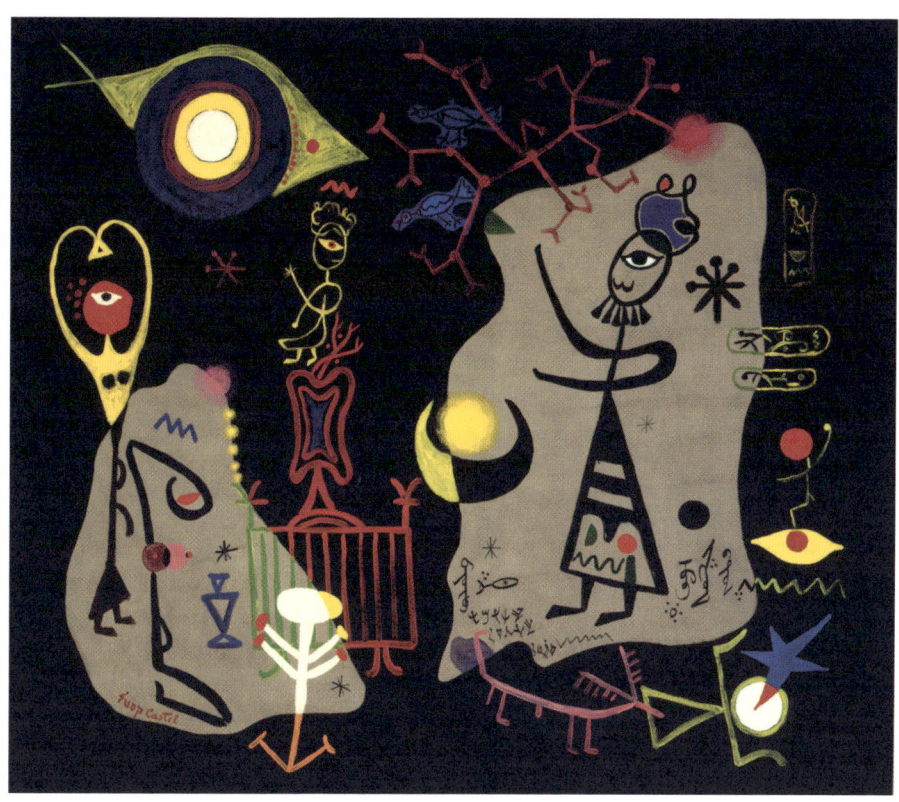

▲ **Cabbalistic Magic Israel**
Moshe Castel, 1953, oil on canvas.

Moshe Castel (1909-1991) was an Israeli artist who made contemporary imagery from ancient Jewish and Arabic letters and archeological artifacts of the Middle East. His work is marked by its depictions of Sephardic life and can be categorised into two distinct styles: vibrantly coloured prints embossed with metallic paints and strong watercolours which are abstract in style.

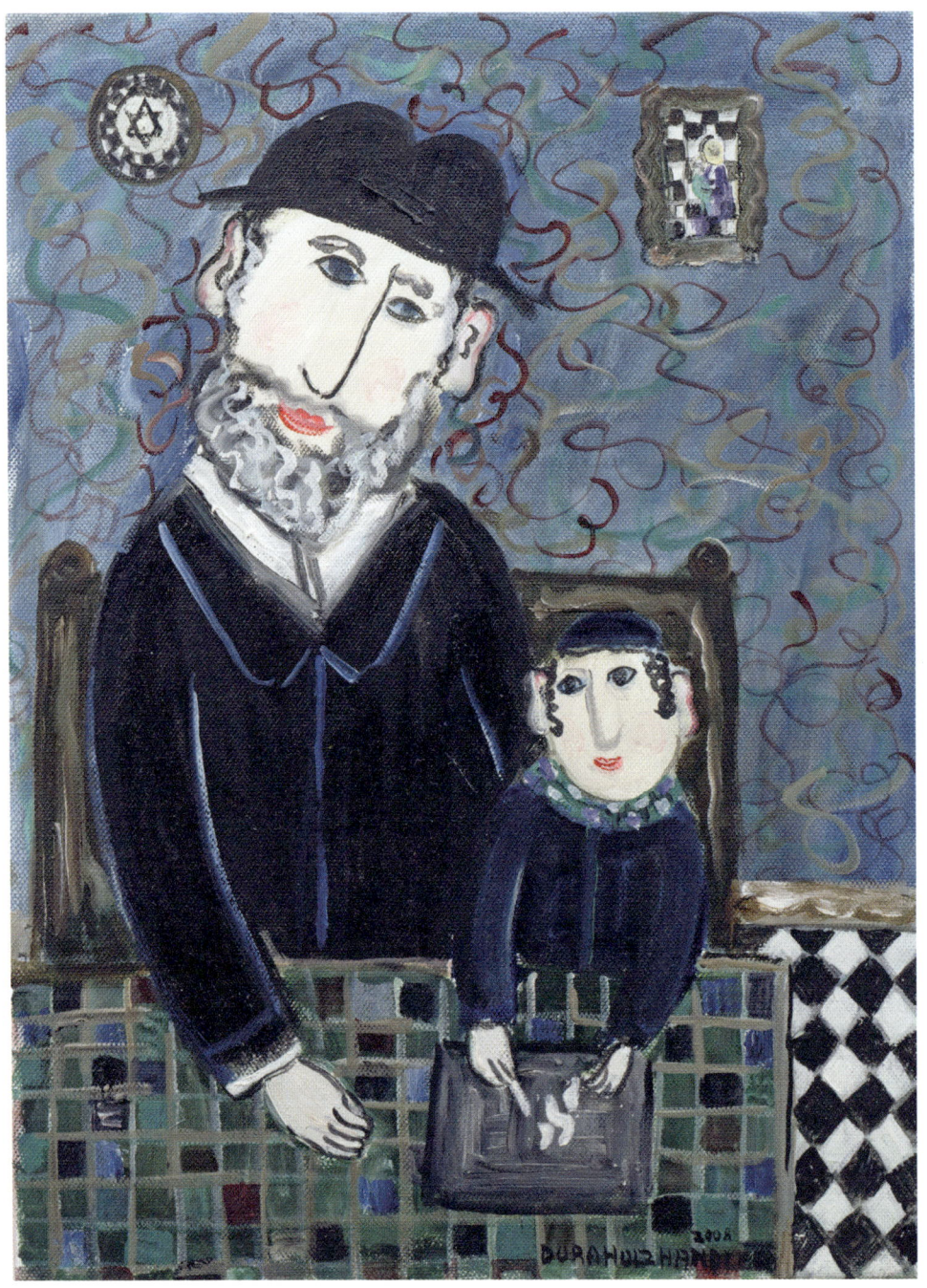

◄ Rabbi studying Kabbalah
Dora Holzhandler,
2008, oil on canvas.

Family and ritual are central to the works
of artist Dora Holzhandler (1928–2015),
who was born into a family of Polish
refugees. Sent to live with a foster family in
Normandy, she endured the war in England
and much of her extended family perished
at Auschwitz. Her childhood memories
and Jewish roots permeate her work, as
did her Buddhist beliefs, and she is said
to have claimed that, 'now, as a Buddhist,
I can really enjoy being Jewish.' Both the
sacred and the mundane play a part in her
simple, timeless artworks teeming with
humanity's celebrations and contemplations.

► 100 Sounds of the Shofar
Avraham Loewenthal,
undated.

Prayer, Jewish Mysticism and contemporary
art are combined in the unique work of
Tzfat artist Avraham Loewenthal (b.1969).
100 Sounds of the Shofar is a meditational
map of the 100 sounds blown on the
shofar on Rosh Hashanah. Each sound
corresponds to a particular aspect of our
consciousness. Kabbalah discusses the
deep spiritual significance of this pattern
of sounds blown since ancient times. Each
progressive sound represents deeper
levels of love and spiritual awareness.

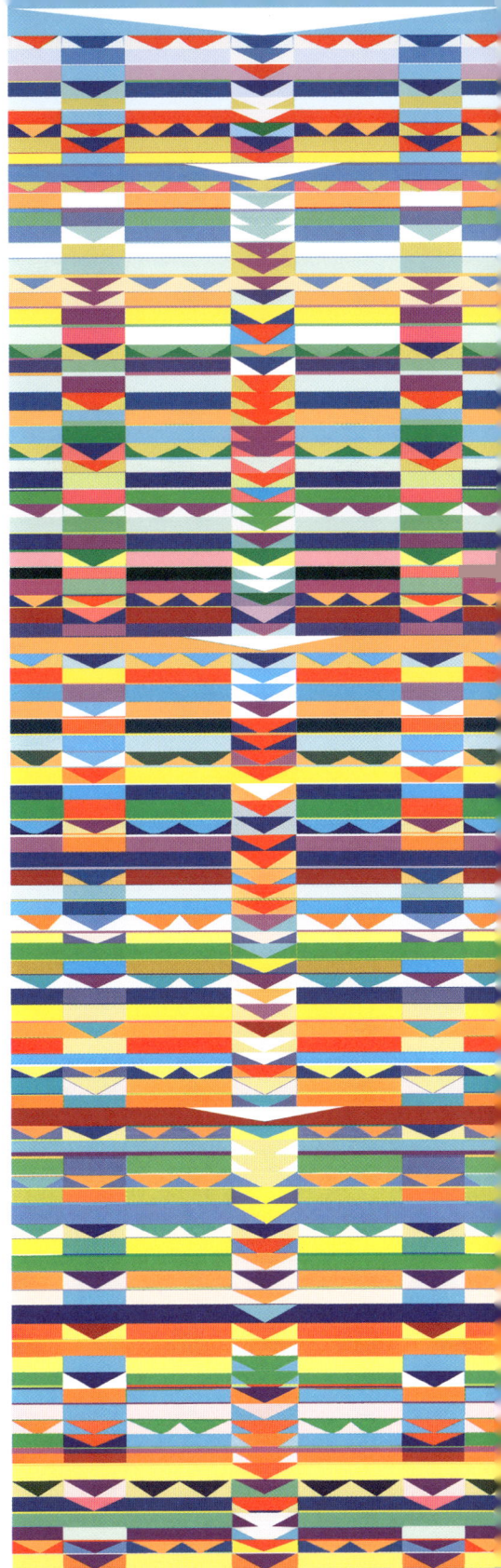

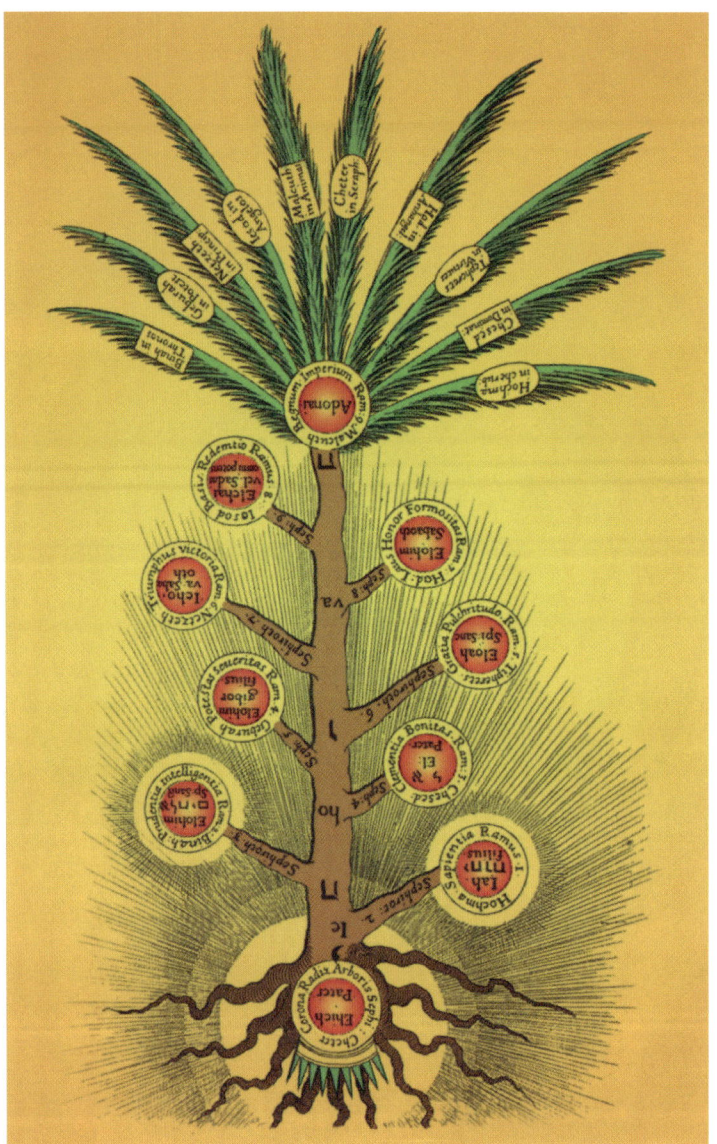

► **Symbol of the Nothing and the All Absolute** undated.

This Kabbalistic symbol presents an interesting conundrum, with no definitive meaning. From a Kabbalistic point of view, it appears to represent the paradoxical relationship between the meaning of Ayin (nothingness) and Yesh (something/being). Other sources reference the enigmatic symbol in relation to Ein-Sof, (the 'Infinite God' or 'without an end'). It remains a mystery – but, after all, exploring the hidden meaning of the art that pricks our senses and piques our curiosity is such a vitally important piece of what the art in this book is all about.

Robert Fludd (1574–1637) was an English mystic, philosopher, alchemist, scientist and published a large number of richly illustrated books – covering both practical and speculative topics in an attempt to reconcile mysticism with 17th-century science. The diagram of the Sephirotic Tree, a central mystical symbol used in the Kabbalah of esoteric Judaism, appears in Fludd's *Philosophia Sacra*.

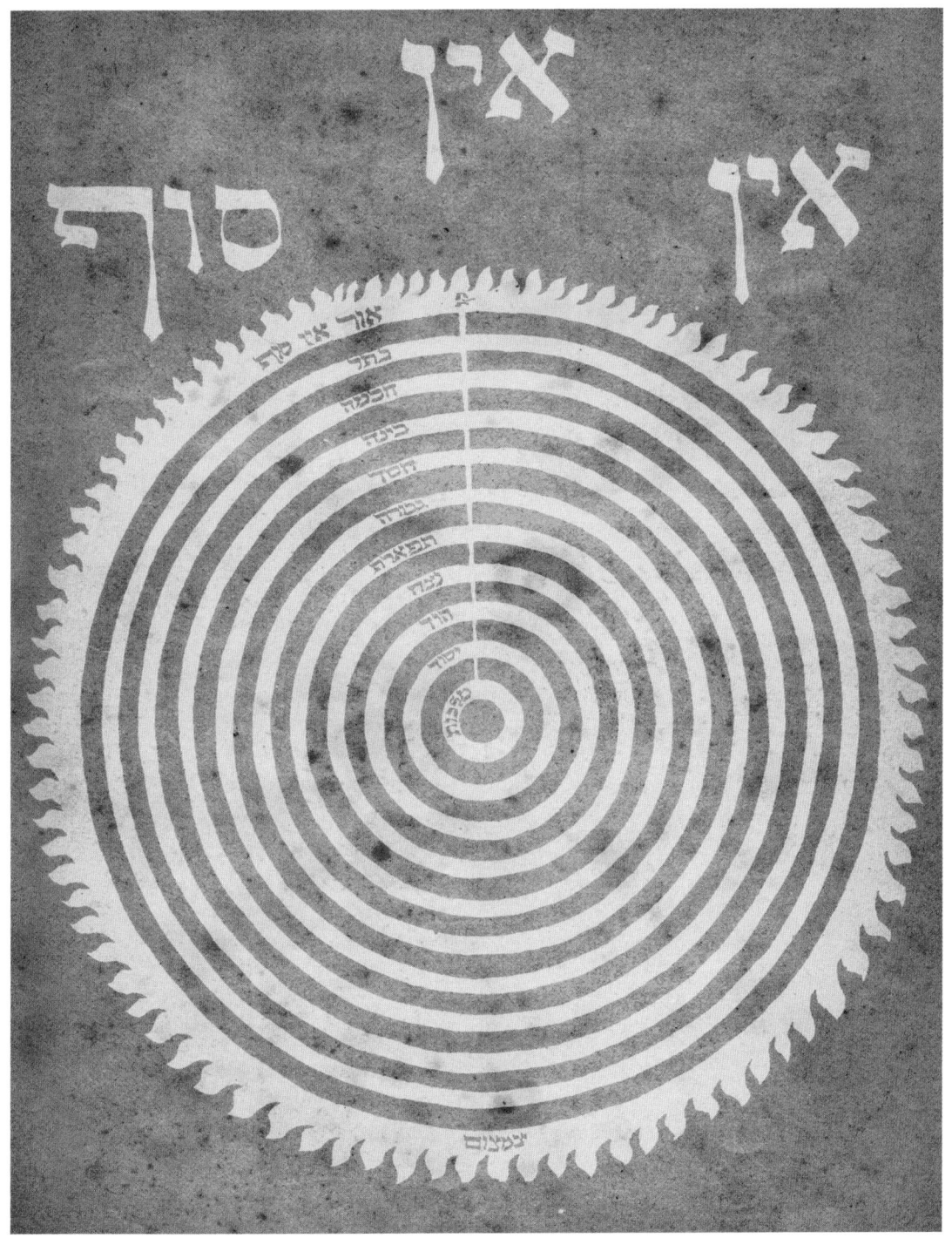

▶ **Everyone Stands Under His Own Dome of Heaven**
Anselm Kiefer, 1970,
watercolour, gouache and
graphite on joined paper.

Born a Catholic in a small village
in the Black Forest during the
last year of World War II, artist
Anselm Kiefer (b.1945) strove for
reunification and reconciliation in
the complex personal cosmology
of his artistic creations. Kiefer's
oeuvre, which explores themes
of German history and the horror
of the Holocaust, in addition to
his artistic interest in Kabbalistic
thought and systems, is described
as 'unquestionably difficult'.

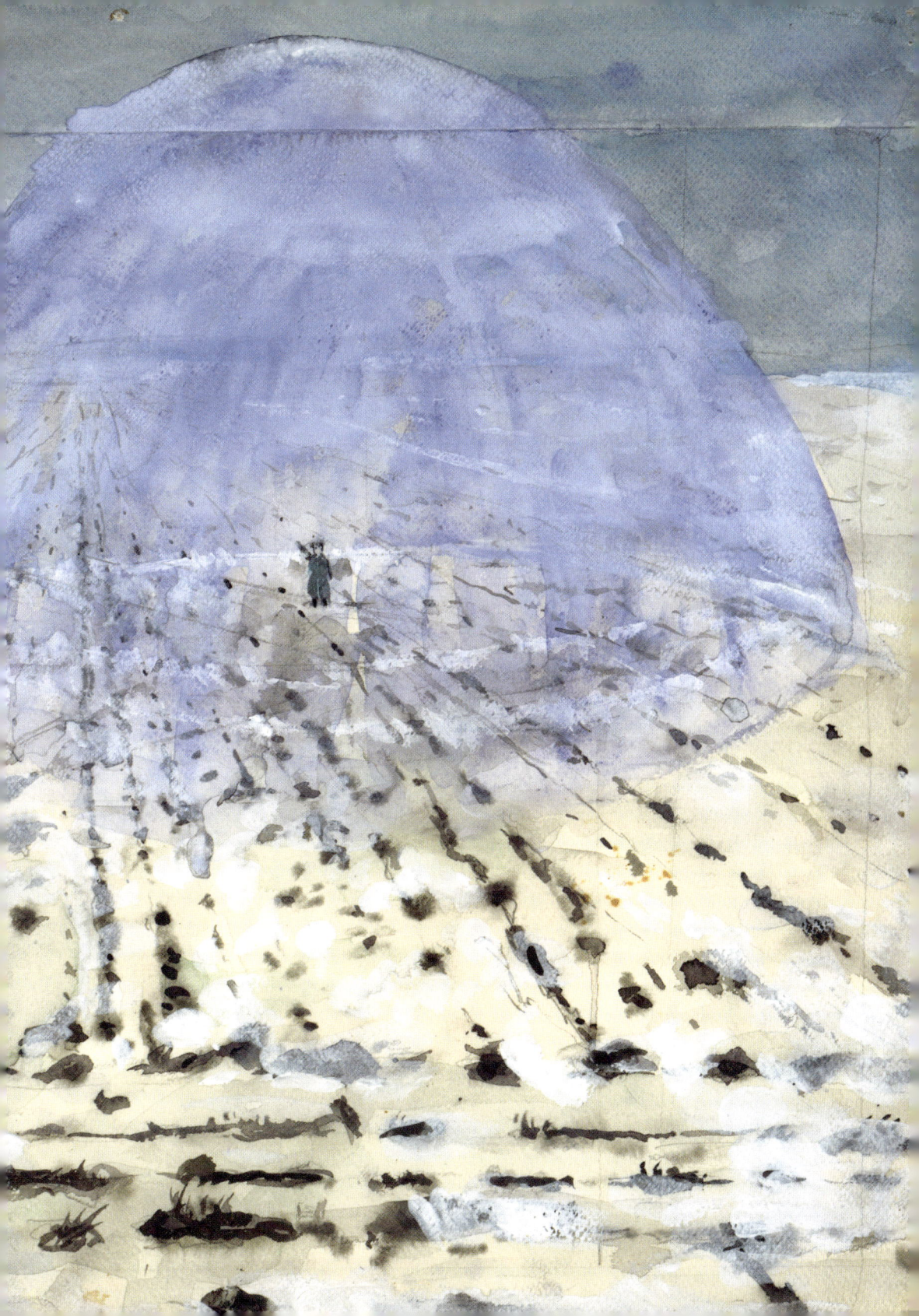

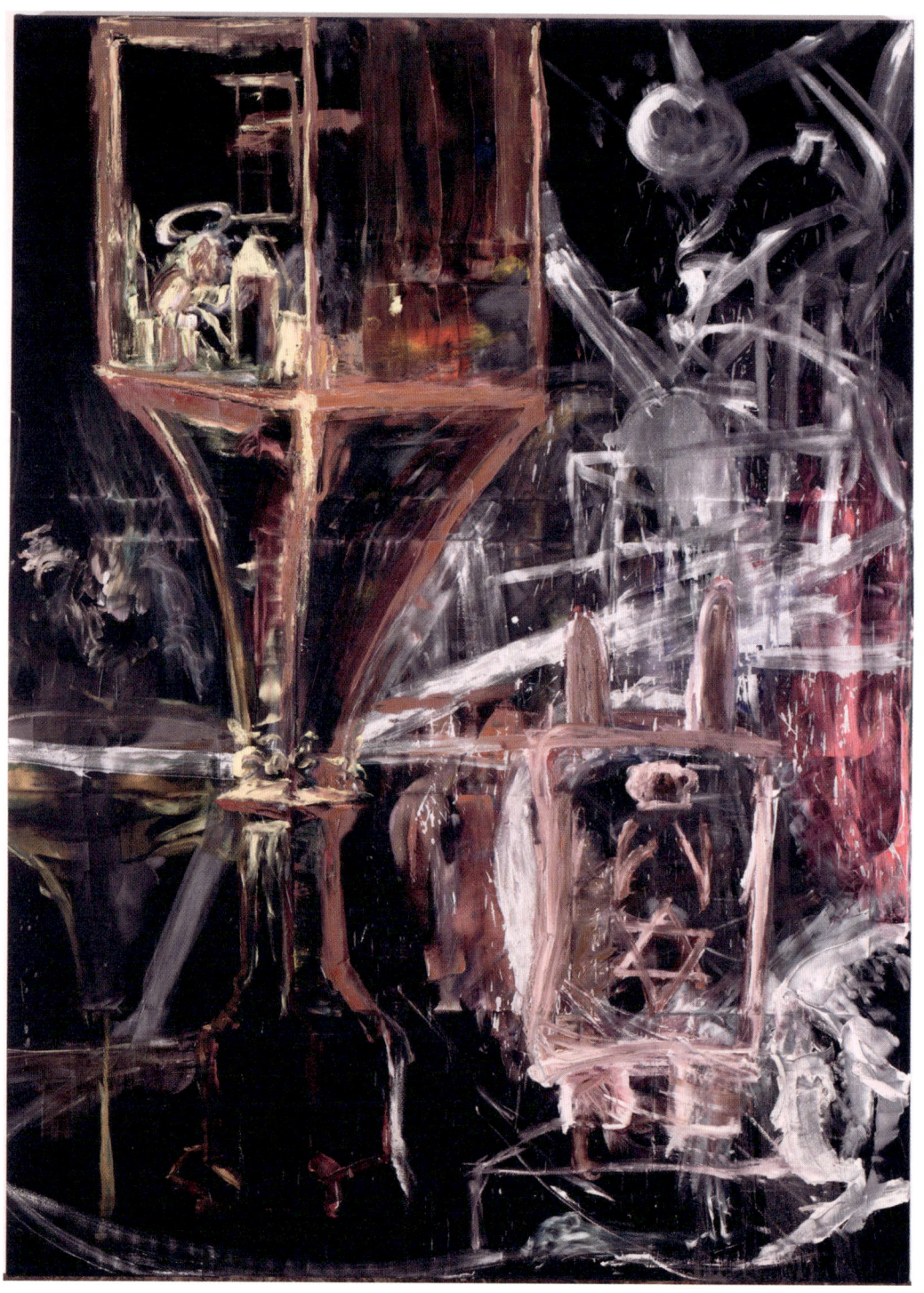

▶ Abraham
Barnett Newman,
1949, oil on canvas.

Painter and theorist Barnett Newman
(1905–1970) is noted as one of the
most intellectual artists of the New York
School. His approach to creating art
was shaped by both his philosophical
studies at The City College of New
York and his political activism. For him,
art was an act of self-creation and
a declaration of political, intellectual
and individual freedom. Described
as a slab roughly the size of a tall
man, Barnet's work *Abraham* is a
dark painting with a black 'zip' placed
off-centre on a brown field. The title
evokes both Newman's own father
and the Old Testament Father, who
nearly sacrificed his son to God.

◀ Kaballistic Painting
Julian Schnabel,
1983, oil on velvet.

Artist Julian Schnabel (b.1951) first
became known for his large-scale
paintings that incorporated unusual
materials, such as wax, velvet and
broken ceramic plates. He is also
an accomplished director whose
cinematic success at times eclipsed his
accomplishments as a painter. Despite
this, the artist remains prolific and sees
himself as a painter first and foremost.
Schnabel's 1983 work, *Kaballistic
Painting*, incorporates imagery from
both the Old and New Testaments,
showing a man seated at a table on
which sits an alembic and a torah.

VII

THEOSOPHICAL THOUGHT MANIFESTED THROUGH ART

THE WORD 'THEOSOPHY', MEANING 'GOD'S wisdom', was first used in writing during the third to the sixth century by the Alexandrian Neo-Platonic philosophers as a term to indicate an experiential knowledge attained through spiritual means. Over time, various mystics and spiritual movements in the West adopted the word 'Theosophy' in their teachings, until in 1875, Helena Petrovna Blavatsky and a group of like-minded colleagues founded the Theosophical Society in New York, thus bringing the term back into the mainstream. These individuals espoused that Theosophy was not a religion but a system synonymous with eternal truth, which underlies not only all religions, but also philosophy and science. The aim of its founders was to 'liberate man from bondage by presenting a philosophy of life that would show him how to find the truth within himself'.

Born to an aristocratic family in Russia in 1831, Mme Blavatsky was a Spiritualist and clairvoyant, and was said to have been possessed of certain psychic powers. From a young age, she had been fascinated by the Hermetic tradition, travelling the world in search of esoteric wisdom. Some people say she visited spiritual masters in Tibet region of China, while others attribute her with less aspirational travels and experiences (she had an illegitimate child, worked in a circus, and earned a living as a medium in Paris.) An extraordinary and controversial character, Blavatsky has been called many things: the fountainhead of modern occult thought, a trailblazing psychologist of the visionary mind, and one of most 'accomplished, ingenious, and interesting impostors in history', whose contributions to the occult are numerous.

In 1877 she published *Isis Unveiled*, which outlined her Theosophical world view, a synthesis of science, religion and philosophy. *The Secret Doctrine*, published in 1888, was an 'influential example' of the revival of interest in occult ideas in the modern age, in particular because of its claim to reconcile ancient Eastern wisdom, such as karma and reincarnation, with modern science. Blavatsky alleged that its contents had been revealed to her by the 'mahatmas' or 'great souls' of India, who had retained the knowledge of humanity's spiritual history, knowledge that it was now possible, in part, to reveal.

The most fundamental teaching of Theosophy, according to the Theosophical Society, is that all people have the same spiritual and physical origin because they are 'essentially of one and the same essence, and that essence is one – infinite, uncreate, and eternal, whether we call it God or Nature'. Its objectives concern forming a universal brotherhood of humanity, without distinction of race, creed, sex, caste or colour; encouraging the study of comparative religion, philosophy and science; and investigating unexplained laws of Nature and the powers latent in human beings.

Considering the casual, yet wonderfully profound philosophies and tenets of Theosophy, one might imagine this liberating way of

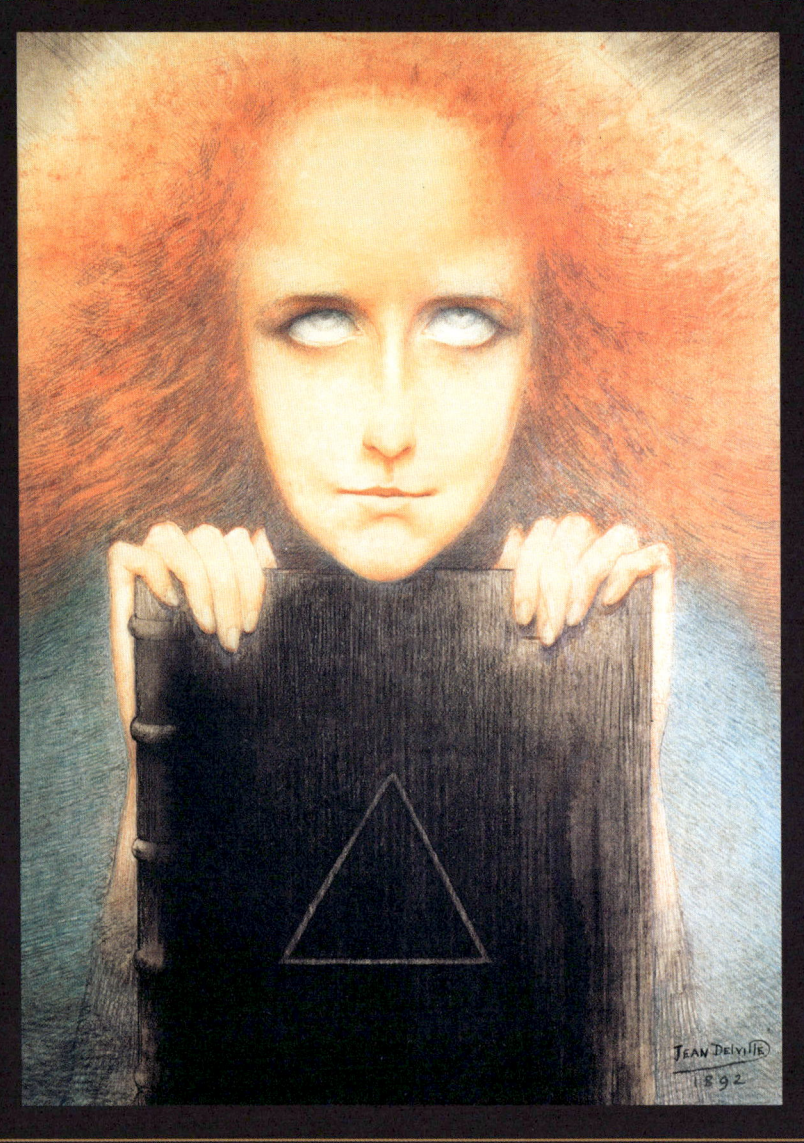

▲ The Portrait of Mrs Stuart Merrill
Jean Delville, 1892, coloured pencil on paper.

Jean Delville (1867–1953) maintained throughout the course of his life that art should be the expression of a higher spiritual truth. Not much other than second-hand accounts are known of the mysterious Mrs. Stuart Merrill in Delville's most enigmatic work (although it is likely her visage appears in other works by Delville), but the artist was obviously struck by her strange beauty and immortalised her otherworldly gaze and dramatic energies for the ages in this portrait.

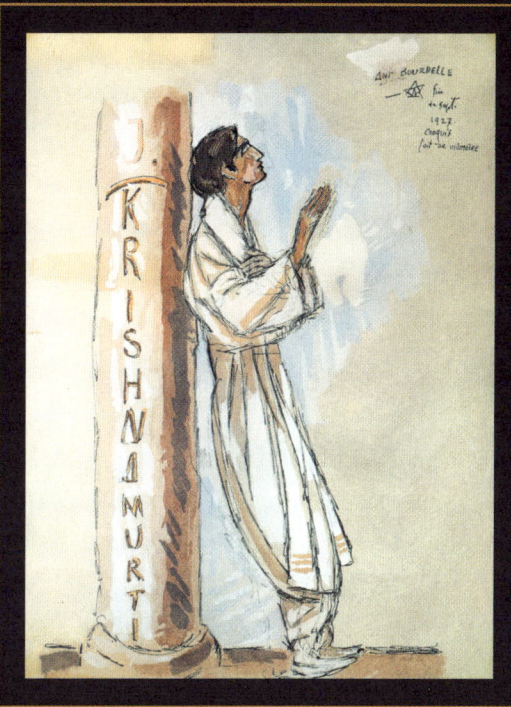

▶ **Krishnamurti**
Emile-Antoine Bourdelle,
1927, gouache on paper.

Influential and prolific French
sculptor Emile-Antoine Bourdelle
(1861–1929) was a student of
Auguste Rodin (1840–1917) and
an important figure in the Art Deco
movement. His portrait of Indian
spiritual leader and philosopher
Jiddu Krishnamurti (considered by
the Theosophical Society to be the
incarnation of Maitreya Buddha)
was apparently drawn from memory.
It is interesting to note that later
Krishnamurti severed his ties to
Theosophy and the Theosophical
Society, declaring independence
from all religious, philosophical, and
cultural disciplines and practices.

thinking would appeal to the free-spirited
souls of the day who possessed an artistic
temperament and creative tendencies, and who
were seeking a higher cosmic truth. And one
would be correct in assuming so, for amongst
the members of the Theosophical Society were
a great number of artists, many of whom are
considered the founders of the modern abstract
art movement: Wassily Kandinsky, Frantisek
Kupka, Piet Mondrian and Hilma af Klint. It was
inevitable that artists might turn their attention
to spirituality at the dawn of the materialistic age
of the twentieth century, and Theosophy gave
them a perspective that became the fundamental
groundwork of their beliefs; from this vantage
point, they believed they were able to see beyond
the natural world into otherworldly realms.
They stood in this doorway between worlds as
messengers, and communicating this knowledge
became the objective of their art.

Mme Blavatsky wrote the following of artists:

> Thoreau pointed out that there are artists in
> life, persons who can change the colour of
> a day and make it beautiful to those with
> whom they come in contact. We claim that
> there are adepts, masters in life who make
> it divine, as in all other arts. Is it not the
> greatest art of all, this which affects the very
> atmosphere in which we live? That it is the
> most important is seen at once, when we
> remember that every person who draws the
> breath of life affects the mental and moral
> atmosphere of the world, and helps to
> colour the day for those about him.

Perhaps she intended it as whimsical musing, but
I prefer to read it literally, as an appreciation for
these creative messengers of higher truths, cosmic
knowledge, the adepts who 'make it divine'.

▼ **Evolution**
Piet Mondrian, 1911,
oil on canvas.

Influential painter, Pieter Cornelis 'Piet' Mondrian (1872–1944), became a member of the Dutch section of the Theosophical Society in 1909 and much of artist's work for the rest of his life was inspired by his search for that spiritual knowledge. While Mondrian was still experimenting with Symbolist art, he painted *Evolution* – a triptych that made use of mystical triangles, hexagons and Stars of David. The images, read from left to right, depict a movement from the material to the spiritual, a common concept in Theosophy.

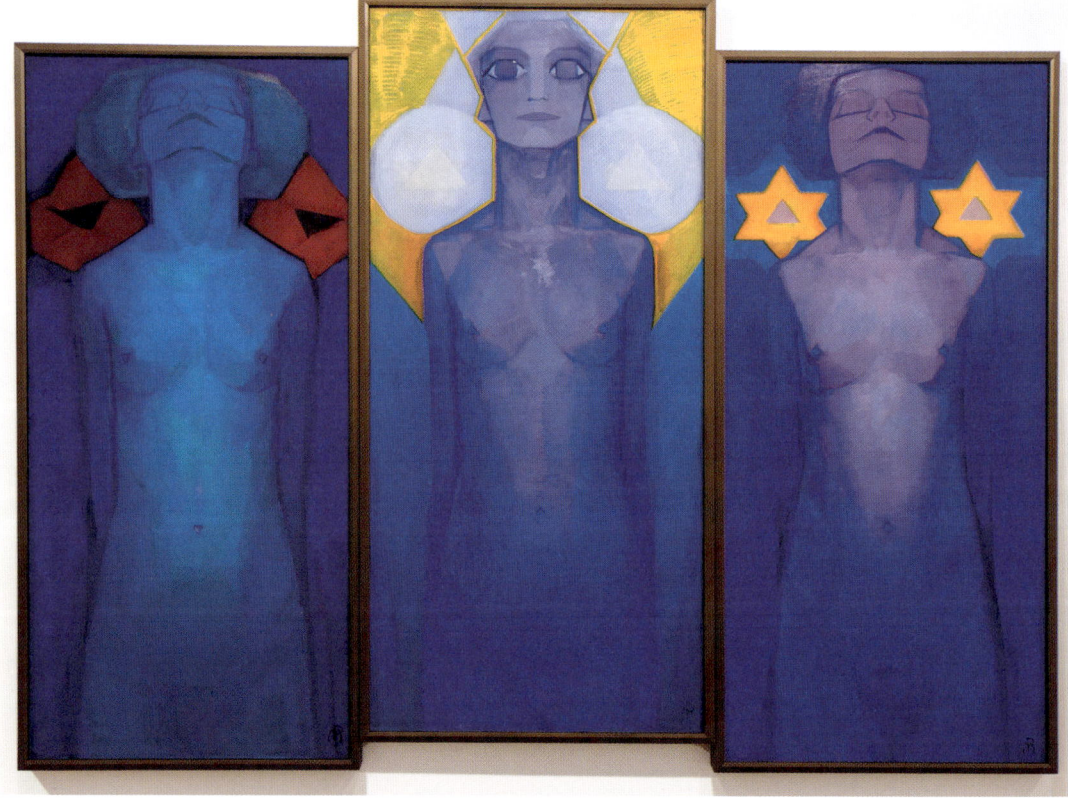

► Music
Luigi Russolo, 1911.

Luigi Carlo Filippo Russolo (1885–1947) was an Italian Futurist painter, composer, builder of experimental musical instruments and the author of the manifesto *The Art of Noises* (1913). He designed and constructed a number of noise-generating devices called Intonarumori. Although Russolo does not mention Theosophy explicitly in his theoretical writings about music, scholars conjecture that the artist and his Futurist comrades had likely absorbed Theosophical ideas through their fascination for late 19th-century French thought; additionally, through his synesthetic investigations he had no doubt devoted intense hours of study to the theory of vibrations, acoustic science, as well as the Theosophical theories about the forms produced by music.

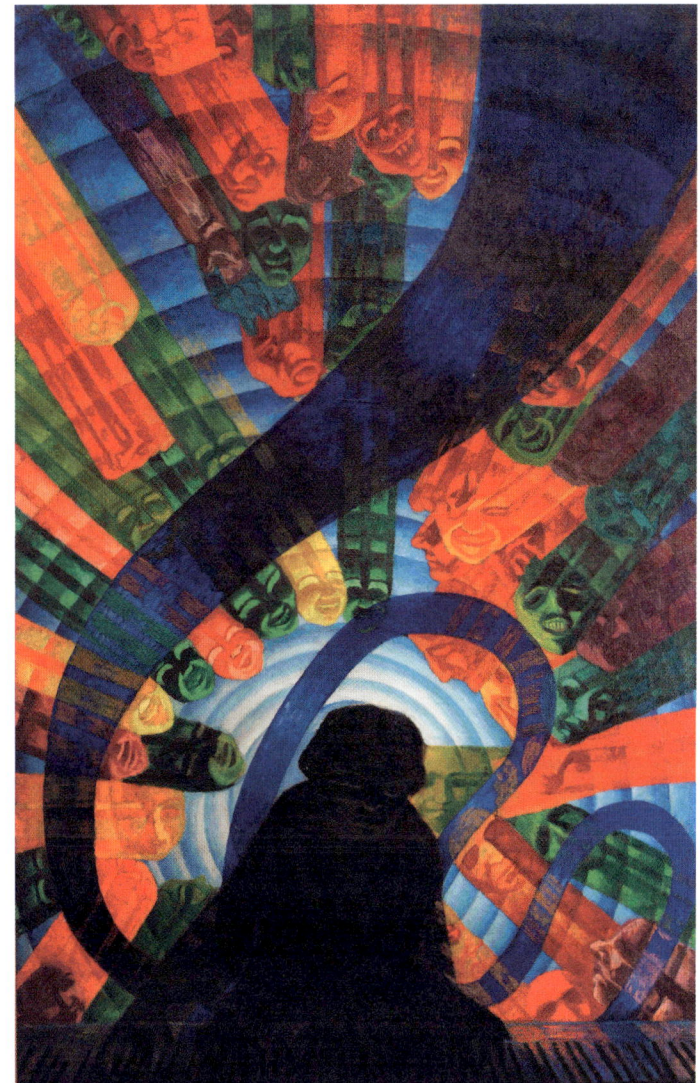

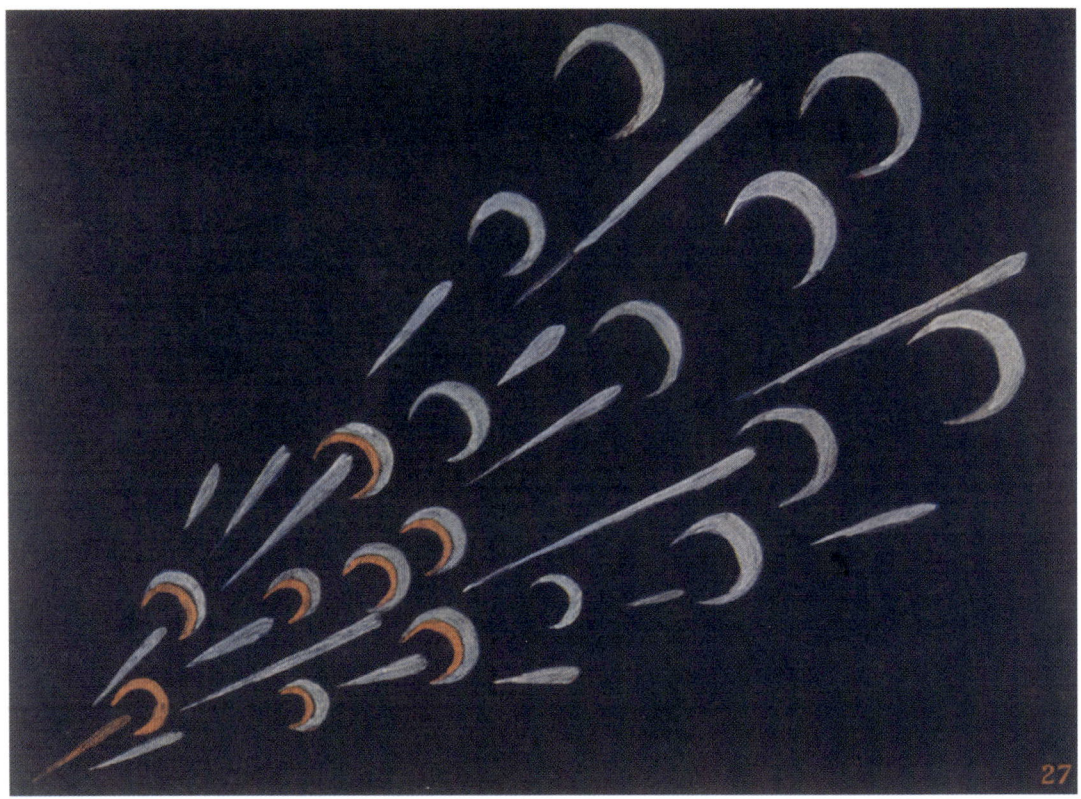

▲ **Sudden Fright**
From *Thought-Forms*
(Annie Besant and C.
W. Leadbeater, 1905)

Thought-Forms: A Record of Clairvoyant Investigation is a
Theosophical book compiled by A. Besant (1857–1933) and
C. W. Leadbeater (1854–1934), members of the Theosophical
Society, regarding visualisation of thoughts, experiences,
emotions and music. Drawings of the 'thought-forms' were
performed by painters Varley, Prince and McFarlane.

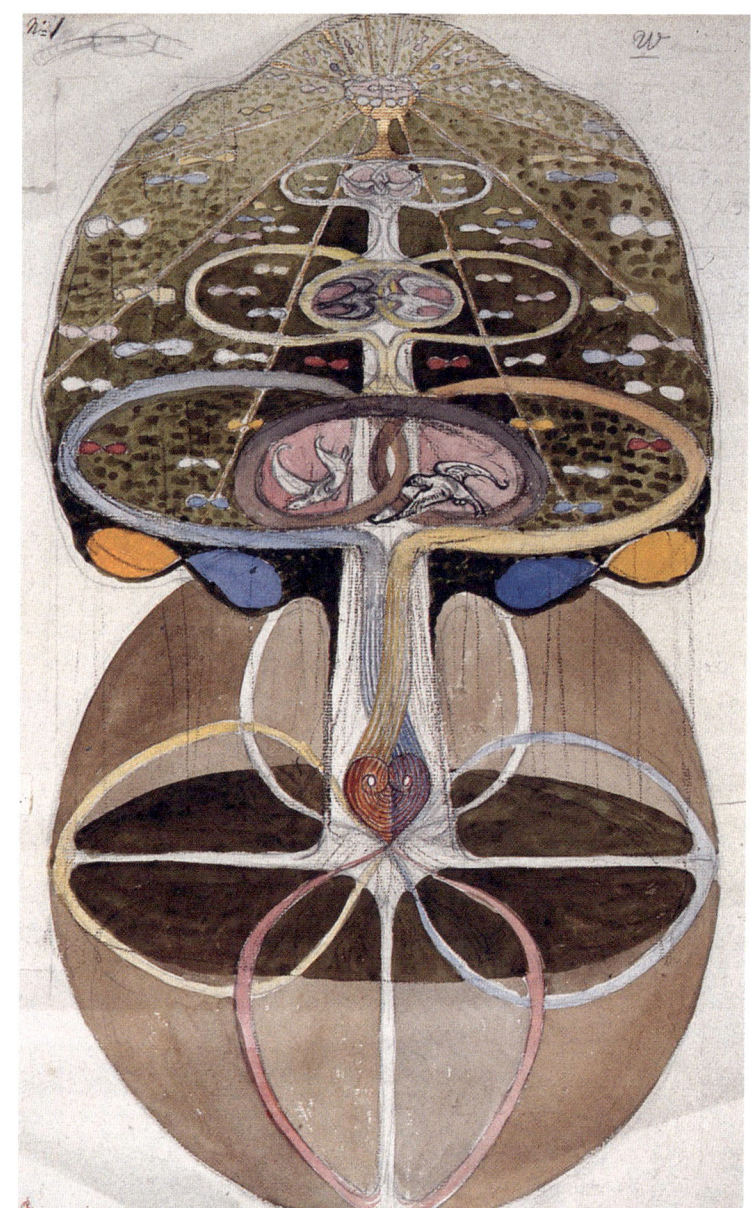

▶ Tree of Knowledge, No. 1
Hilma af Klint, 1913, watercolour, gouache, graphite, metallic paint and ink on paper.

Hilma af Klint (1862–1944) was a Swedish artist, Spiritualist and seeker whose ecstatic works have become known as some of the first examples of abstract art. Af Klint became greatly involved in various religious and philosophical movements in her lifetime, but it was Theosophy that would shape her and her work for years to come.

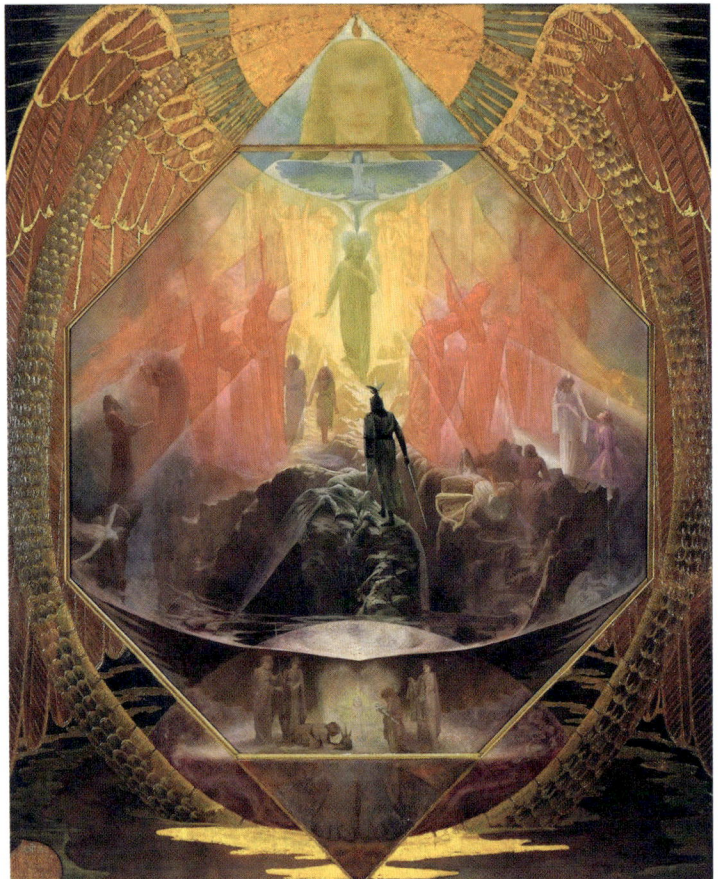

► **Oversoul**
Emil Bisttram, c.1941,
oil on masonite.

Emil Bisttram (1895–1976) was an American artist who lived in New York and Taos, New Mexico, and was known for his modernist work. Bisttram brought a fascinating array of spiritual, philosophical and scientific traditions to his painting. A Theosophist who founded The Transcendental Painting Group, he wrote of universalism and 'the essential oneness of all things' and explored these concepts in works such as *Oversoul*.

▲ **The Path**
Reginald W. Machell,
c.1895, oil and
gesso on canvas.

Reginald Willoughby Machell (1854–1927) was an English painter whose best-known work is *The Path*. He joined the Theosophical Society after meeting Helena Petrovna Blavatsky in London, after which the scope of his work began to change toward mysticism and symbolism. In the artist's words, 'The Path is the way by which the human soul must pass in its evolution to full spiritual self-consciousness.' The work hangs at the headquarters of the Theosophical Society, in Pasadena, California.

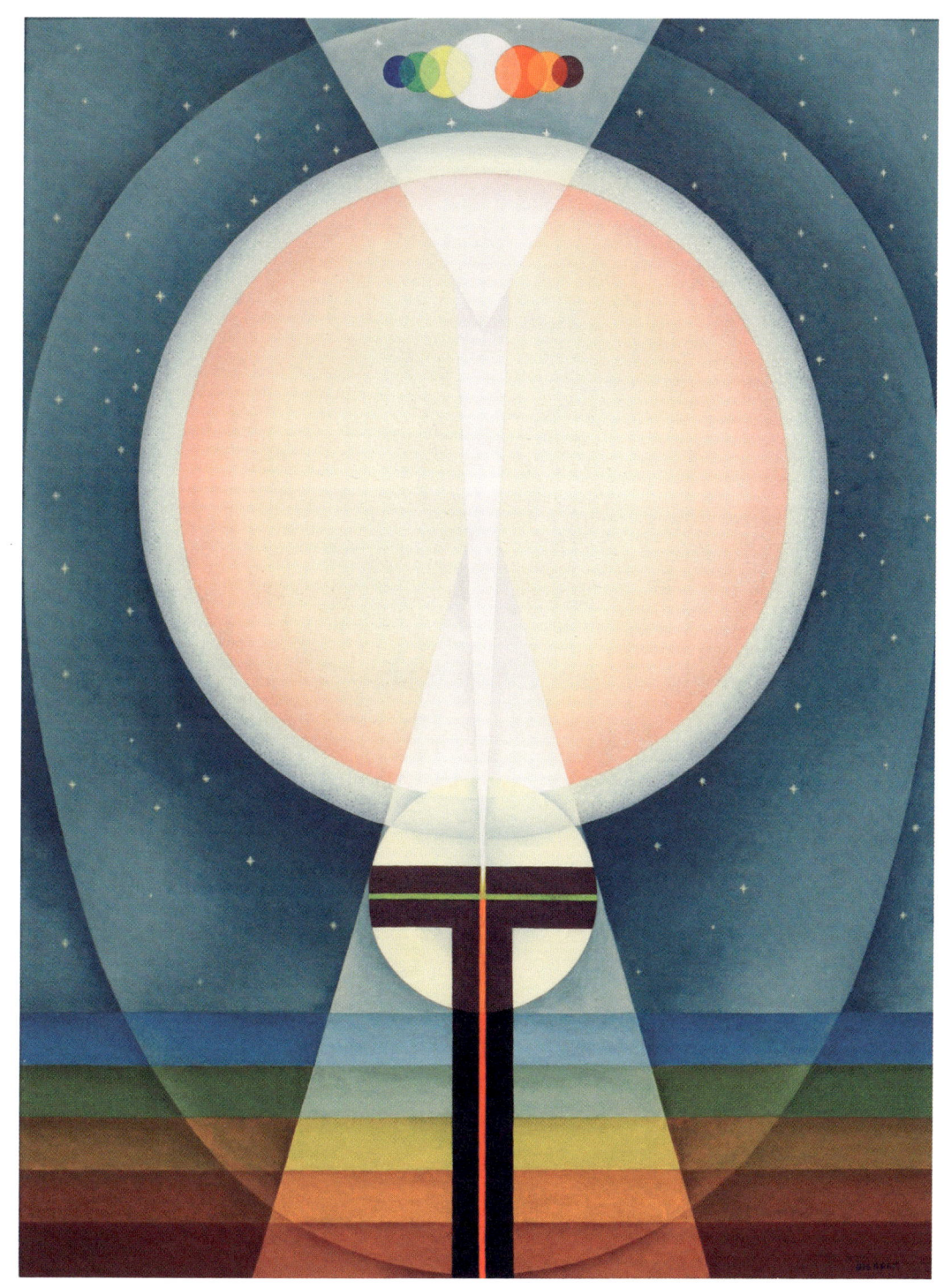

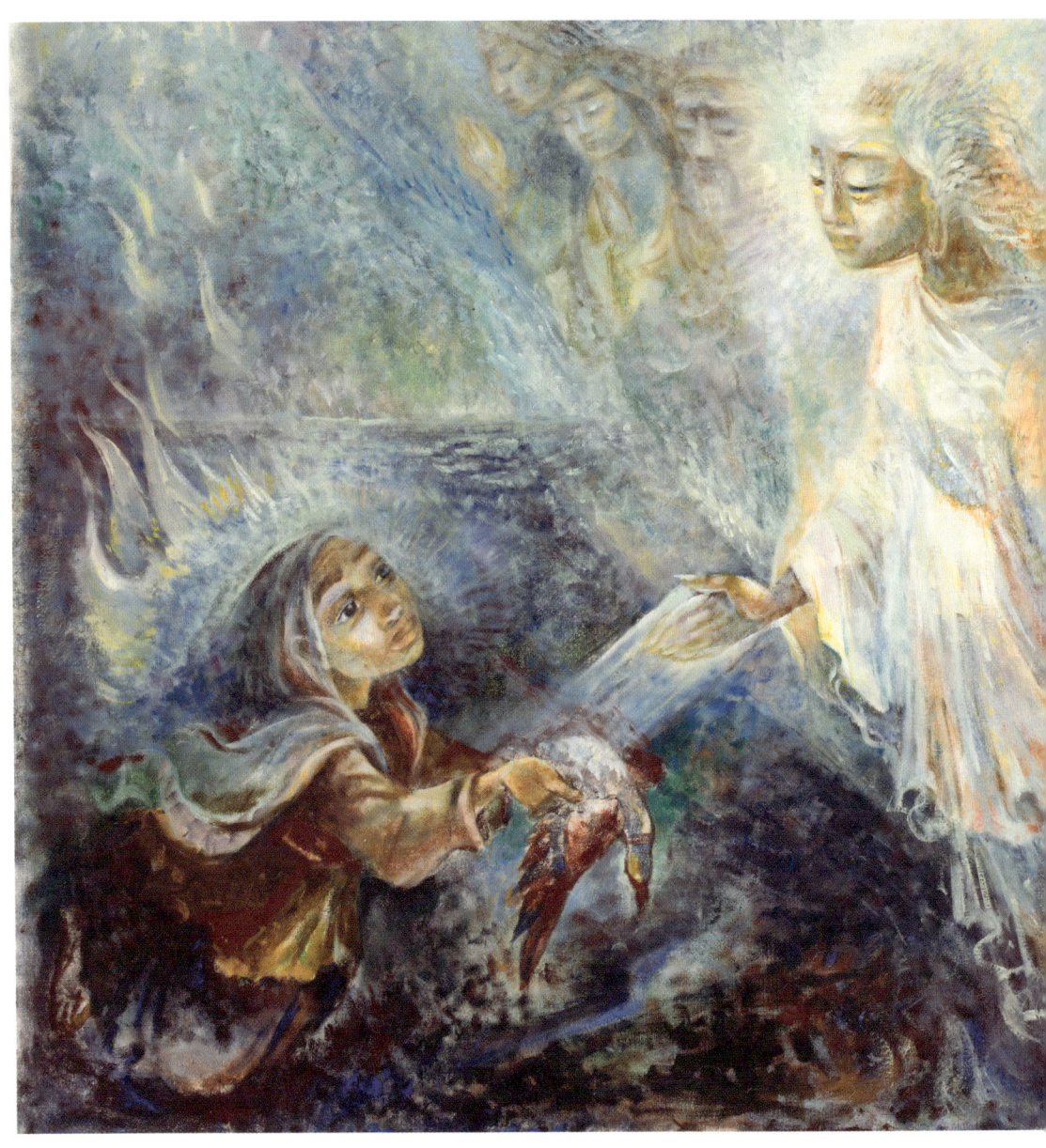

▲ Enlightened
Ilona Harima, 1939,
oil on canvas.

Finnish artist Ilona Harima (1911–1986) was fascinated with oriental art forms and cultures and was particularly interested by the visual world of Indian and Chinese art. In 1936, she became a member of the Theosophical Society, where she was encouraged by the artist Hilma af Klint to read the writings of Rudolf Steiner. She later produced some large paintings under that specific influence.

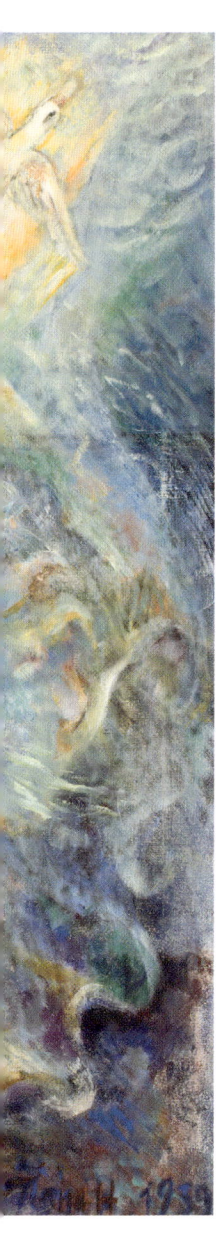

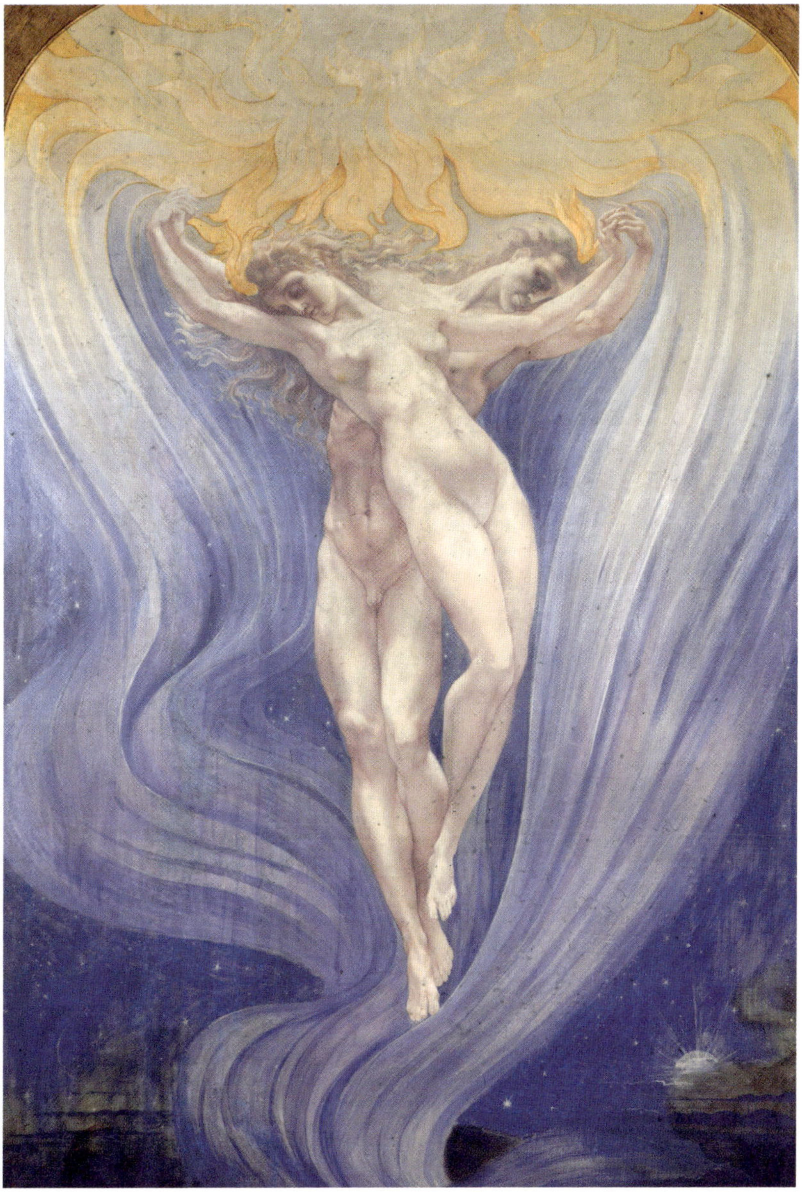

▲ **L'amour des âmes**
Jean Delville, 1900,
tempera and oil
on canvas.

In *L'amour des âmes* (The Love of Souls) Theosophist and
Belgian painter Jean Delville's (1867–1953) distinctive
style is seen to great effect in his use of gentle curves,
contours and subtle contrasts. This painting suggests a
theme of male and female energy being united to form
a state of wholeness and complete unity of being.

▼ The Yellow Cape
Odilon Redon, 1895,
pastel on paper.

Odilon Redon (1840–1916) was a French Symbolist painter, whose evocative works are the stuff of mysteries and nightmares. Redon explored Buddhist and Hindu writings, as well as religious syncretic and Theosophical texts from French writers like Edouard Schuré. Redon said of his works, 'My drawings inspire, and are not to be defined. They place us, as does music, in the ambiguous realm of the undetermined.'

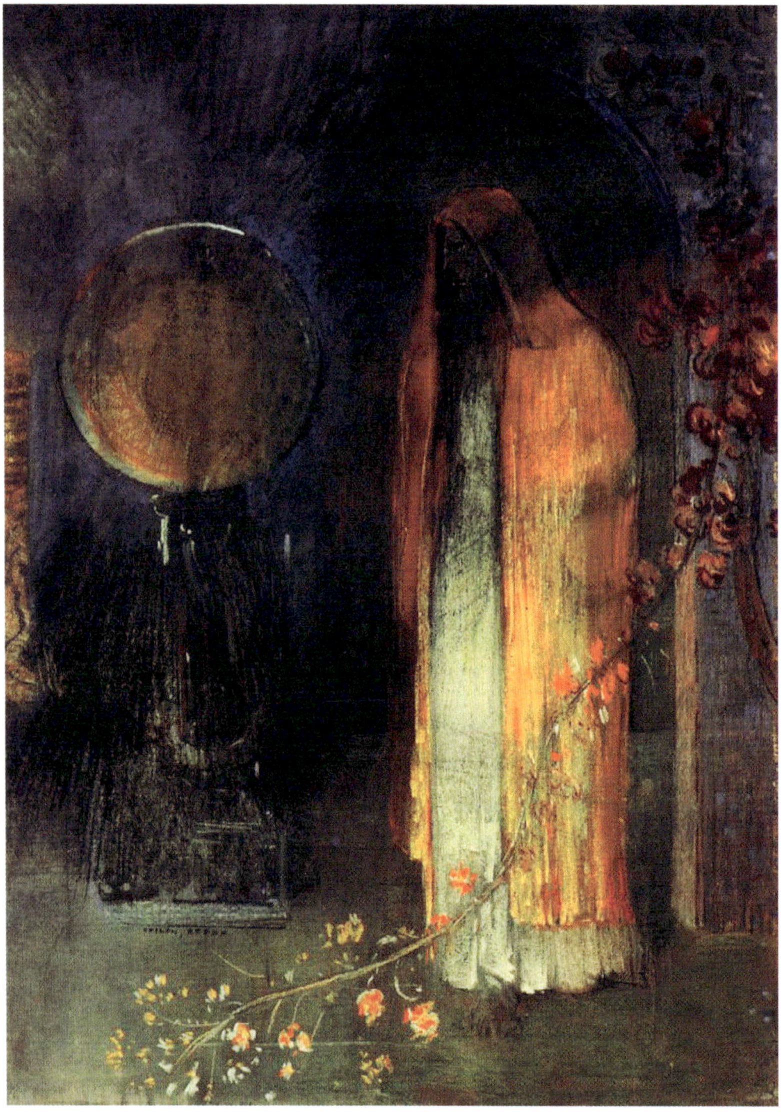

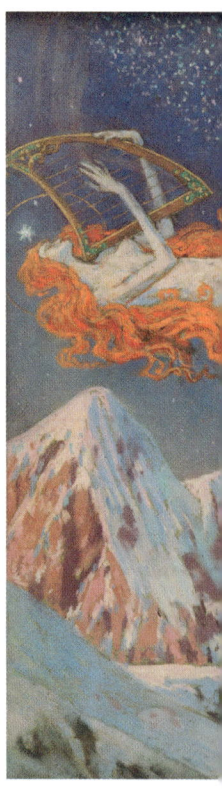

▼ Heiliger Turm im Gebirge mit den vier Quellen der Lebensströme
Melchior Lechter, 1917, pastel on cardboard.

Artist and publisher Melchior Lechter (1865–1937) is best known for his glass paintings, drawings and decorative designs for books, calendars, catalogues, ex libris and posters, whose symbolic style combined Gothic elements with Art Nouveau. In his paintings and writings, Lechter integrated 'ideas of both the medieval German and the ancient Indian mystics'. His travels to India intensified his long-held interest in Theosophy and Buddhist mysticism – themes which later became prevalent in his work – although he continued his involvement with Catholic mysticism and theology.

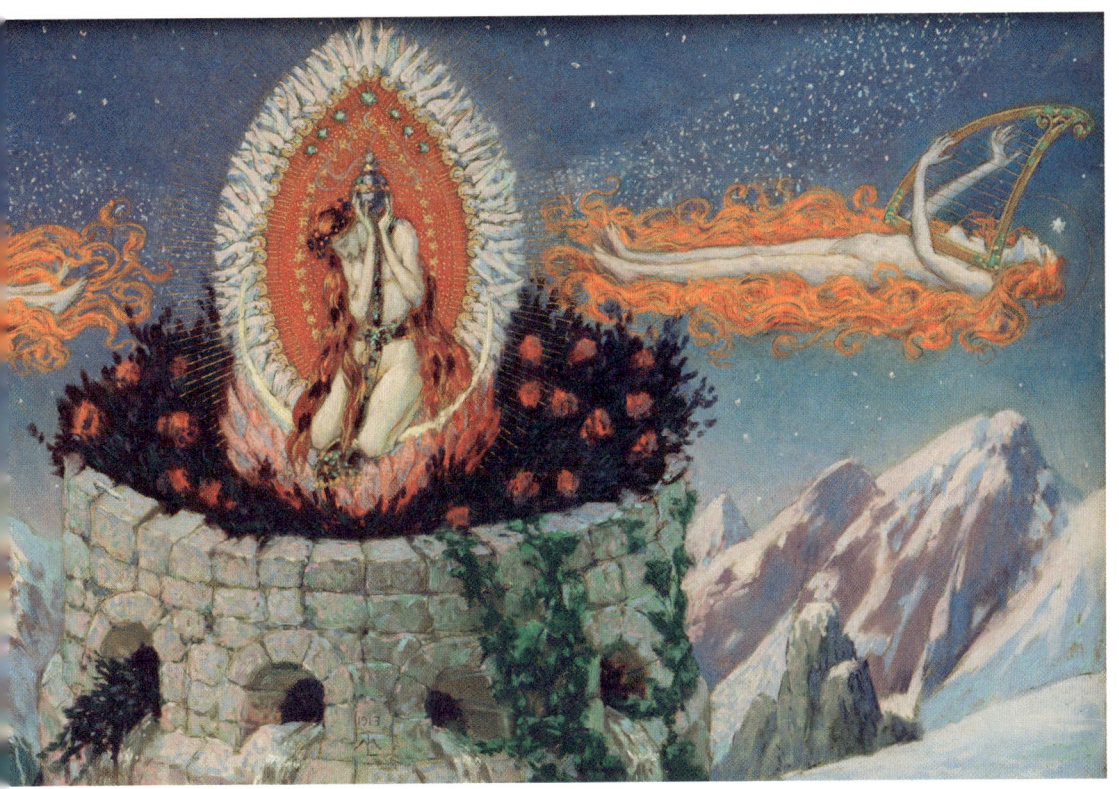

THEOSOPHICAL THOUGHT MANIFESTED THROUGH ART

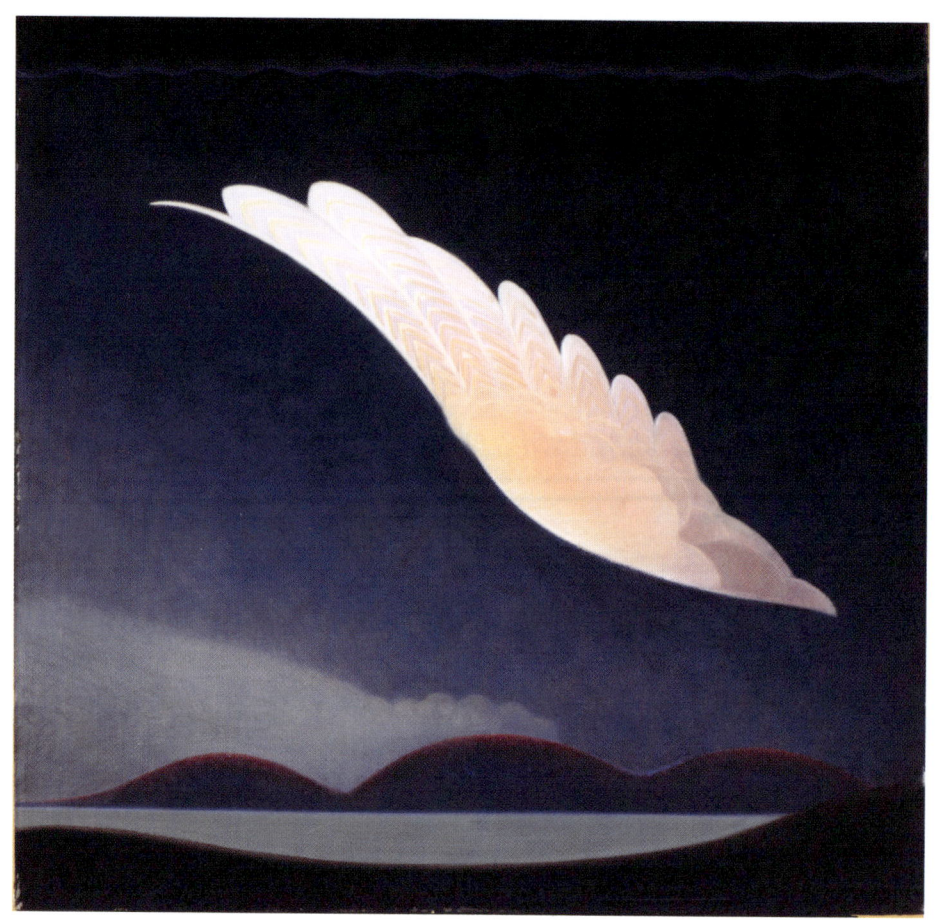

▲ The Primal Wing
Agnes Pelton, 1933, oil on canvas.

Agnes Pelton (1881–1961) was a visionary Symbolist painter whose abstract art – full of deep solitude, gentle, healing colour and mystical symbolism – were creative works arrived at via extensive meditation and trance. For most of her career, Pelton chose to live away from the distractions of a major art centre; her isolation from the mainstream meant that her paintings were relatively unknown during her lifetime and in the decades thereafter.

▶ Centre Cosmique
Frantisek Kupka, 1932–33, oil on canvas.

Czech painter and graphic artist František Kupka (1871–1957) was a pioneer and co-founder of the early phases of the Abstract Art movement and Orphic Cubism. Kupka started out as Spiritualist medium, widening his interests as an adult into Eastern religions, astrology and Theosophy. Though it should be noted that he did not become a Theosophist, nor did he embrace all its tenets.

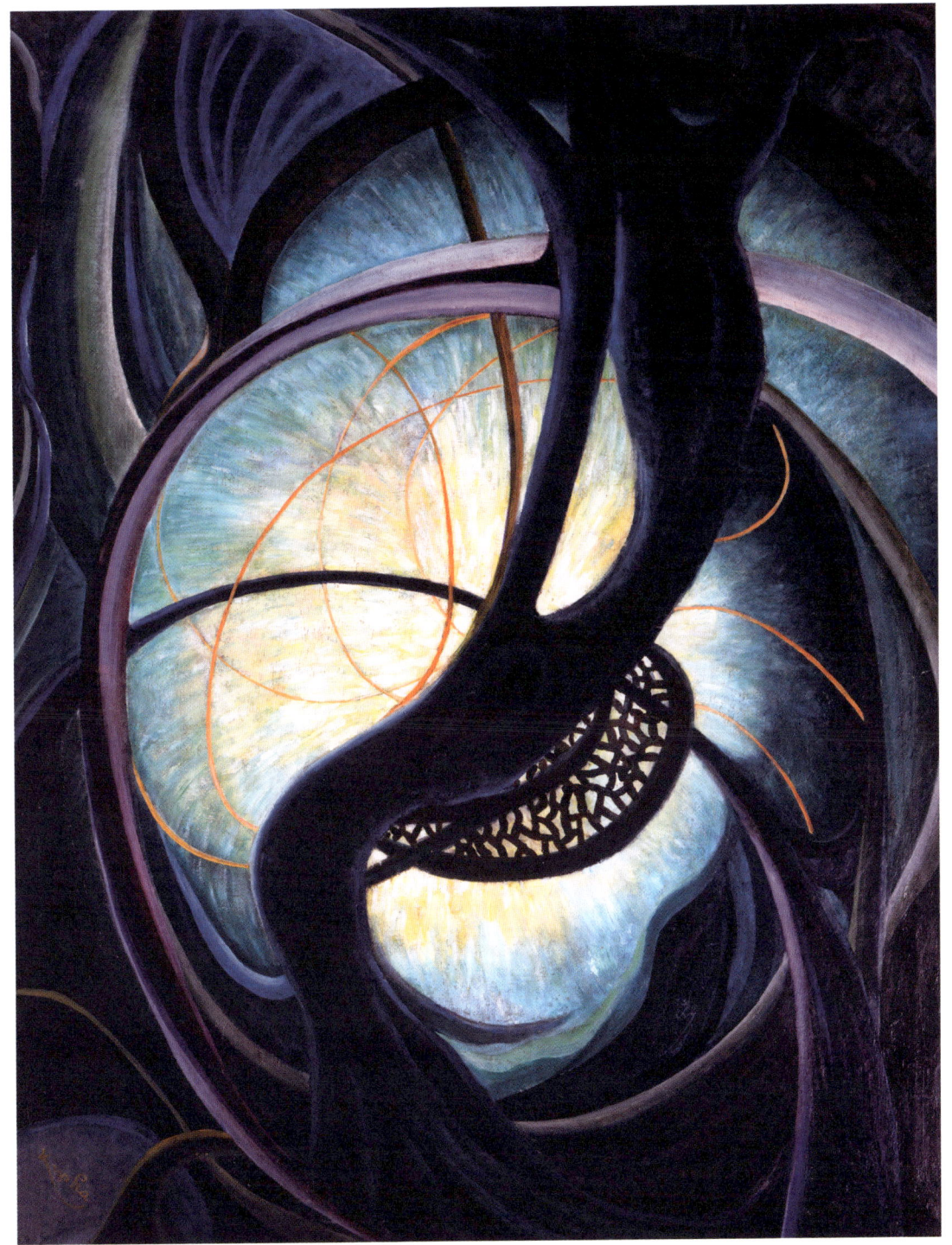

VIII

THE HERMETIC
TRADITION
AND THE ARTS

THE MOTTO OVER ONE OF the entrance gates of a Greek temple at Delphi reads: *Nosce te ipsum* (Know thyself). Yes, well, who could argue with that? There's no denying that to know one's self is indeed a lovely sentiment, but perhaps we should start by getting to know the philosopher who purportedly uttered these words: the legendary Hermes Trismegistus, 'thrice-greatest Hermes', himself.

The mythical Hermes Trismegistus looms large in the tradition of Western esotericism, and his origins can be traced back to Thoth, the Egyptian god of magic and writing. A new cult was born when the Greeks, under Alexander the Great, conquered Egypt in 332BC and saw in Thoth the equivalent of their god, Hermes, who, coincidentally, was also a god of magic and writing.

Hermes Trismegistus is first referred to in the Greek magical papyri: in one such reference he is called 'Hermes the Elder, chief of all magicians'; in another he is referred to as 'thrice-great', for in Ancient Egypt the superlative was constructed by repeating a word three times, an epithet derived from the god with which Hermes had become assimilated, 'Thoth the great, the great, the great'.

The Hermetica are the surviving writings attributed to Hermes Trismegistus, and are mostly presented as dialogues in which a teacher, generally identified as Hermes Trismegistus, enlightens a disciple. The texts form the basis of Hermeticism. The Asclepius and the Corpus Hermeticum are the most important of the Hermetica and contain philosophies of the divine, the cosmos, mind and nature. Some, considered more practical or technical, discuss astrology, magic, alchemy, and related concepts. Another famous tract is the Emerald Tablet, a cryptic piece of the Hermetica reputed to contain the secret of the prima materia and its transmutation. It was highly regarded by European alchemists as the foundation of their art and taught the much-recognised occult maxim 'as above, so below'. According to the Emerald Tablet, the wisdom of the universe can be subdivided into three spheres: alchemy, astrology and theurgy.

Many Hermetic texts were lost to Western culture during the Middle Ages, but rediscovered in Byzantine copies and popularised in Italy during the Renaissance. The Hermetica provided an electrifying impetus in the development of Renaissance thought and culture, having a profound impact on alchemy and modern magic as well as influencing philosophers of the day. Much of the importance of Hermeticism arises from its connection with the development of science during the time 1300–1600AD. The significance that it lent to the idea of influencing nature led many scientists to look to magic (alchemy, astrology) which, it was thought, could put nature to the test by employing experiments.

The concept of Hermeticism as a religious, philosophical and esoteric tradition also gave rise to several occult organisations and movements.

Rosicrucianism was a Hermetic/Christian movement dating back to the fifteenth century. The Rosicrucian Order consisted of a system in which members moved up in rank and gained access to more knowledge; once a member was deemed able to understand the knowledge, they moved on to the next grade. There were three steps to their spiritual path: philosophy, Kabbalah and divine magic. Their movement was symbolised by the rose (the soul) and the cross (the body of four elements). Thus, the Christian symbolism of the cross was reinterpreted as representing the human soul crucified on the 'cross' (four elements) of the material plane.

Freemasonry emerged in the seventeenth century as another iteration of the interest in the occult that led to Rosicrucianism. It describes itself as a 'beautiful system of morality, veiled in allegory and illustrated by symbols', and while it does not deal directly with magic, it does touch upon it closely. Much of the Freemasonry philosophy stems from the self-knowledge/understanding inherent to Hermeticism, and some of its rituals recreate the cycle of birth and death found in alchemy.

The Hermetic Order of the Golden Dawn was a magical order of the late nineteenth and early twentieth centuries, which practised various forms of theurgy and spiritual occultism. It is noted as possibly the single most considerable influence on twentieth-century Western Hermeticism. The Golden Dawn system was based on an initiated hierarchal order similar to that of a Masonic Lodge, however women were admitted on an equal basis with men.

From the tracing boards used in the instruction of new members to a Masonic Lodge; to the various arcane symbols and glyphs of the Golden Dawn; to the more abstract forms of symbolism and metaphysical iconography used by contemporary artists such as Pilar Zeta, the Western Hermetic tradition is associated with artistic works of cryptic obscurity and enigmatic visual images rich in emblem and allegory. These images, notes writer A.C. Evans, reflect an 'instinctive understanding of the role of the artist as a receiver of visions and an explorer of the innermost recesses of the human mind'. We might also say that these artists and initiates have taken Hermes Trismegistus's adage of 'know thyself' very much to heart.

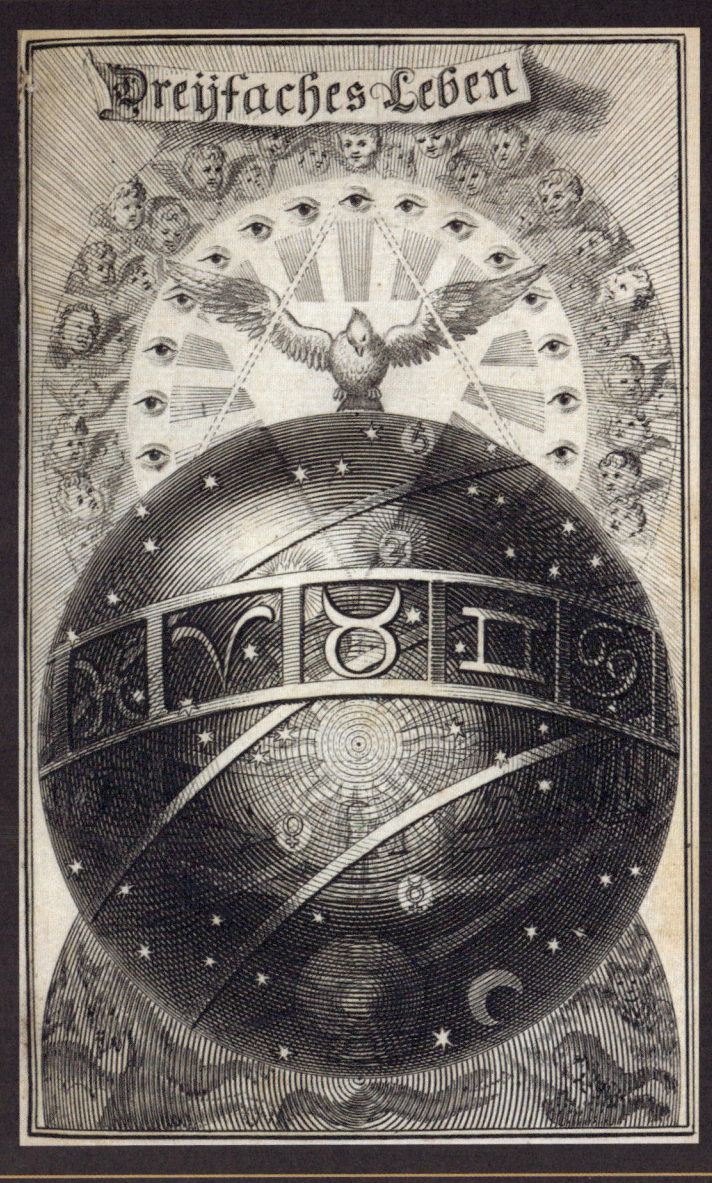

Dreyfaches Leben

▲ A Sphere with Occult Symbols
From *Des gottseeligen hocherleuchteten* (Jakob Böhme, 1682), engraving.

In trying to find a language to communicate his mystical perceptions, German philosopher, Christian mystic and Lutheran Protestant theologian, Jakob Böhme (1575–1624) drew upon alchemical ideas and Hermetic imagery. Böhme was an important influence on the ideas of the English Romantic poet, artist and mystic William Blake, in addition to Swiss psychiatrist and psychoanalyst Carl Jung, who made numerous references to Böhme in his writings.

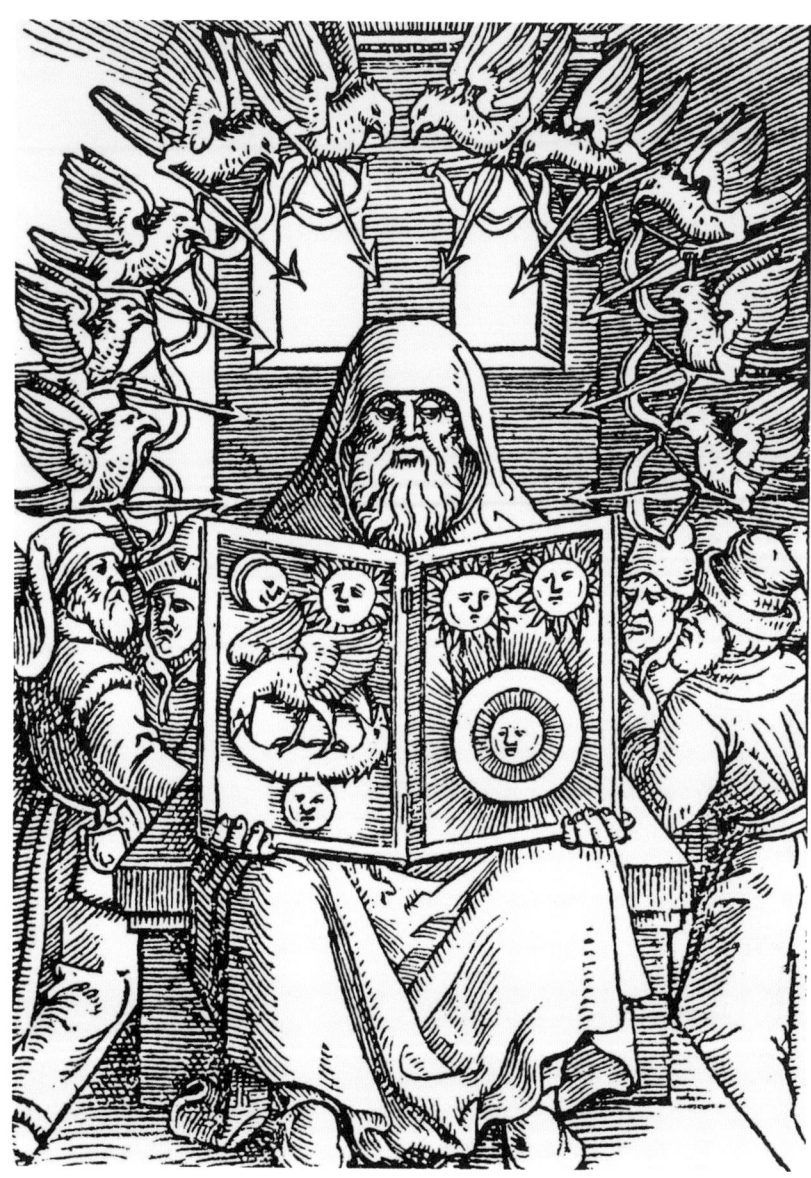

▲ **Hermes Trismegistus**
2nd or 3rd century.

Hermes Trismegistus (Thrice-Great Hermes) is the alleged author of the sacred texts forming the basis of Hermeticism. Many Christian writers considered him to be a wise pagan prophet who foresaw the coming of Christianity. The addition of 'thrice-great' was added to his name because he knew the three parts of the wisdom of the universe: alchemy, astrology and theurgy.

HIGHER BEINGS

▼ Rosicrucian symbol of the Hermetic Order of the Golden Dawn English School, 19th century.

Rosicrucianism is a spiritual and cultural branch of Hermeticism combining references to Kabbalah, alchemy and Christian mysticism. Elements of Rosicrucianism were combined in the The Hermetic Order of the Golden Dawn, a secret society devoted to the study and practice of the occult, metaphysics, and paranormal activities during the late 19th and early 20th centuries. The Rosicrucian symbol of the Hermetic Order of the Golden Dawn was created around the 19th century.

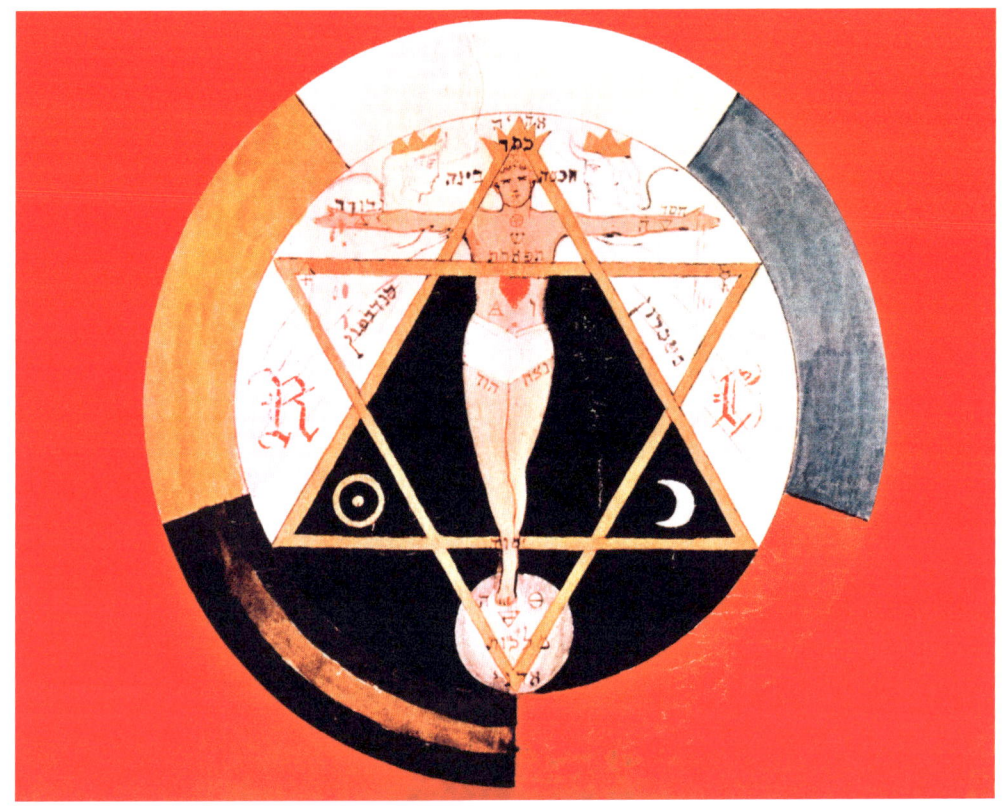

THE HERMETIC TRADITION AND THE ARTS

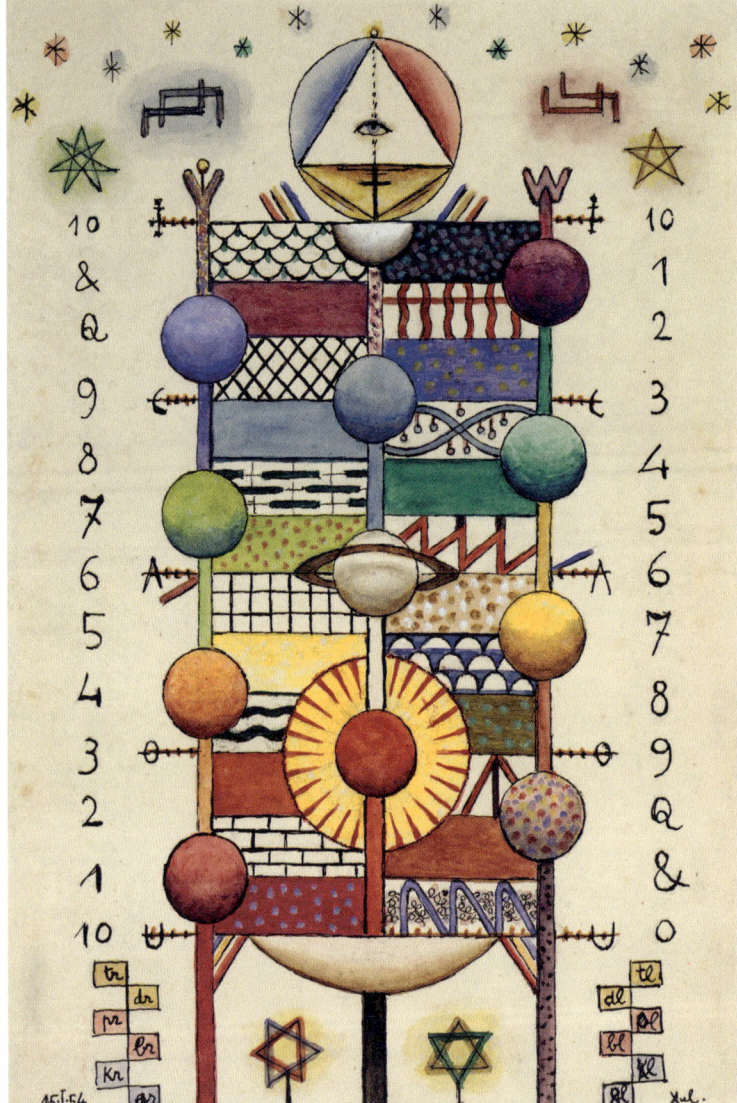

◀ **Pan Tree**
Xul Solar, 1954, watercolour
and ink on paper board.

Xul Solar was the adopted
name of Oscar Agustín
Alejandro Schulz Solari
(1887–1963), an avant-
garde occultist, painter,
sculptor, writer and inventor
of imaginary languages.
A mystic who sought out
spiritually-minded individuals
throughout his life, Xul Solar
learned a secret method
for attaining mystic visions
derived from the practices
of the Hermetic Order of the
Golden Dawn, taught to him
by Aleister Crowley himself.

▶ **Illustration
showing the Hermetic
Philosophy of Nature**
From *Opera 392 Chemica*
(Ramon Llull).

Ramon Llull (c.1235–1315) was a mathematician, philosopher,
theologian, mystic and writer from the Kingdom of Majorca. In
this illustration depicting the Hermetic Philosophy of Nature from
his *Opera 392 Chemica*, we can see the Hermetic tree of life
with the seven main branches and ten heads symbolising the
seven planets and the ten spheres of Kabbalistic tradition.

HIGHER BEINGS

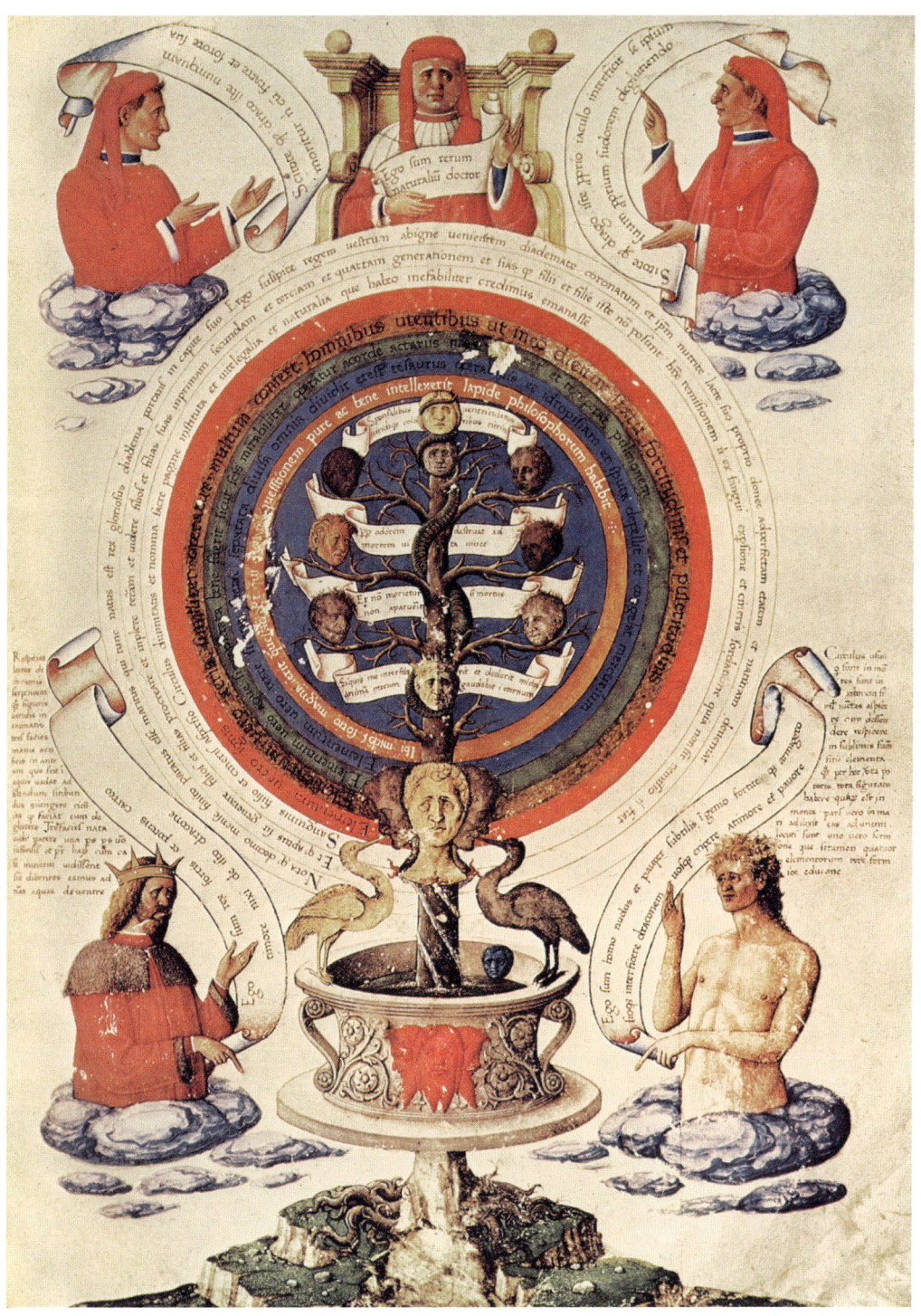

▼ Call of the Heaven. Lightning
Nicholas Roerich, 1935–36, tempera on canvas.

As prolific a writer as he was a painter, Nicholas Roerich (1874–1947) – visionary and world citizen – writes in *Fiery Stronghold* (1933) of the immeasurably powerful mountains of India, '… over the snowy peaks of the Himalayas burns a bright glow, brighter than the stars, and the fantastic flashes of lightning.'

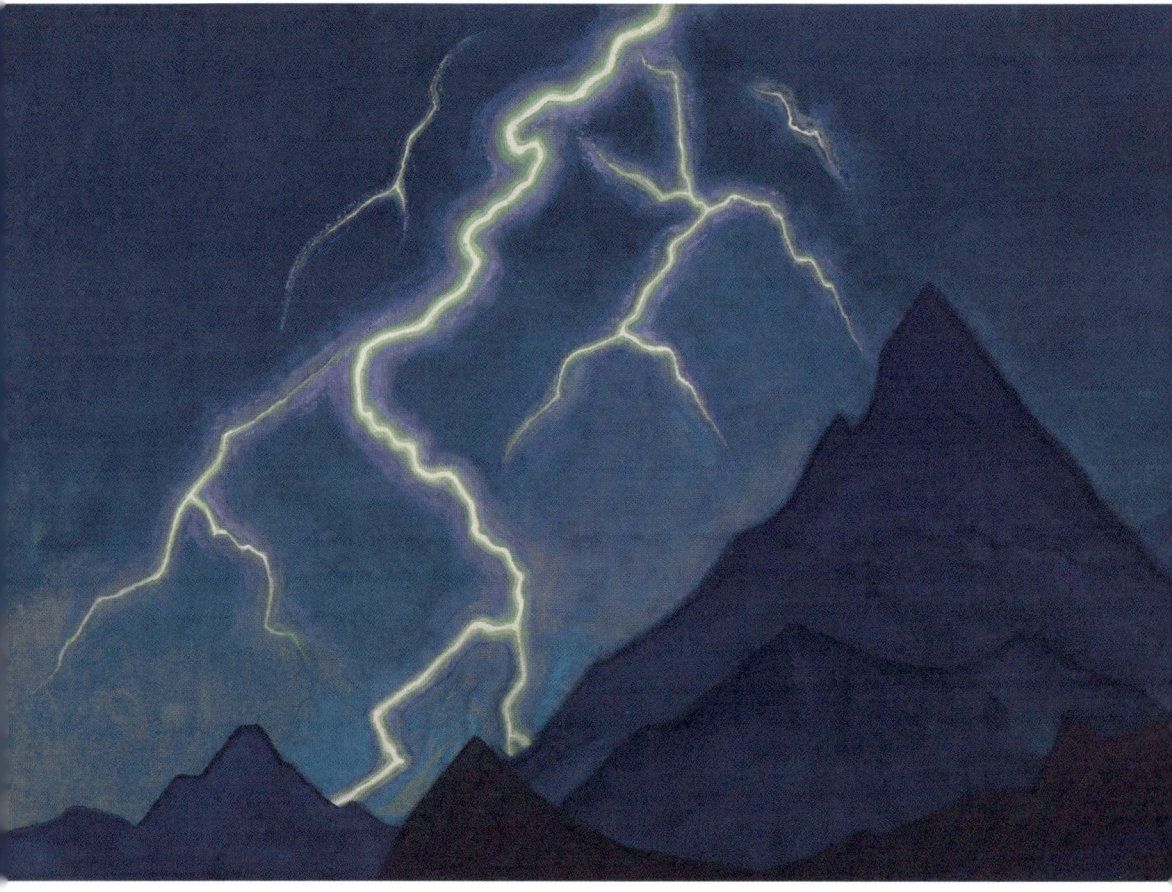

▼ The Hermetic Principals
Pilar Zeta, 2011,
digital collage.

Fuelled by a lifelong love of the paranormal, visual and sonic, artist Pilar Zeta's (b.1986) metaphysical iconography and music exist in futuristic, surreal and elegant spaces. Her work functions as a form of practical magic in a machine-centric world, connecting different mediums through a singular, transcendent vision.

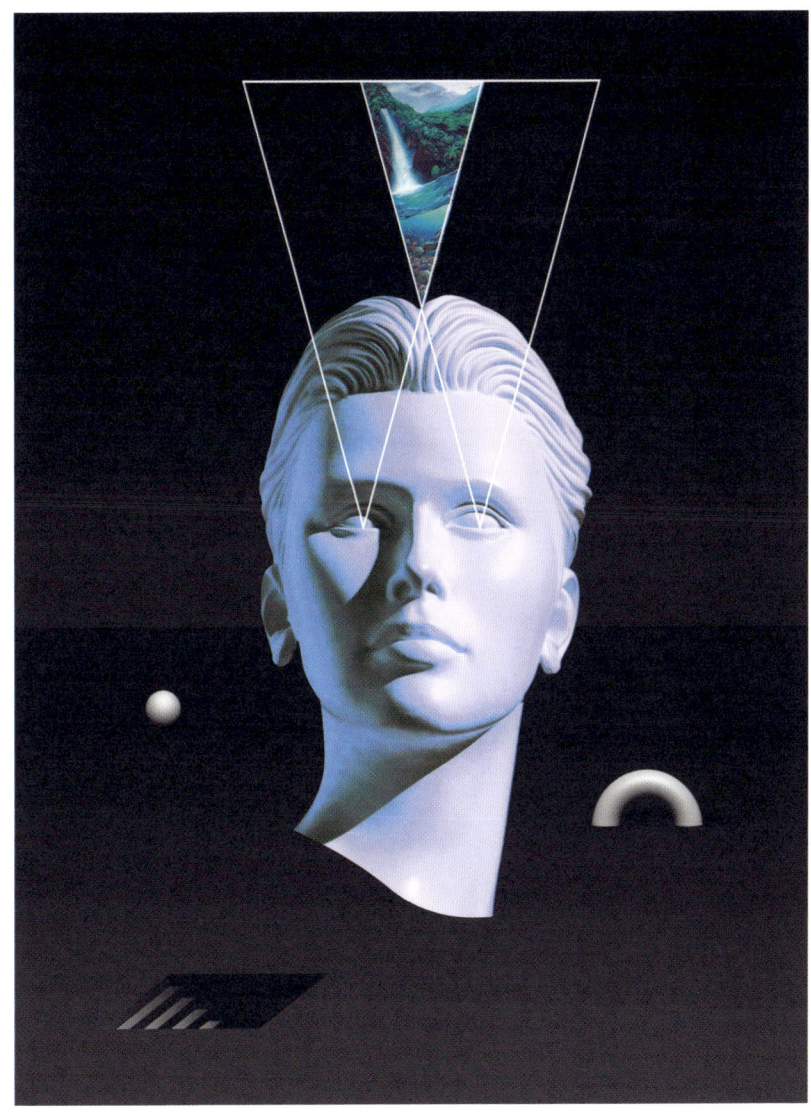

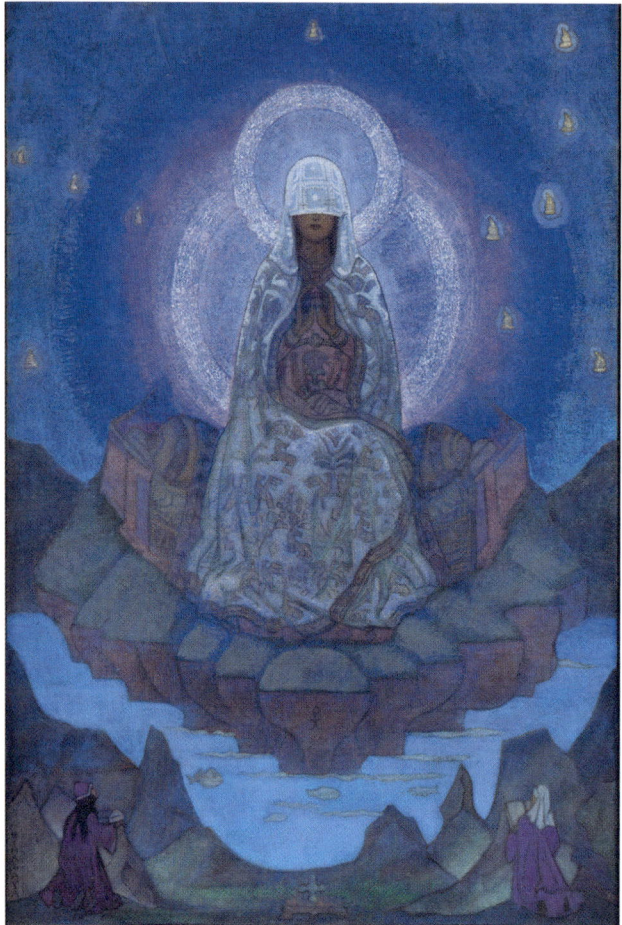

This tracing board by Josiah Bowring (1757–1832) is an example of one of the artist and Freemason's popular recurring designs. Used by Freemasons as visual aids during ceremonies, tracing boards are intricately painted or printed illustrations depicting the various emblems and symbols of the masonic journey. They can be wooden; painted and gilded; drawn on cloth or paper; or even made out of stone. Typically, there is a tracing board for each of the three ceremonies: Apprentice, Fellowcraft and finally, the degree of Master Mason. Some tracing board designs became particularly popular, leading to some repetition of favoured design features, and the boards by Josiah Bowring were said to have raised the standard for all who came after.

▲ **The Mother Of The World**
Nicholas Roerich, 1924, tempera on canvas laid on cardboard.

'The Mother of the World. How much of that which is tremendously stirring and moving is blended in this sacred image of all ages and all peoples.' Thus wrote spiritually-inspired artist and poet Nicholas Roerich (1874–1947) in *TO WOMANHOOD* (1930). These feelings are stunningly expressed in this work, Roerich's most inspiring images, rendered with tender majesty in deep tones of blue and violet.

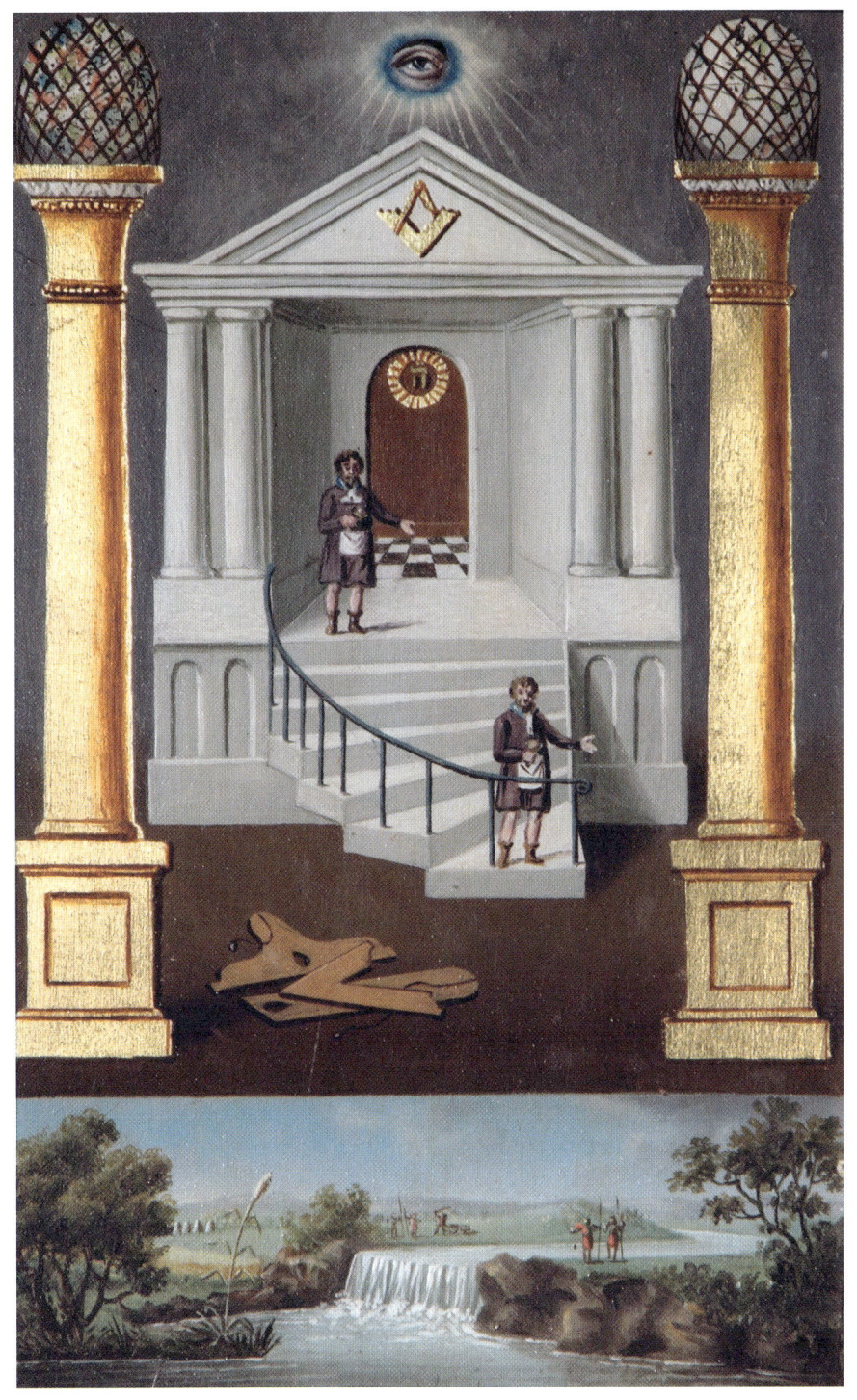

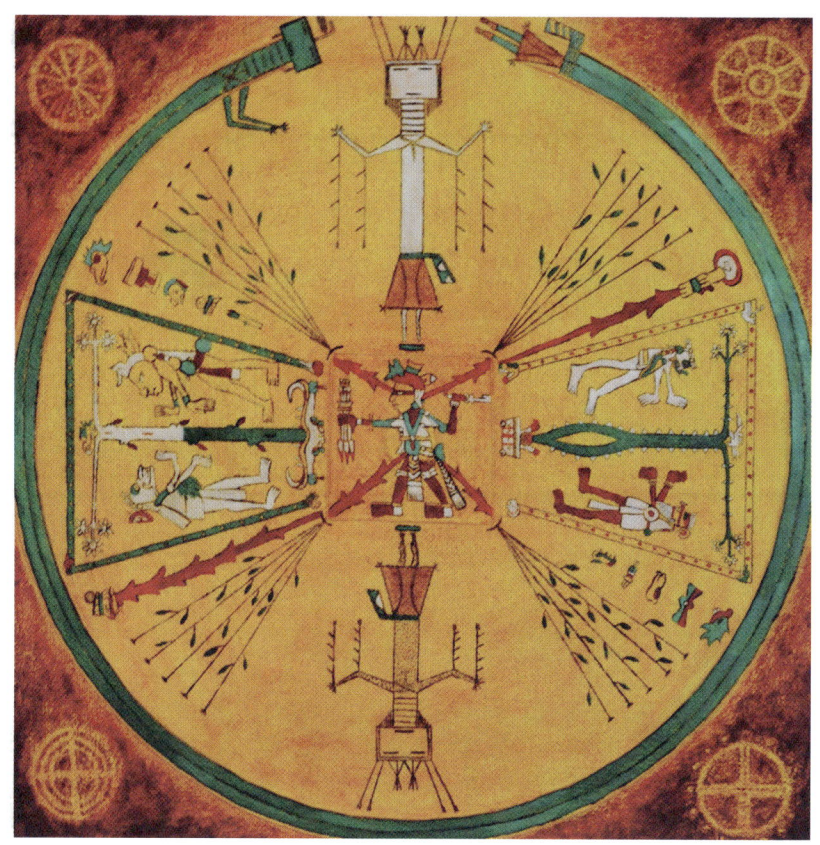

▲ **Hermetic**
William Jones, undated,
oil on panel.

The paintings of artist William Jones (b.1957) are each the result of an investigation of a spiritual tradition, practice or personal experience. Including a variety of symbols from different traditions, because of the commonalities of what they represent, he notes, 'My figurative pieces are allegorical and the abstract pieces are esoteric'.

▼ Telesmatic angelic figure
W. A. Ayton, c.1892, watercolour on paper.

A general telesmanic figure is an illustration of an angel or diety contructed according to a predetermined set of correspondences, colours and symbols. The image, then consecrated and charged, becomes a sacred icon. By utilising the chosen colours and symbolism, anyone, according to *Golden Dawn Magic* (Chic and Sandra Tabatha Ciceros, 2019), can then create a general telesmanic image of a given angel. William Alexander Ayton (1816–1909) was a British Anglican clergyman and member of the successor Order of the Golden Dawn who did just that.

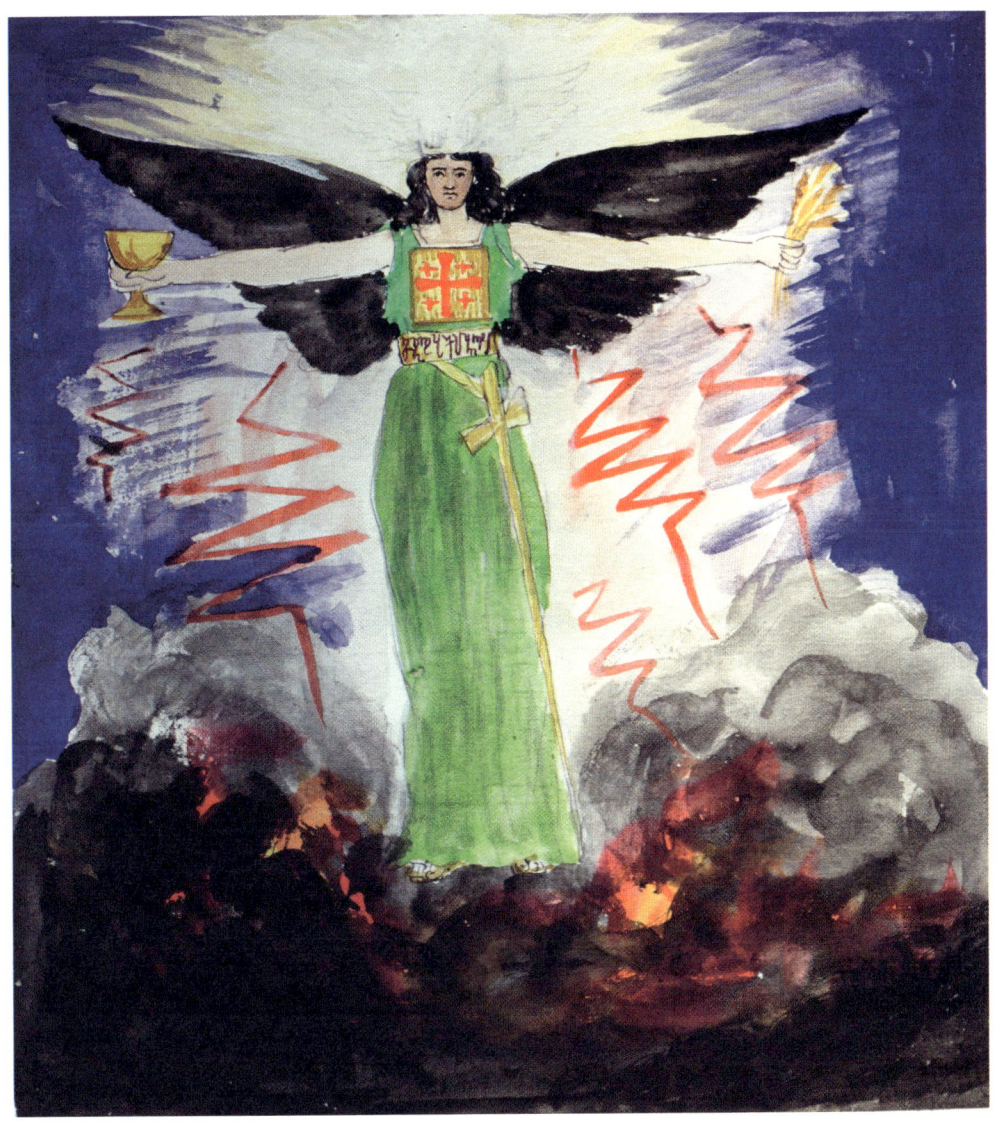

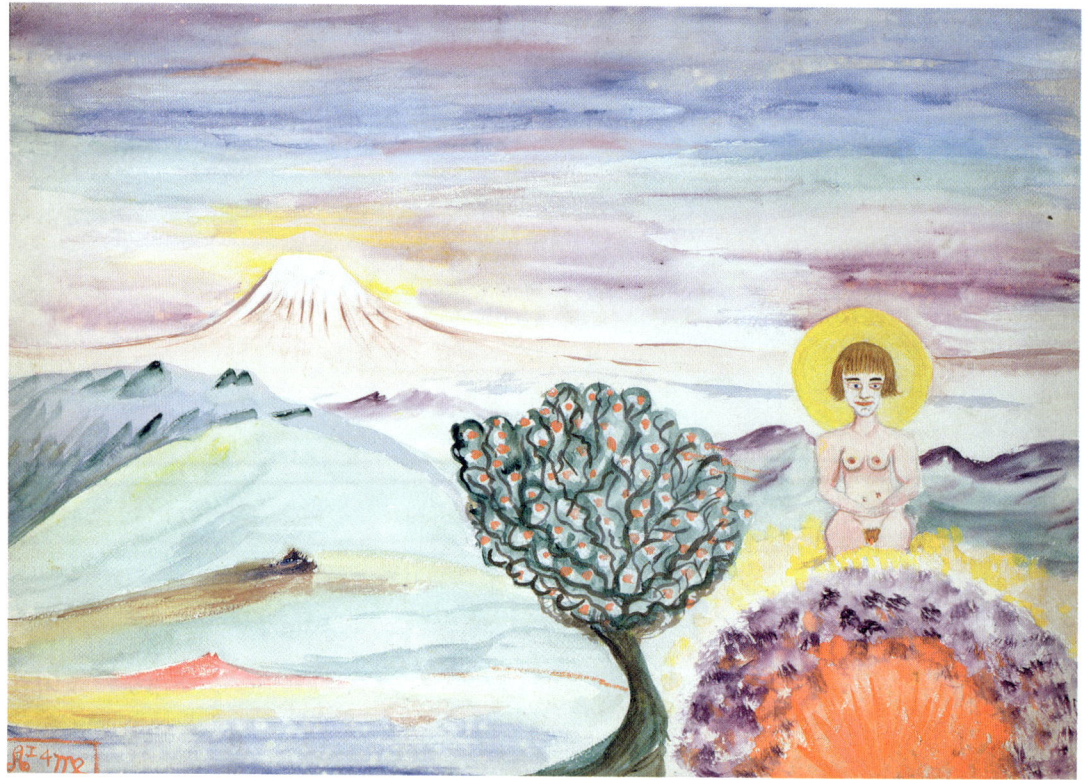

▲ Untitled
Aleister Crowley, c.1920,
watercolour on paper.

Aleister Crowley (1875–1947),
occultist, ceremonial magician,
poet and painter, described by one
newspaper as 'the wickedest man in the
world', apparently liked to paint a nice
landscape. Who knew? Known more for
his occult reputation, his landscapes,
portraits and trance paintings were
created as part of his occult practice,
and were influenced by Symbolism
and Expressionism. For Crowley, art
was not about replicating observed
subjects but about expression. He
noted, 'One should not paint "Nature"
at all; one should paint the Will.'

▶ Trumps, Mercury as
the Magus
Lady Frieda Harris, 1938–1943,
watercolour tarot card.

Marguerite Frieda Harris (1877–1962) was an artist and
feminist, who later became an associate of the occultist Aleister
Crowley. She is best known for the design of Crowley's Thoth
tarot deck, which, by Crowley's own admission, was originally
intended to be traditional. However, Harris encouraged him
to commit his own views to the project. With allusions to
astrology, the Kabbalah and Egyptian mythology, the Thoth
Tarot is a luminous embodiment of both Harris's artistic skills
and Crowley's symbology. This is a prototype created for the
infamous deck, but it didn't make it into the final edition. Neither
Harris nor Crowley lived to see their tarot deck published.

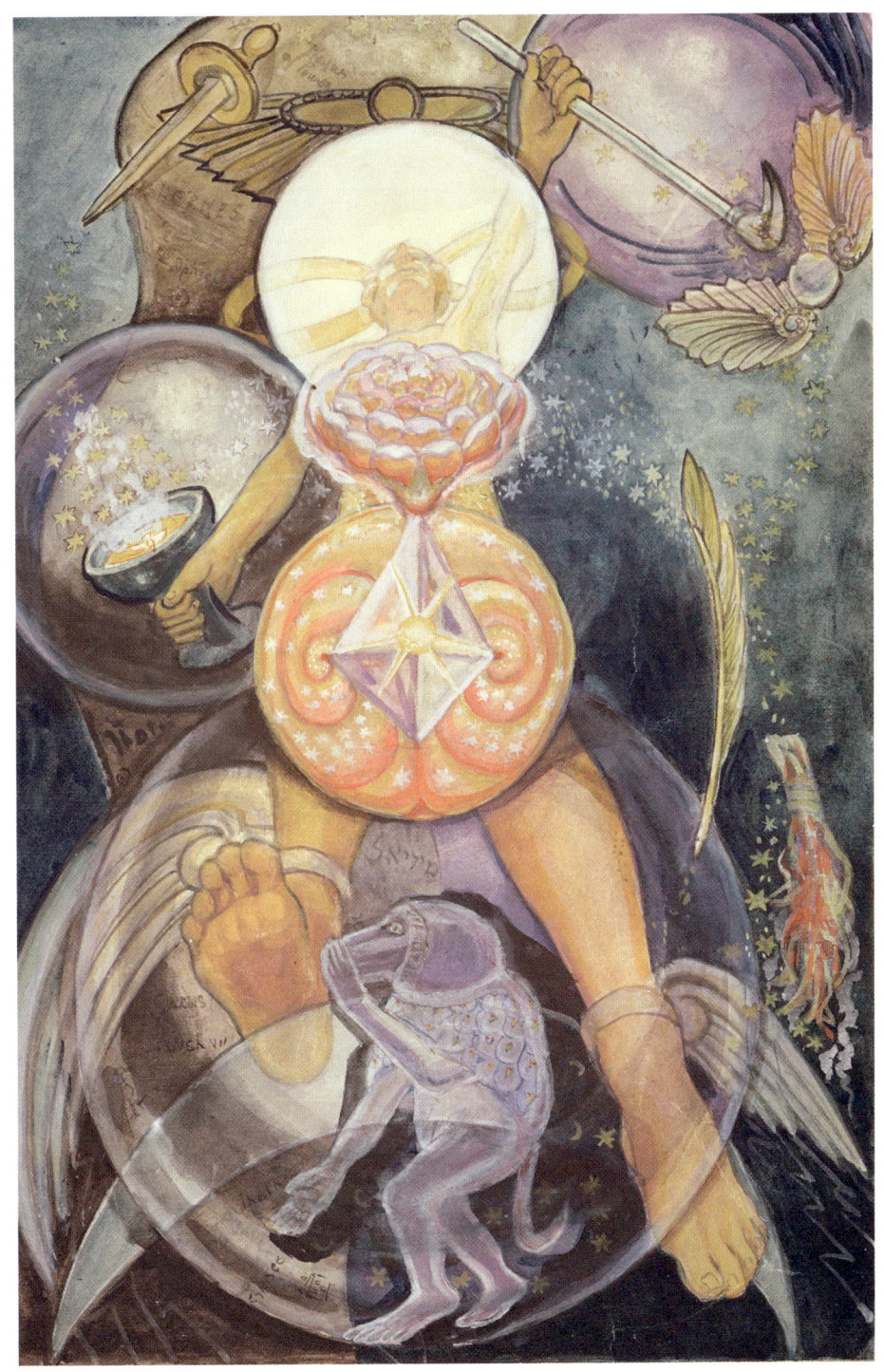

PART THREE

PRACTITIONERS

'The artist must be clairvoyant:
he must see that which others do
not see; he must be a magician,
he must possess the power to
make others see what they do not
themselves see, but which he does.'

— P.D. OUSPENSKY

F OR THOSE WILLING TO LOOK, a vital key to unlocking the
cryptic mysteries of magical history and occult philosophy can
be found in the many artistic depictions of the enigmatic entities
who engage in the practice of mystical endeavours. Whether in
performance of a ritual, inducing an altered state, divining for truth
and meaning, or engaging in a path of or the act of creation, the
rites of prophets and seers, witches and magicians, Spiritualists and
mediums, and all of the pomp, ceremony and tools of the trade that
may accompany them, have inspired and influenced visual artists –
some of them scholars and practitioners of these same philosophies
– for centuries.

By their nature, such magical pursuits are quite clandestine
undertakings, but in closely studying the evocative, ecstatic works
of art they inspire, we can begin to glimpse thrilling understandings
of their theoretical and practical secrets. These artistic
representations can take many forms: an intricate and complex
invocation of angels or conjuration of demons, hand-illustrated
in a cracked, leather-bound grimoire; an exquisite oil painting
of a lustrous-haired young woman in sweeping velvets, staring
pensively into a crystal ball (or an old woman, furrowed of brow,
staring inscrutably at you as she divines your destiny in a similarly-
shaped quartz orb); mediums producing miraculous watercolour
canvasses, channelled through their hand by guardian spirits from
'the other side'; the abstract and alien drawings generated by artists
and Spiritualists in trance states; the multi-faceted, mythic and
many-layered portrayals across history of the witch, a staggeringly
powerful archetype that provokes the imaginations and piques the
curiosities of traditional and contemporary artists alike.

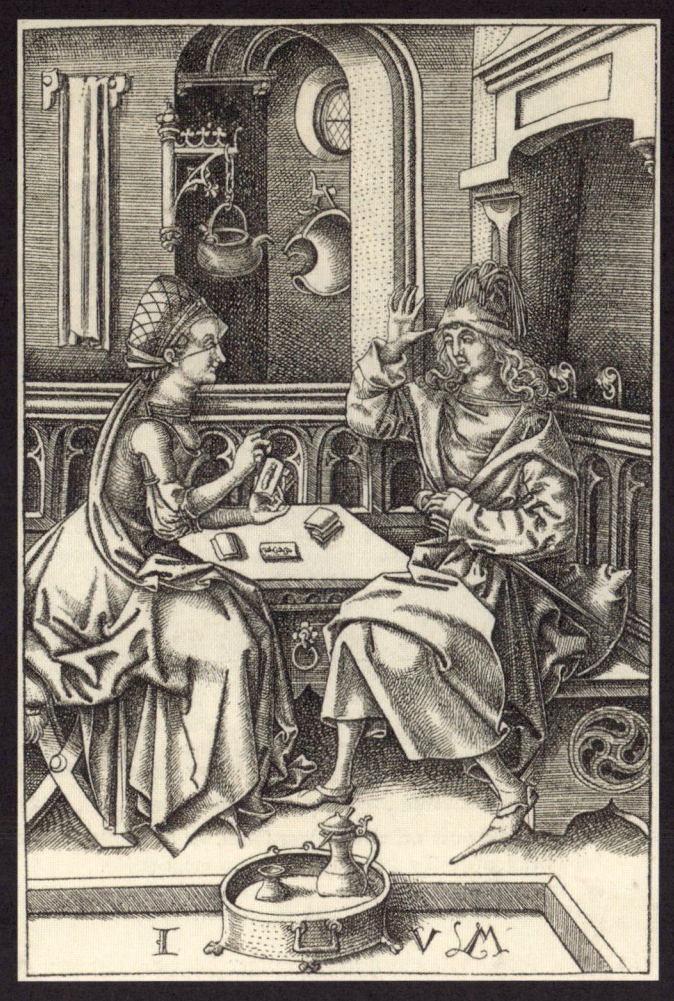

These fantastical images stir our senses and engage our perceptions in a profound way that transcends time and place, and much as I assume our ancestors might have felt, we never tire of imagining the extraordinary powers wielded by the subjects – not to mention the transformative results of their magical undertakings. Through the unique creative abilities of the artists who are attracted to these occult practitioners and their esoteric activities, even if we don't entirely understand what they're all up to, we are able to share, at least vicariously, in some of those same magics.

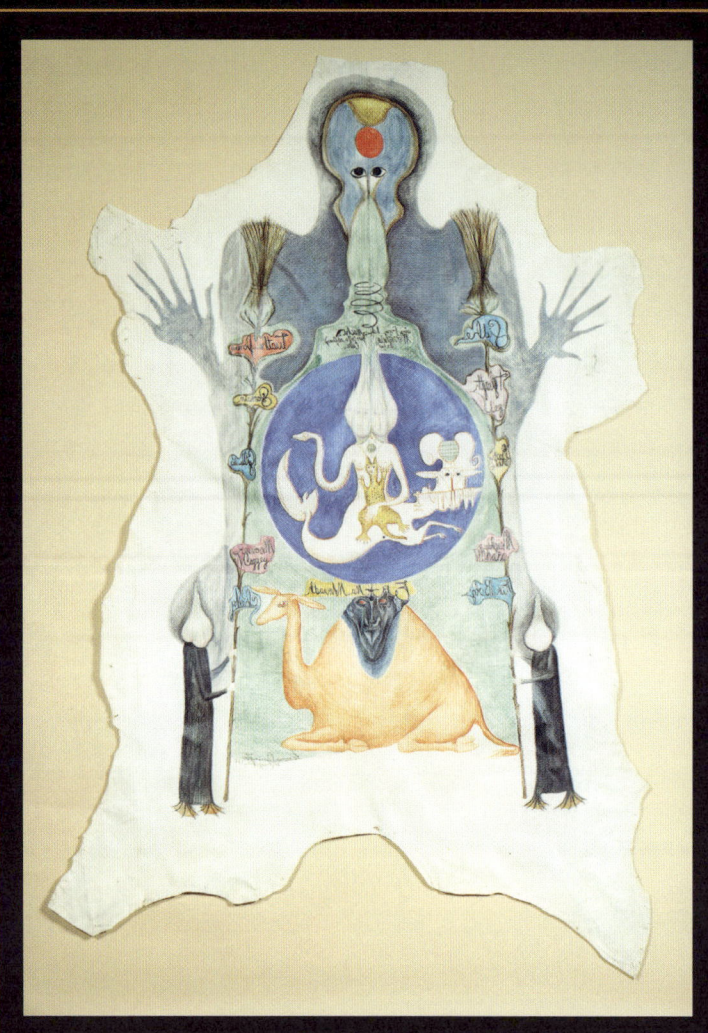

▲ **La Bruja Magica**
Leonora Carrington, 1975, gouache on vellum.

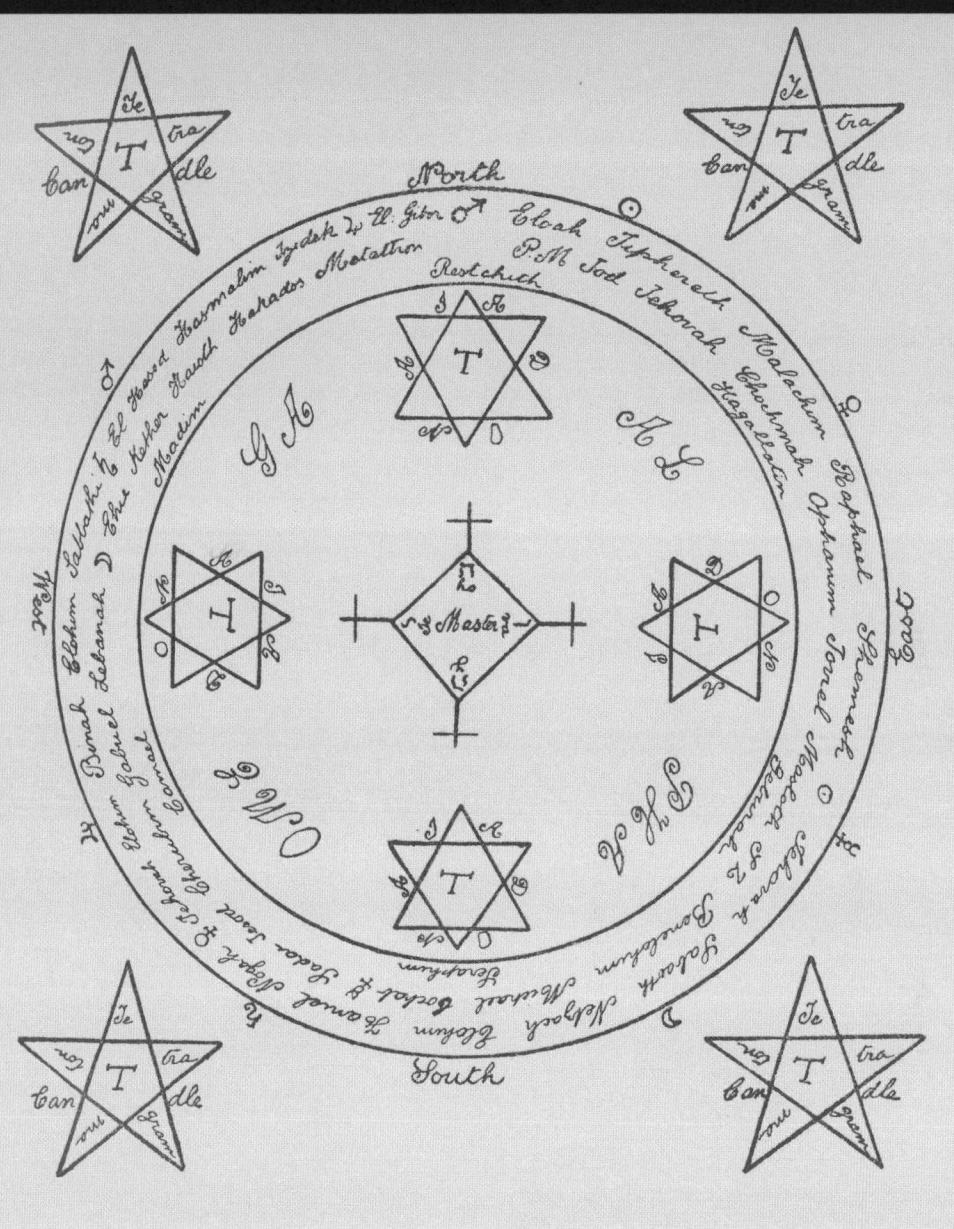

IX

POTIONS, PERSECUTION AND POWER

Witches and Witchcraft in Art

YOU ARE NO DOUBT FAMILIAR with ominous images of witches attending black masses and midnight sabbats; glamorous witches cooking up spells and coyly casting clever magic circles; shadowy, cloaked figures in pointy hats; insouciant old crones zipping through the skies on broomsticks, or trotting blithely – backwards, even – on a goat; witches having salacious relations with Old Scratch himself . . . Really, what manner of mischief and monkeyshines don't witches get into?

'Witches have always walked among us, populating societies and storyscapes across the globe for thousands of years,' writes Pam Grossman in *Waking the Witch*, a reflection on women, magic and power. And it's true – can you conjure forth a single folk or fairytale, myth or legend worth its salt circle that doesn't contain a witch or some witchy archetype stirring up trouble and sowing supersensory seeds of discontent? The witch provides the element that surprises, startles and scares, provides struggle and strife, a snag in the story, a shift in the narrative.

Historical representations of witches and their craft span several centuries and, much like the above examples, are typically an exploration in extremes, depicting the witch as a wrinkled, wretched, hideous hag, or the saucy, seductive sorceress. They are objects of devilment and desire, downfall and deliverance, and whatever form they take, witches set our imagination as well as our apprehensions and anxieties alight.

Scholars note that the classical figure of the witch in art history functioned as a symbolic means of examining and understanding the negative feelings of desire, fear and confusion that witches arouse, and, as such, contribute to a great deal of both social and religious unrest. In the sixteenth and seventeenth centuries, folklore imagined witches as a very real threat to society: 'The land is full of witches,' Chief Justice Anderson, a witch hunter, told an English court in 1602, 'they abound in all places.' But negative depictions of the witch predate the witch hunts and trials, and many of the stereotypes that persisted then were also present in the Classical era. Medea, for example, is frequently presented as dark, dangerous and unpredictable, and whether she's engaged in wanton sexual gratification or bending the gods to her will, she is characterized as ready to destroy the social order and return the cosmos to chaos at a moment's notice.

The fear surrounding witches, and the hostility and hatred directed towards them, in both Classical and early modern eras, had its basis not only in the various religious thoughts and beliefs of the times, but also the beliefs and philosophies regarding the nature of the different genders. For of course, the popular figure of the witch – synonymous with sorcery, transgression and wickedness – is almost always female. These perceptions, frequently unfavourable to the point of dangerous and harmful stereotyping, became

Angelo Caroselli (1585–1672) was an Italian painter of the Baroque period who created religious works, allegories, portraits and landscapes; he also returned regularly to scenes of witchcraft and sorcery. Though there is no documentation to support this, various art historians have theorised that Caroselli was linked to the secret circles of magic, occultism and alchemy. The fantastical elements and the strange mood of this painting would at least point to, if nothing else, a healthy fascination with the subject.

so culturally widespread and deep-rooted that they were reflected in art and material culture.

These impulses and fears anchored in themes of 'dangerous' female pleasure and power have been an inspiration to artists at various times throughout history. In early religious art, witches were enemies of Christianity; in the seventeenth century, Salvator Rosa specialised in paintings of witches – his work seethes with night-time horrors and a push-pull dynamic of both intense fear and fascination. In the Romantic period of the late eighteenth and early nineteenth centuries, artists such as Goya, Blake and Fuseli explored witchcraft in darkly imaginative, emotionally fraught works, dabbling in madness and superstition as a reaction to the science and rationalism of Enlightenment philosophy. Later in the century, artists of the Symbolist movement were interested in witchy women as femme fatales: coldly seductive, sexually powerful females, hell-bent on consuming and destroying men. Clearly, sex and magic combine for an eerie and potent brew in portrayals of witchcraft.

The archetype of the witch is an evocative canvas on to which some of the greatest artists have projected their most intensely bizarre imaginings, and this fascination for witches has gripped numerous Western artists from the sixteenth century to modern times. Many continue to draw inspiration from the dark and cruel origins of the classic image of the witch; the perceived terrors and very tangible, tragic history of the witch continues to instill fear and provoke anxieties in contemporary creators, inspiring powerful artwork steeped in magic and superstition.

However, as nineteenth- and twentieth-century feminists have addressed the history of the witch as a history of female suppression, artists' bias and intentions have evolved; what was once a shadowy social outcast and symbol of fear has been reclaimed by women as a fierce feminist ally, a symbol of independence and resistance against patriarchal oppression and institutional inequality. Artists are more empowered than ever by the witch in all of her guises.

I started this chapter by telling you that we can count on the witch to shift the narrative. In actual fact, a witch shifts the paradigm. A witch shifts the power.

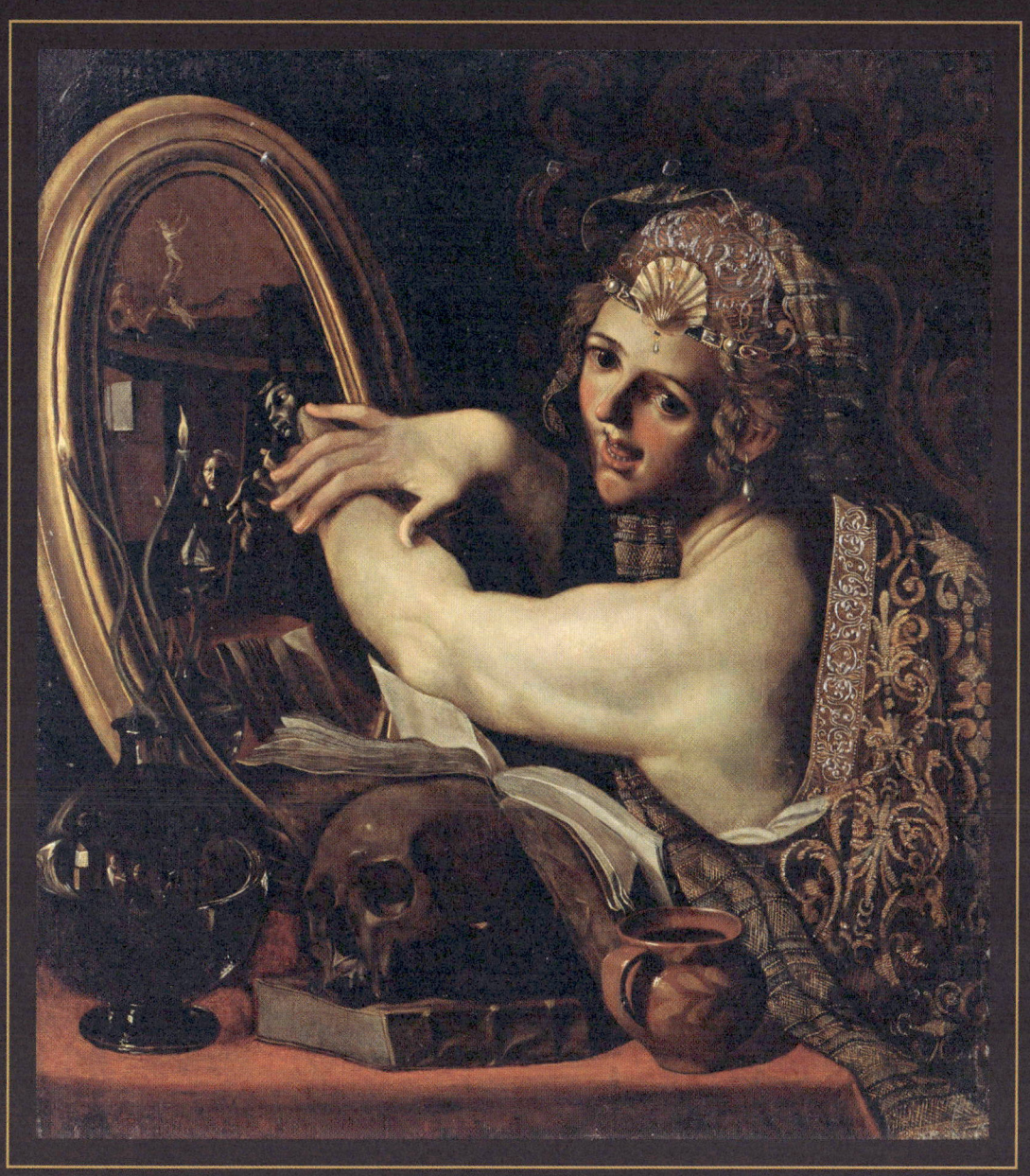

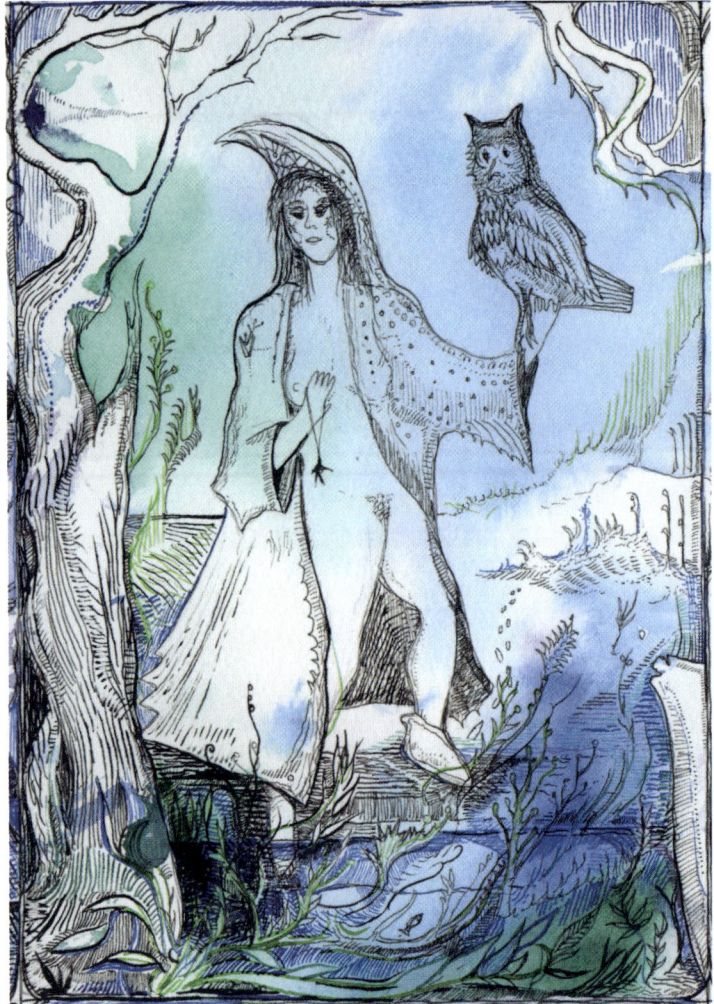

Francisco José de Goya y
Lucientes (1746–1828)
was a Romantic painter
and printmaker considered
to be the most important
Spanish artist of the
late 18th and early 19th
centuries. *Witches
Sabbath* depicts the devil
in the form of a garlanded
goat, surrounded by
a coven of expectant
witches in a moonlit
landscape. Interest in
the supernatural was a
feature of Romanticism,
and Goya's paintings
have been seen as a
protest against the
values of the Spanish
Inquisition. They reflect
the artist's disdain for
what he saw as medieval
fears exploited by the
established order for
political capital and gain.

▲ **Witch**
Max Razdow, 2018,
ink, paper and pen.

Artist, writer and teacher, Max Razdow (b.1978)
captures mythical universes in his works
across various media, including detailed pen
and ink drawings, paintings, text pieces and
sculptures. Using techniques of 'ink-scrying'
to form his symbolic poetic creations, Razdow
introduces us to an imaginative world of
mysticism, mythology and fantastical creatures.

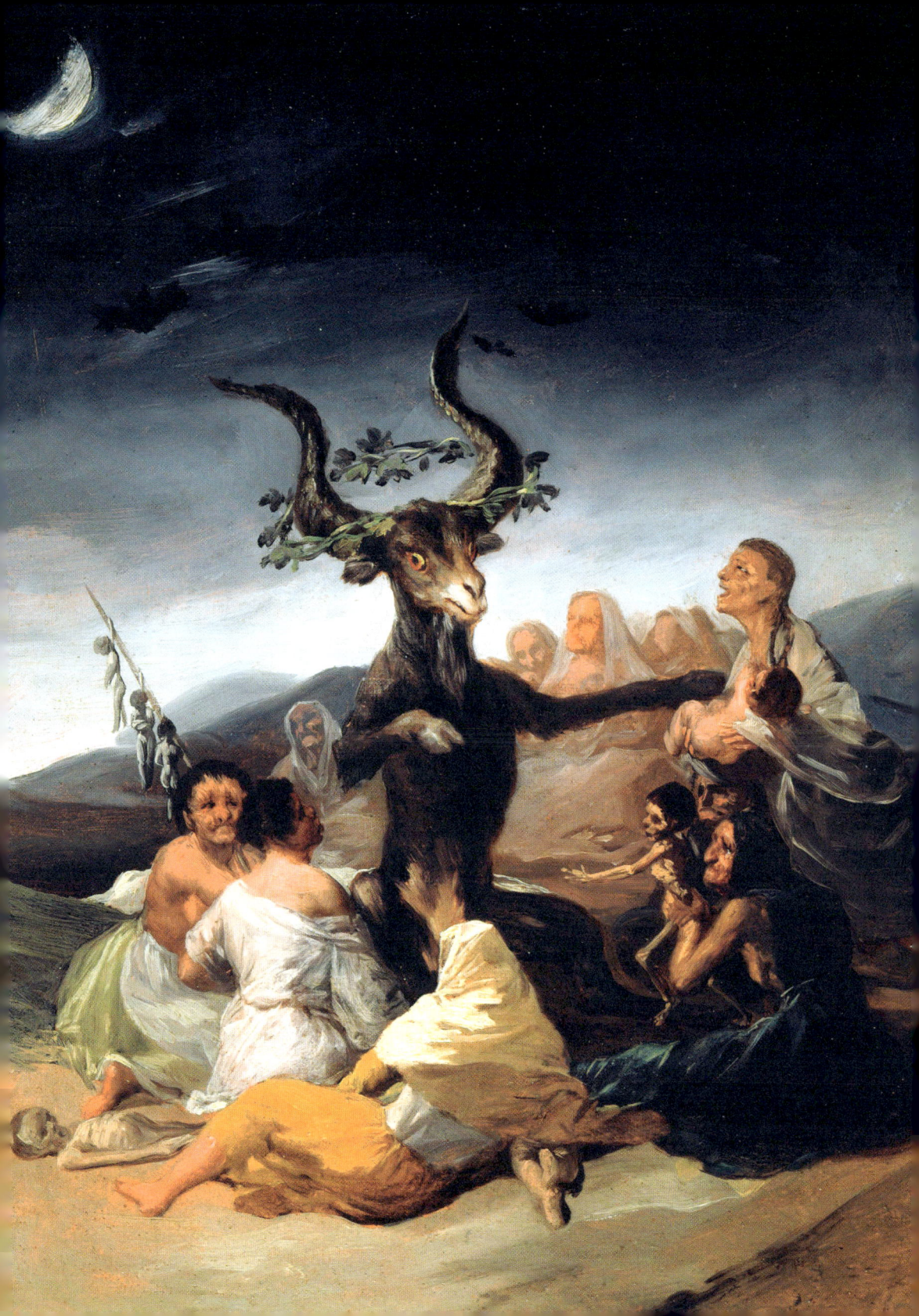

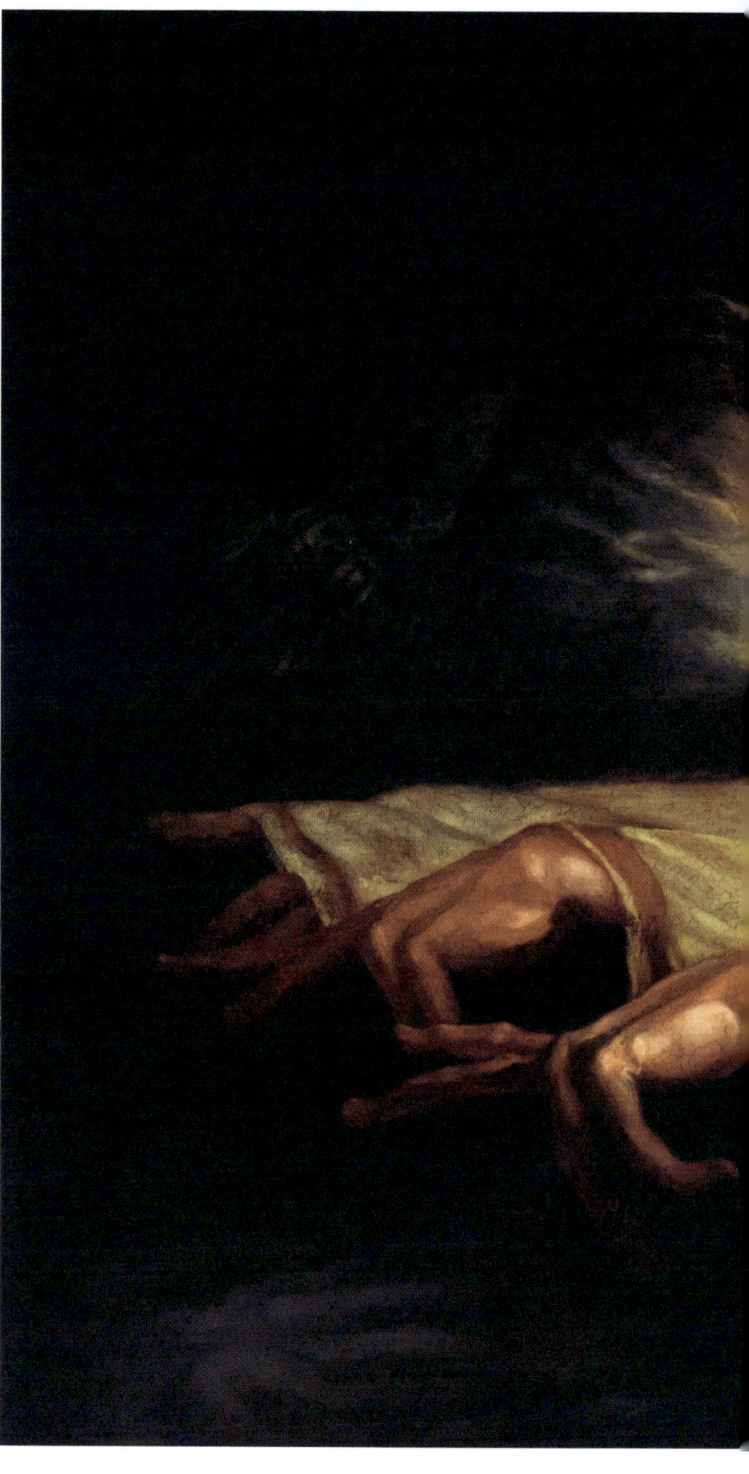

► The Three Witches
Henry Fuseli, 1783,
oil on canvas.

Much of Swiss painter,
draughtsman and writer,
Henry Fuseli's (1741–
1828) work revels in
the macabre, delights
in ominous moods and
dealt with supernatural
subject-matter. In one
of his best-known
compositions, Fuseli
paints a dramatic portrayal
of a critical moment from
Shakespeare's tragedy
Macbeth, when the
protagonist encounters
the trio of witches
who foretell his fate.

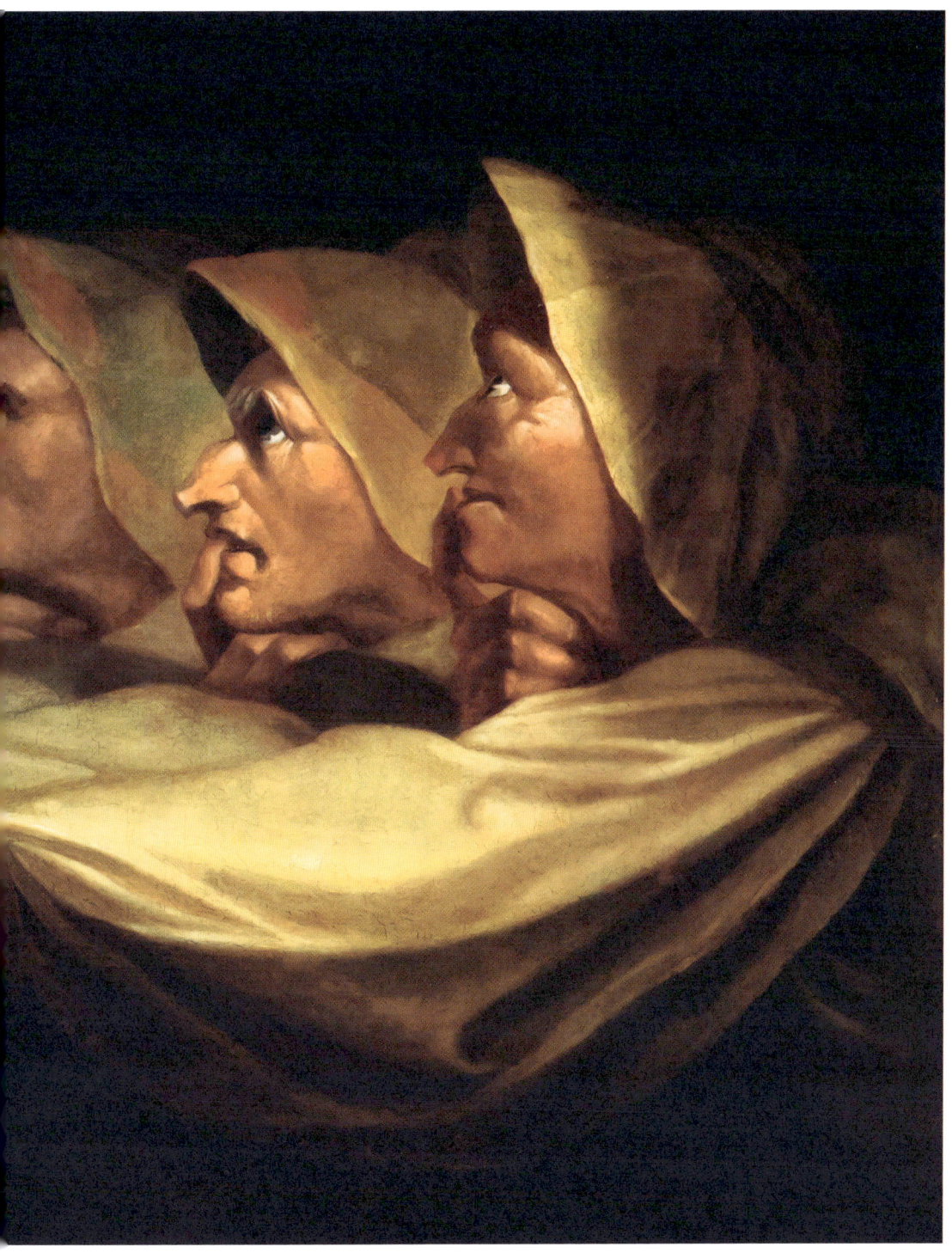

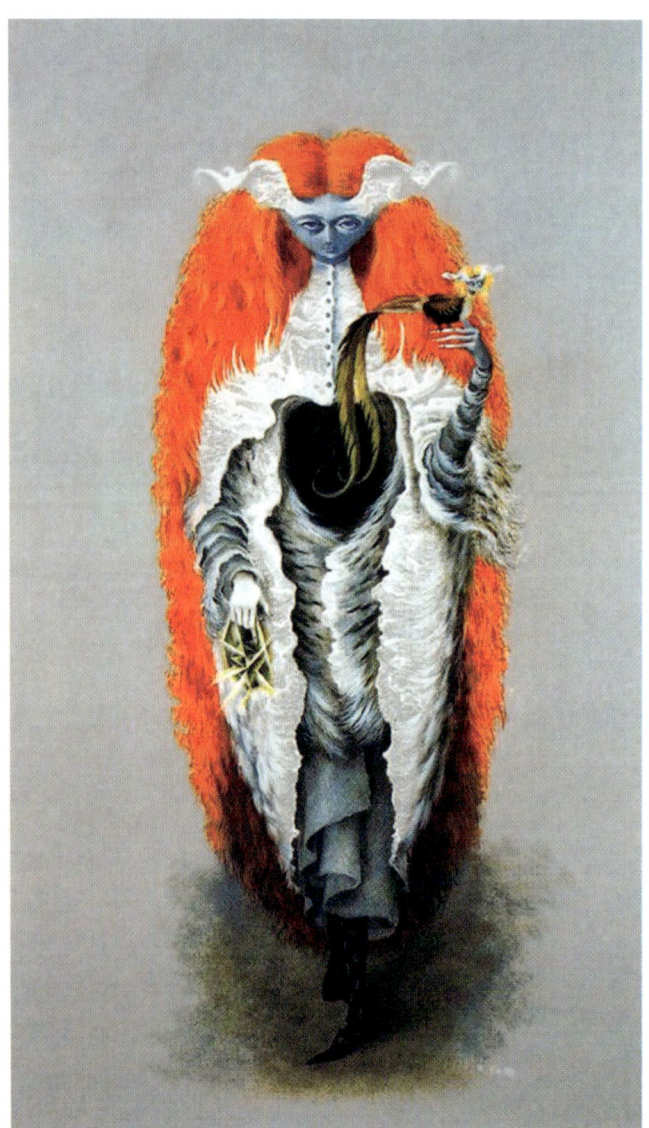

◀ Witch going to the Sabbath
Remedios Varo, 1957, oil on canvas.

A single female figure bedecked in vaporous finery, crowned with a cascade of fiery crimson tresses, carrying an elegant plumed familiar and a glimmering crystal clutch – this is the vision of Surrealist artist Remedios Varo (1908–1963). With this fabulous painting, Varo set a very high bar for your next haute couture sabbath ensemble.

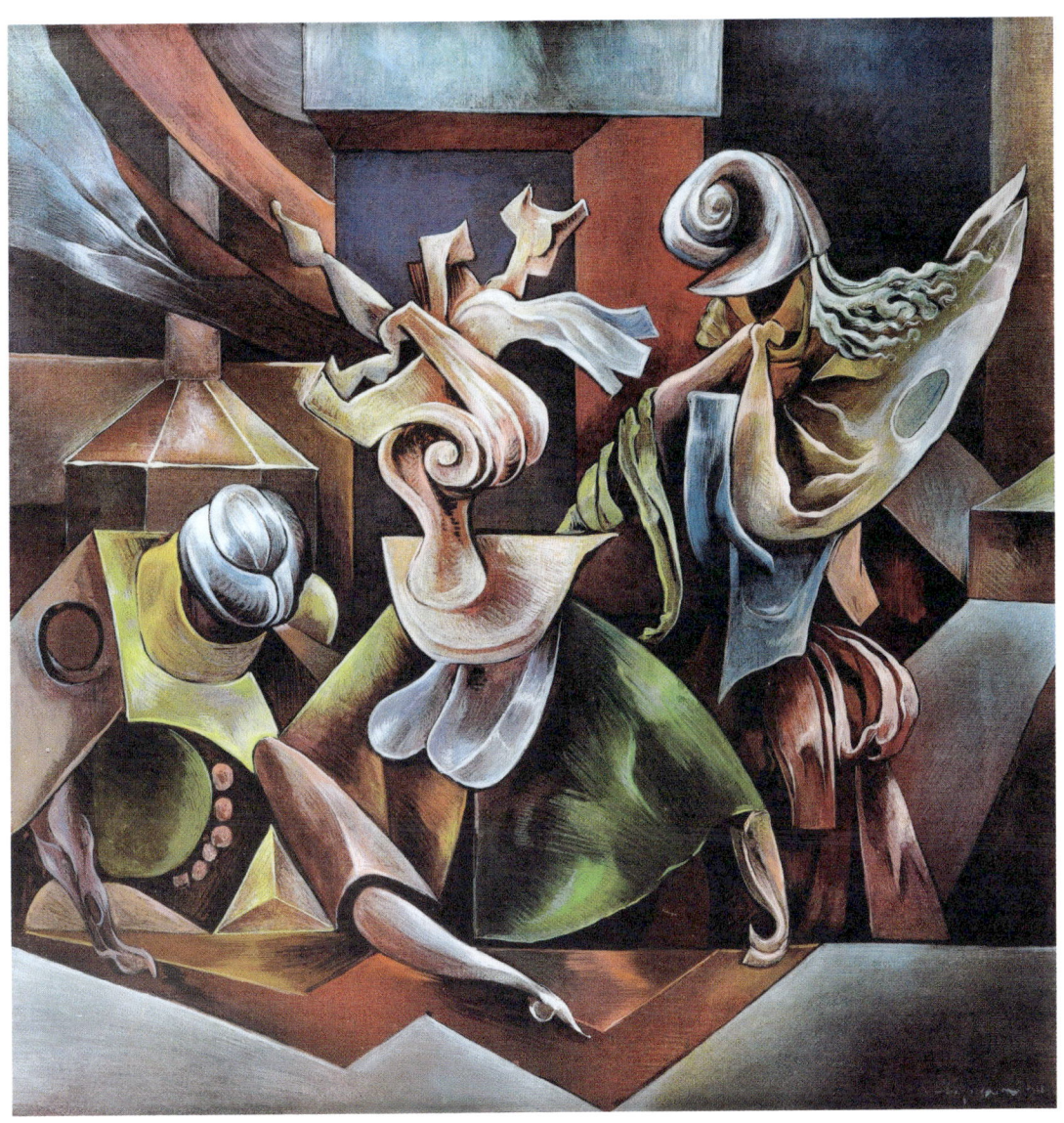

▲ Witches
Kurt Seligmann, 1950,
oil on canvas.

Kurt Seligmann (1900–1962) was a Swiss-American Surrealist painter and expert on magic, known for his monumental role in the popularisation of Surrealism in the United States. Seligmann's initial style was abstract, often using flowing organic shapes and dark, richly coloured scenes in which one may glimpse secret, fantastical plots. In 1937 he met with André Breton (1896–1866) and became a member of the Surrealist group.

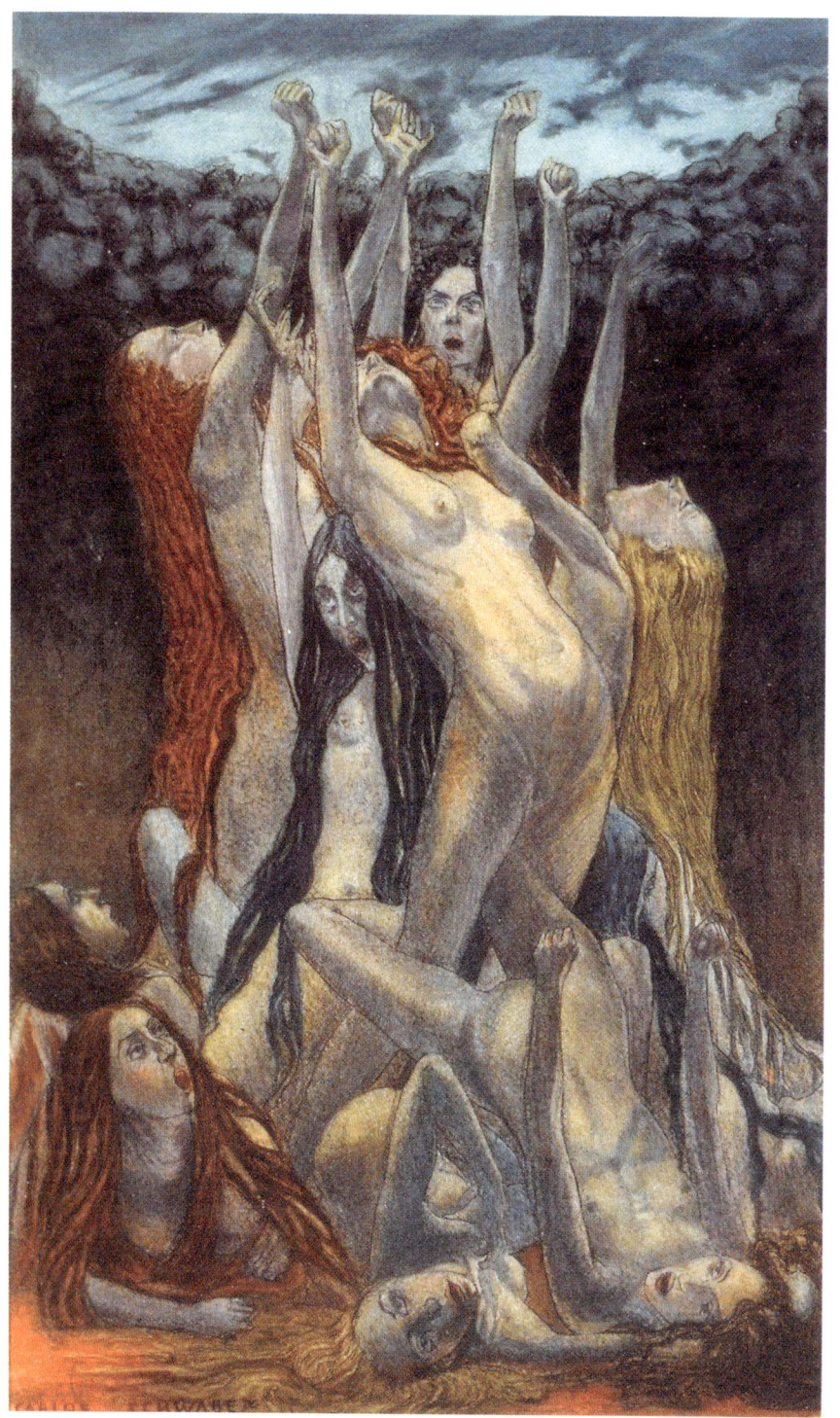

◄ Revolte
Carlos Schwabe, 1900.

Carlos Schwabe (1866–1926) was a Swiss Symbolist painter and printmaker whose paintings typically featured mythological and allegorical themes with a very personal vision. The fearsome reveries of his piece accompanied, along with other works from the artist, the poems of Charles Baudelaire's (1821–1867) decadent *Les Fleurs du mal* (1857).

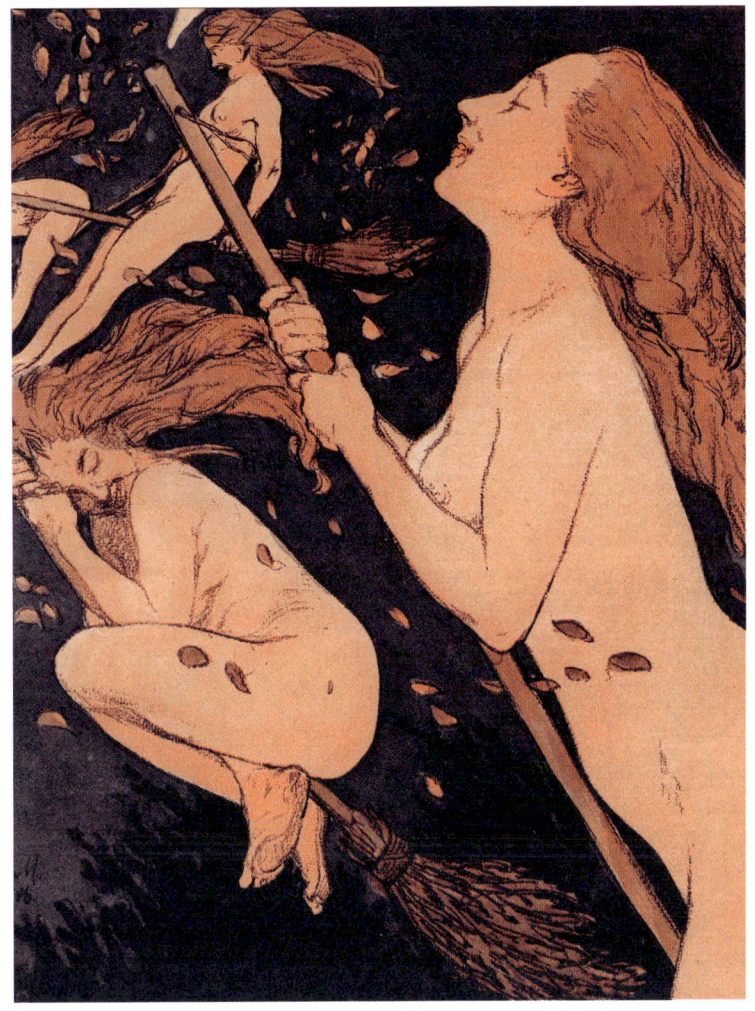

▲ Walpurgis Sabbath
Adolf Münzer, 1906, colour engraving.

Adolf Münzer (1870–1953) was a German painter and graphic artist who contributed a number of works to *Jugend*, a German art magazine that was created in the late 19th century and which featured many famous Art Nouveau artists. In German folklore, Walpurgis Night was believed to be the night of a witches meeting on the Brocken, the highest peak in the Harz Mountains. In this image we see ecstatic witches mounted on their brooms in anticipation of all manner of Walpurgisnacht revelries and devilries.

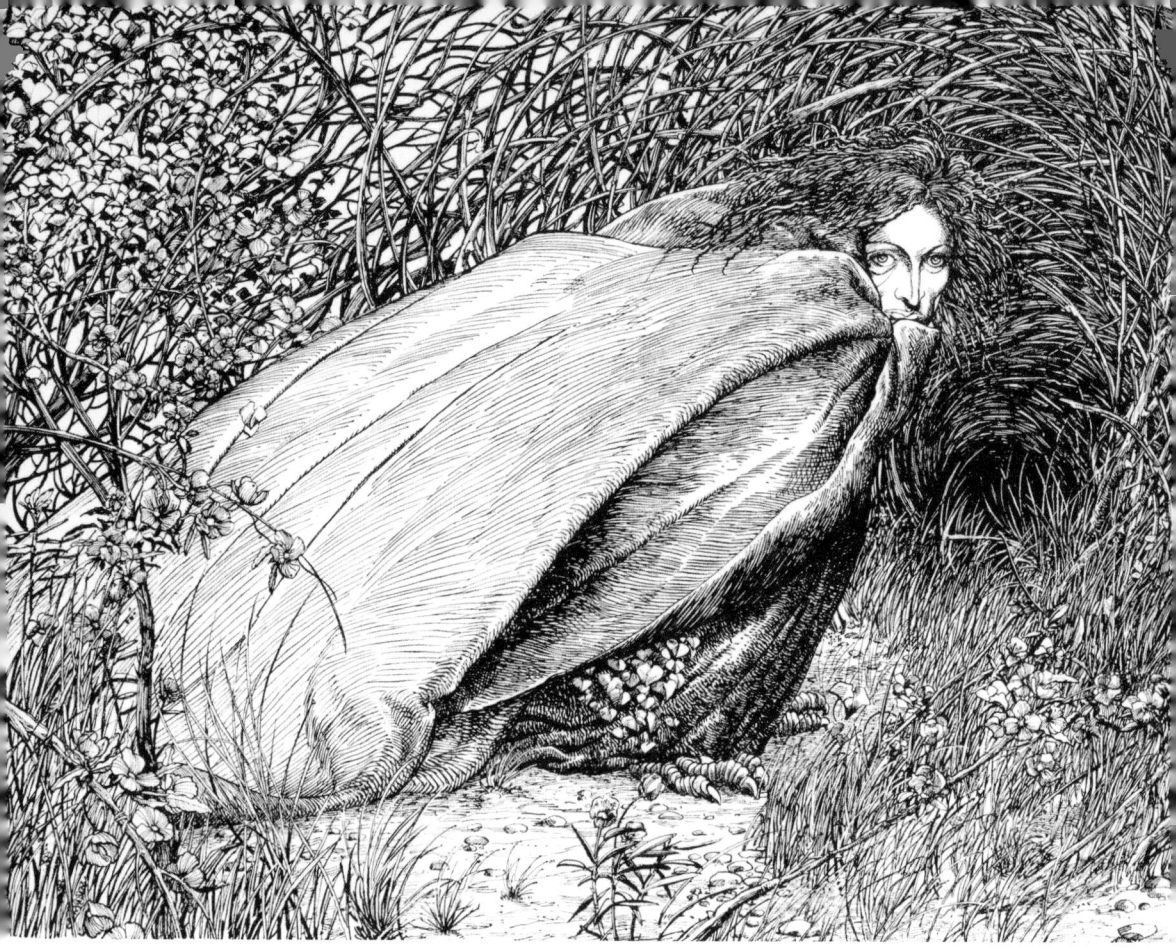

▲ The Witch
Barry Windsor-
Smith, 1978.

The legendary Barry Windsor-Smith (b.1949) has been
creating distinctive comics, art and stories since his
first published works in 1967. In a collected series of
works, the artist reveals his lifelong encounters with
'High Strangeness', or transcendental human experience
– strange glimpses of which perhaps can be gleaned
from haunting works such as *The Witch*. Intricate and
eerie, in his signature sophisticated style, this image
of the harpy-like witch hiding in a thicket of brambles
is mesmerising; her unflinching gaze hints at uncanny
sights, perhaps things known only by the artist himself.

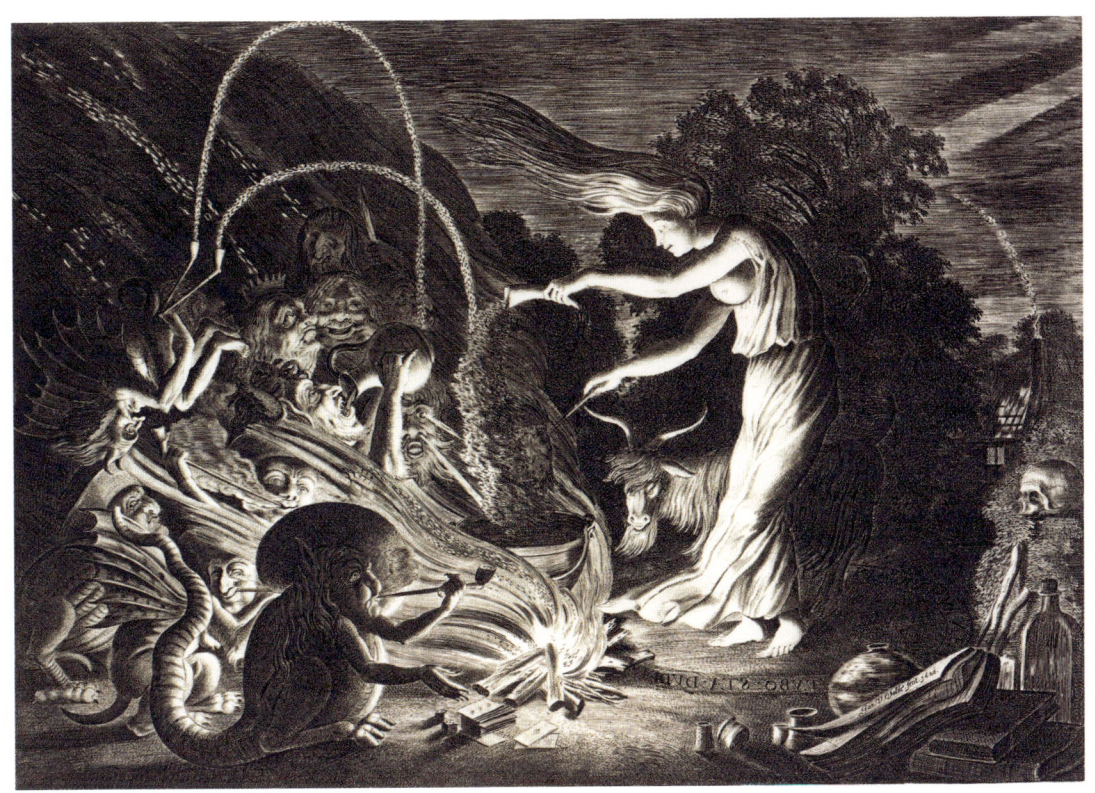

▲ The Sorceress
Jan van de Velde II,
1626, engraving.

Jan van de Velde the younger (1593–1641) was a
Dutch Golden Age painter and engraver of animal,
landscape and still-life subjects. Jan van de Velde II
came from an artistic family. In this dramatic, flickering
scene we see many features that were attributed to
witches in early modern times, as a classically garbed
young witch stands before her smoking cauldron as a
small troupe of monstrous familiars cavorts nearby.

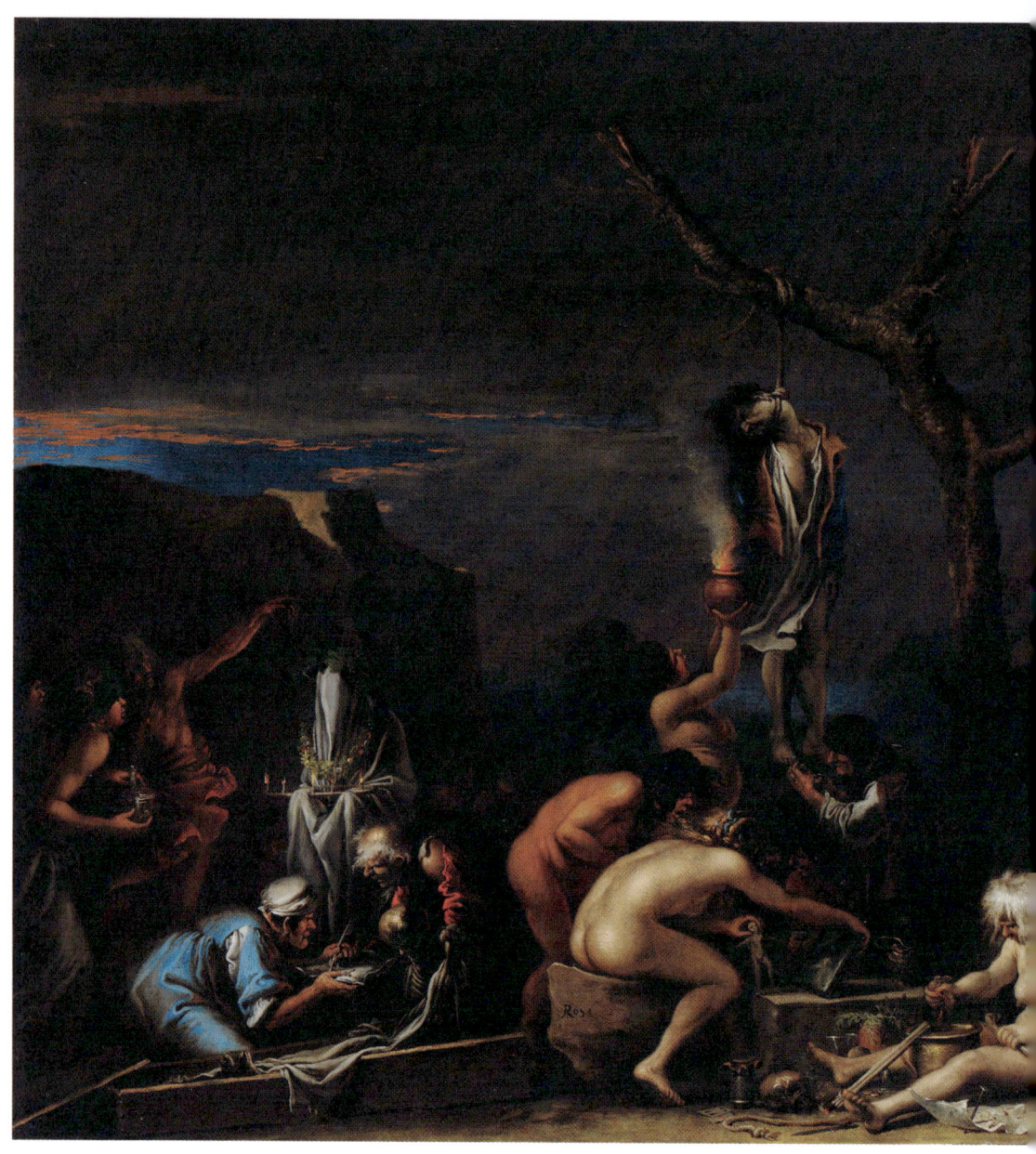

▲ **Witches at their Incantations**
Salvator Rosa, c.1646,
oil on canvas.

Salvator Rosa (1615–1673) was a Baroque painter, poet and printmaker described as 'unorthodox and extravagant'. His painting *Witches at their Incantations*, with its portrayal of nightmarish nocturnal revelries in the gloomy dead-of-night darkness of the Italian countryside, is indeed an exercise in malefic extravagance and in it is a terrifyingly evocative 17th-century exploration of witchcraft in Italian painting.

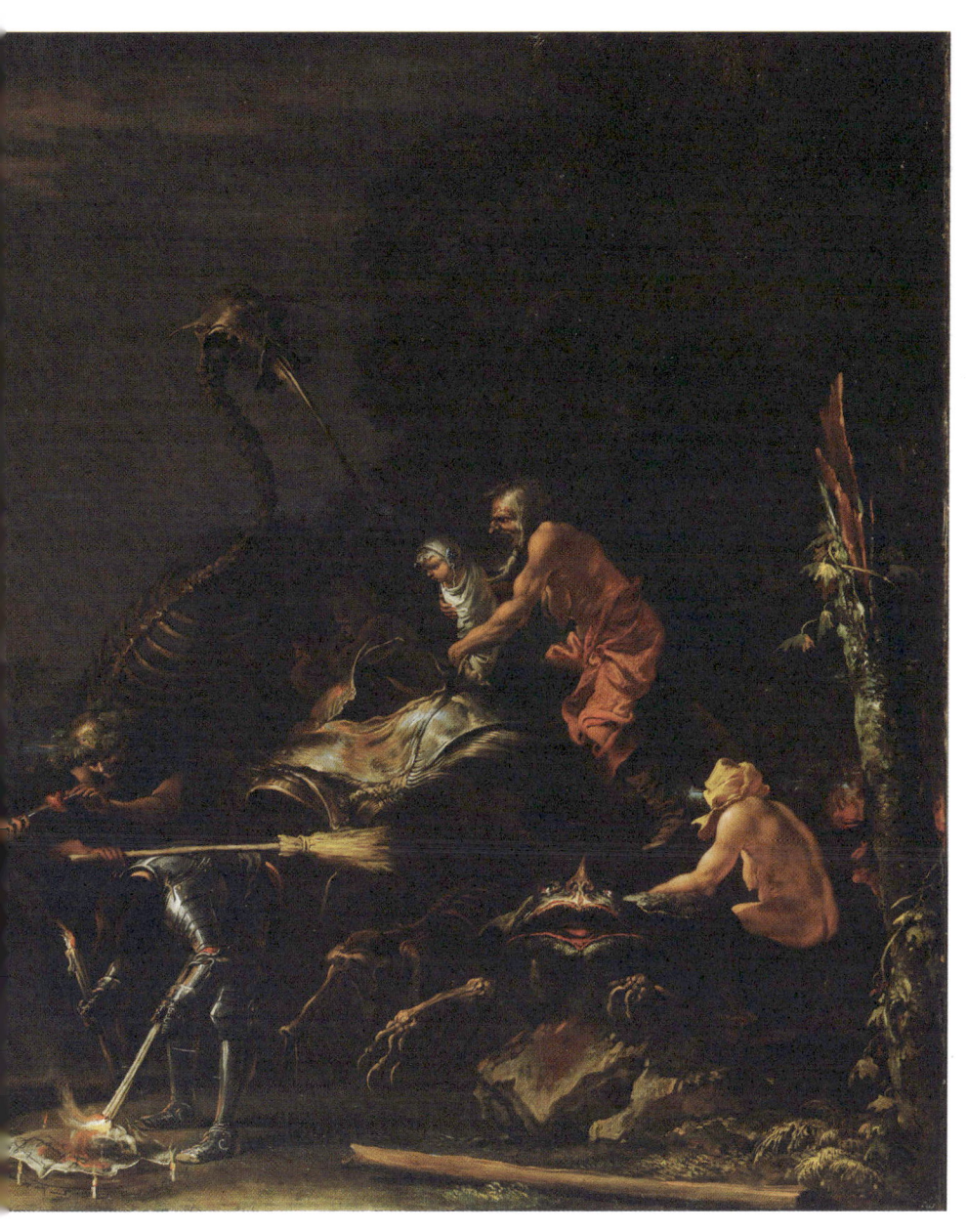

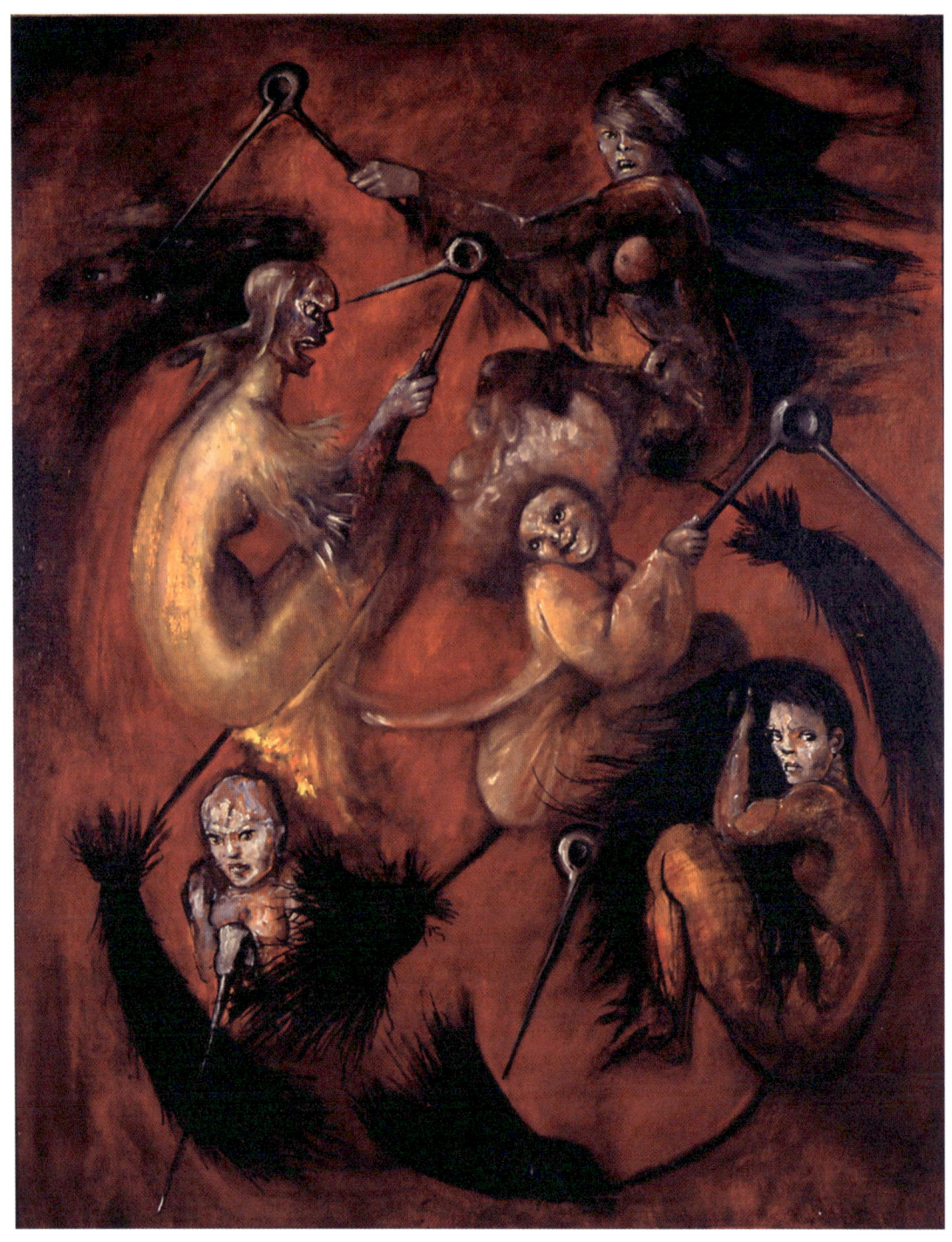

◀ Les Sorcières
Leonor Fini, 1959, oil on panel.

Leonor Fini (1907–1996) – an eccentric and flamboyant Argentinian painter, designer, illustrator and author – is frequently labeled a Surrealist, though she was never an official member of the movement. Known for fantastical paintings that explore female sexuality and power, Fini often seemed to depict women as either priestesses or as sorceresses. In *Les Sorcières*, we see this latter theme in the form of five frenzied witches swarming on their broomsticks through a swirling blood-red sky.

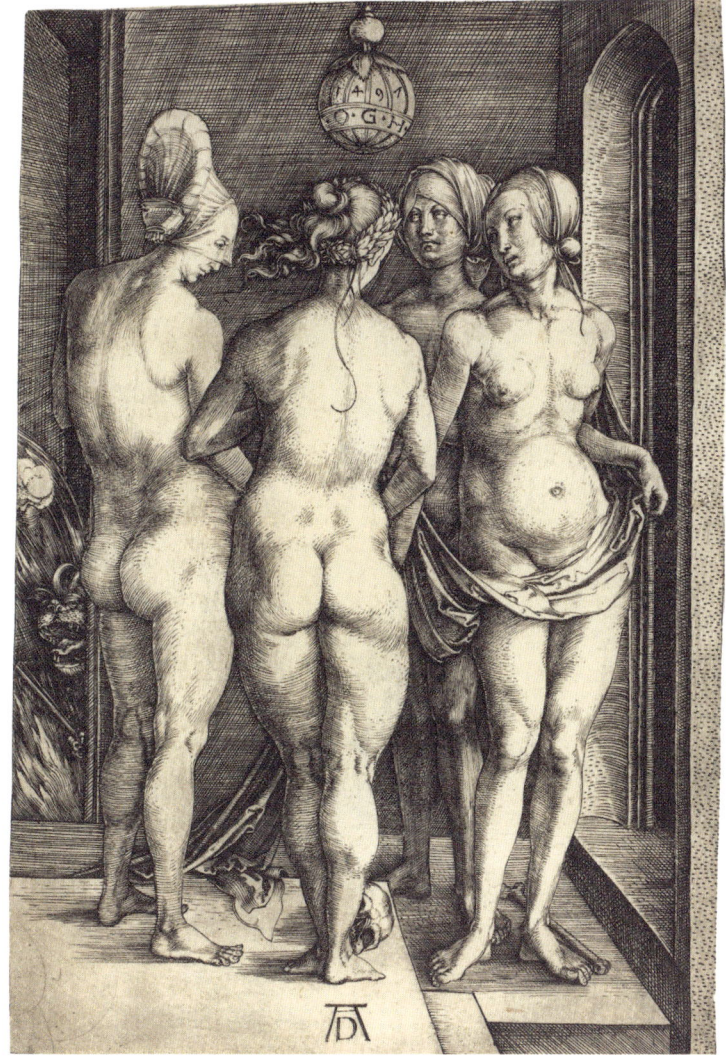

▲ The Four Witches
Albrecht Dürer, 1497, engraving.

Also known as *The Four Naked Women*, *The Four Sorceresses* or *Scene in a Brothel* – this work has as many titles as it does possible interpretations. Four nude women stand in a bathhouse, gathered in a circle with skulls and bones at their feet – a devil lurking in the doorway. There is a suggestion of magic and invocation. Or could it be that it's just a bathhouse, and these enigmatic ladies have got the good gossip?

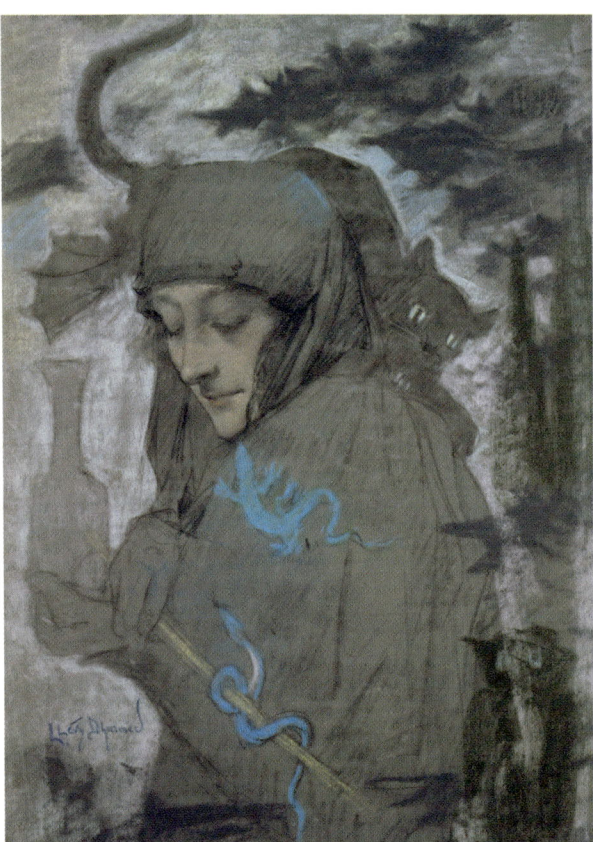

◄ **La Sorcière**
Lucien Lévy-Dhurmer,
1897, pastel on paper.

Lucien Lévy-Dhurmer (1865–1953)
was a French Symbolist and Art
Nouveau artist. His academic attention
to detail earned him high praise. A
Symbolist at heart, he often rejected
realism in favour of mysticism and
spirituality. *La Sorciere*, with its
melancholic haze of diffused colours
and textures, which seem to shimmer
and swim with deeper meaning, is one
of my favourite images in this collection.
The inclusion of that wily-eyed feline
only gilds this gloriously moody lily.

▶ **Untitled in the Rage (Nibiru Cataclysm)**
Juliana Huxtable, 2015, inkjet print.

As a self-confessed 'cyborg, witch and Nuwaubian princess',
Juliana Huxtable (b.1987) combines and reinvents cultural
histories. She questions the presentation and perception
of identity in artworks that often use her own body both
boldly celebrating it, and frankly interrogating normative
attitudes toward gender and queer sexuality. In *Untitled in
the Rage (Nibiru Cataclysm)* the surrounding landscape
and the references to Nubian and Egyptian cultures
highlight a triumphant portrayal of black identity, while
Huxtable gazes away from us, towards a utopian future.

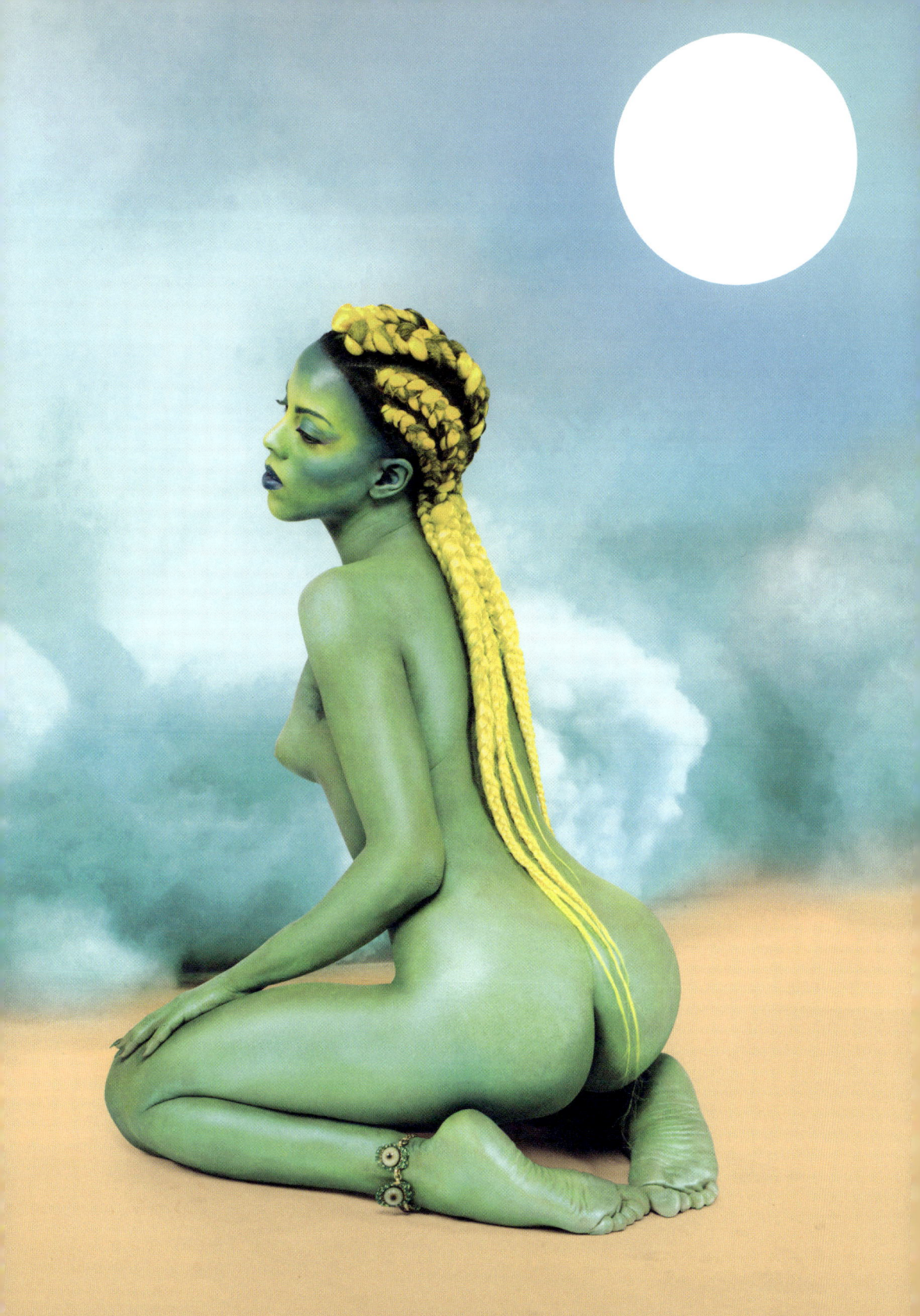

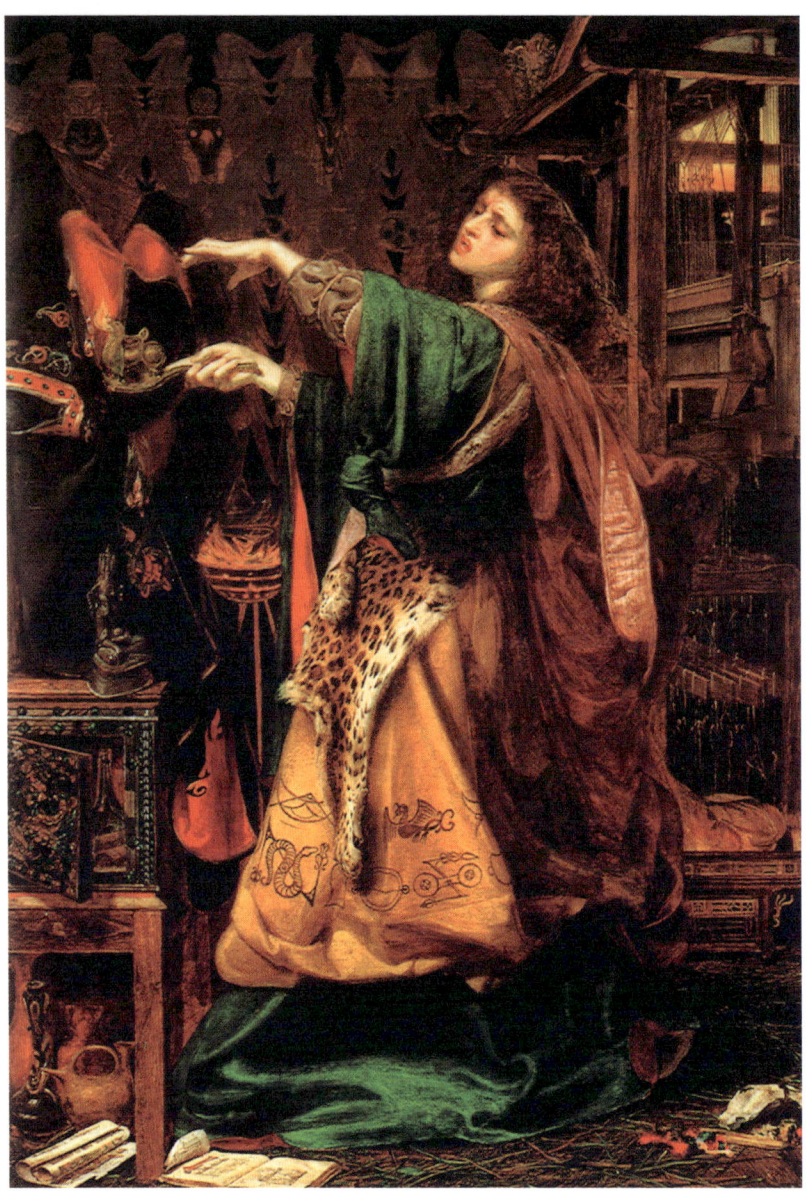

▲ Morgan-le-Fay
Frederick Sandys, 1863.

Anthony Frederick Augustus Sandys (1829–1904), was an English painter associated with the Pre-Raphaelites. It is difficult to tear one's gaze from the jewel-hued, symbolically intense painting of legendary Arthurian sorceress Morgan-le-Fay. Its lush brushstrokes are fraught with archetypal passions, unseen occult forces and grim fate.

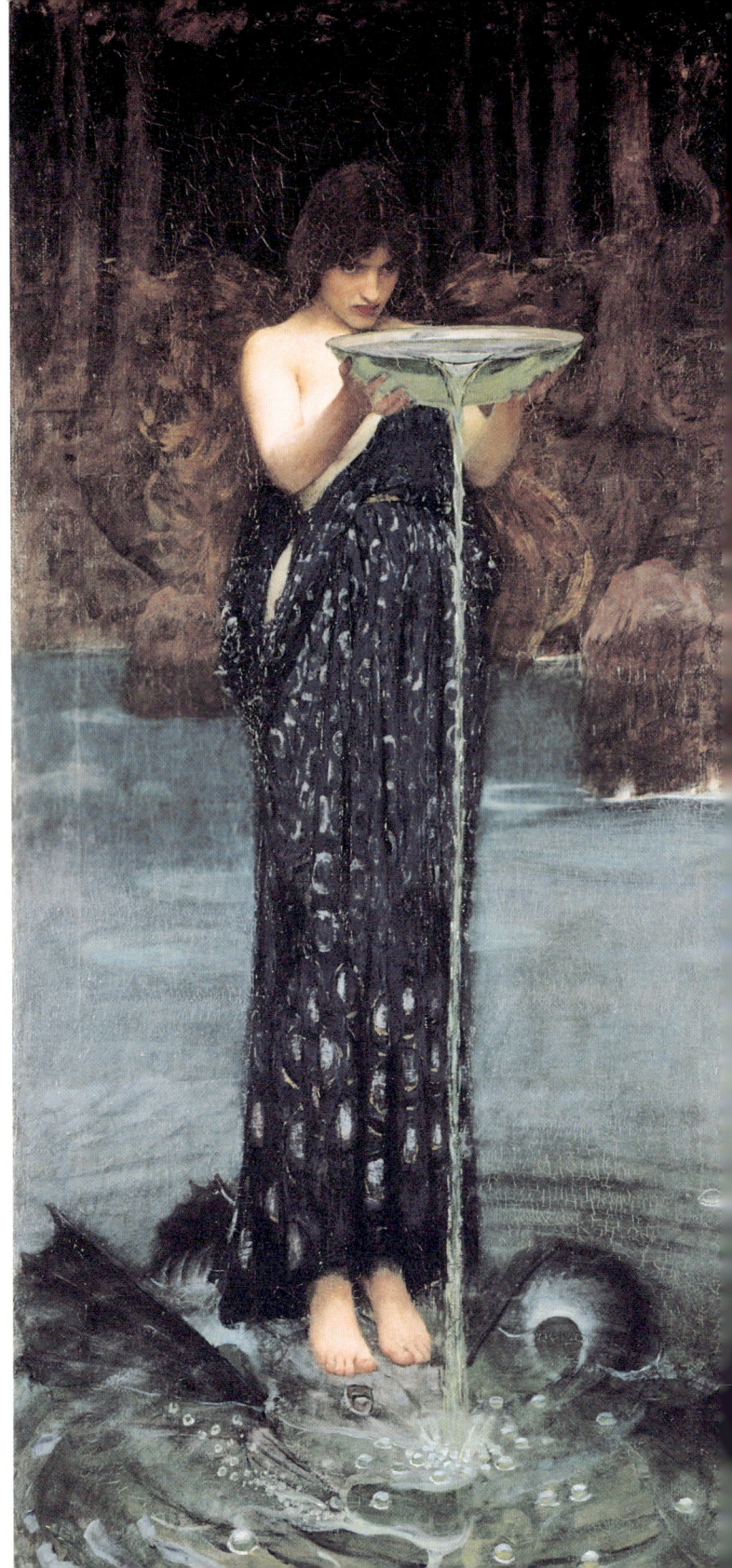

► **Circe Invidiosa**
John William Waterhouse
1892, oil on canvas.

John William Waterhouse
(1849–1917) was
an English painter of
classical, historical and
literary subjects, as well as
other themes associated
with the Pre-Raphaelites
– particularly tragic or
powerful femmes fatales.
Waterhouse painted
Circe Invidiosa in 1892
– one of three paintings
featuring the mythological
Greek sorceress. In
this scene, Circe is
poisoning the water to
turn Scylla, Circe's rival
into a hideous monster.
Is there one amongst us
who can look upon the
anger and determination
on this elegant, fearsome
woman's face, and not
relate to a moment of
such searing jealousy?

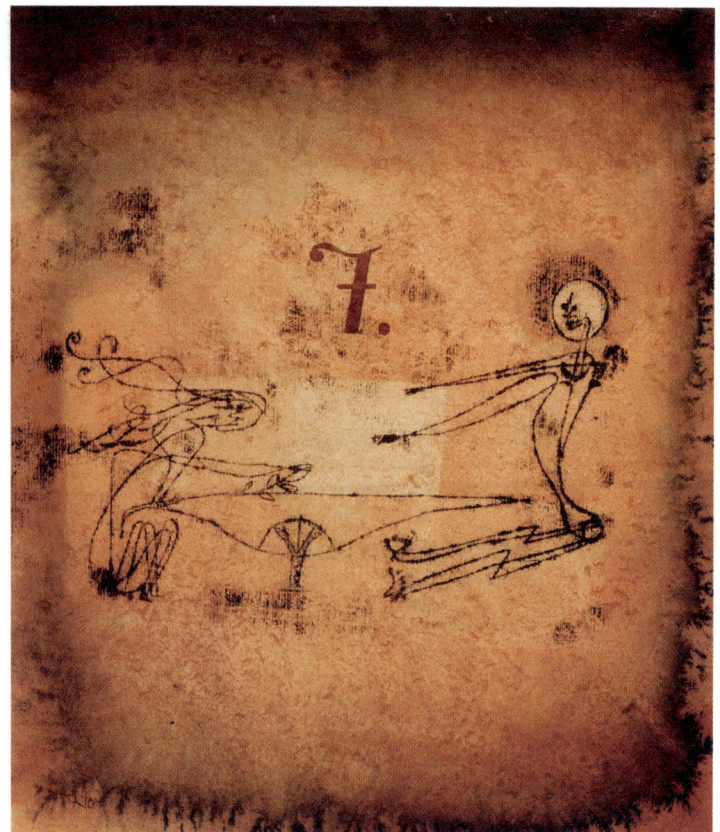

▶ **Witch of Atlas**
Vali Myers, 1993, fine pen,
black ink, burnt sienna
ink and watercolour.

Australian visionary artist,
dancer, bohemian and
indomitable spirit, Vali Myers
(1930–2003) – also known
as 'The Witch of Positano' –
has been described as ' … a
unique spirit born out of time'.
She is said to have inspired
generations of existentialists,
beatniks, hippies, punks,
rebels and dreamers.
Vali Myers referred to her
paintings as 'spirit drawings'
and in these intimate and
otherworldly visions, one
can glimpse what appears
to be archetypal reflections
of Myers herself: a funhouse
mirror of phantasmagorical
fancies, and fierce, feral,
feminine forces.

▲ **Brauende Hexen (Witches Brewing)**
Paul Klee, 1922, oil transfer and watercolour
on paper on cardboard.

Born in Munchenbuchsee, Switzerland, Paul Klee's (1879–
1940) large body of work, with its highly individual style, was
influenced by Cubism, Expressionism and Surrealism and is tied
to numerous groundbreaking 20th-century movements, from
German Expressionism to Dada. Witches often employ potions to
effect their spells, and in Klee's *Witches Brewing* one observes
a scene like a mystical hieroglyph, with witches gathered around
a cauldron, and the large number seven hovering over it.

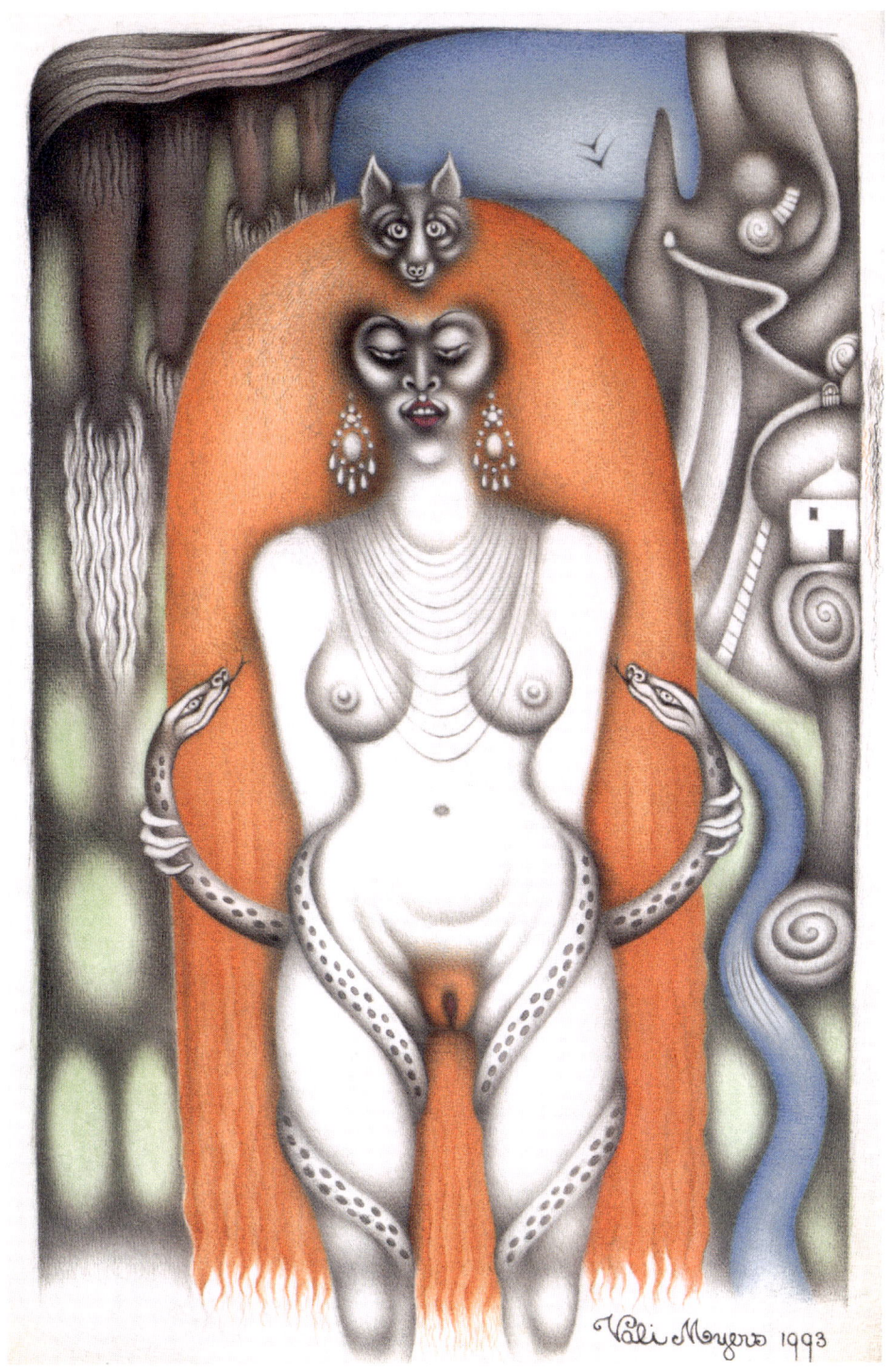

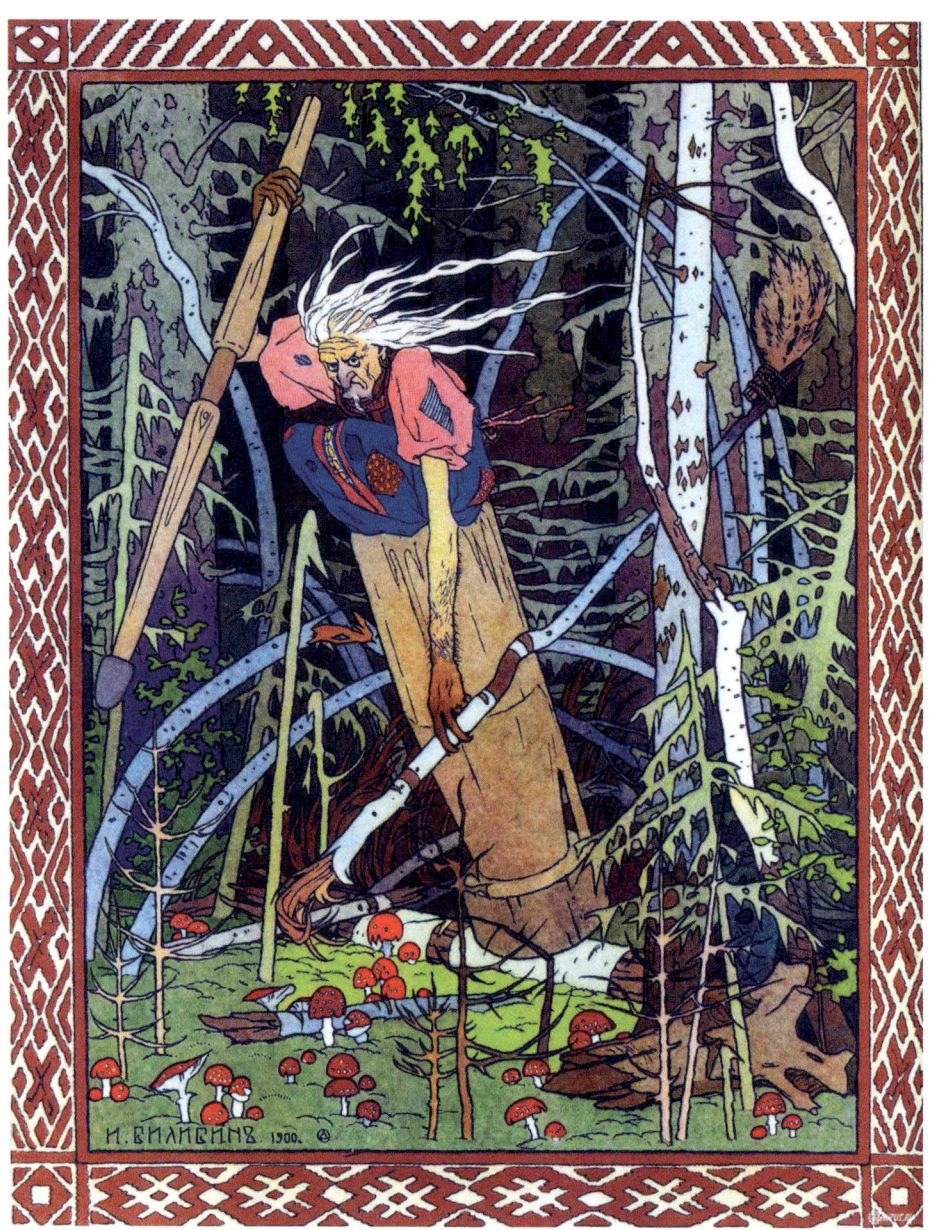

◄ Baba Yaga
Ivan Bilibin, 1900.

Ivan Yakovlevich Bilibin
(1876–1942) gained
popularity with his illustrations
of Russian folk tales and
Slavic folklore. His vivid
illustration for the children's
tale *Vasilissa the Fair* depicts
a menacing-looking Baba
Yaga weaving through an
eerie forest landscape in a
wooden mortar and wielding
a pestle. But don't be so
quick to assume the worst.
In folklore, Baba Yaga is an
enigmatic supernatural being,
a crone that transcends
definition. Is her intent to
help or to harm? Well, I
guess that depends on you.

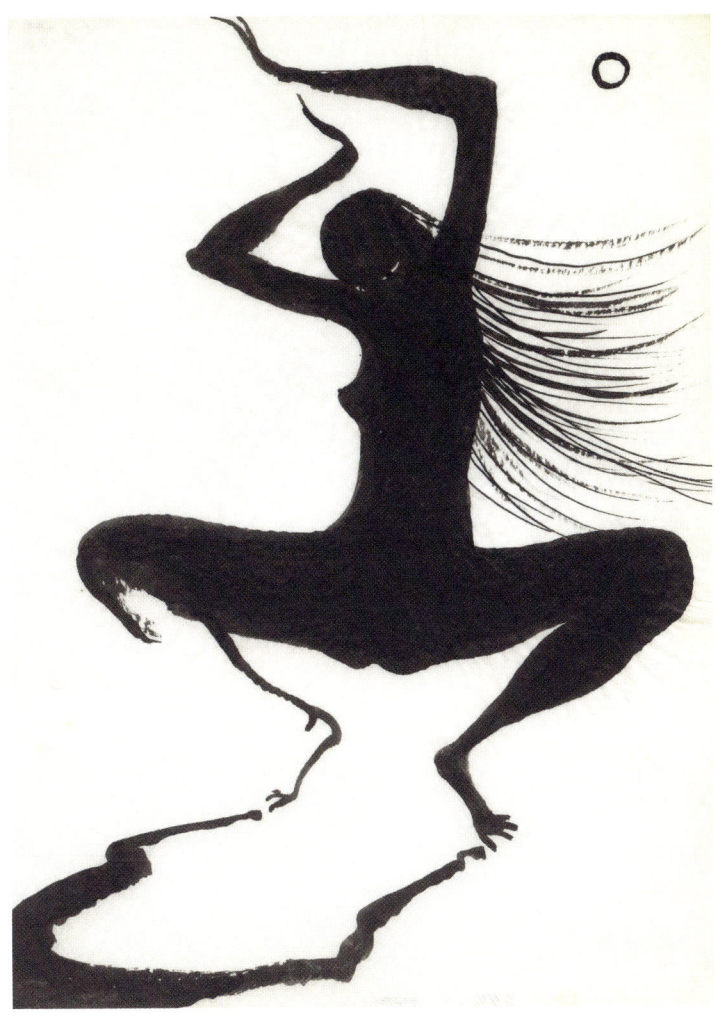

▲ From Songs For The Witch Woman
Marjorie Cameron, undated, ink on paper.

Marjorie Cameron (1922–1995) was an
artist, performer, poet and occult practitioner.
This countercultural icon's singular aesthetic
and strong feminist spirit can be seen in
her fanciful and often darkly expressionistic
works depicting mythic figures of her own
creation, engaged in ritualistic, symbolic acts.

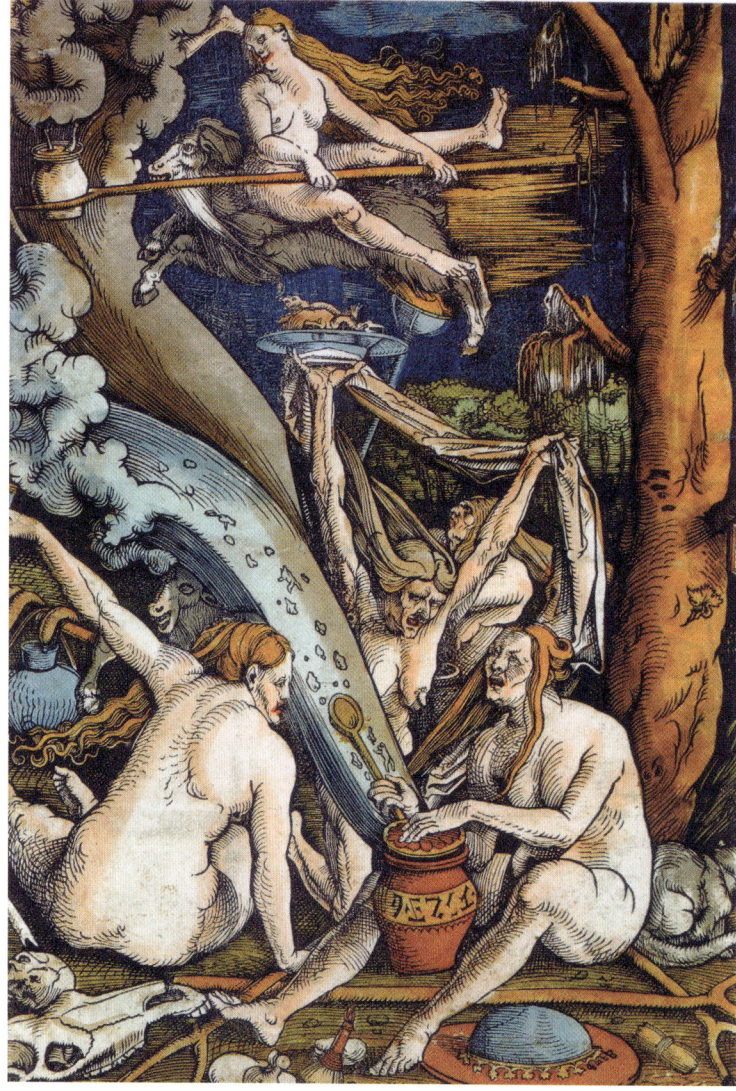

▶ **Witches Sabbath**
Rik Garrett, from
Earth Magic (Fulgur
Press, 2014).

Chicago-based artist
and photographer Rik
Garrett's work teems
with powerful symbolism
and deep sense of spirit,
energy and connection.
Witches Sabbath, as well
as the related works in
Earth Magic, explores
historical and personal
relationships between
witchcraft, femininity and
nature through a series
of images created using
the traditional wet plate
collodian process.

▲ **Witches**
Hans Baldung Grien, 1508, woodcut (colourised version).

Hans Baldung Grien (1484–1545) was a German painter and printmaker,
considered the most gifted student of Albrecht Dürer. His distinctive style, full of
colour, expression and imagination, can be seen in an extensive variety of work.
A 'masterpiece of German chiaroscuro', the original woodcut of *Witches* with a
scene of both hellish glow and nocturnal gloom is one of his best-known prints.

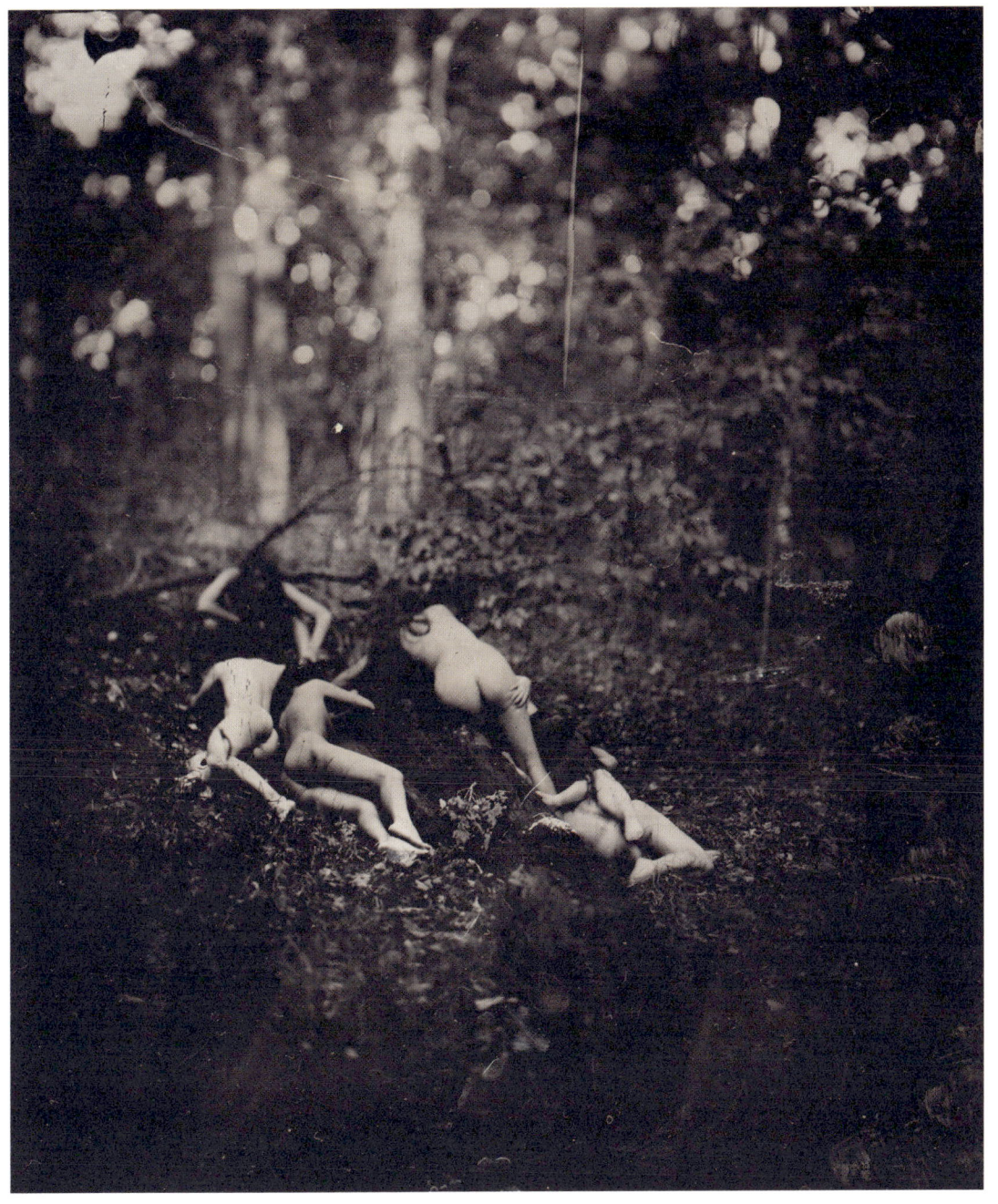

X

SPIRIT ART AND SPIRITUALISM

ALTHOUGH THE BELIEF THAT THE dead can communicate with the living has its roots in ancient religion and spirituality, and no doubt dates back to prehistory, it was in the mid-nineteenth century that it became a widespread and recognised religious and cultural movement across Europe and North America. Its origin is often attributed to the mysterious wall rappings of the Fox sisters of Hydesville, New York, and was fuelled by the religious beliefs of Swedish theologian and mystic Emanuel Swedenborg, and some of the theories and trance-like techniques of Anton Mesmer. Spiritualism was concerned with the idea that the spirits of the dead exist and have both the ability and inclination to communicate with the living, usually through a medium.

Spiritualists believed in a continued future existence, that souls survive bodily death and live in a spirit world, and that people who have passed on into the spirit world can and do communicate with us. The afterlife is seen by Spiritualists not as a static place, but as one in which spirits continue to evolve. These beliefs – that contact with spirits is possible, and that spirits are more advanced than humans – led Spiritualists to adopt the view that spirit beings are aware of and interested in the lives of those they have temporarily left behind in the material world, and that they are capable of providing useful knowledge about moral and ethical issues, as well as about the nature of God. Some Spiritualists speak of a concept which they refer to

as 'spirit guides' – specific spirits, often contacted, who are relied upon for spiritual guidance.

The Spiritualist movement grew quickly, spreading across America and into England, and from there to the European continent. Its followers were not only religiously-inclined country folk, but members of the urban middle classes: intellectuals, scientists, politicians, aristocrats and artists. Spiritualism flourished for a half-century without canonical texts or formal organisation; it didn't dictate what one should believe, or how one should interpret religious philosophy, and it spread through periodicals and the penny press, tours by trance lecturers, camp meetings, and the missionary activities of accomplished mediums. As Spiritualism grew in popularity in the mid-nineteenth century, women became recognised as the more spiritual sex, with an increasing number granted authority as mediums. In fact, many prominent Spiritualists were women, which allowed them to recognise their own oppression and advocate for women's rights through the lens of the spirit. By the late 1880s, however, the credibility of the informal movement had weakened due to accusations of fraud perpetrated by mediums, and more formal Spiritualist organisations began to appear. Today, Spiritualism is practised primarily through various denominational Spiritualist churches in the United States, Canada and the United Kingdom.

Perhaps one of the greatest legacies of the Spiritualist movement is its indelible mark on the

▶ **Group X, No.1, Altarpiece**
Hilma af Klint, 1915, oil and
metal leaf on canvas.

art world: a wondrous and varied profusion of
artistic creations, some of them quite literally
(or at least allegedly) produced by the vaporous
hands of the spirits themselves, and others
wherein the spirits are said to have guided a
human hand. This 'spirit art' historically falls
into three categories. The first is 'precipitation'
of artistic expression that materialised on canvas
or other media, seemingly without the use of
a human artist and presumably created by the
spirits directly during a Spiritualist séance,
such as the 'Precipitated Spirit Painting of Azur
the Helper'. Azur the Helper was the spirit
guide of Lily Dale mediums Allen Campbell
and Charles Shourds, better known as the
'Campbell Brothers'.

A second category is 'spirit portraits',
wherein mediums sketched portraits of spirits
they claimed were present during the séances.
Frank Leah was one such psychic artist and
clairvoyant who dedicated 40 years to sketching
the spirits he perceived accompanying his sitters.
The third category of 'spirit art' includes works
of painting, sculpture and architecture created
by spirits guiding the hands of the artist. Among
those mediums who painted or drew in trance
states or during séances, reportedly under the
influence of spirits, were Anna Mary Howitt,
Madge Gill and Hélène Smith. Their work
ranged from abstract shapes to portraits to alien
flora, yet while their styles differed, these 'spirit
artists were unified by one purpose: to use their
unique creative abilities and psychic sensibilities
in artistic mediumship for the purpose of sharing
the prevailing truth that the spirit world existed
and that spirits could interact with us, the living.

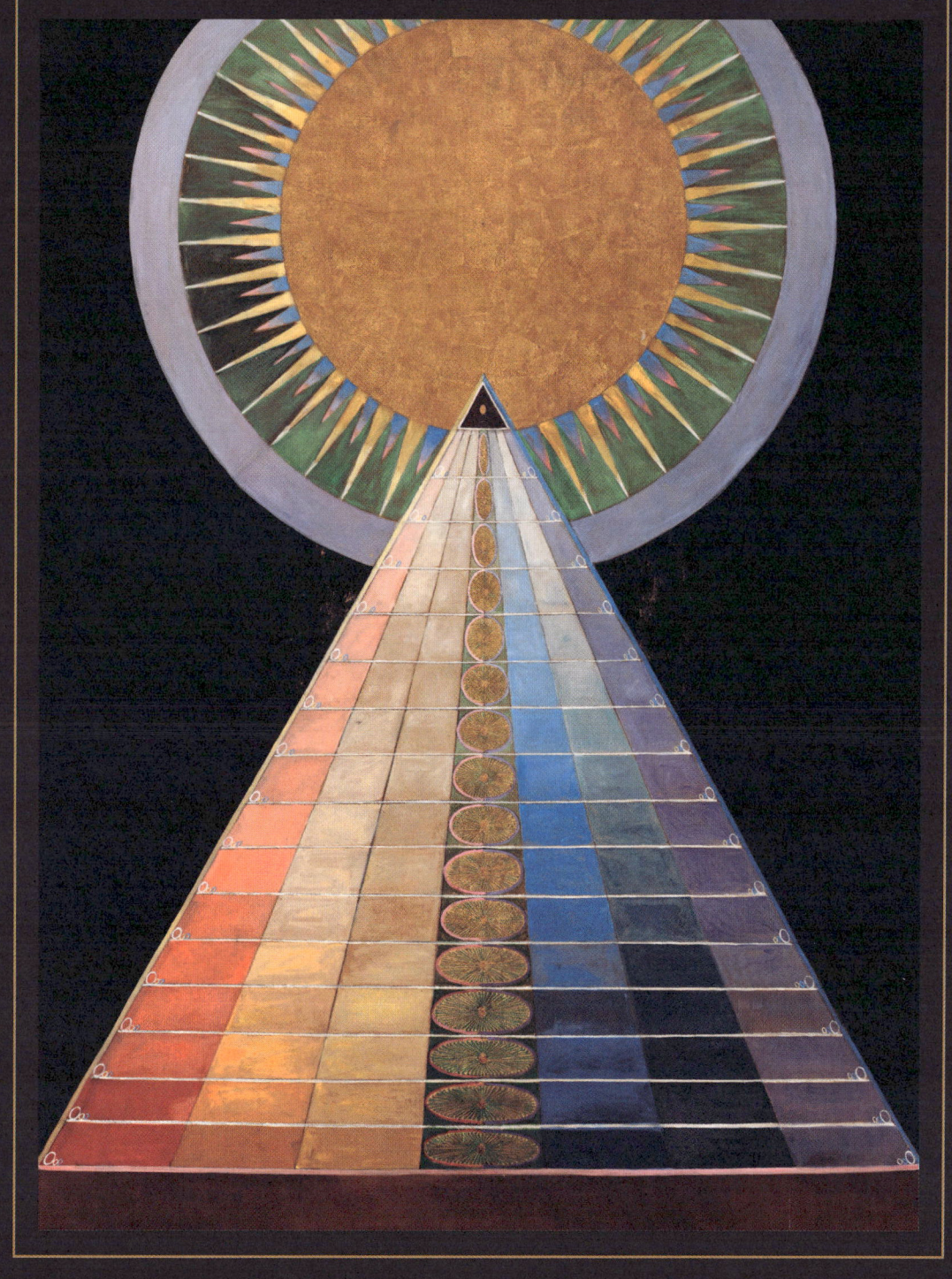

▼ The Three
Madge Gill, c.1940,
pen and ink on card.

Madge Gill (1882–1961), born Maude Ethel Eades, was an English outsider and visionary artist. Gill believed herself 'possessed' by a spirit she called Myrninerest (my inner rest), under whose power she drew in a trance-like state, creating up to 100 images at a time. Mostly black-and-white ink drawings and embroidered textiles, Gill's works often feature a girl's face or figure surrounded by swirling lines and patterns.

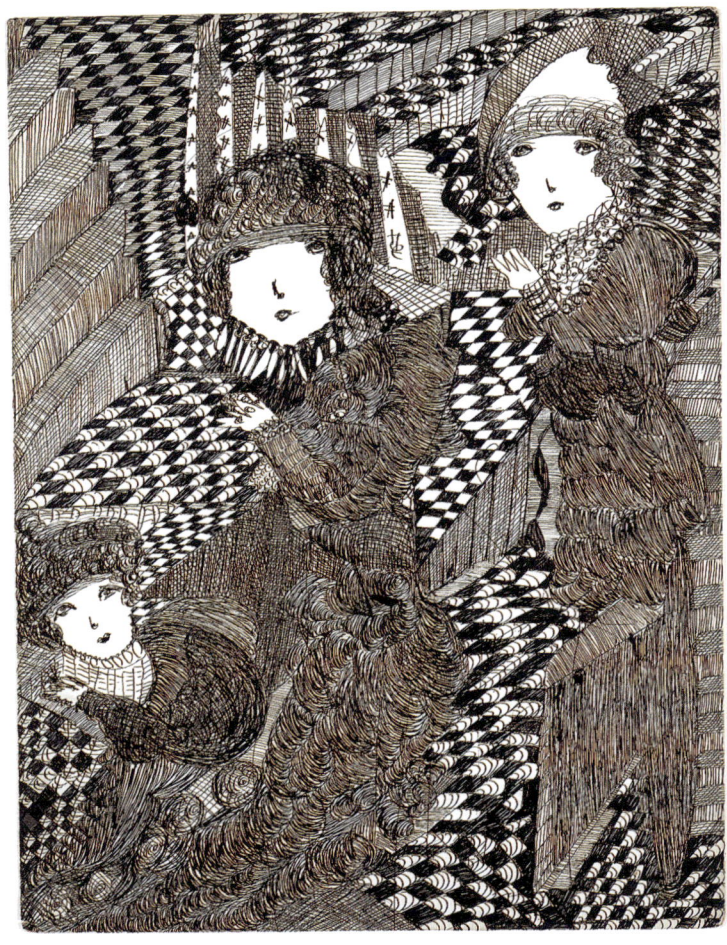

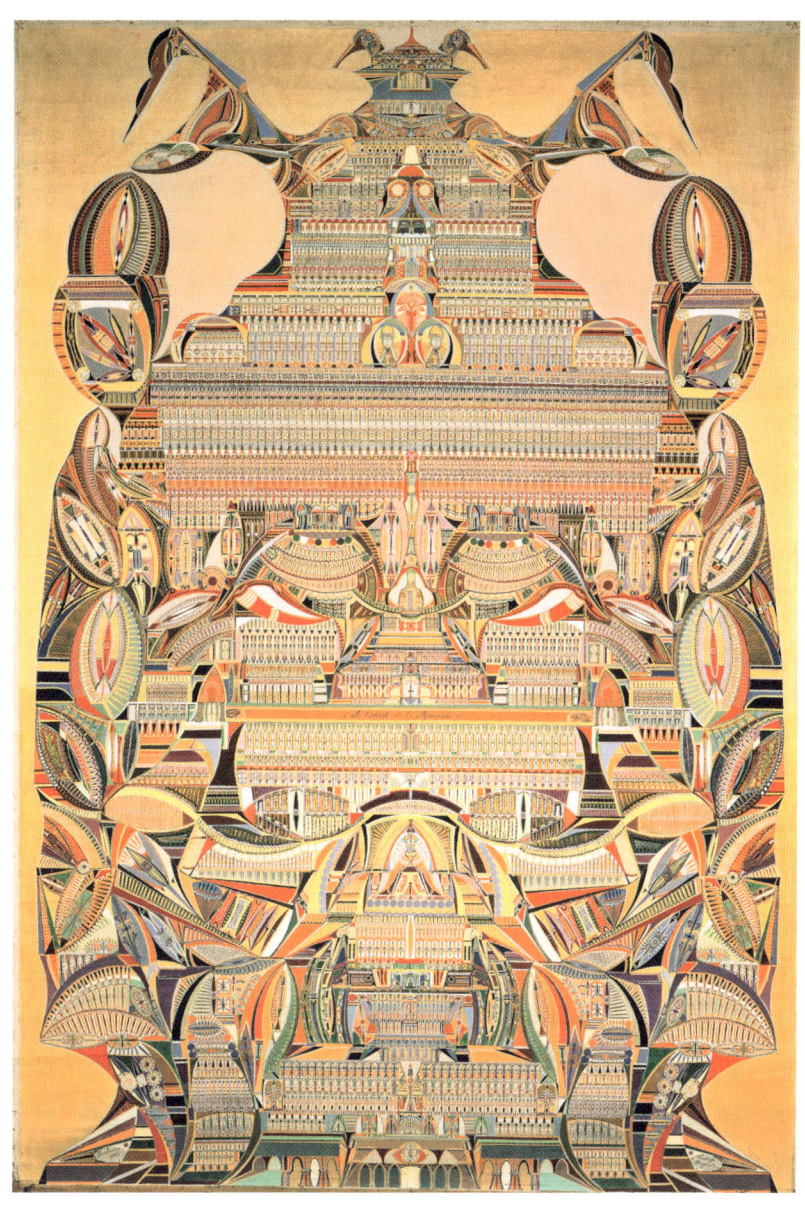

▲ Untitled
Augustin Lesage,
1946, oil on canvas.

Augustin Lesage (1876–1954) was a French coal miner who became an artist
through the help of what he considered to be spirit voices. He produced his first
drawings during a series of séances, guided by voices of the dead. 'I never have
an overview of the entire work at any point of the execution,' Lesage claimed.
'My guides tell me; I surrender to their impulse.' His finely-detailed compositions
most frequently depict highly symmetrical, imaginary architectural structures.

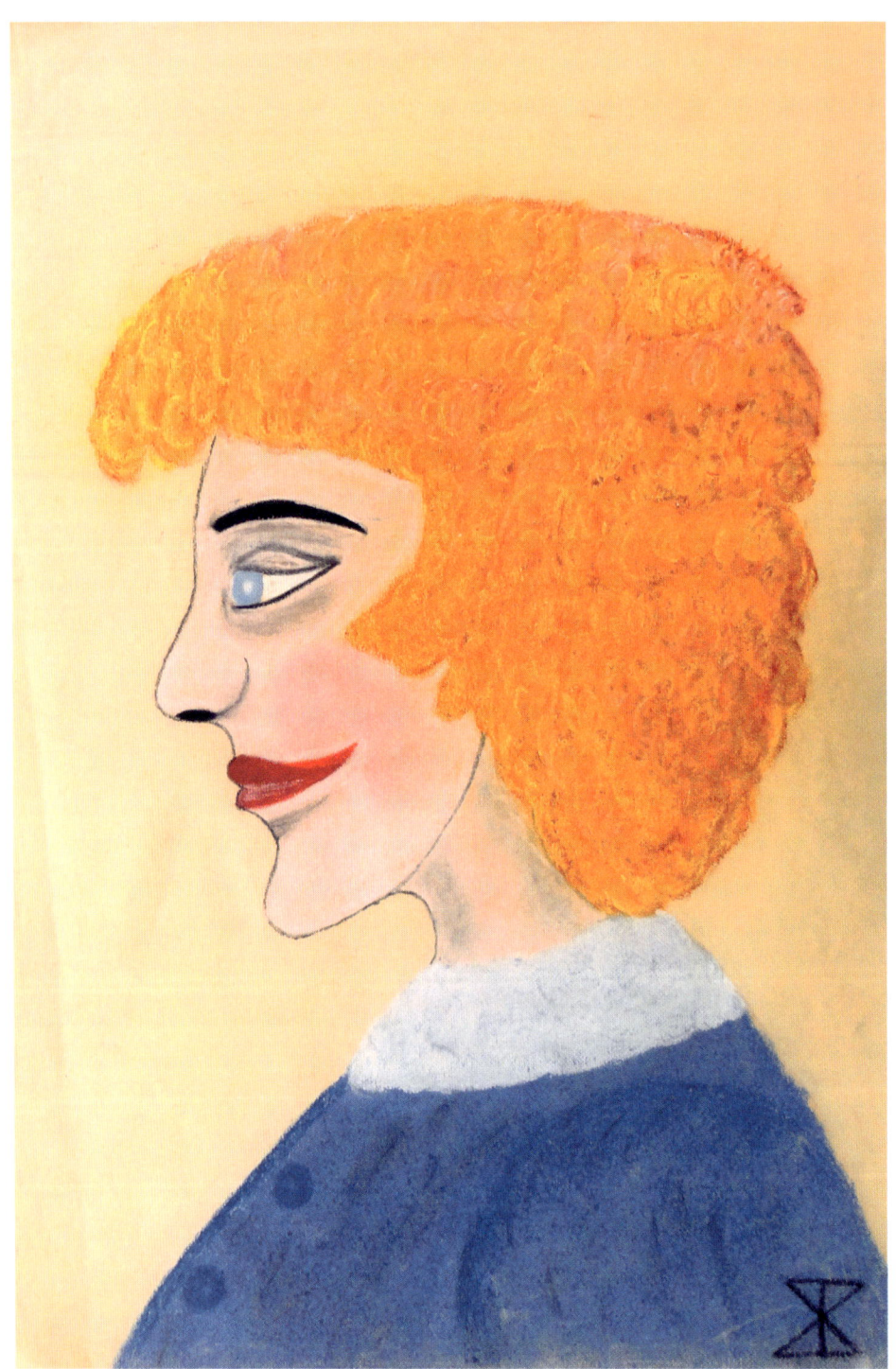

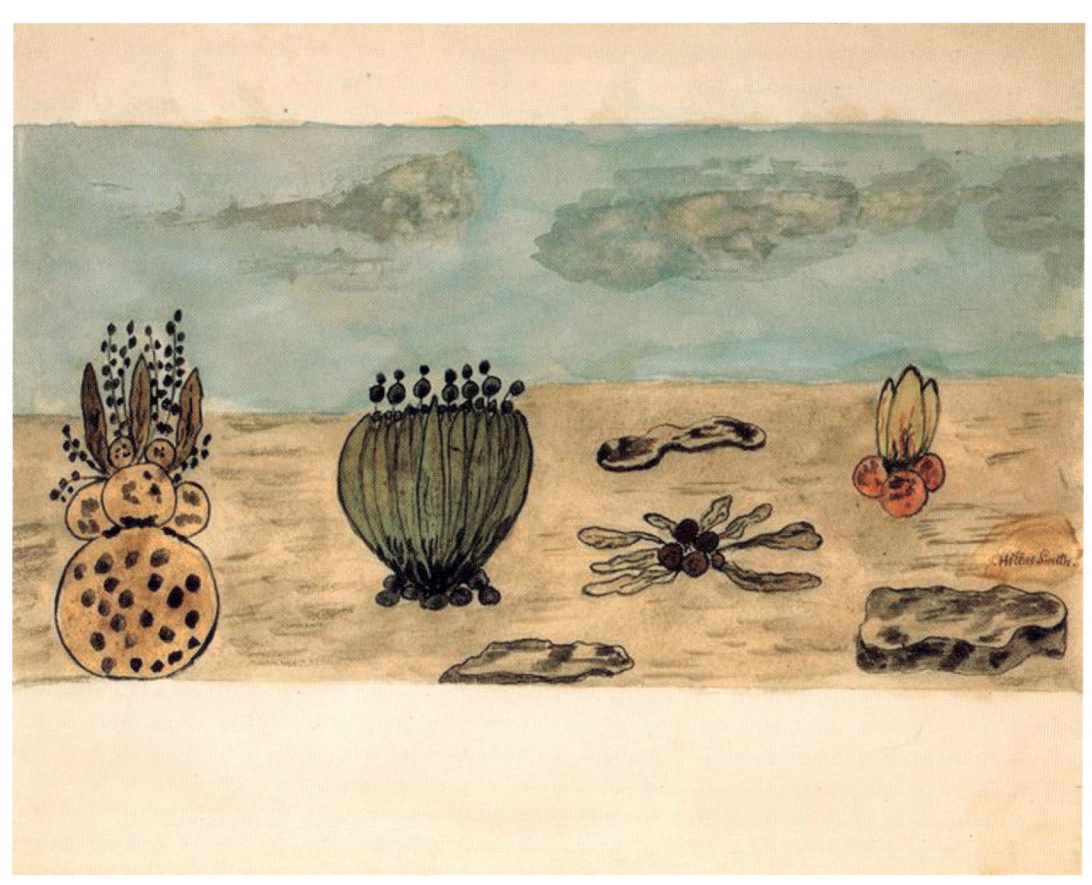

▲ Alien Plants
Hélène Smith, undated,
gouache on paper.

Claiming to communicate with Martians, and to be a reincarnation
of a Hindu princess and Marie Antoinette, Hélène Smith (1861–
1929) was a famous late 19th-century French medium, also
known as 'the Muse of Automatic Writing' by the Surrealists.

**◄ Nr. 253, Eine
Griechin, beim
Zeichnen Zuschauer**
Margarethe Held,
undated, chalk on paper.

Margarethe Held (1894–1981) was born in Mettingen,
Germany. She married at the age of 27 but lost her husband
after only four years of marriage. After the World War II she
became interested in occult practices. In 1950, during an
attempt to communicate with her deceased husband, a spirit
known as 'Siwa, God of the Indians and Mongols by order
of the Most Heavenly God' contacted her. Under Siwa's
instructions, she brought hundreds of mediumistic drawings
into the world. The faces drawn by Held have the appearance
of masks, representing the dead, gods, spirits and elves.

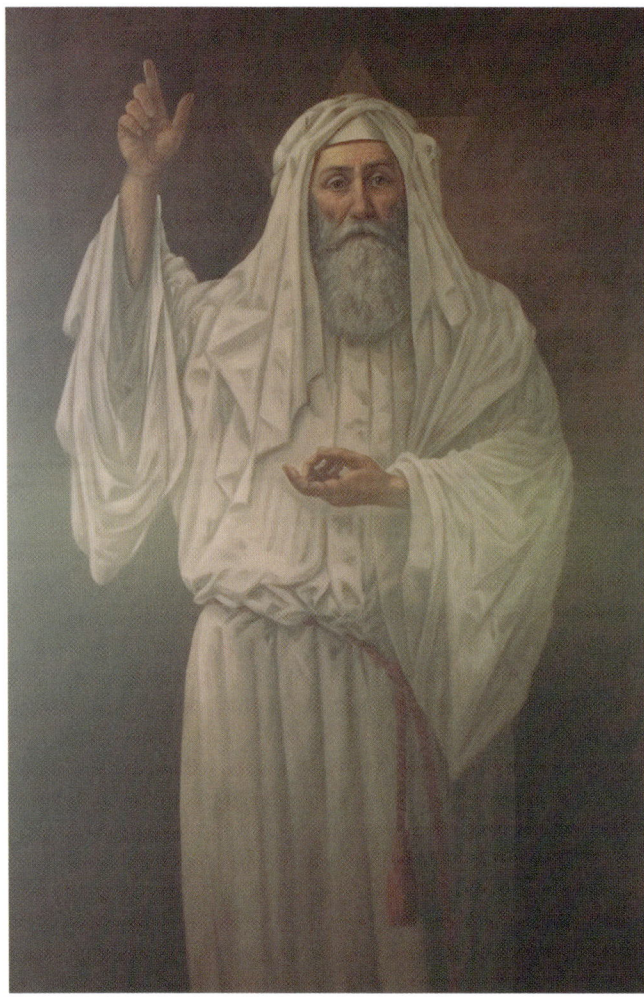

► **Photograph from Séance**
Shannon Taggart, from *Séance* (Fulgur Press, 2019).

Shannon Taggart (b.1975) is an artist based in Brooklyn, New York, who explores the intersection between photography, ethnography and the immaterial. *Séance* is an eighteen-year journey, 'part documentary, part ghost story' that has taken her around the world in search of 'ectoplasm' – the elusive substance that is said to be both spiritual and material.

▲ **Precipitated Spirit Painting of Azur the Helper**
1898, oil on canvas.

Azur the Helper was the Spirit Guide of Allen Campbell (1833–1919) and Charles Shourds (d.1926), better known as the Campbell Brothers. In 1898, during a session, Allan channeled Azur's spirit into a 40" x 60" oil painting, having never touched the canvas. The room was dark with a minimum light – enough for those present to witness the portrait emerging. To ensure there was no fraud each guest was encouraged to place personal marks on the back of the canvas. Allan, in a trance, commanded Azur's portrait and during this time it gradually developed as the guests watched in awe.

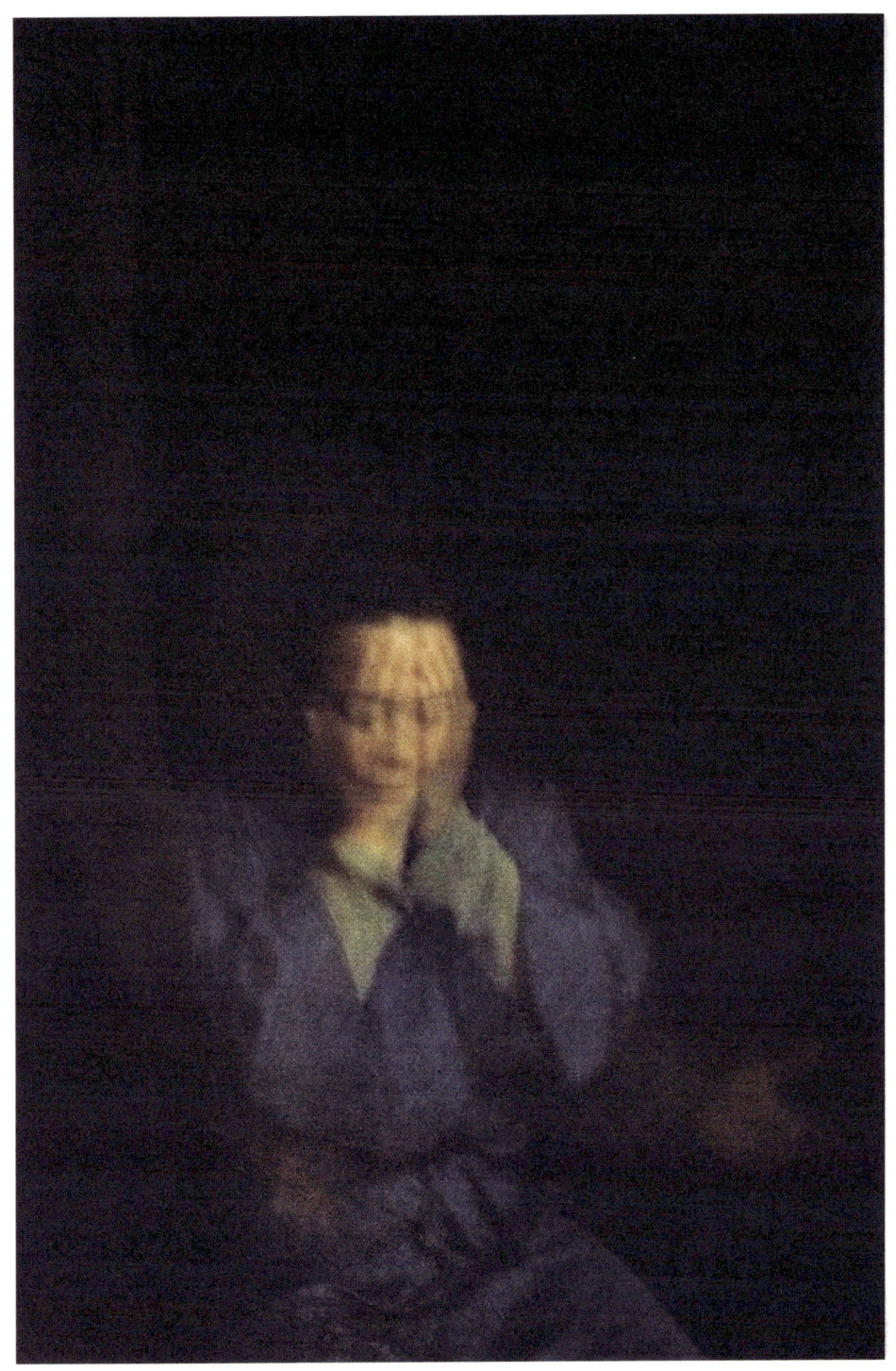

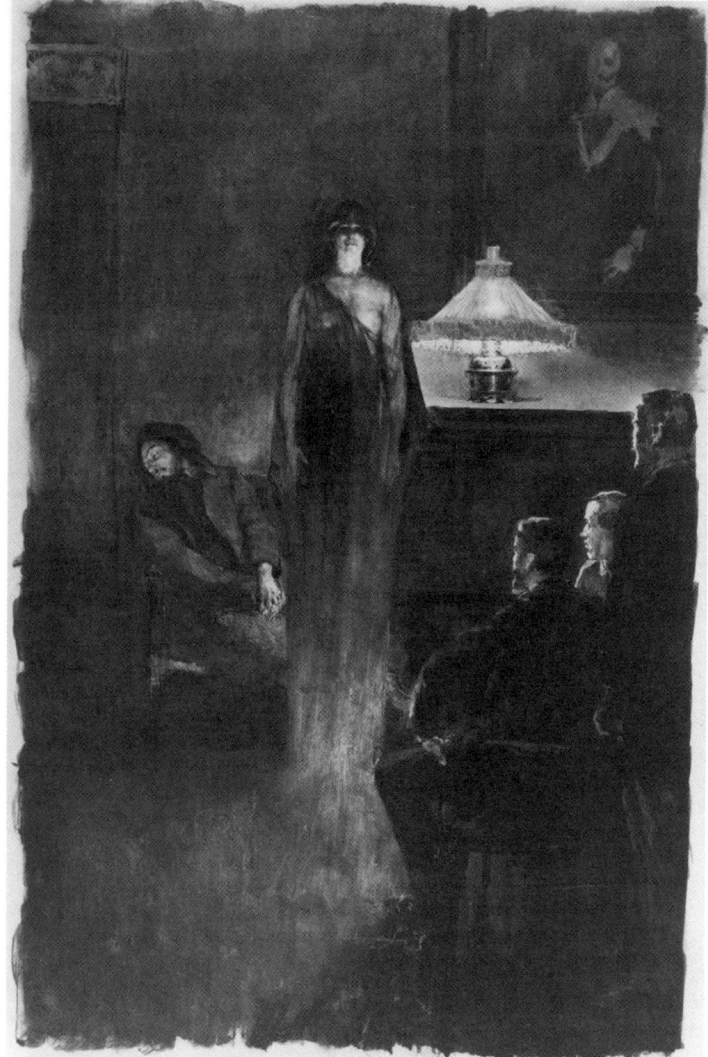

Swedish painter and poet Ernst Josephson (1851–1906) became involved in spiritism after a summer spent with with painter and engraver Allan Österlind (1855–1938) and his family. In visionary states, possibly inspired by Österlind's interest in occult phenomena, or perhaps due to the delusions and hallucinations brought on by the progression of his syphilis, he wrote poems and created paintings that he signed with the names of dead artists. Some of his best known and most influential works were created during this period.

▲ **The Séance**
Alexandre Lunois, c.1900, lithograph.

An accomplished artists of the belle époque, Alexandre Lunois (1863–1916) was an autodidact and considered the re-inventor of the lithotint technique. Inspired by his travels, most of Lunois' works leaned more to colour lithography, having an almost 'touristy' feel. This rendering of the solemn apparition and the eerie atmosphere of *The Séance* a bit of a mysterious occult odd duck amidst his other works.

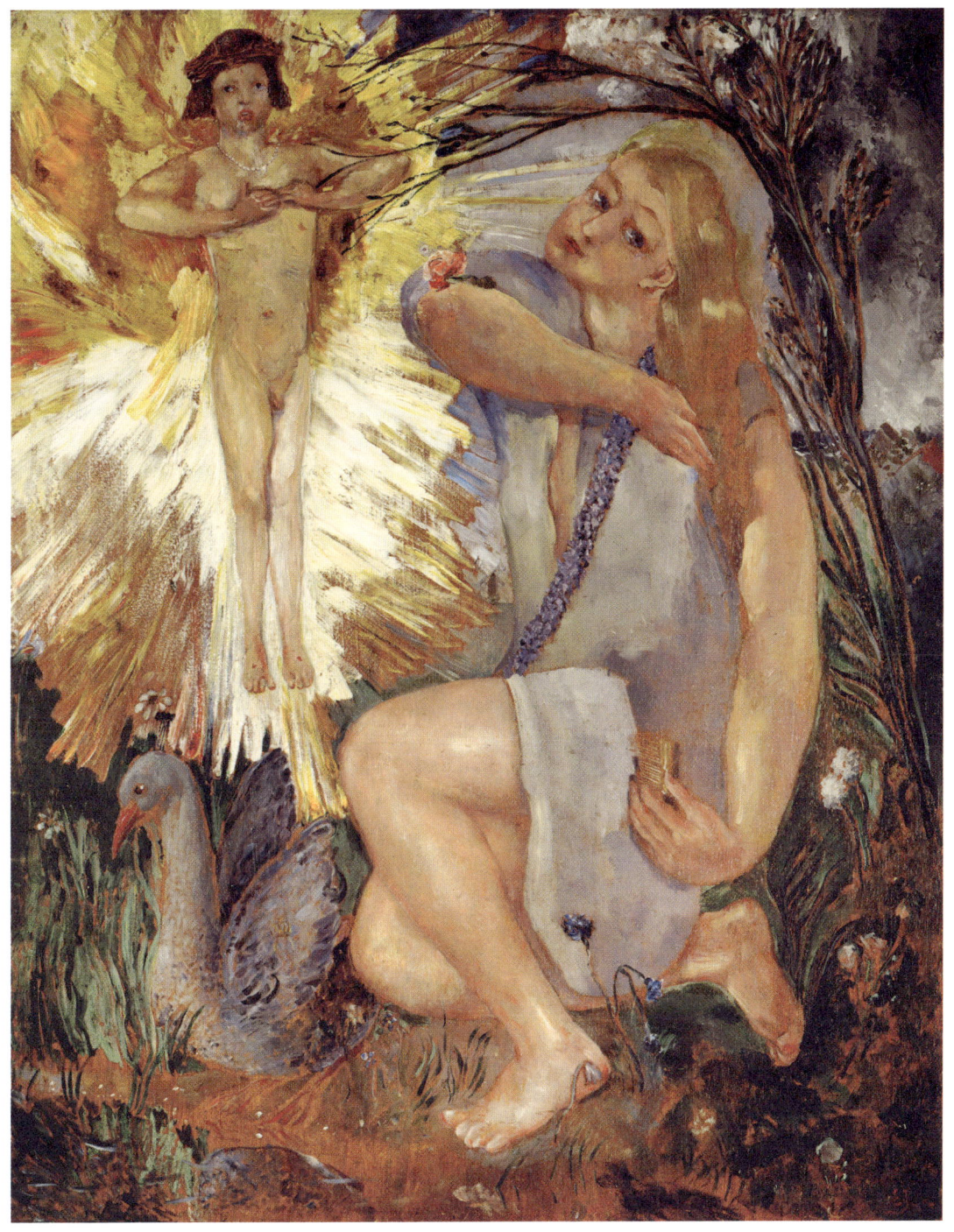

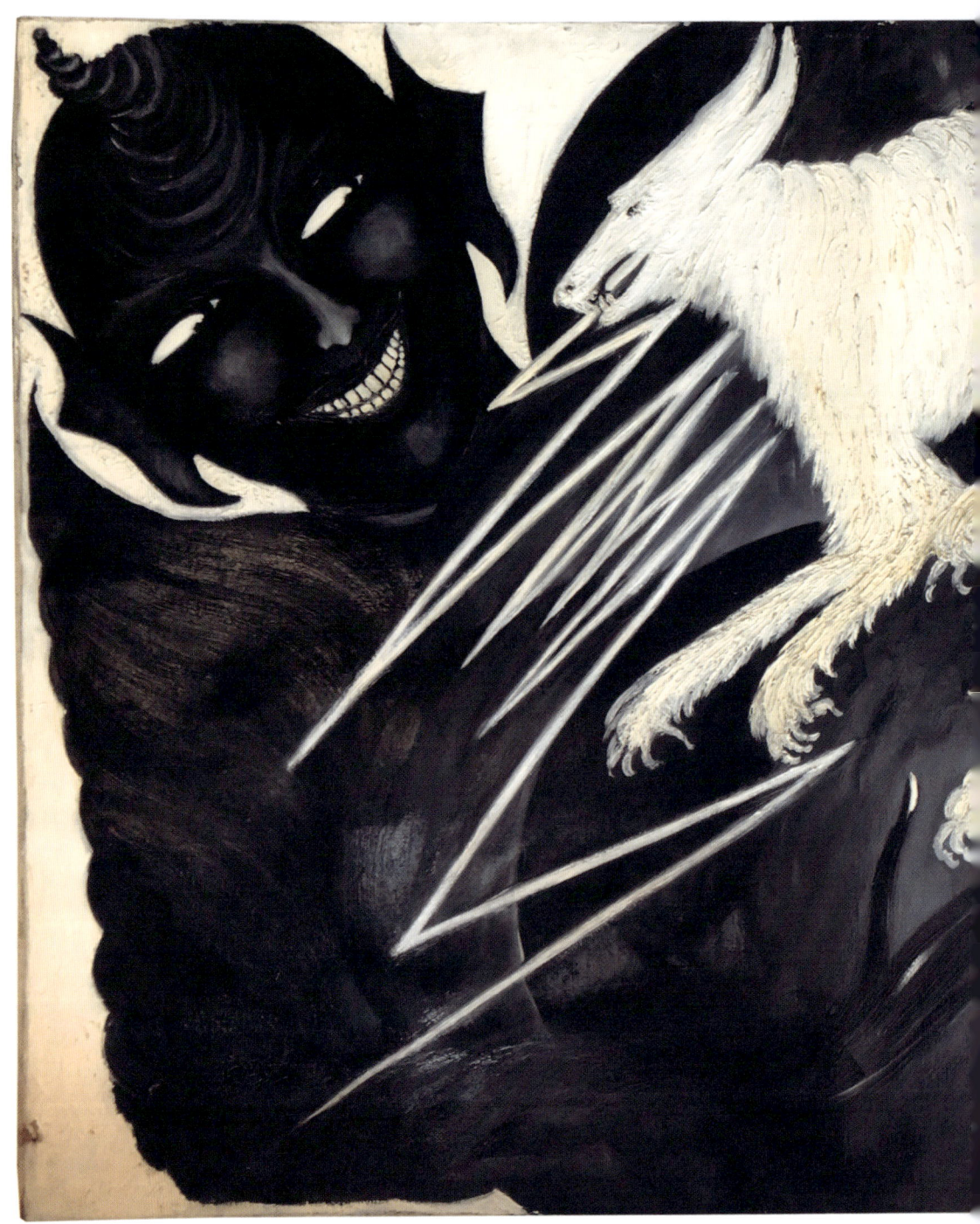

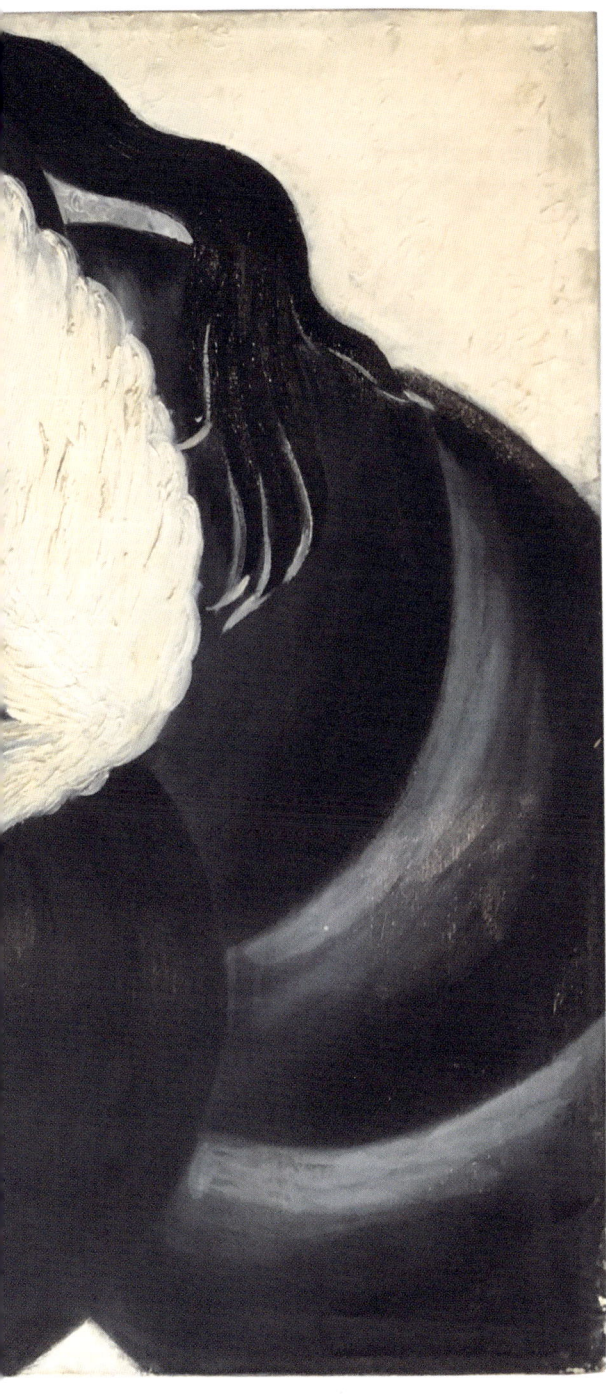

◄ **Thunder and lightning**
Marian Spore Bush,
c.1938, oil on canvas.

In the 1920s, Marian Spore Bush (1878–1946) left her successful Michigan dental practice for a studio in Greenwich Village, New York, to become a self-taught painter. She claimed her large surrealistic works were inspired by long-dead artists who were communicating with her from 'beyond the veil'. Her predictions of the future, unusual artwork, philanthropy and her marriage to industrial tycoon Irving T. Bush, incited much interest in the national press.

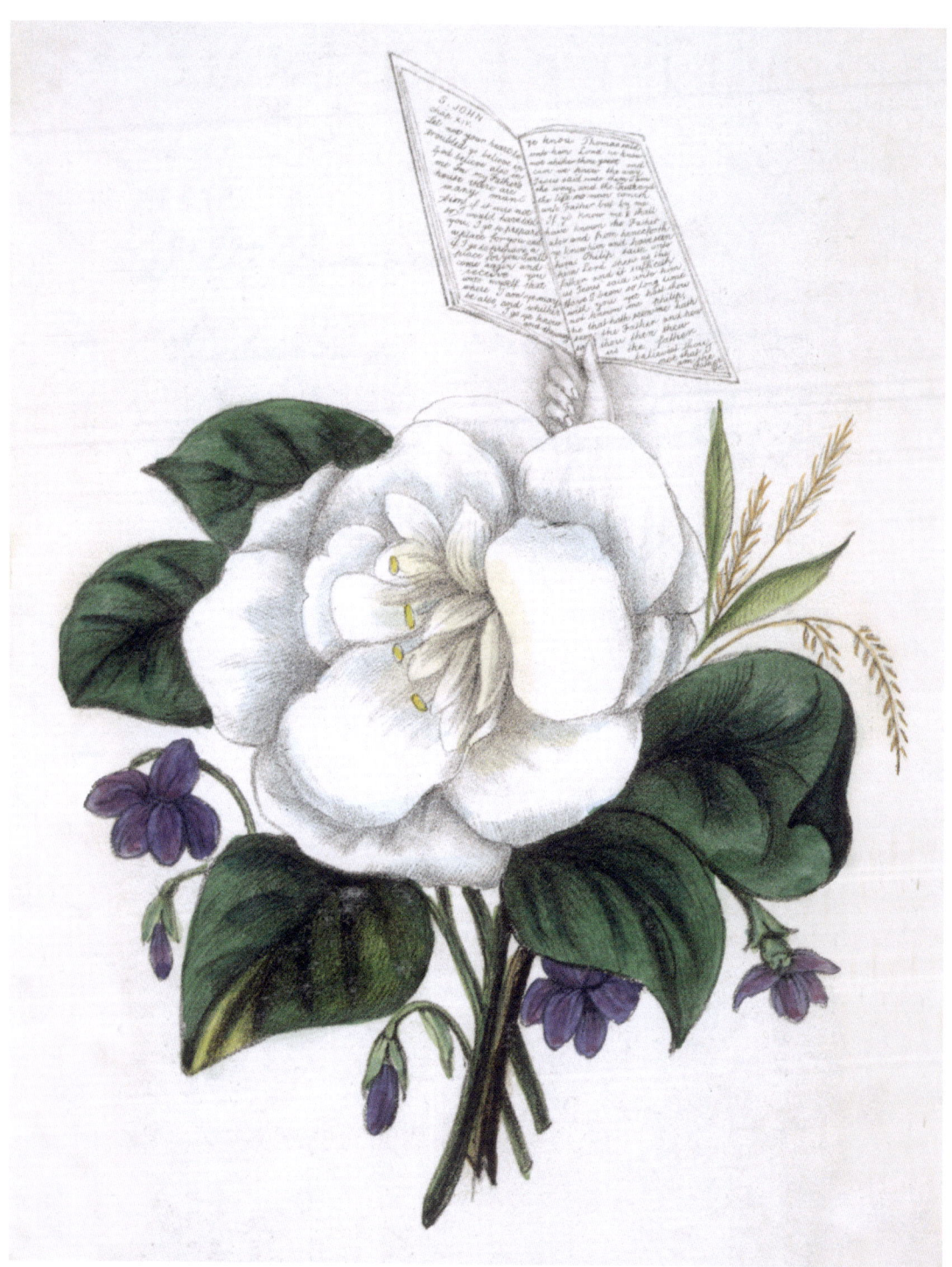

◄ Untitled

Mrs E. J. French, 1861, reproduced in *Spiritualism in America* (Coleman, 2018).

New York medium Mrs E. J. French (c.1860) specialised in psychic painting and, inspired by the spirits, claimed to create this drawing in 11 seconds. Typically her imagery took the form of flowers, birds or insects and were produced in a curtained-off dark cabinet under a small table, with prepared pencils, brushes and paints. The speed of her artistry was said to have been remarkable, producing works in less than 15 seconds.

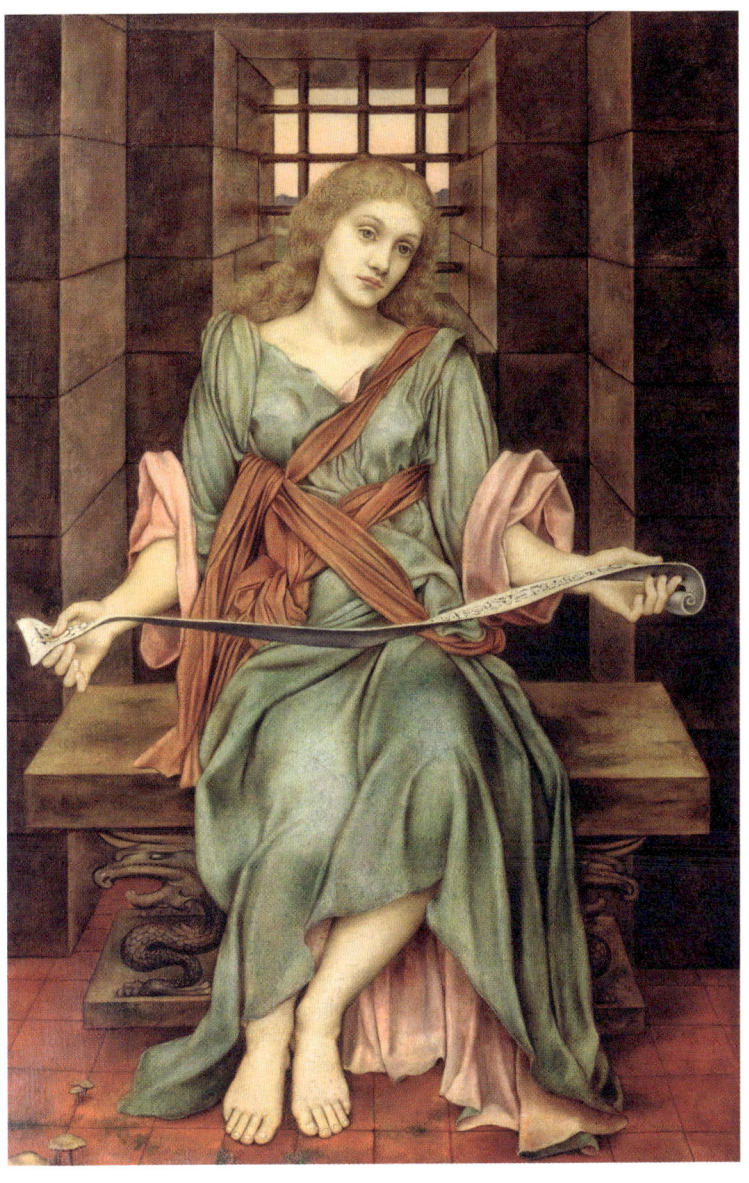

▲ The Soul's Prison House

Evelyn De Morgan, 1888, oil on canvas.

English artist and suffragette, Evelyn De Morgan (1855–1919) painted richly coloured canvases inhabited by beautifully draped female figures – exploring mythological and allegorical themes, while delivering messages of feminism and spirituality. *The Soul's Prison House* echoes the painter's belief that the body is merely an earthly shell, which the spirit longs to cast off in death.

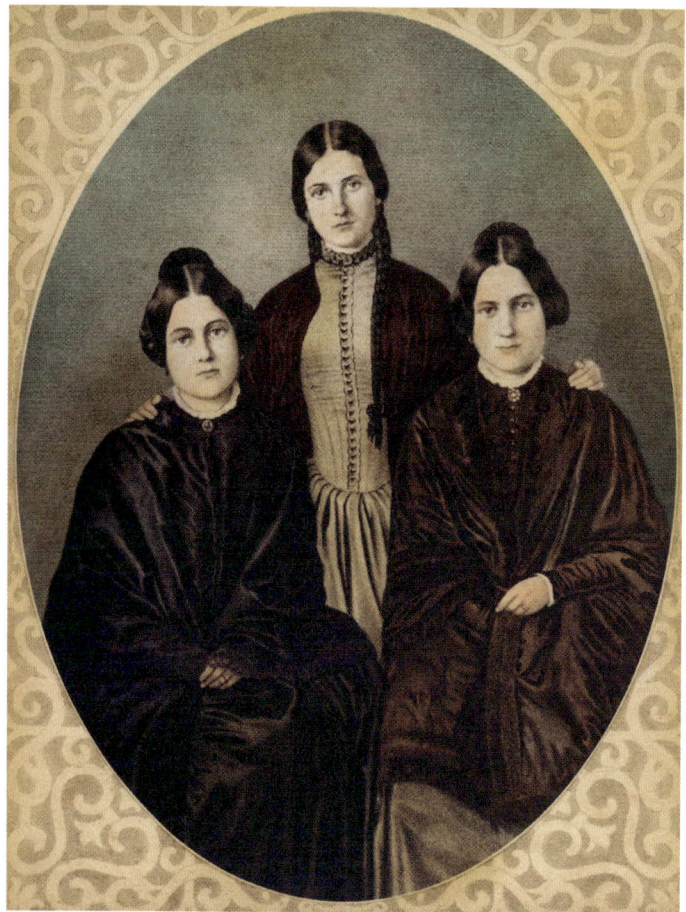

▶ **Photograph
of a Thought**
Charles Lacey,
c.1894, albumen
and gelatin silver print.

Spiritualists and psychics
used the new medium of
photography to produce
such images that they
claimed showed the effect,
or presence, of human
thoughts, or spirits. Pictured
here is a 'Thoughtograph',
or psychic photograph,
produced by British
Spiritualist Charles Lacey,
with the ghostly figure of a
human visible in the centre.

▲ **The Fox Sisters**
19th century, print taken from a portrait photo.

It's funny, and fascinating to ponder that one of the most important
religious movements of the 19th century began with two sisters scheming
to frighten their mother. Younger Fox sisters, Maggie (1833–1893)
and Kate (1837–1892), used 'rappings' to convince their family
and neighbours that they were communicating with spirits. News of
the unearthly communications quickly spread, and the sisters, both
alleging to possess mediumistic powers, gained popularity in public
and Spiritualist circles. Suddenly, others began to discover their own
mystical powers, and mediums and séances became fashionable. The
Fox Sisters continued to perform séances until the late 1800s when
non-believers forced them to confess it was all a fraud. Despite their
admissions, the Spiritualism movement continued to grow in popularity.

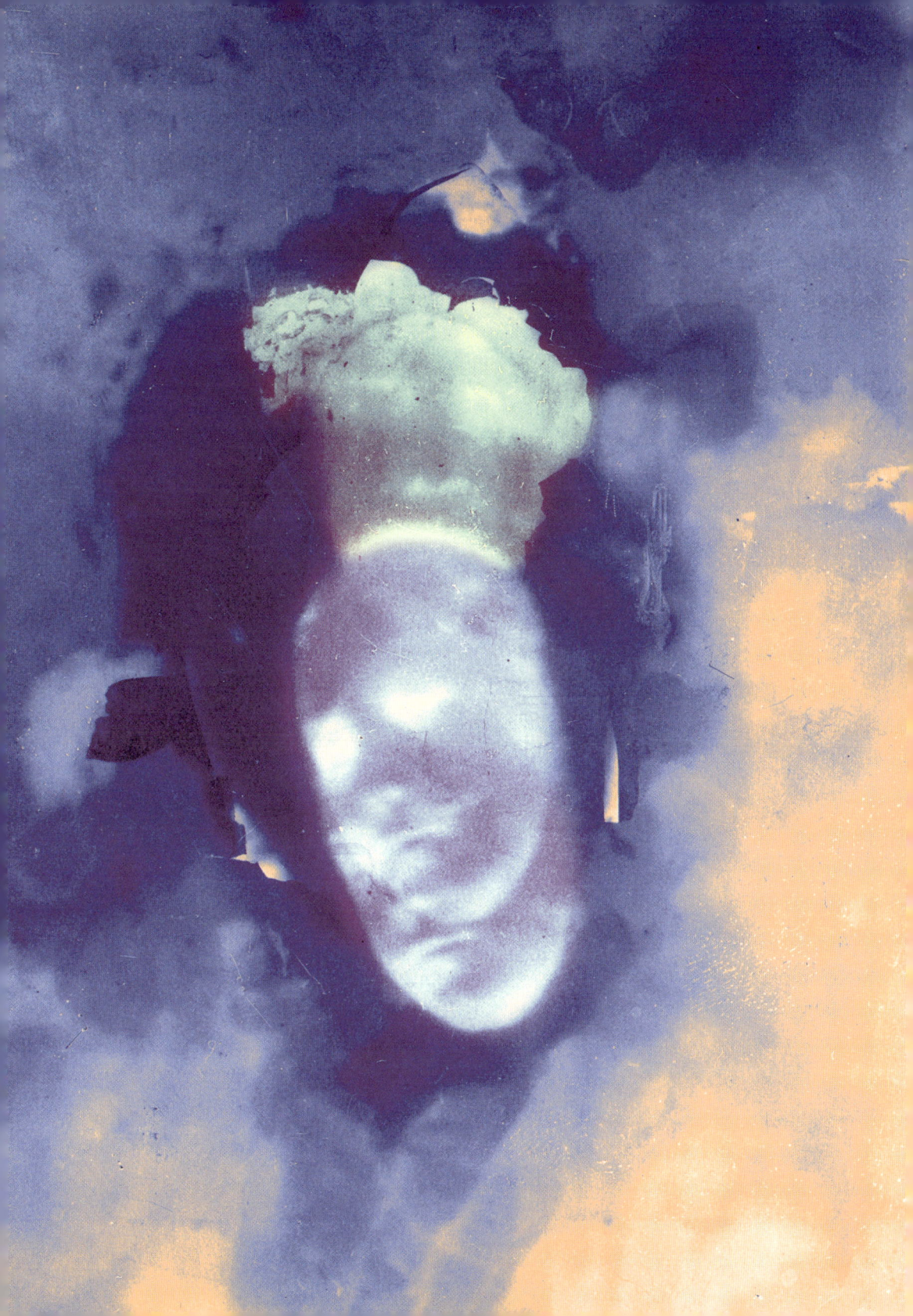

XI

EMBLEMS OF INSIGHT AND DIVINE INSPIRATION

Divination in the Arts

ONE OF THE OLDEST FORMS of magic, and certainly the most widely practised, divination is the attempt to gain insight into questions or situations, discover hidden knowledge, or foresee future events, typically by the interpretation of omens or by the aid of supernatural powers. Many sources seek to make a distinction between divination and fortune-telling, though in principle (if not in practice) it can be argued that they are nearly identical in scope. The difference is that the term 'divination' is used for predictions considered part of a religious ritual, invoking deities or spirits, while 'fortune-telling' implies a less serious, informal, everyday setting where a belief in the occult workings behind the prediction carries less importance than the concept of empowering an individual to know their options. But whether one is consulting an oracle through whom a certain God or Goddess is thought to speak, or visiting a local tarot reader who instinctively intuits the meaning of the cards laid out before them, aren't both prophets, externally or internally, tapping into the divine? After all, the word 'divination' means 'to be divinely inspired'. For the purpose of this chapter, this is how I have chosen to interpret and align these divergent opinions.

We have been obsessed with predicting the future for as long as humankind has walked the earth; there is archaeological evidence, writes Paul O'Brien, that 'a need to know and deep spiritual seeking are universal human traits, and that some

form of divination has been used since the earliest times, to support this quest'. Many cultures – including Chinese, Mayan, Mesopotamian and Indian – and people – from medieval kings to modern presidents – have looked upwards to the heavens, not only for purposes of telling time and understanding the seasons, but also for portents and predictions, or to decipher occurrences owing to divine action. Astrology was one of the first sophisticated forms of divination, dating back to Ancient Mesopotamian times, and we still consult our horoscopes in the newspaper or on the internet today. Other cultures have looked inwards, such as the Australian aborigines with their dreamtime, or have used entheogenic plants for vision quests, such as the Mazatec Indians of Mexico. Across the globe, throughout history, every culture has tried to make sense of their world through a variety of methods designed to tap into the unknown and unseen, in order to gain prophetic insight and learn what awaits them.

Particular divination methods vary by culture and religion. The Egyptians, Druids and Hebrews used scrying, or the practice of gazing into a reflective surface, in the hope of detecting significant messages or visions. The Romans practised augury (interpreting the flight of birds) and haruspicy (inspecting the entrails of sacrificed animals), while the Greeks had oracles who spoke for the gods. The biblical prophets used various forms of divination in reading the future: in the Hebrew Old Testament, Joseph's household

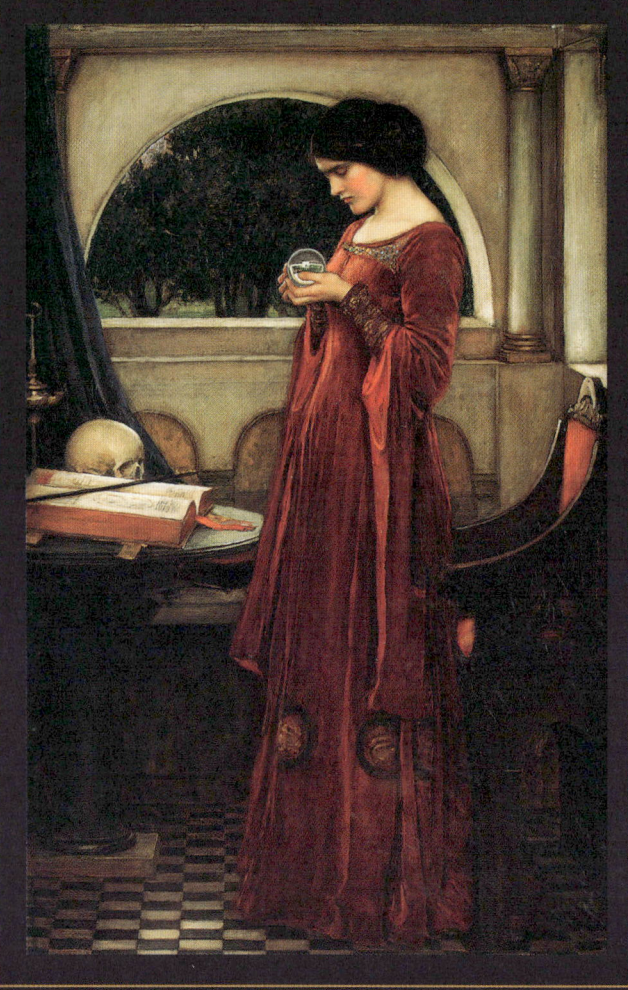

▶ **The Fortune Teller**
Jehan Georges Vibert, late
19th century, oil on canvas.

Jehan Georges Vibert or Jean
Georges Vibert (1840–1902)
created *The Fortune Teller* in the
style of Academic art, influenced by
the standards of the French style
of true-to-life, but high-minded,
realist painting and sculpture.
There is a strong emphasis on the
intellectual element, combined
with a fixed set of aesthetics.

▲ **The Crystal Ball**
John William Waterhouse, 1902, oil on canvas.

John William Waterhouse (1849–1917) paints a young woman
peering into a crystal ball, giving no hint as to what she might be
seeing and thinking. It is perhaps up to the viewer to imagine what
fate has in store for her. Crystal balls such as the one depicted here
have been used by numerous cultures over the centuries for scrying,
the practice of gazing into a translucent surface with the intention of
seeing images that can then be interpreted at the scryer's discretion.

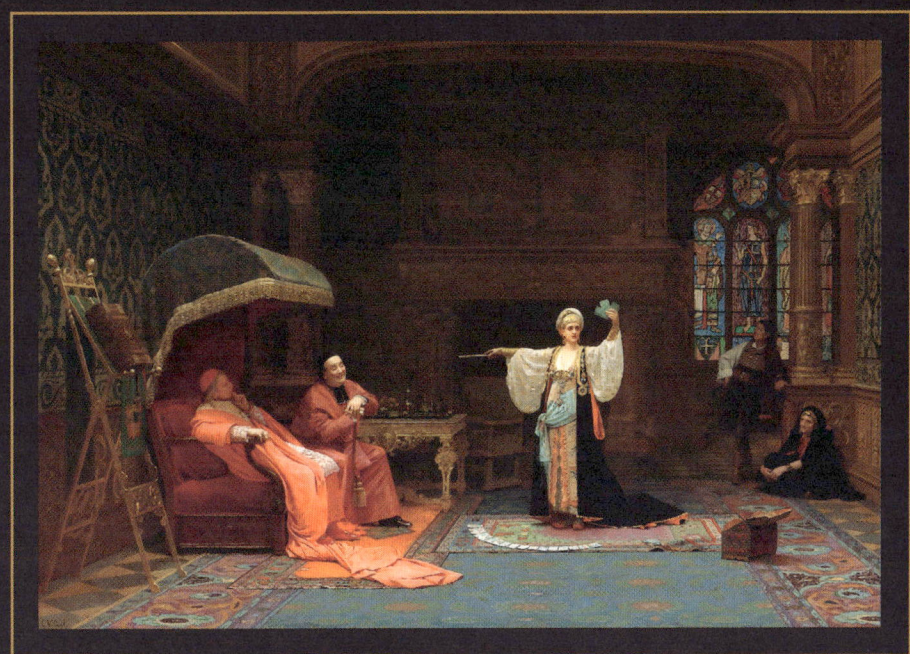

manager refers to a silver drinking cup '. . . in which my lord drinketh and whereby indeed he devineth'; in the New Testament, the magi read the signs in the heavens to find the Christ child. Grain, sand and seeds were tossed into fields in the Middle Ages to glean the patterns in which they fell in order to divine the year's crops. Chinese Taoists read patterns on tortoise shells, which evolved into the hexagrams of the I Ching, and another ancient Chinese divinatory practice still used today is feng shui or geomancy, which concerns spatial arrangement and orientation in relation to the flow of energy. African tribes used bones in divination rituals for hundreds of thousands of years, while Germanic tribes consulted the runestones.

The emblems and iconography of divinatory practices – the glint of the crystal ball or black scrying mirror, the primal symbolism of the runes, the intriguing archetypes of the tarot – conjure evocative associations for artists, even today, when our need for such things is less

a superstitious mediation of the future than a contemporary desire to quell uncertainty. And there is much uncertainty in the world today. The oracular exemplifications associated with divination are numerous and varied and contribute to a rich source of inspiration for artists interested in creating prophetic portraits, sibylline sculptures, or moments of divine insight captured on canvas. Whether we look to Pre-Raphaelite painter John William Waterhouse's somewhat straightforward work, *The Crystal Ball*, wherein a classically beautiful woman contemplates her destiny with the help of the crystal ball; or Leonora Carrington's elusive *Casting the Runes*, in which two hooded female figures seem to engage in an ancient ritual, perhaps to divine the future of the golden creature in their care; or we engage with Surrealist artist Salvador Dalí's kitschy enchantment of a tarot deck, the magic and promise of divinatory practices and of learning what fate has in store for us remains, even in our modern era, too much of a temptation to resist.

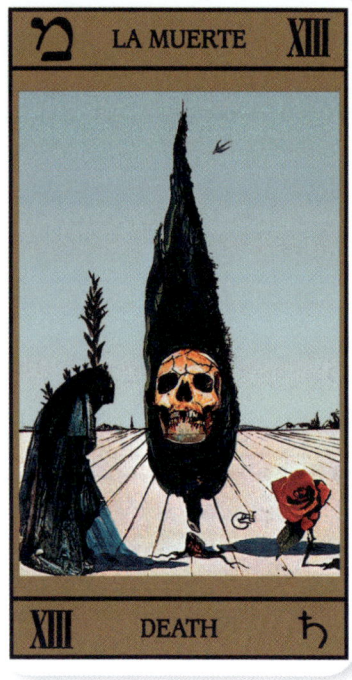

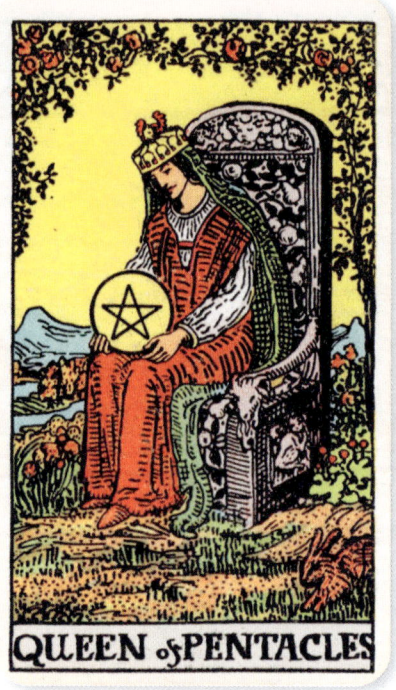

▲ The Death Card
Salvador Dalí, early 1970s, from
the Salvador Dalí tarot deck.

Surrealism meets Symbolism in Salvador
Dalí's (1904–1989) tarot deck, in which
Dalí poses as the Magician and his wife
Gala becomes the Empress. It was initially
undertaken by Dalí for the film *Live and
Let Die*. It did not appear in the movie, the
deck was eventually completed in 1984.

▲ Queen of Pentacles
A. E. White and Pamela Colman Smith, c.1909,
from the Rider-Waite-Smith tarot deck.

Pamela Colman Smith (1878–1951) was a British artist,
illustrator, writer and occultist. In 1909 her involvement with
the Order of the Golden Dawn led to a commission from
A. E. Waite to create a tarot deck. She was, he wrote, 'a most
imaginative and abnormally psychic artist'. As universal and
beloved as the images on the cards have become, Colman
Smith received little recognition and outrageously, until recent
years, her name was left off most editions of the deck.

▶ Tea Leaf Reading
Gina Litherland,
2014, oil on wood.

Contemporary artist Gina Litherland's (b.1955) layered technique of
working gives way to revelatory results, with worlds often emerging out of
nowhere. In *Tea Leaf Reading*, two women are engaging in a speculative
bit of tasseography, a divination method that interprets patterns in
tea leaves, while some animal companions look on supportively.

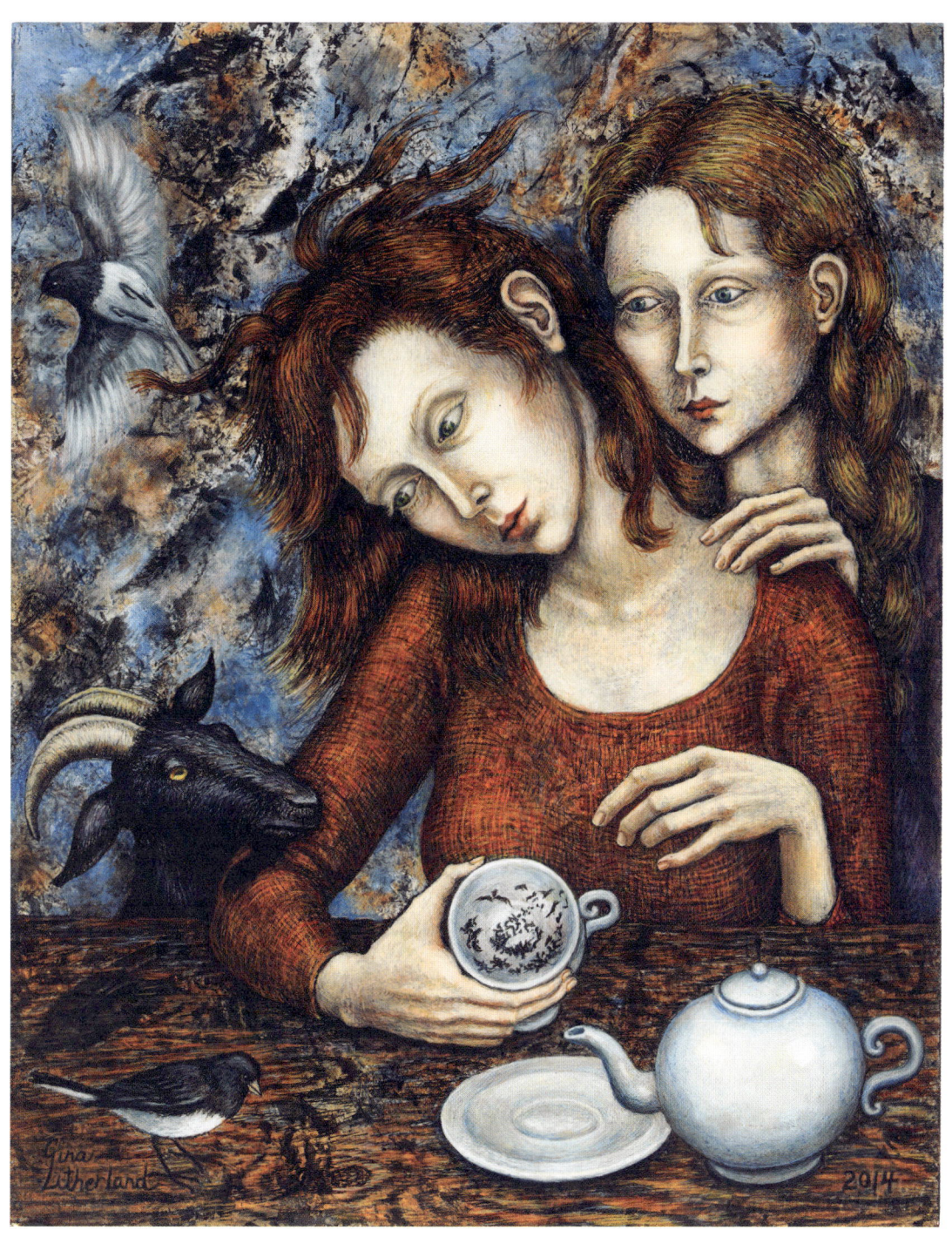

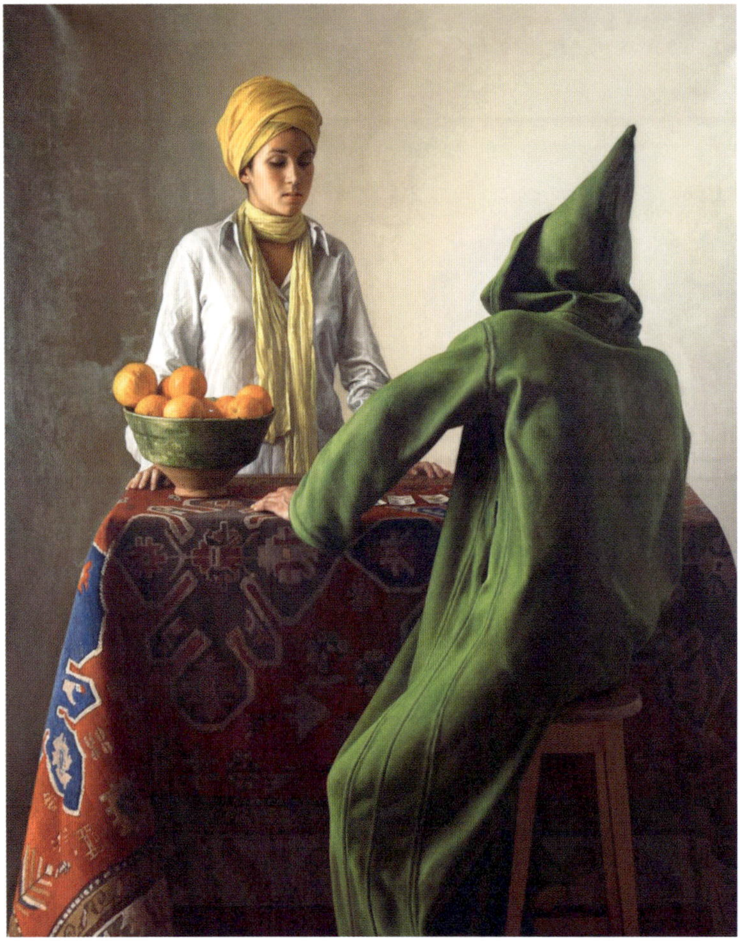

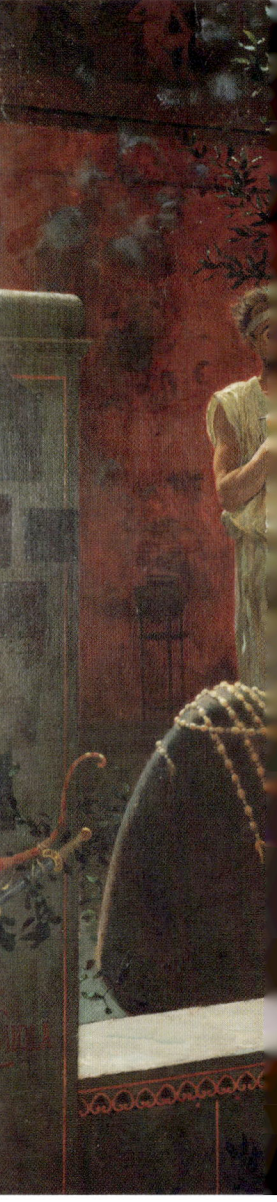

▲ The fortune-teller
Claudio Bravo, 1981.

Claudio Bravo (1936–2011) was a celebrated Chilean painter,
noted for his hyperrealist still lifes and figurative paintings. Equally
representational of a uniquely Chilean convention as it is of art
historical reference, Bravo's work was influenced by Baroque and
Surrealist styles. Despite receiving no formal artistic training, he would
go on to achieve international recognition. In *The Fortune Teller*, a
robed figure has their back to the viewer, ostensibly reading the cards
for the individual facing us. It's interesting that we can see neither
the reader's face, nor the details of the cards. Perhaps the hooded
stranger is the one receiving the reading? Mysteries abound in what
would at first glance appear to be a straightforward work of art.

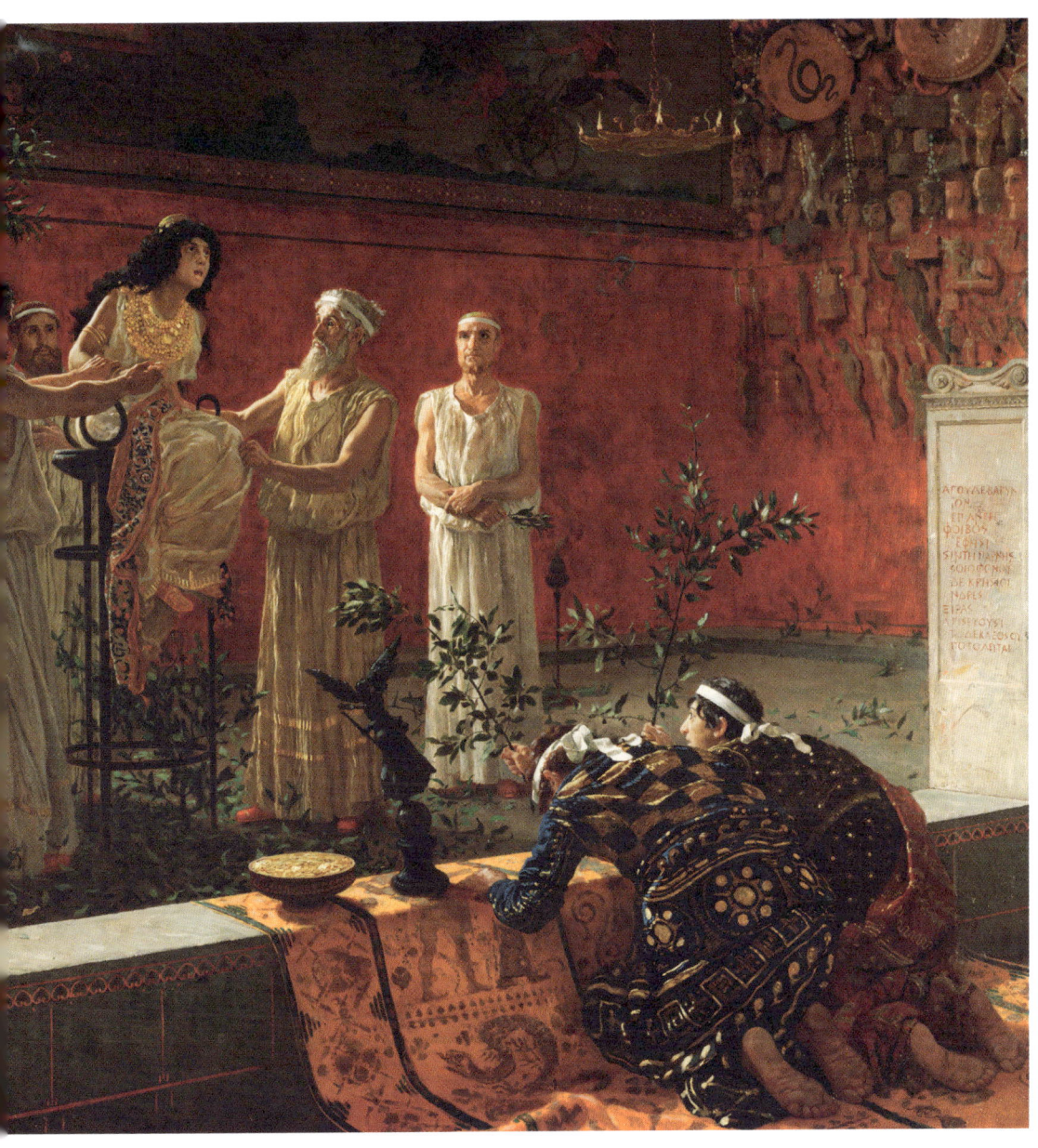

▲ **The Oracle,**
Camillo Miola, 1880,
oil on canvas.

Camillo Miola (1840–1919) was an Italian painter who often painting exotic Neo-Pompeian and Orientalist subjects. In *The Oracle* we see *The Pythia* – a virgin from the local village selected in ceremonies that established her as the god Apollo's choice – sitting atop the sacred tripod as the Delphic oracle. The ancient Greeks considered the Delphic oracle the final authority on almost any matter, regardless of the details.

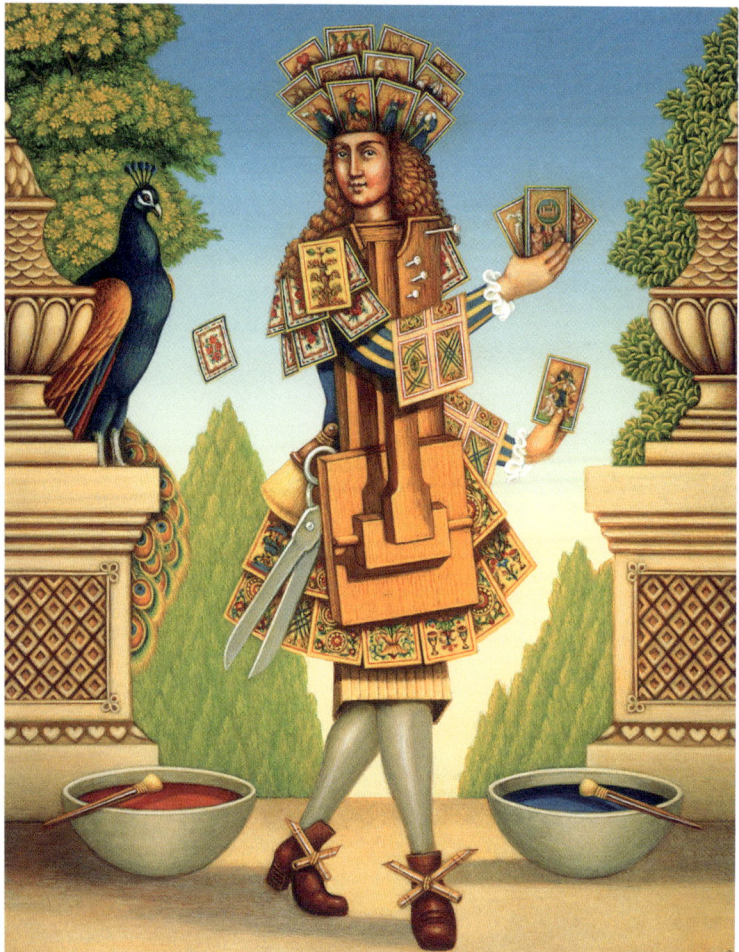

▶ **The Fortune-Teller**
Jean Metzinger 1915,
oil on canvas.

Jean Dominique Antony
Metzinger (1883–1956) was
a French painter, theorist,
writer and prominent member
of the French avant-garde.
Metzinger was best known
for Cubist paintings which
combined Divisionist
techniques with modeled
forms and multiple angles.
A consequential theorist,
Metzinger passionately
argued against traditional
approaches in art and the
need for portraying multiple
perspectives to better
understand reality and time
in a static picture. In *The
Fortune-Teller*, we await
our fate under a frank and
faceted gaze as destiny is
doled out on the table in
the form of playing cards.

▲ **Cartomancy**
Frances Broomfield,
2004.

Frances Broomfield (b.1951) creates work that
has been described as 'sophisticated naive' and
whose imaginative art is tinged with mystery,
humour and eccentricity. This whimsical painting
brims with bold colours and a jaunty fellow
whose beckoning gaze (and entire outfit, really)
hints at unlimited possibilities just within reach.

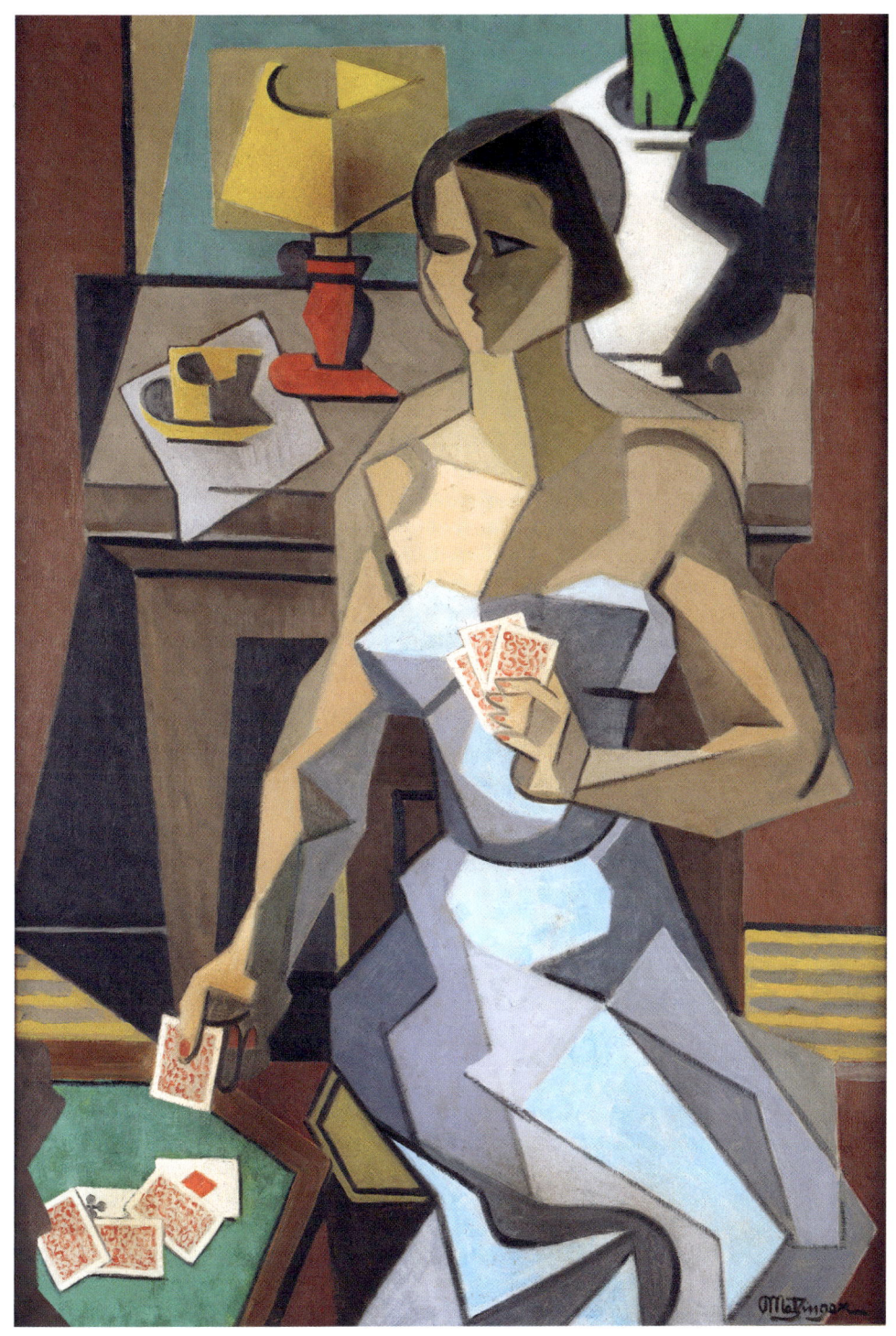

EMBLEMS OF INSIGHT AND DIVINE INSPIRATION

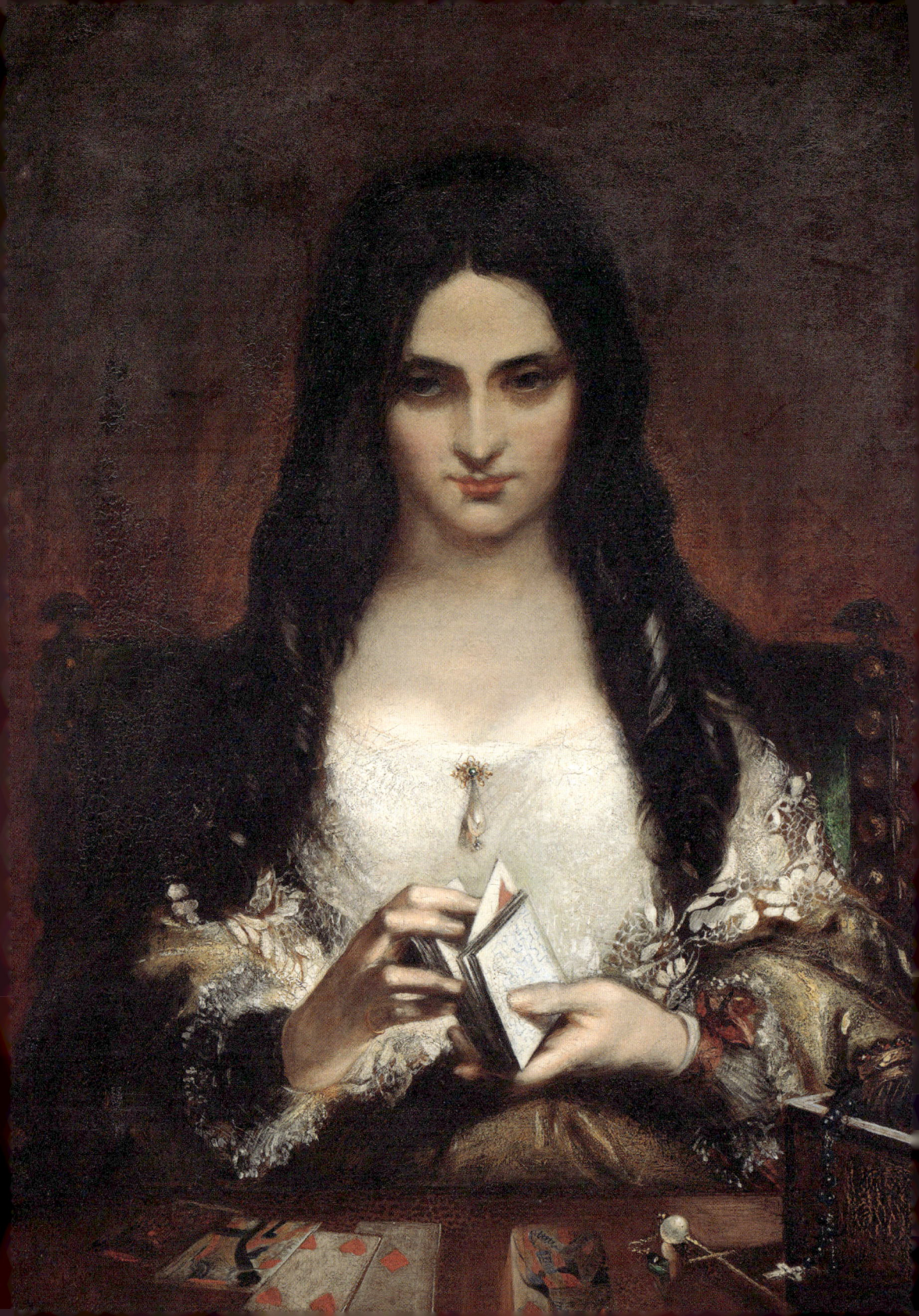

◄ The Wish
Theodor von Holst.
1840, oil on canvas.

The London-born painter
Theodor von Holst
(1810–1844) is said to
occupy a unique position
in the history of British
Romantic art, between his
eccentric master Henry
Fuseli (1741–1825) and
his most important admirer
Dante Gabriel Rossetti
(1828–1882). Von Holst's
painting *The Wish* is a
moodily and exquisite
piece depicting fortune
teller as femme fatale. It
was the inspiration for
Dante Gabriel Rossetti's
poem 'The Card Dealer'.

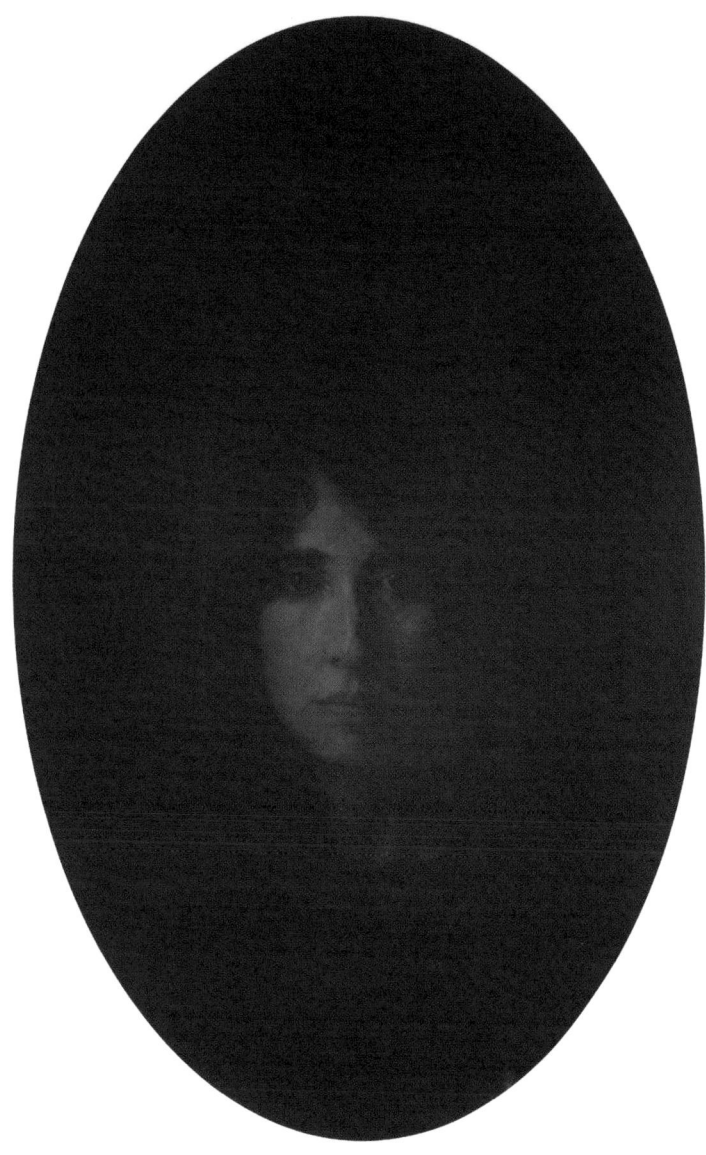

▲ Scrying Mirrors
– Renata
Paul Benney, 2014,
oil on board.

Paul Benney (b.1959) is a British artist born in London, England. In
his works Benney explores the personal and mystical themes that
have occupied him throughout his career, engaging with a wide range
of media. His widely exhibited, dark, highly personal and symbolic
paintings explore the 'shadowlands of the soul', examples of which
have been acquired by the Metropolitan Museum of Art, New York.

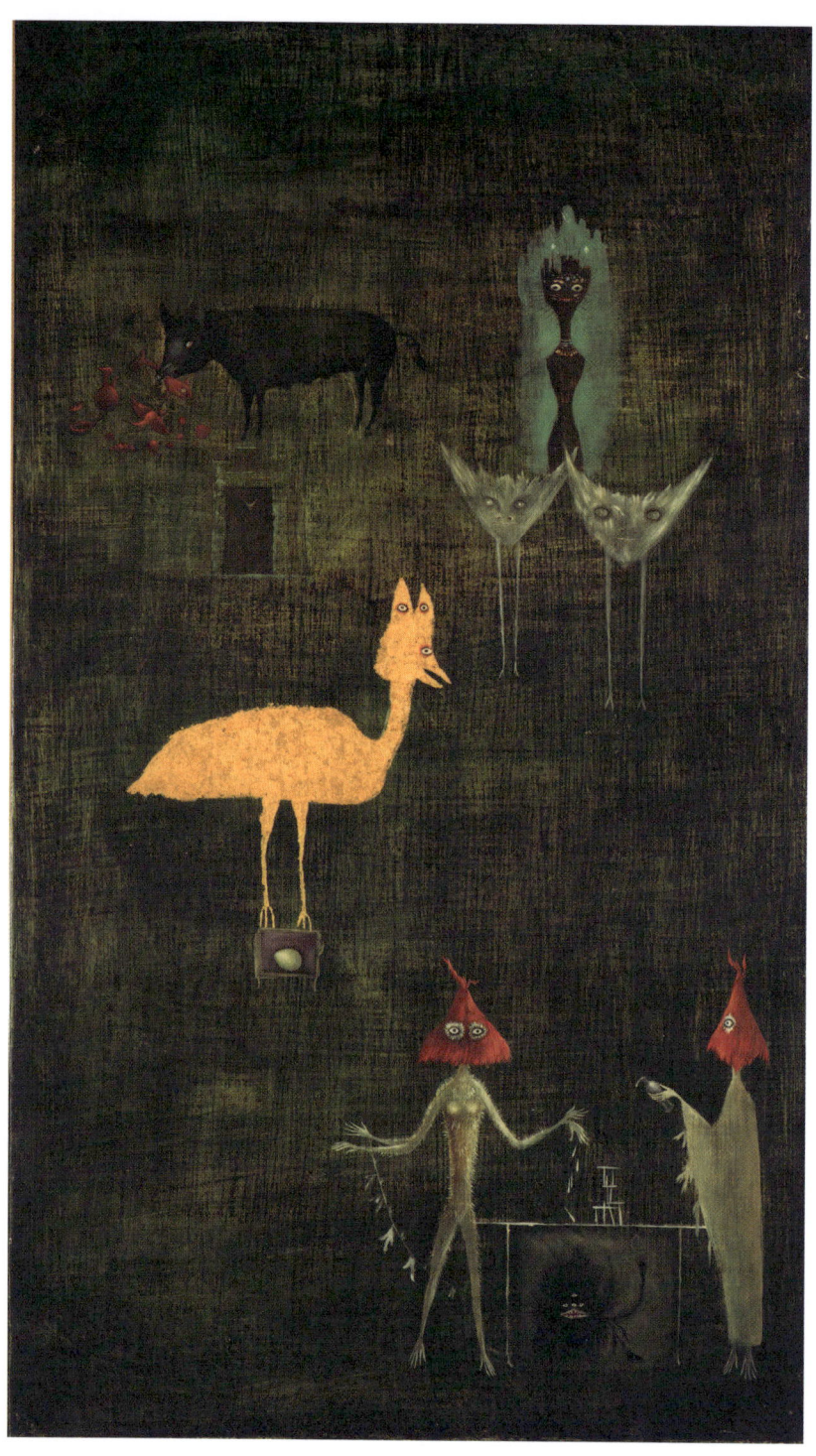

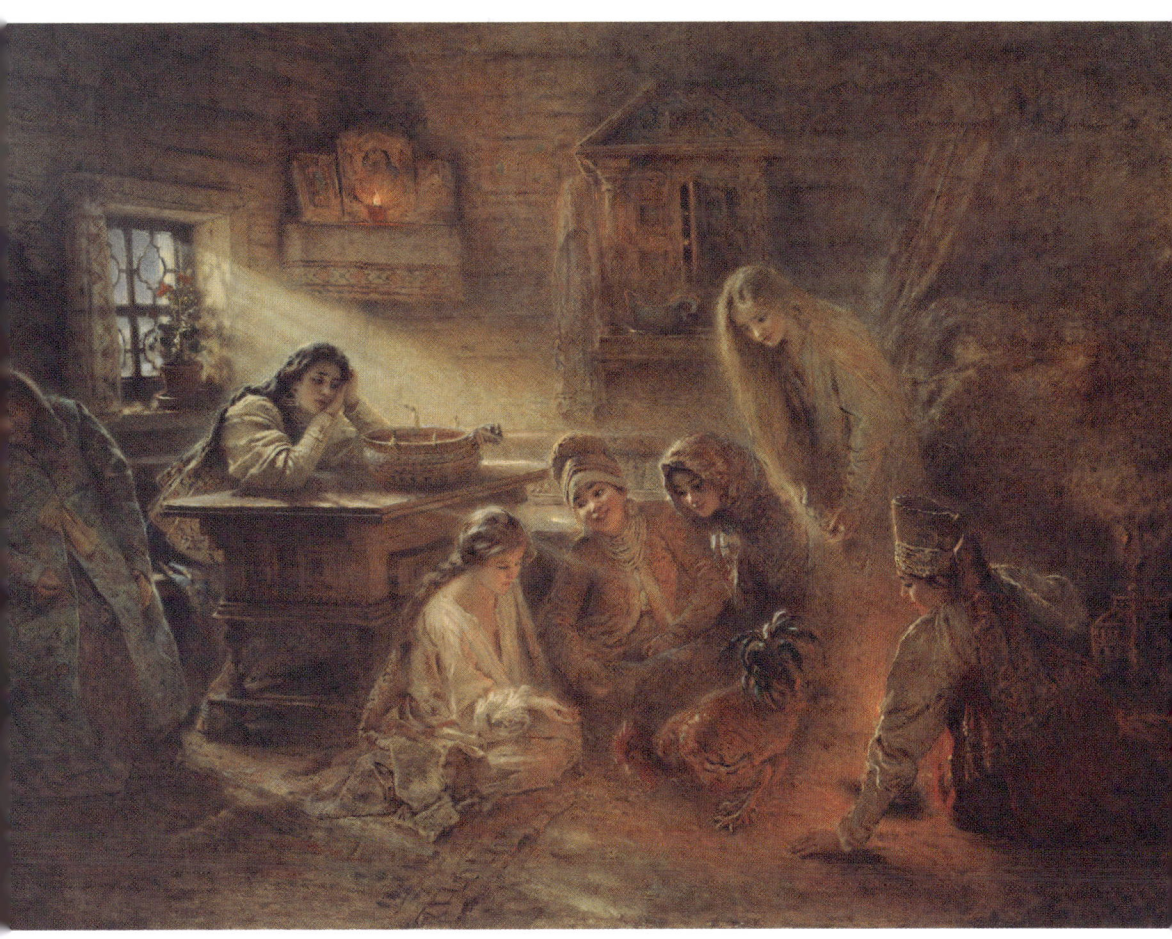

▲ Christmastide Divination
Konstantin Makovsky, c.1905, oil on canvas.

Konstantin Yegorovich Makovsky (1839–1915) was an influential Russian painter, affiliated with the Peredvizhniki (Wanderers) – a cooperative of Russian realist artists. In *Christmastide Divination* we are privy to a moonlit holiday scene of Russian folk divination during Eastern Orthodox Christmastide. In a rural log home, women are gathered for a bout of alectryomancy, a form of divination in which the diviner observes a bird pecking at grain that the diviner has scattered on the ground.

◄ Casting the Runes
Leonora Carrington, 1951, mixed oil, tempera and gold leaf on three-ply.

Leonora Carrington (1917–2011) settled in Mexico in 1943, joining a group of fellow Surrealist émigrés. Informed by a broad spectrum of inspiration ranging from ancient history and Celtic mythology, to Mexican healing traditions, her otherworldly paintings are often observed to have elusive meanings. In *Casting the Runes*, two hooded female figures seem to engage in an ancient ritual involving runes, perhaps to divine the future of the golden bird-like creature in their care.

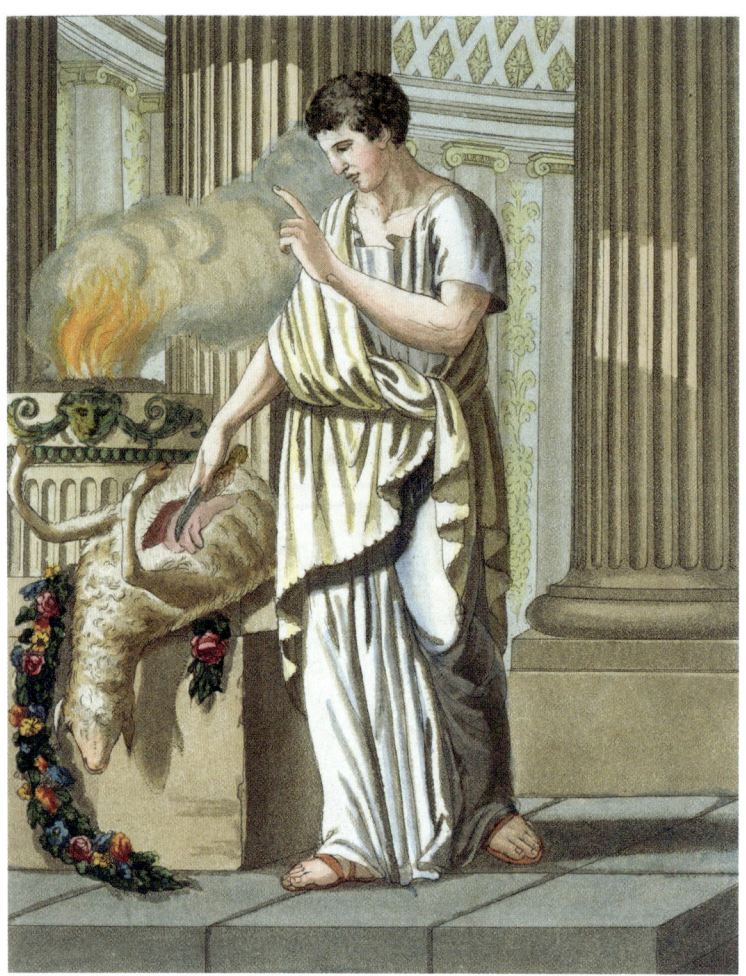

▲ Aruspice
Jacques Grasset de
Saint-Sauveur, from
***L'Antique Rome* (1796).**

In this deceptive illustration from Jacques
Grasset de Saint-Sauveur's (1757–1810)
1796 book on historical and picturesque
ancient Rome and Roman people, we can
observe the practice of haruspicy – in
which the bowels of an animal sacrifice
were inspected as a form of divination.

▼ Dregs in the cup
William Sidney Mount, 1838.

William Sidney Mount (1807–1868) was an American painter best known for his genre paintings, although he also painted landscapes and portraits. In this light-hearted scene of tasseomancy (divination by reading tea leaves), an older woman gazes bemusedly into a dainty teacup while the younger struggles with that distinctive, 'please tell me! No, I don't want to know!' look upon her face.

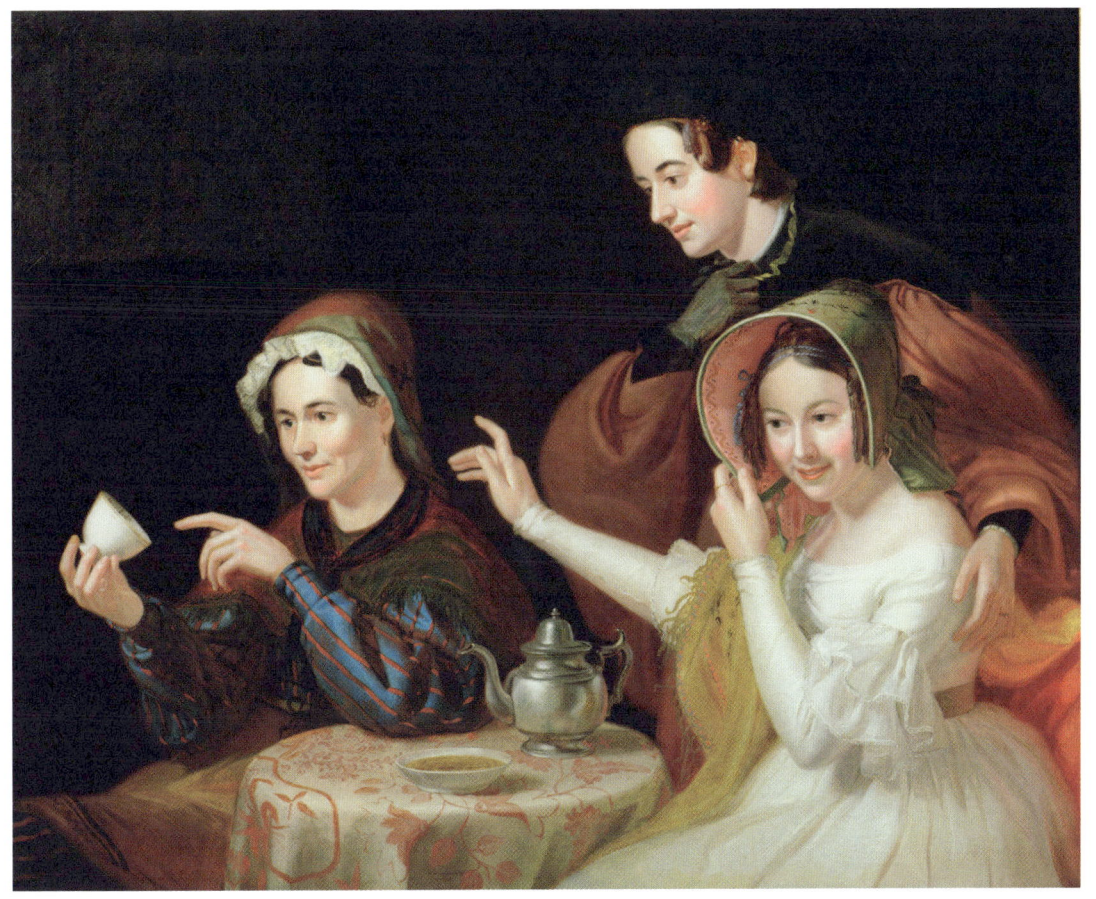

XII

CEREMONIAL MAGIC

Invoking the Artistic Spirit

I N THE WESTERN OCCULT TRADITION, there is a distinction between 'ceremonial magic' (or 'high magic'), which seeks to bring about change through elaborate and complex ceremony and rituals, and often involves the invoking and control of spirits and other entities, and 'natural magic', which concerns itself with nature and natural forces directly, such as astrology and alchemy. According to Manly P. Hall's *The Secret Teachings of All Ages*, those who practised ceremonial magic 'did so largely with the hope of securing from the invisible worlds either rare knowledge or supernatural power'. And what learned scholar could resist the heady allure of power?

A term coined in relation to sixteenth-century Renaissance magic, ceremonial magic referred to practices described in various medieval and Renaissance grimoires. A 1569 translation of Heinrich Cornelius Agrippa's *De incertitudine et vanitate scientiarum* (On the Uncertainty and Vanity of the Arts and Sciences) refers to '…The partes of ceremonial Magicke be Geocie, and Theurgie' (goetia and theurgy). This mention was the first recorded use of the term ceremonial magic, although the practice had existed for at least a century or two before, and in collections such as that of Johannes Hartlieb, a physician of late medieval Bavaria who had written of the 'seven artes magicae' in 1456; these seven prohibited disciplines included practices ranging from palm-reading to black magic.

Various European occultists studied and practised many of the rituals and ceremonies still being used today. Late-eighteenth-century Englishman Francis Barrett studied metaphysics, the Kabbalah, natural occult philosophy and alchemy. His work, *The Magus*, is a compendium of esoteric knowledge and ceremonial magic that was heavily influenced by Agrippa's writings and remains a rare and highly sought-after tome. French occultist Alphonse Louis Constant, perhaps better known by his pseudonym Éliphas Lévi, lived in the 1800s and developed an interest in both the Kabbalah and magic, as part of a group of radicals who believed that 'magic and the occult were essentially a more advanced form of socialism'. He wrote a number of works on ceremonial magic, as well as books on Spiritualism and the secrets of the occult. Lévi's take on magic became a great success, especially after his death. He had a profound impact on the magic of the Hermetic Order of the Golden Dawn and, later, English author and occultist, Aleister Crowley. It was, to a great extent, through this impact that Lévi is remembered as one of the 'key founders' of the twentieth-century revival of magic.

The practice of ceremonial magic frequently requires tools made or explicitly consecrated for these uses, and which are necessary for a specific ritual or series of rituals. In *Magick (Book 4), Part II*, Aleister Crowley lists the representative tools required as: a circle outlined on the ground inscribed with the names of God; an altar; a

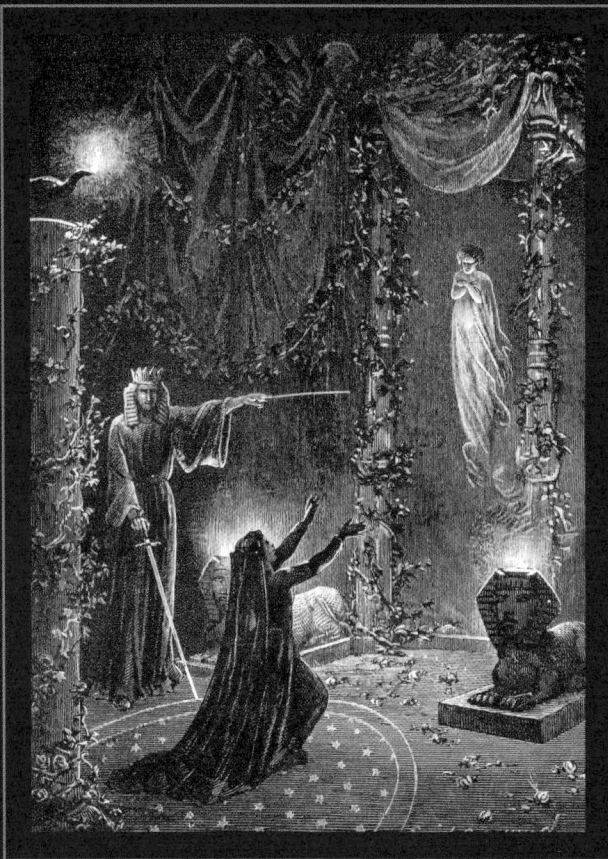

◀ **Summoning the Beloved Dead**
Émile Bayard, from *Histoire de la magie* (Paul Christian, 1870).

Paul Christian's (1811–1877) study of occult history encompasses subjects ranging from the mysteries of the pyramids and the ancient oracles, to magic from the Christian era and end of the Middle Ages. *Summoning the Beloved Dead* is one of many exquisite images by French artist Emile Bayard (1837–1891) which illustrate this arcane tome.

wand, cup, sword and pentacle. On the altar there should be a vial of oil to represent the practitioner's aspiration, and for consecrating items to their intent. The magician has nearby a scourge, dagger and chain intended to keep his intentions pure. Additionally, an oil lamp, book of conjurations, and bell are needed, as well as a crown to affirm divinity, a robe to symbolise silence, and a lamen (pendant or breastplate) to declare the work. Finally, the book of conjurations provides a magical record of the rites. These books, of course, were no invention of Crowley's; books of magic record, or grimoires, are accounts of magical experiments and philosophical musings, giving instructions for invoking angels or demons, performing divination and gaining magical powers, and have circulated throughout Europe since the Middle Ages.

Popularised again by the Hermetic Order of the Golden Dawn, ceremonial magic as we know it today draws on various grimoires and such schools of philosophical and occult thought as Hermetic Qabalah and the Enochian system of angelic magic of John Dee and Edward Kelley, who claimed that their information, including the revealed Enochian language, was delivered to them directly by various angels.

From a visual and artistic perspective, these ceremonies and rituals must certainly conjure a fanciful spectacle, and between the imagery of magicians in their vestments and mystical paraphernalia, the arcane ciphers, symbols and seals that comprise their spell work, and the exultant (or terrifying) host of angelic and demonic visitations they coax forth from places divine or infernal, our notions of the practices and processes involved in traditional ceremonial magic provide no lack of inspiration for the artist's palette. From woodcut art depicting gleefully cavorting demons, to shadowy illustrations of raising one's beloved from the dead; from the dizzying array of cryptic symbology copied from the brittle pages of dusty grimoires, to the present-day interpretations of ritual and ceremony by the hand of contemporary artists viewing these practices through an abstract lens, ceremonial magic, with its murky promises of knowledge and power untold, hold the modern imagination no less spellbound than it did in years long past.

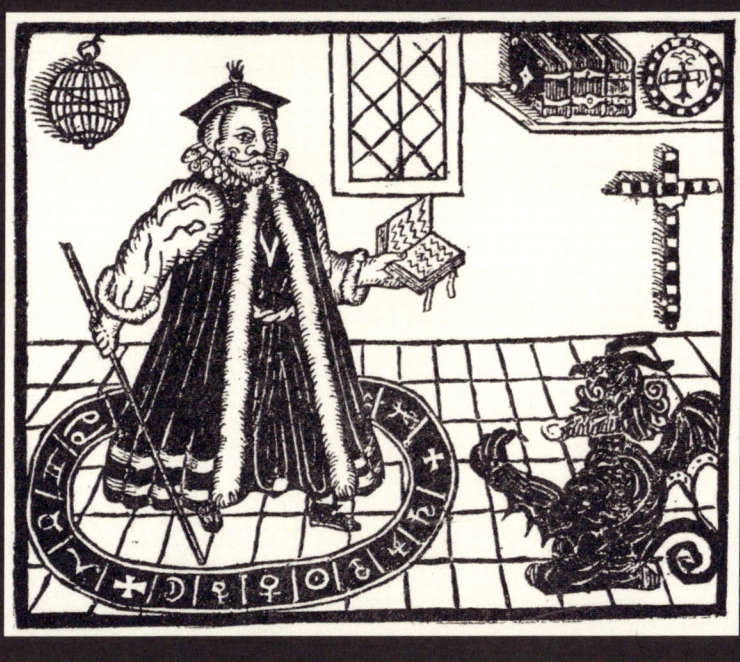

▶ **Faust and Mephistopheles**
From *The Tragicall Historie of the Life and Death of Doctor Faustus*, (Christopher Marlowe, 1631 ed.), woodcut.

Faustus, the theologian who became interested in black magic, is depicted in the centre of his magic circle, at the moment when his conjurations have summoned the diabolical Mephistopheles.

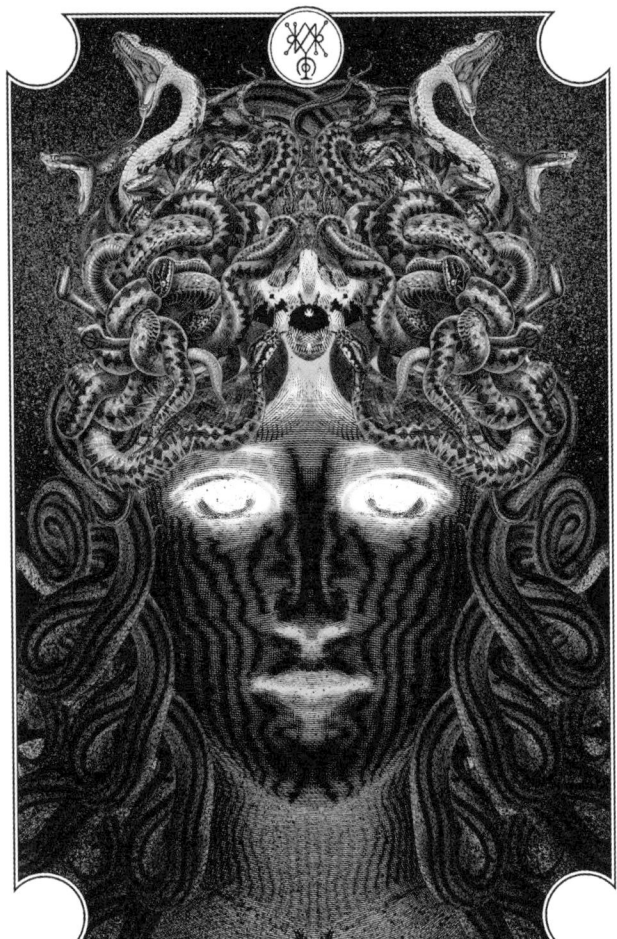

▶ **Bachelor machine, from behind and below (Guyotat version)**
Elijah Burgher, 2013, colour pencil on paper.

Chicago-based artist Elijah Burgher's (b.1978) precisely detailed drawings and large drop-cloth paintings sit at 'the intersections of representation and language, imaginary and real worlds,' and indoctrinate viewers into a mystical cult of queer sexual energies. In his figurative and abstract drawings. paintings and prints of sigils, Burgher utilises ideas from magic and the occult to address sexuality, sub-cultural formation and the history of abstraction.

▲ **Abyzou**
John Coulthart,
From *The Demons of King Solomon* (JournalStone, 2017).

John Coulthart (b.1962) is a British illustrator, graphic designer and writer who works with various styles and media in his singular, chimeric aesthetic and is known for his striking and complex 'genre-defying' artistry. Abyzou is the name of a female demon blamed for miscarriages and infant mortality and was said to be motivated by envy, as she herself was infertile.

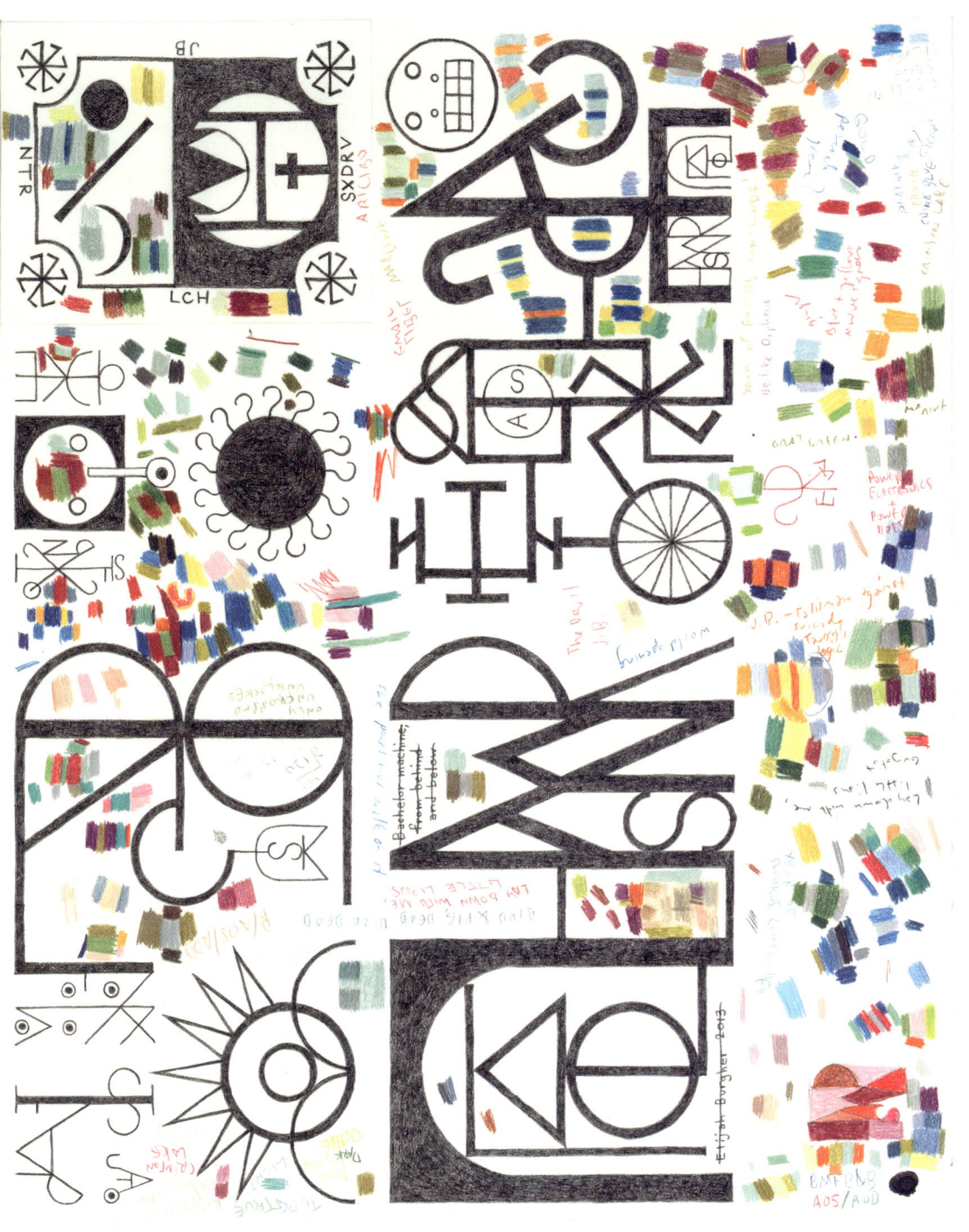

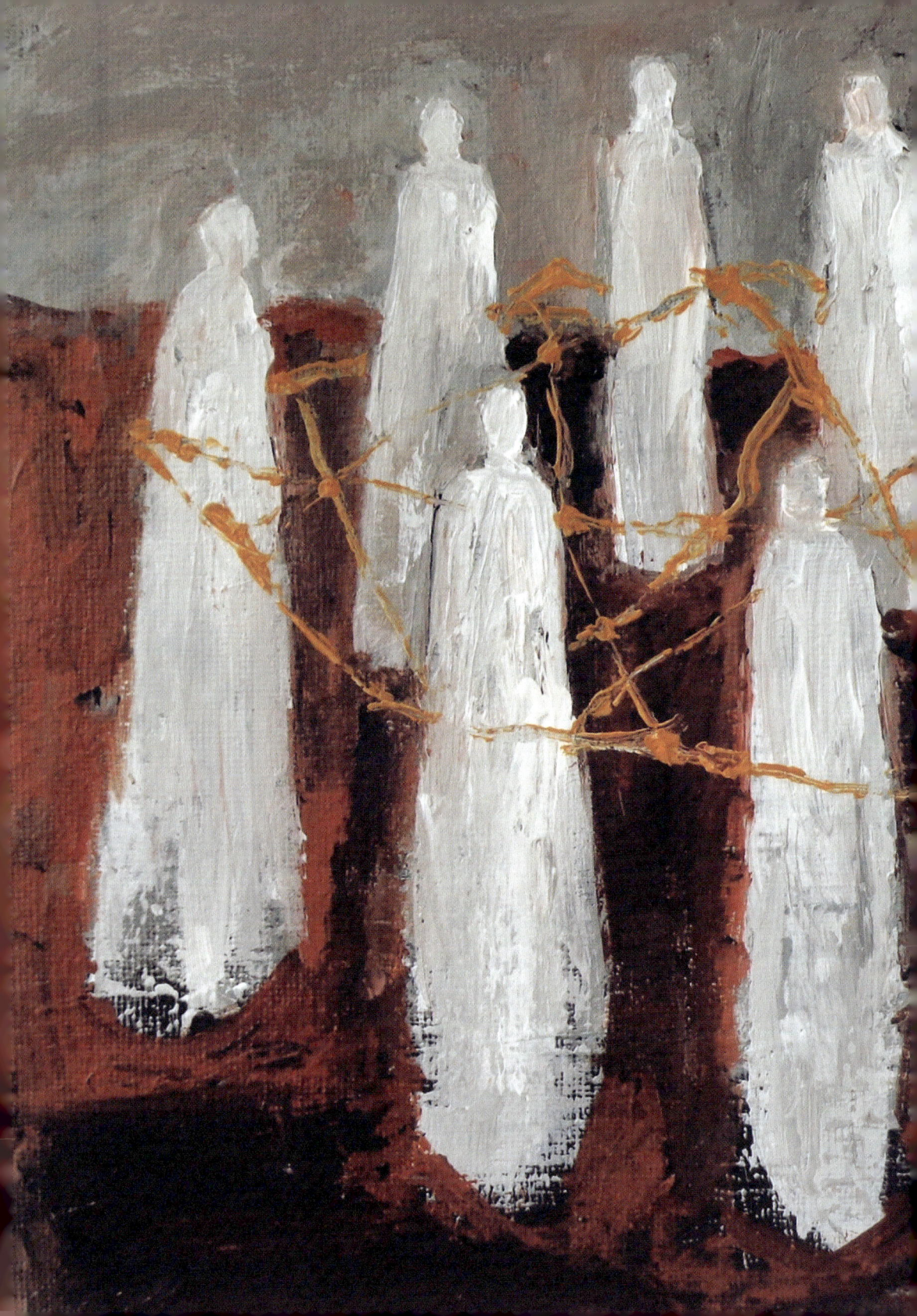

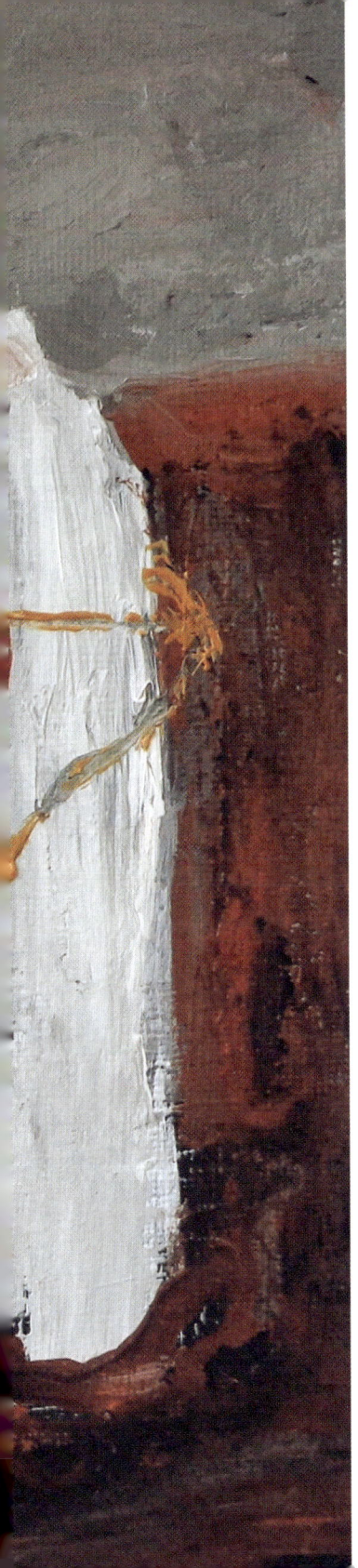

◄ **Warp and Weft**
Jeanie Tomanek,
undated, acrylic
on canvas.

Drawing upon themes that first developed
in her poetry, contemporary artist Jeanie
Tomanek (b.1949) explores various feminine
archetypes from myths, folk-tales, fairy tales
and her own experiences. She paints to explore
the significance of ideas, memories, events,
feelings, dreams and images. In her painting
Warp and Weft we are presented with a circle
of white robed initiates connected by a circle or
symbol of golden, glowing thread-like energy.

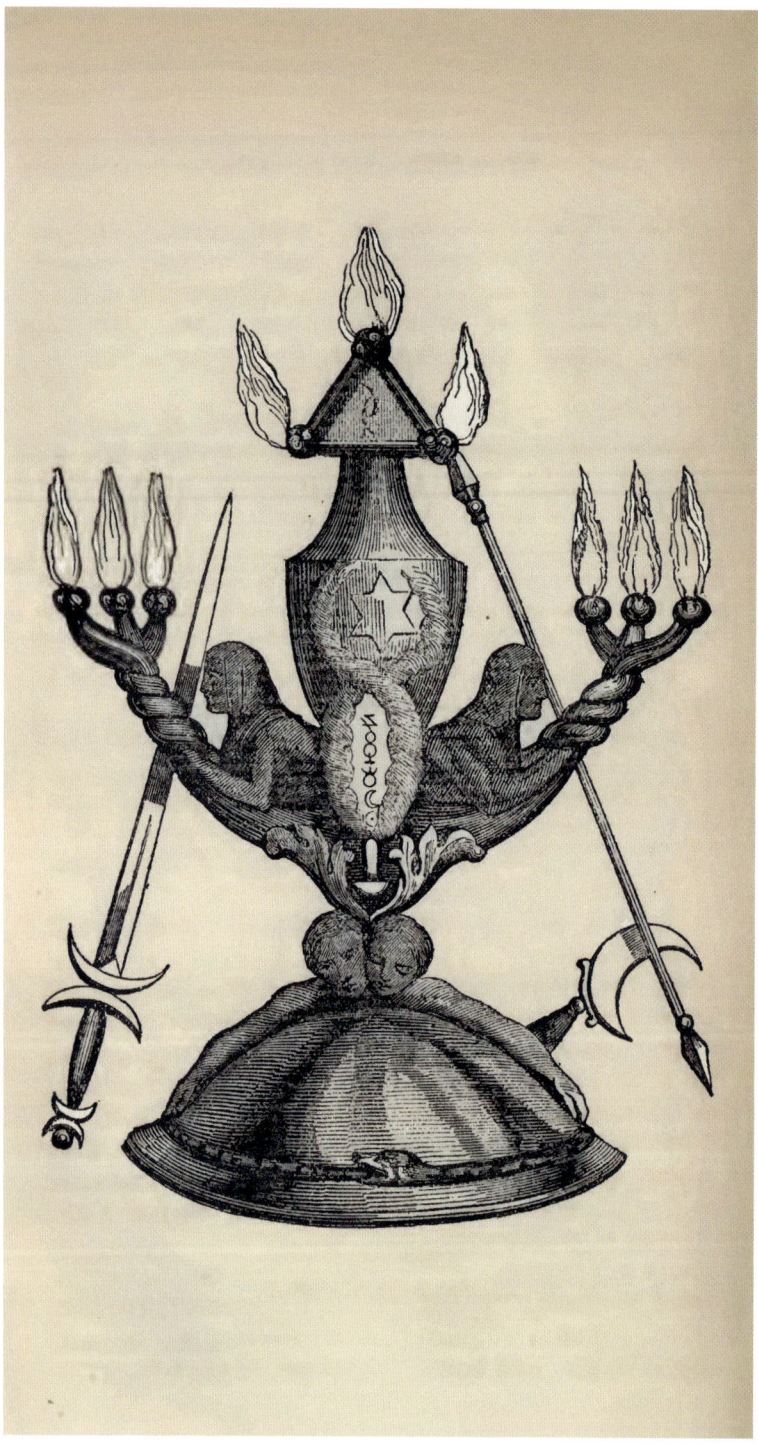

◄ **Magical instruments. Lamp, rod, sword and dagger**
From *Transcendental Magic, its Doctrine and Ritual* (Eliphas Levi, 1896).

An illustration of magical tools from Eliphas Levi's (1810–1875) first treatise on magic. Lévi rejected views that magic or religion is inherently irrational and instead he posits magic as an 'esoteric science', suggesting that Hermeticism could be adapted to find the underlying truth behind all magical systems. Levi had a deep impact on the magic of the Hermetic Order of the Golden Dawn and later on the ex-Golden Dawn member Aleister Crowley. It was largely through the occultists inspired by him that Lévi is remembered as one of the key founders of the 20th century revival of magic.

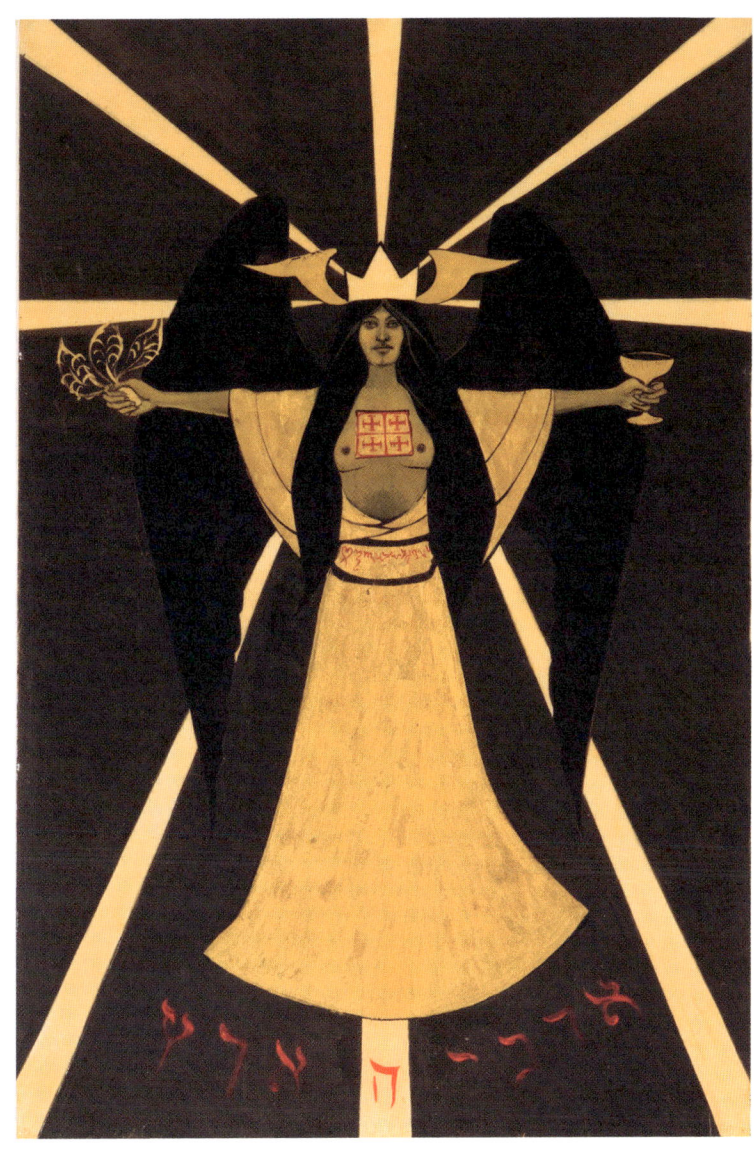

**▲ Holy Guardian
Angel According to
Aleister Crowley**
Marjorie Cameron,
1966, case in and gold
lacquer on board.

Marjorie Cameron Parsons Kimmel (aka Cameron) (1922–1995) was a poet
and mystic whose work blended 19th-century occultism, kabbalistic symbolism,
and the hedonistic spiritualism of mid-century Los Angeles. Cameron's *Holy
Guardian Angel* is derived from a mystical concept put forward by English
occultist Aleister Crowley. According to Crowley, we each have an appointed
Holy Guardian Angel to watch over us. Summoning and consciously connecting
with these personal guardian angels through a process called 'Knowledge
and Conversation' is the essential step in discovering our highest selves.

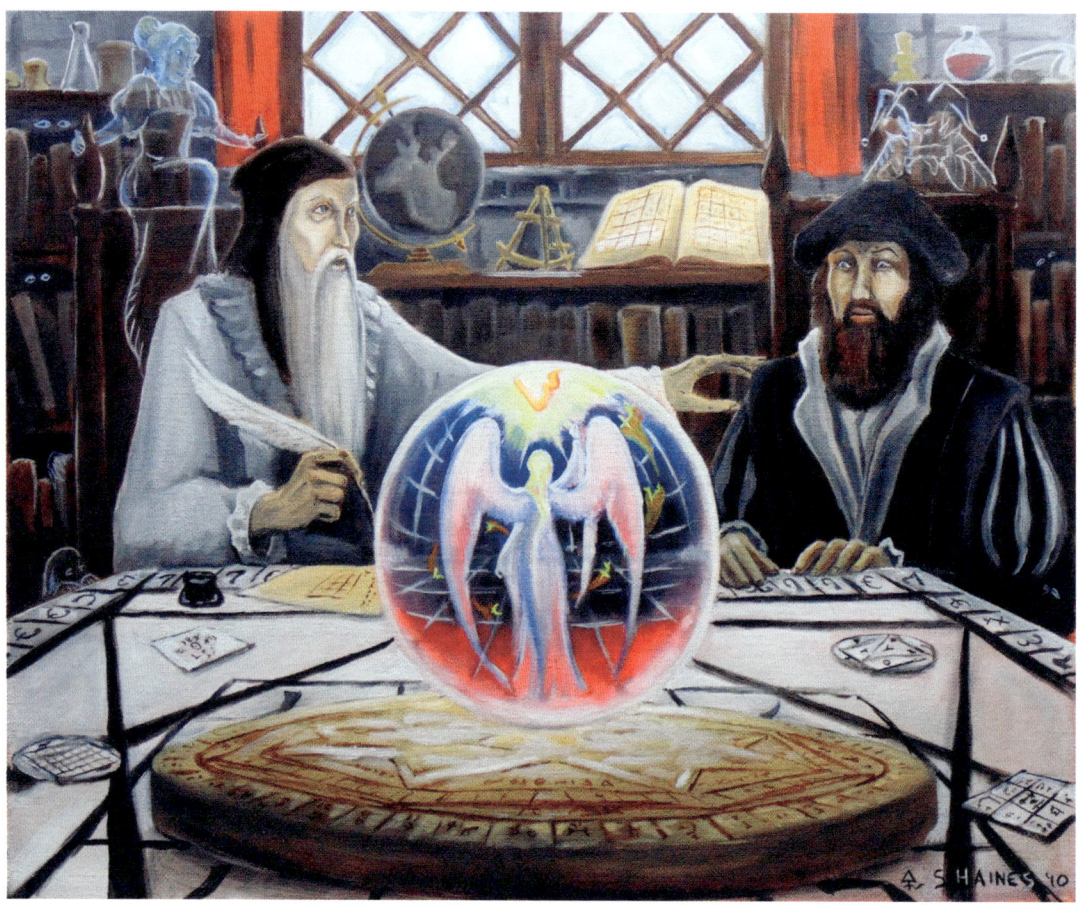

▲ **Dee and Kelley**
Sebastian Haines,
2010, oil on canvas.

US-based contemporary painter Sebastian Haines is
a self-taught artist who paints primarily in the tarot,
mythology and fantasy genres. In this scene we
observe mathematician, philosopher, and astronomer
John Dee (1527–1608/9), alongside the slightly less
decorated English Renaissance occultist and self-
declared spirit medium, Edward Kelley (1555–1597/8).
Theirs was strange partnership spent engaged in
alchemical cahoots, and encounters with angels.

▼ History of Magic, Part II … Initiation
Alison Blickle, 2014, oil on canvas.

Los Angeles-based contemporary artist Alison Blickle (b.1976) creates richly detailed oil on canvas paintings with subjects draped and dissolved in opulent avant-garde textiles, reminiscent of Byzantium or European folk art. Fantastical women engaged in elaborate ritual populate these transportive scenes that unfold out of a familiar place and time. Initiation, along with the other works in Blickle's *History of Magic* series, tells a story that is part creation myth, part heroic journey and which references French occultist and writer Eliphas Levi's 1860 book on the historical use of sacred imagery in art.

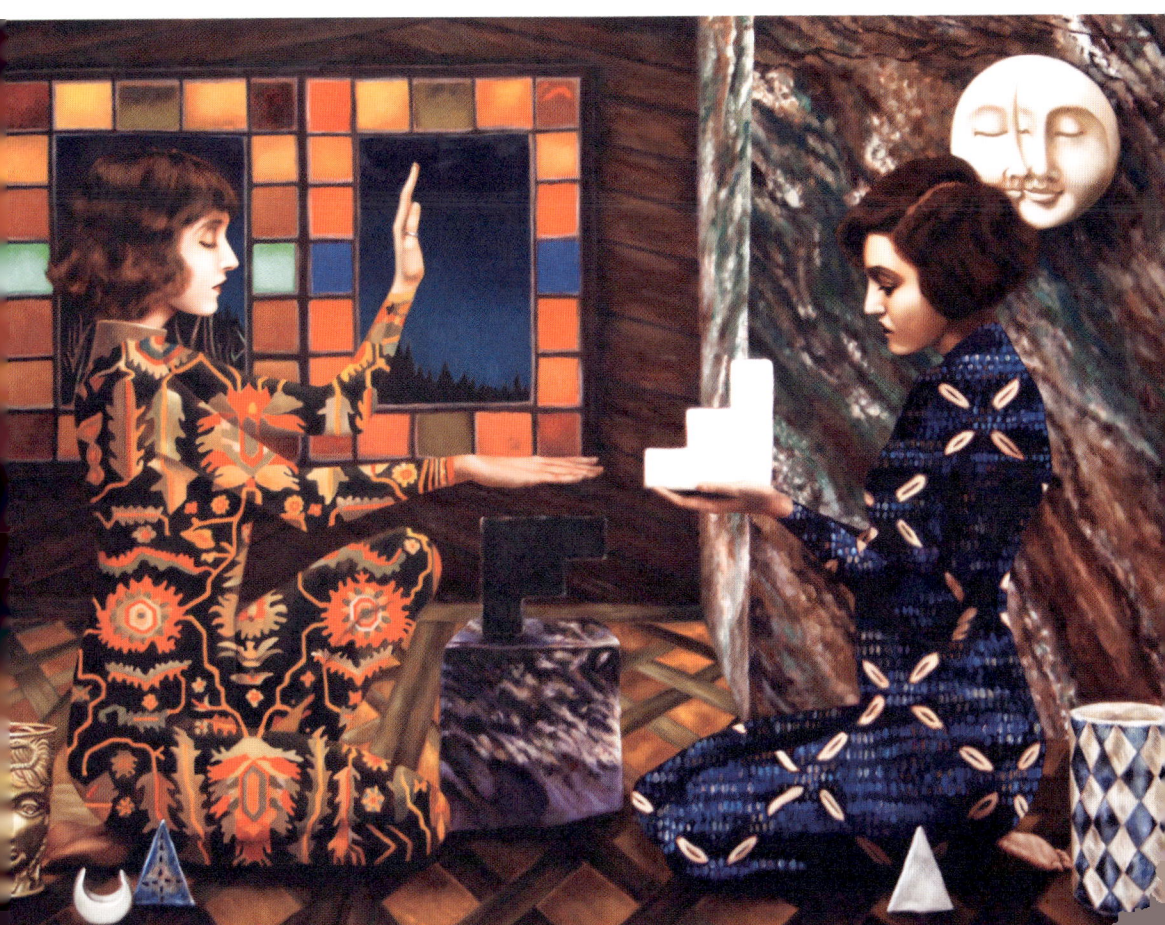

FURTHER READING

A Curious Future: A Handbook of Unusual Divination and Unique Oracular Techniques by Kiki Dombrowski, 2018

Agnes Pelton: Desert Transcendentalist by Gilbert Vicario, 2019

American Grotesque: The Life and Art of William Mortensen by William Mortensen, Larry Lytle , et al, 2014

Austin Osman Spare: The Occult Life of London's Legendary Artist by Phil Baker and Alan Moore. 1994

Divination: Sacred Tools for Reading the Mind of God by Paul O'Brien, 2007

Earth Magic by Rik Garrett, 2014

Enchanted Modernities: Theosophy, the Arts and the American West by Sarah Victoria Turner, Rachel Middleman, et al. 2019

Femme Fatale: Images of Evil and Fascinating Women. Patrick Bade, 1979

Georgiana Houghton: Spirit Drawings by Lars Bang Larsen, Simon Grant, 2016

Hilma af Klint: Paintings for the Future, by Tracey Bashkoff, Hilma af Klint, et al, 2018

Illuminations of Hildegard of Bingen by Matthew Fox, 2002

Kabbalah in Art and Architecture by Alexander Gorlin, 2013

Leonora Carrington: Surrealism, Alchemy and Art by Susan Aberth, 2010

Letters, Dreams, and Other Writings by Remedios Varo, Margaret Carson, 2018

Luigi Russolo, Futurist: Noise, Visual Arts, and the Occult by Luciano Chessa, 2012

Nicholas Roerich: The Life & Art of a Russian Master by Jacqueline Decter, 1989

Night Flower: The Life & Art of Vali Myers, by Vali Myers, Martin McIntosh, et al, 2012

Odilon Redon: Prince of Dreams, 1840-1916 by Douglas W. Druick and Odilon Redon. 1994

Pamela Colman Smith: The Untold Story by Stuart R. Kaplan, 2018

Pan's Daughter: The Magical World of ROSALEEN NORTON by Nevill Drury, 1988

Sacred Geometry: Deciphering the Code, Stephen Skinner, 2006

Shannon Taggart: Séance.by Andreas Fischer, Tony Oursler, et al, 2019

Songs for the Witch Woman by John W. Parsons, Marjorie Cameron, 2014

Surrealism and the Occult: Shamanism, Magic, Alchemy, and the Birth of an Artistic Movement by Nadia Choucha, 1992

The Complete Stories of Leonora Carrington by Leonora Carrington and Kathryn Davis, 2017

The Fated Sky: Astrology In History by, Benson Bobrick, 2005

The Mystery Traditions: Secret Symbols And Sacred Art by James Wasserman, 2005

The Occult, Witchcraft, and Magic: An Illustrated History by Christopher Dell, 2016

The Perfect Medium: Photography and the Occult by Clément Chéroux, Pierre Apraxine, et al. 2005

The Secret Teachings Of All Ages, by Manly P. Hall 1928

The Spiritual Image in Modern Art by Kathleen J. Regier, 1995

Transcendental Magic: Its Doctrine and Ritual by Eliphas Levi and Arthur Edward Waite, 1923

Understanding Aleister Crowley's Thoth Tarot by Lon Milo DuQuette, 2003

Visions of Enchantment: Occultism, Magic and Visual Culture: Select Papers from the University of Cambridge Conference. by Nathan Timpano, Antje Bosselman-Ruickbie, et al, 2019

Waking The Witch: Reflections On Women, Magic, and Power, by Pam Grossman, 2018

What Is A Witch by Pam Grossman and Tin Can Forest, 2016

Witches, Sluts, Feminists: Conjuring the Sex Positive, by Kristen J. Sollee, 2017

Women of the Golden Dawn: Rebels and Priestesses: Maud Gonne, Moina Bergson Mathers, Annie Horniman, Florence Farr by Mary K. Greer, 1996

World Receivers: Georgiana Houghton - Hilma af Klint - Emma Kunz by Karin Althaus , Matthias Mühling, et al, 2019

INDEX

PICTURE CREDITS

The publishers would like to thank the institutions, picture libraries, artists, galleries and photographers for their kind permission to reproduce the works featured in this book. Every effort has been made to trace all copyright holders but if any have been inadvertently overlooked, the publishers would be pleased to make the necessary arrangements at the first opportunity.

4 Wikicommons/South Australian Government Grant 1892 11 Bridgeman Images 14 Bridgeman Images 16 Luisa Ricciarini/Bridgeman Images 17 Pictures from History/Bridgeman Images 20 FineArt/Alamy 21 Peter Barritt/Alamy 22 David M. Benett/Getty 23 Courtesy of the Artist 24 Courtesy of the Artist 25 Courtesy of the Artist 27 Courtesy of the Artist 28 Bridgeman Images 29 Courtesy of Galleri Riis, Photo: Jean-Baptiste Béranger 30 Courtesy of the Artist 31 Heritage Images/Fine Art Images/akg-images 32 Jodi Simmons/Bridgeman Images 33 Wikicommons 37 Wellcome Collection 38 Patrizia Laporta/Bridgeman Images 39 Courtesy of the Artist 40 Tate 41 Courtesy of the Artist 43 Bridgeman Images 44 © RMN-Grand Palais/Photo: Madeleine Coursaget/Musée national Picasso, Paris, France 45 Courtesy of the Artist 46 Luisa Ricciarini/Bridgeman Images 47 Heritage Image Partnership Ltd/Alamy 48 Courtesy of the Artist 49 © Jake Baddeley – www.jakebaddeley.com 50 INTERFOTO/Alamy 51 Vintage Images/Alamy 54 Heritage Image Partnership Ltd/Alamy 55 Charles Walker Collection/Alamy 56 World History Archive/Alamy 57 Artnet 58 Collection of KAWS 59 Courtesy of the Artist 61 Courtesy of the Artist 62 akg-images/Science Source 63 Courtesy of the Artist 64 © William Johnstone/National Galleries Scotland 66 Christie's Images/Bridgeman 67 Courtesy of the Artist 70 The Picture Art Collection/Alamy 71 Wikicommons 72 akg-images/De Agostini/G. Amoretti 73 Bridgeman Images 74 Artnet 75 Courtesy of the Artist 77 Bridgeman Images 79 Courtesy of the Artist 80 Courtesy of the Artist 81 Courtesy of the Artist 82 Courtesy of the Artist 83 "The Hermaphrodite and the World Egg", colour pencil on paper: from the book, "THE SPLENDOR SOLIS", illustrated by Laurie Lipton (www.laurielipton.com) 84 Index Fototeca/Bridgeman Images 85 Alchemist with Golden Dragon from Orryelle Defenestrate-Bascule's 'Coagula' (Gold Book of the Tela Quadrivium bookweb, Fulgur 2011) 89 Bridgeman Images 90 The Museum of Modern Art, New York/Scala, Florence 94 Artnet 95 The Leiden Collection 97 Bridgeman Images 98 'With the Milk of Gazelle, Hathor Heals Hoor's Eyes on the Horizon'. Originally published in 'Distillatio' (Fulgur 2015) 99 Art Collection 3/Alamy 101 Courtesy of the Artist 102 akg-images 103 akg-images 104 INTERFOTO/Alamy 105 Christie's Images, London/Scala, Florence 106 The Stapleton Collection/Bridgeman Images 107 Collection of Jan Jones 110 A. Dagli Orti/De Agostini Picture Library/Bridgeman Images 111 Bridgeman Images 112 Bridgeman Images 113 Getty Research Institute 114 akg-images/Fototeca Gilardi 115 The Jewish Museum/Art Resource/Scala, Florence 116 Estate of Dora Holzhandler/Bridgeman Images 117 Avraham Loewenthal, www.kabbalahart.com/ 118 akg-images/Science Source 119 akg-images/Fototeca Gilardi 121 The Metropolitan Museum of Art/Art Resource/Scala, Florence 122 Founders Society purchase, W. Hawkins Ferry fund/Bridgeman Images 123 The Museum of Modern Art, New York/Scala, Florence 126 Peter Willi/Bridgeman Images 127 Archives Charmet/Bridgeman Images 128 Peter Barritt/Alamy 129 Heritage Images/Fine Art Images/akg-images 130 Mary Evans Picture Library 131 Historic Images/Alamy 132 Wikicommons 133 Private Collection; Courtesy of Michael Rosenfeld Gallery LLC, New York, NY 134 Finnish National Gallery/Ateneum Art Museum Photo: Finnish National Gallery/Hannu Pakarinen 135 The Stapleton Collection/Bridgeman Images 136 Art Heritage/Alamy 137 akg-images 138 Gift of the Artist/Bridgeman Images 139 A. Dagli Orti/De Agostini Picture Library/Bridgeman Images 143 Album/Alamy 144 akg-images/Science Source 145 Bridgeman Images 146 Gift of Fundacion Pan Klub, Museo Xul Solar, Buenos Aires/Bridgeman Images 147 Bridgeman Images 148 Fine Art Images/Heritage Images/Scala, Florence 149 Courtesy of the Artist 150 Bridgeman Images 151 Bridgeman Images 152 Artspan 153 Bridgeman Images 154 Bridgeman Images 155 Bridgeman Images 159 Mary Evans Picture Library 160 Christie's Images, London/Scala, Florence 161 Lebrech History/Bridgeman Images 165 Heritage Image Partnership Ltd/Alamy 166 Courtesy of the Artist 167 Wikicommons 169 Peter Barritt/Alamy 170 ArtHive 171 MutualArt 172 The Picture Art Collection/Alamy 173 © Archives Charmet/Bridgeman Images 174 Heritage Auctions 175 Gift of Mrs. Murray S. Danforth/Risdmuseum 176 The National Gallery, London/Scala, Florence 178 Courtesy Galerie Minsky 179 Wikicommons 180 Peter Willi/Bridgeman Images 181 Solomon R. Guggenheim Museum, New York Purchased with funds contributed by Stephen J. Javaras, 2015 © Juliana Huxtable 182 Universal Images Group North America LLC/Alamy 183 Wikicommons/South Australian Government Grant 1892 184 akg-images 185 Vali Myers Art Gallery Trust/http://www.outregallery.com/collections/vali-myers 186 Wikicommons 187 Jeffrey Deitch Gallery, NYC 188 Wikicommons 189 Courtesy of the Artist 193 The Picture Art Collection/Alamy 194 Henry Boxer Gallery, London 195 Outsider Art Fair 196 The Museum of Everything 197 Historic Images/Alamy 198 World Religions and Spirituality Project 199 Courtesy of the Artist 200 akg-images 201 akg-images/Erich Lessing 202 The Museum of Everything 204 Mary Evans Picture Library 205 Bridgeman Images 206 akg-images/Fototeca Gilardi 207 akg-images/Science Source 210 Heritage Images/Getty 211 Painters/Alamy 212l © Salvador Dalí, Fundació Gala-Salvador Dalí 212r © 1971 U.S. Games Systems, all rights reserved (courtesy U.S. Games Systems, Inc., Stamford, Connecticut) 213 Courtesy of the Artist 214 WikiArt 215 Wikicommons 216 Frances Broomfield/Portal Gallery, London/Bridgeman Images 217 Bridgeman Images 218 Wikicommons 219 Courtesy of the Artist 220 Blanton Museum of Art, The University of Texas at Austin, Gift of Judy S. and Charles W. Tate, 2016 © Leonora Carrington/Artists Rights Society (ARS), New York 221 Wikicommons 222 The Stapleton Collection/Bridgeman Images 223 Bridgeman Images 226 Mukange Books 227 Culture Club/Getty 228 Courtesy of the Artist 229 Courtesy of the Artist 230 Courtesy of the Artist 232 Wellcome Collection 233 Jeffrey Deitch Gallery, NYC 234 Courtesy of the Artist 235 Courtesy of the Artist

ACKNOWLEDGEMENTS

First and foremost, I would like to thank everyone who has supported my writing over the years, whatever form it might have taken, and through all of its evolutions and incarnations.

To my incredible inner sanctum: My partner, Ývan; my sisters, Mary and Melissa; my best good friend, Violet; and my dear sweet spoods, Maika, Sonya, and Jo – I could not have even embarked on a project like this without your unflagging motivation, encouragement, humour, epicurean cheeses and edible fruit arrangements. And of course, my brother-in-law, David, who took the press photos for this project!

To the witches, poets, perfumers, writers and creators I admire: Meredith, Angeliska, Pam, Beth, Flan, Sam, Tom, Lisa, Jess. All of you have been so helpful and so inspirational – some over the course of many years, and some of you more recently. But all of you in various and wonderful ways.

My dear blog island friends. Remember that place? We've followed each other on so many journeys since then! Minna, Jessica, Robyne. You befriended me at a time I needed it most, and it was then that I began writing in earnest. Your love and support over the years has kept me afloat and guided me ever forward.

To my lovely and knowledgeable editors at Quarto – Alice, your feedback and insights were invaluable to me. Thank you for taking my words and making them better, every step of the way. Joe, your tireless assistance with the imagery featured in this book made an initially insurmountable task seem entirely possible. Paileen, your keen eye for composition and design has elevated these words and images into something wholly wondrous.

To those who have helped shaped this book and who shaped me into a person who would write it. My beloved, departed grandparents, Mawga and Boppa. I don't even want to think of the direction my life might have taken if not for your love and guidance. Jim and Steve, whose appearances in my life at formative points, though brief in the grand scheme of things, influenced me in weird and wonderful ways I can't even begin to describe to you. Thank you both for loving my mother for a time and loving my sisters and I as well. And Elaine. Oh, Mom. Oh, chaos charmer of complicated mayhem and magic. You remain a mystery to me, your secrets silent and knowledge hidden. Maybe in the next life our paths will cross and I will have much to learn from you, but until then, and because of your influence – I will never stop seeking in this one.

ABOUT THE AUTHOR

S. Elizabeth is a writer, curator and frill-seeker. Her essays and interviews about esoteric art have appeared in *Coilhouse*, *Dirge Magazine*, *Death & The Maiden* and her occulture blog Unquiet Things, which intersects music, fashion, horror, perfume and grief. Born of the strange and fraught relationship between an astrologer and an architect, S. Elizabeth draws upon the magic in her blood and lifelong passion for the visual arts to explore her obsessions through her writing. She is the co-creator of *The Occult Activity Book* (volume 1 and 2) and a staff writer at *Haute Macabre*. She lives in the Florida swamps with a Viking named Ývan and an imaginary corgi named Cheese Tray.